Foundation Version Control for Web Developers

Chris Kemper and Ian Oxley

friendsof ⊘™

DESIGNER TO DESIGNER™

an Apress® company

FOUNDATION VERSION CONTROL FOR WEB DEVELOPERS

Copyright © 2012 by Chris Kemper and Ian Oxley

ISBN-13 (pbk): 978-1-4302-3972-7

ISBN-13 (electronic): 978-1-4302-3973-4

Trademarked names, logos, and images may appear in this book. Rather than use a trademark symbol with every occurrence of a trademarked name, logo, or image we use the names, logos, or images only in an editorial fashion and to the benefit of the trademark owner, with no intention of infringement of the trademark.

The use in this publication of trade names, service marks, and similar terms, even if they are not identified as such, is not to be taken as an expression of opinion as to whether or not they are subject to proprietary rights.

While the advice and information in this book are believed to be true and accurate at the date of publication, neither the authors nor the editors nor the publisher can accept any legal responsibility for any errors or omissions that may be made. The publisher makes no warranty, express or implied, with respect to the material contained herein.

Distributed to the book trade worldwide by Springer Science+Business Media New York, 233 Spring Street, 6th Floor, New York, NY 10013. Phone 1-800-SPRINGER, fax (201) 348-4505, e-mail orders-ny@springer-sbm.com, or visit www.springeronline.com.

For information on translations, please e-mail rights@apress.com or visit www.apress.com.

Apress and friends of ED books may be purchased in bulk for academic, corporate, or promotional use. eBook versions and licenses are also available for most titles. For more information, reference our Special Bulk Sales–eBook Licensing web page at www.apress.com/bulk-sales.

Any source code or other supplementary materials referenced by the author in this text are available to readers at www.apress.com. For detailed information about how to locate your book's source code, go to www.apress.com/source-code/.

Credits

President and Publisher: Paul Manning	**Coordinating Editor**: Tracy Brown
Lead Editor: Louise Corrigan	**Copy Editors**: Elizabeth Berry, Tiffany Taylor
Technical Reviewer: Tom Barker	**Compositor**: Mary Sudul
Editorial Board: Steve Anglin, Mark Beckner, Ewan Buckingham, Gary Cornell, Morgan Ertel, Jonathan Gennick, Jonathan Hassell, Robert Hutchinson, Michelle Lowman, James Markham, Matthew Moodie, Jeff Olson, Jeffrey Pepper, Douglas Pundick, Ben Renow-Clarke, Dominic Shakeshaft, Gwenan Spearing, Matt Wade, Tom Welsh	**Indexer**: SPi Global **Artist**: SPi Global **Cover Image Artist**: Corné van Dooren **Cover Designer**: Anna Ishchenko

To my family, friends, and Lauren

—Chris Kemper

To Rachel, Stewart, and Adam

—Ian Oxley

Contents at a Glance

Contents

About the Authors

Photo credit: Graham Smith

Chris Kemper was born and bred in the North of England. Growing up taking computers apart and putting them back together, it's no surprise he got into web development in his early teens. Graduating in 2008, Chris secured a job at one of the leading web design agencies in the North East, building awesome Drupal-powered websites for some big names.

Moonlighting as a freelance web developer, Chris always stays on the cutting edge of web development—which means he also has a lot of big ideas and not enough time to develop them.

On the rare occasion Chris isn't on his MacBook, he can be found exploring the realms of Skyrim and beyond, travelling the country for various web conferences, and drinking fine ales.

You can catch Chris on Twitter at @ChrisDKemper or by checking out his personal site at www.chrisdkemper.co.uk.

Ian Oxley is a web developer who's been writing front-end and back-end code professionally since 2004. He's based in Newcastle-upon-Tyne, England, and can often be found attending, and on occasion speaking at, local user groups and meetups. When he's not programming, Ian enjoys playing the guitar, photography, badminton, and spending time with his wife and family.

About the Technical Reviewer

Tom Barker is a software engineer, solutions architect, and technical manager with over 13 years of experience working with ActionScript, JavaScript, Perl, PHP, and the Microsoft .Net Framework. Currently he is the manager of web development at Comcast Interactive Media where he leads the craftsmen responsible for www.xfinity.com and www.xfinitytv.com. He is also an adjunct professor at Philadelphia University, where he has been teaching undergraduate and graduate courses on web development since 2003. When not working, teaching, or writing, Tom likes to spend time with his family, read, and play video games until very early in the morning.

About the Cover Image Artist

Corné van Dooren designed the front cover image for this book. After taking a brief hiatus from friends of ED to create a new design for the Foundation series, Corné worked at combining technological and organic forms with the results now appearing on this and other book covers.

Corné spent his childhood drawing on everything at hand, and then he began exploring the infinite world of multimedia—His journey of discovery hasn't stopped since! His mantra has always been, "The only limit to multimedia is the imagination," a saying that keeps him constantly moving forward.

Corné works for many international clients, writes features for multimedia magazines, reviews and tests software, authors multimedia studies, and works on many other friends of ED books. You can see more of his work and contact him through his website at: www.cornevandooren.com.

Acknowledgments

To all my friends who have offered kind words to me at times of stress, I thank you. My mam practically bullied her way in here, but I love her all the same! My brother Kane also gets a mention, because of his support, and helping me suck less at Battlefield. To my dad, who would quite happily listen to me talk about the book without any knowledge of what the hell I was talking about, thanks! Phil Sherry gets a big mention, as he's always offered words of advice (although most of them look like "$!#@) and he got me in touch with the right people to start this whole process off. I owe you a beer, my good man. Craig Tweedy gets a mention, mainly because he's Craig Tweedy. Ian Oxley also has to get a shout out, since he came and helped me out and produced two cracking chapters for the book in the process. Cheers, man! Finally, I have to thank my partner, Lauren Thompson, for putting up with all the late nights, stress, and pointless conversation, as well as even helping me write and proof various parts of the book; you get hugs and a Nandos.

Introduction

Since you happen to be reading through the opening pages of *Foundation Version Control for Web Developers* then it's safe to say you have some interest in finding out a little bit more about version control. It may be true that this new interest isn't actually your own, but instead comes from a friend, colleague, or employer who thinks getting a bit more knowledge on the subject would be beneficial to you. Either way, throughout the course of this book you'll be walked through the basics of version control using Subversion (SVN), Mercurial, and Git, getting to know each of them a little better as the chapters go on. I'll cover setting up a development environment first, just in case you're really new to the development scene, then the programs you can use for versioning your code (Chapter 5), and even how to dive into Terminal and all your versioning needs with commands (Chapter 9). Don't worry if any of this seems daunting. As you progress through the chapters you'll feel your confidence in version control growing, and before long you'll be a versioning master!

Who this book is for

Foundation Version Control for Web Developers is a book to help those with little to no knowledge of version control get a leg up on one of key components of modern-day development. Whether you are just getting started in the field, a pro who hasn't been versioning code until now, or even a designer wanting to expand your knowledge of the field, this book is for you. And whether you're a freelancer or a full-time agency worker, you'll always have a need for versioning your code. Knowing more about your chosen field is always a good thing under any circumstance.

How this book is structured

As mentioned previously, I'll start off by showing you how to get a development environment of PHP and MySQL set up on your Windows, Mac, or Ubuntu machine. In Chapter 2, you'll be learning about what version control actually is and why it's so important, as well as some history on where the books featured systems came from. Then in Chapter 3, it'll be time to get SVN, Mercurial, and Git installed on your machine, to get you ready for the rest of the book and versioning your code in general.

Chapter 4 will introduce the real benefits of version control, showing many other potential situations where having access to some kind of versioning system would make life so much easier. Next, you'll dive into the world of programs you can utilize to harness the power of version control, without having to go near a Terminal window! The level will come down a little in Chapter 6, where you'll learn that you shouldn't version everything using these systems, and I'll show you some alternatives, just in case you have a need for it. In Chapter 7, I'll try and make your life a little easier by showing how you can integrate version control into some of your favorite development applications and take you on a tour of the features for those that already boost integration. Conflict management is the topic of Chapter 8, showing how to resolve the pesky conflicts that you'll get from time to time, both in the code and using applications.

The applications will go away in Chapter 9, where I'll take you into Terminal and show how to get your version control on with just the commands you need to get started! With your confidence from the previous chapter, it'll be time to create your own server, which you can use to store all of those remote repositories you'll want to be using! If that isn't your thing, then Chapter 11 will be just right for you, in which I'll cover some of the packages out there that have done the hard work for you and created some great repository hosting services, with all the trimmings. In Chapter 12, Ian Oxley will be taking you through why branching is so awesome, and how to go about utilizing those awesome features. Ian will then lead you into Chapter 14, detailing what commit hooks are and how they can be really useful in your versioning workflow. Finally, in the last chapter in the book I'll bring you in for the close, with a chapter on upgrading your CVS repository, if you happen to have one, and how to migrate from SVN to Git or Mercurial, if you fancy a change.

What will I need?

As far the book goes, as long as you have either an up-to-date Mac, PC, or Ubuntu installation, you'll have no problem using these great applications and bettering your version control knowledge. The only other thing you'll need is a desire to learn some awesome new techniques and to make sure that your code stays safe and is backed up.

Contacting Chris Kemper

Chris Kemper can be contacted at either hey@chrisdkemper.co.uk or through his Twitter account @chrisdkemper.

Chapter 1

Are You Set Up? Creating a Basic Development Environment

Have you ever experienced that moment when someone asks you to help out with a current website build, or to help start off a new project, and you realize you just aren't set up to cope with it? If you've ever been caught in this situation, without even knowing where to start, this chapter will help. Although I'm not going to cover how to get you set up with every development environment, I will get you started with the most common. Knowing you have it all set up and working on your machine can give you the confidence you need to grab that new project by the horns.

I know you're itching to get started learning about version control, even if you're not set up yet, but you have to be patient. If you're just getting into the whole writing code thing, don't worry, I'll be guiding you through the entire process from start to finish. You don't have to worry about any developers judging your knowledge here; we're all starting from the same page. You can work through it at your own pace, or even come back to it if need be.

Even though people always try and avoid alienating new colleagues, or even people new to the industry, you can still feel self-conscious when it comes to asking for help or just taking those first steps. The web design field, by nature, is very friendly, but it can still be nerve-wracking for some people to have to ask someone about the basics. If you are one of those people, this book will help you. You can try all setting this all up at home, on your own time, without any fear. Plus, when you're through, I'll bet you'll be able to show everyone else a thing or two.

When it comes to developing anything, whether it's a website, an application, or a framework, you might be using a totally different environment than the one I'm about to walk you through. To get us all on the same page, I'll take you through a basic PHP/MySQL/Apache setup—or as it's known in the Linux world, a LAMP stack (Linux, Apache, MySQL, and PHP). I've chosen this environment because it's a great way to get started in development and, just like Brick Tamland from the movie *Anchor Man*, I love LAMP. (I'm sure you've heard of Wordpress. Well that's built using PHP and MySQL; a lot of designers and developers who are looking to get started with web design, find trying to build a blog for themselves a good place to start. You can find a few good books on the subject, such as *Blog Design Solutions* by Andy Budd (Friends of ED, 2008), which I highly recommend.

Now comes the time to start getting ready to go, and the first stop is with Windows. As Barney Stinson on television's "How I Met Your Mother" would say, "new is always better," so I'll be showing you how to get set up in Windows 7. Don't worry if you're not running Windows 7. These steps will work regardless of your version of Windows (as long as you're not running Windows 98). If there's something you should know, I'll be sure to tell you.

Once I've shown you how to get started with Windows it'll be time to take a trip to Mac town. I'll get you all set up on your Mac, step by step, so it's nice and simple. For you hardcore programmers out there, I'll be continuing through to Linux land, in the form of Ubuntu. While going over Ubuntu, I'll show you how easy it is to apt-get yourself started (it's a clever Linux pun, you'll see). Finally, when you're all set up, I'll get into the good stuff: getting your files version controlled.

So with that said, it's time to set up Windows.

Microsoft Windows

There are a few options available to get you set up on Windows, and a lot of them have a nice and easy install interface. Some of the more popular solutions are Easy PHP, xampp, WAMP, and Wamp Developer Pro. The latter is a paid solution, but all of the previous products are free and open source. If you were to scour the Internet for reviews, you would no doubt find glowing reviews of one solution or another. Although I have no real bias between these packages (I use a Mac), I'll be using Windows, Apache, MySQL, and PHP (WAMP) for the Windows 7 walkthrough. Don't let that stop you from trying others, though; once you've mastered the techniques in this book you'll be able to try any of the solutions I've mentioned, or even ones I don't know about.

Getting the package

Before you can install anything, you'll need the package, so jump into your favorite browser (which I hope isn't Internet Explorer) and head on over to www.wampserver.com. When you land, navigate to the Downloads page. You will have the option of choosing either 32 bit or 64 bit here. If you're unsure which your system is, open up your computer's Properties, which you can find by opening up Start, then right-clicking Computer and choosing Properties. As you can see in Figure 1-1, I'm using a 64-bit system, so I'll be downloading the 64-bit version of the application.

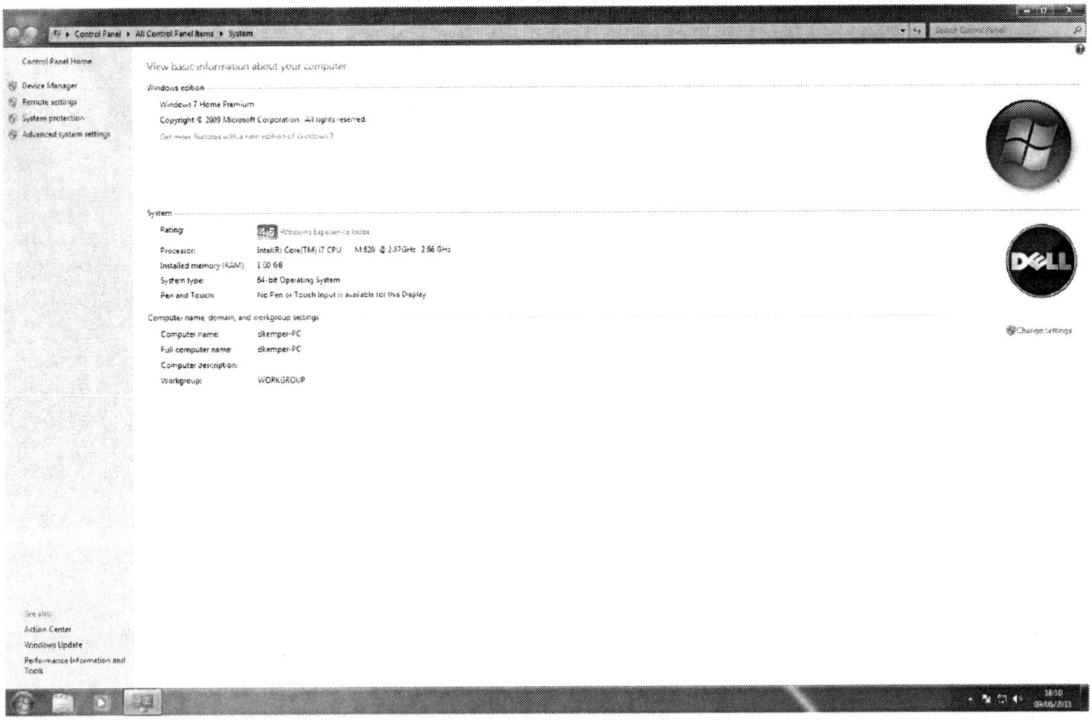

Figure 1-1. The Windows 7 configuration screen, in this instance showing that the system is 64 bit

Getting your install on

Once you have the file downloaded and you give it the good old double-click, you'll see the lovely screen shown in Figure 1-2. Click Next and move onto the license screen, have a nice read, and move on.

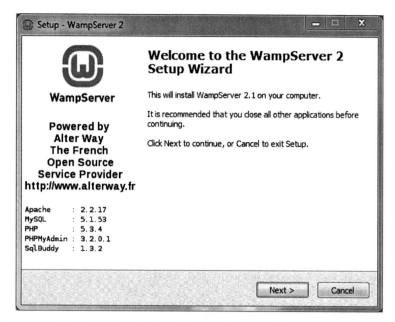

Figure 1-2. The first screen of the WAMP installation which also shows the different versions of Apache, MySQL, PHPMyAdmin, and SqlBuddy

Once you've finished going through the license agreement, you'll see what's pictured in Figure 1-3.

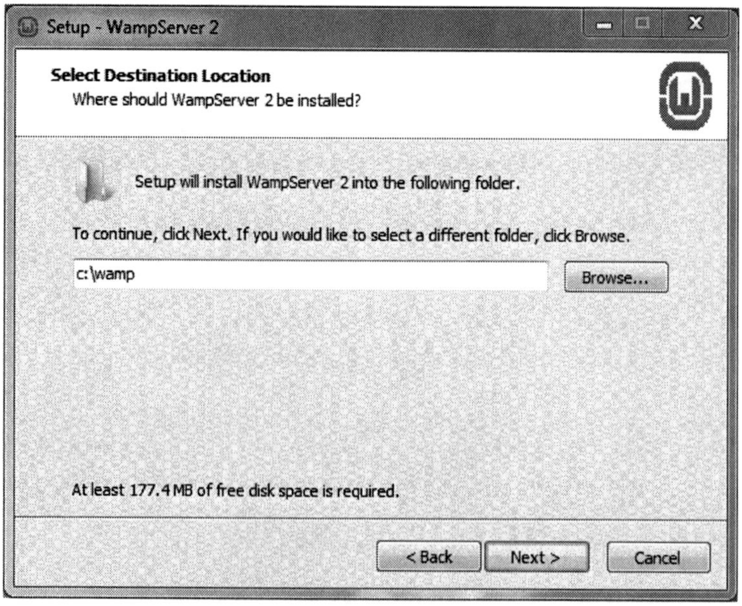

Figure 1-3. The installation directory for WAMP, which defaults to c:\wamp

As you can see, the program suggests you install WAMP straight onto C:, not directly into the program files as with most other applications you'd install. I suggest leaving it where it is, because it makes life much easier by giving easy access to the directory. However, you can move the directory to another location by clicking Browse... I used to have my WAMP install onto my D: drive; the main advantage of this is that it is safe from any potential operating system crashes or problems. It also means that if you want to upgrade your system, you can wipe your operating system drive and your sites will all be safe, which is great!

Working through Windows prompts

Throughout this installation you'll be seeing a lot of those Windows security prompts that ask for your permission before allowing files to be installed on the system, or if something you're installing wants to make changes to your system. You can say yes to all of these requests, as they pose no threat to your system. The most important is the firewall prompt, which will ask permission for Apache to be allowed to transfer information through the firewall, which you will encounter once you reach the end of the installation. Be sure to allow this to avoid problems while running sites in your WAMP installation.

You'll then be prompted to choose if you want a desktop shortcut, or if you'd like WAMP to be added to the quick launch bar. Adding either of these gives you a quick link, either on the desktop or the bottom menu bar, to start the application. If you choose not to create the shortcut, you can always start it via the Start menu. You will then see the setup ask for confirmation about all the previous options, and away it goes to copy across all the files.

Configuring PHP settings

Once that's all done you'll be asked to configure your PHP SMTP settings. For the sake of a basic install, and to get you up and running with a basic environment, I would suggest just leaving these as they are. If you're planning on testing PHP's mail function or using this machine as a live web server, you won't really need these settings, so they can be left as default.

Choosing the default browser

You'll also be prompted to find your default browser, which is Internet Explorer. If you'd like to change this to another browser, navigate to it via the popup window. If you're unsure where your browser is located, you can always open the Properties window of a shortcut to it (such as a Start menu item, or Desktop shortcut), which will show you its location, or you can just leave it as the default. It's possible to change this at a later date, but it requires editing one of the applications configuration files. Don't let that worry you though; I'll mention how to do that a little later. If you'd like to use a different browser, such as Firefox, here's how: when the popup window opens, go back to C:, then Programs Files (x86) ➤ Mozilla Firefox and double-click to select it. (You can see what this folder looks like by checking out Figure 1-4.) Once you've selected your default browser (whatever that is) and clicked Next, you're ready to launch the application. That's it for the setup. Hooray!

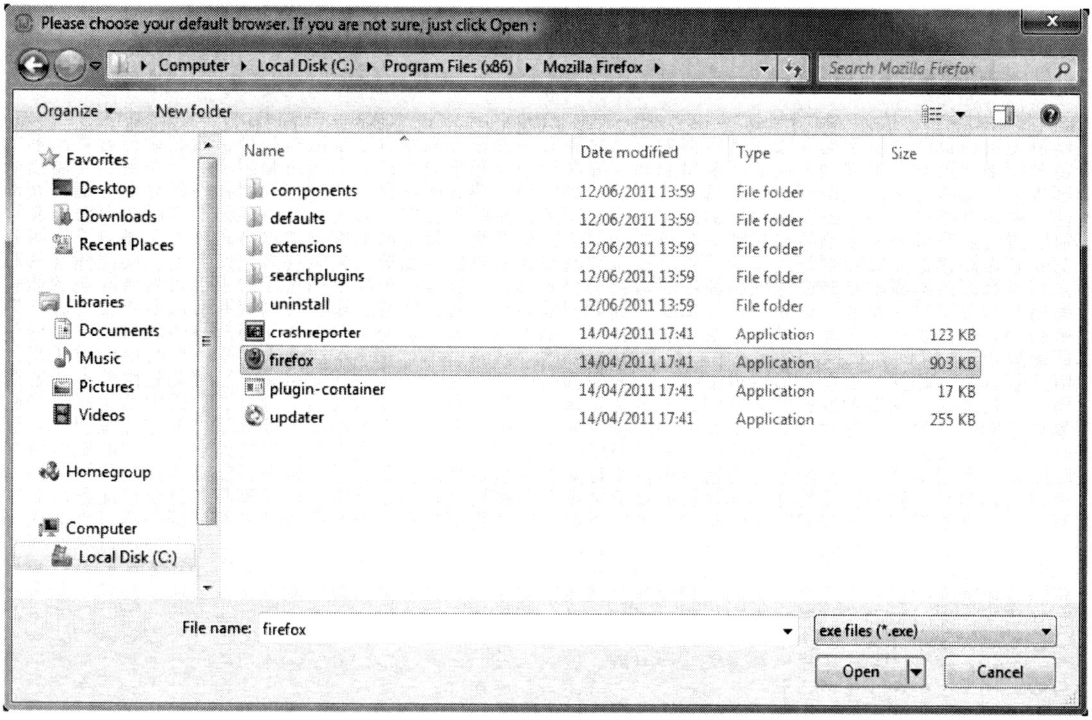

Figure 1-4. Selecting a default browserbrowser, which in this instance is Firefox

Running WAMP

You're now pretty much ready to go. If it's not already running, open WAMP by navigating to it in the Start menu (Start ➤ All Programs ➤ WampServer ➤ Start WampServer), or double-clicking one of the shortcut icons you may have opted to use during the setup process. You will also get another Windows prompt asking for your permission to run the program. You'll see this prompt every time you want to open WAMP, so be sure to accept it, or WAMP won't start up. Once it's running, if you check out the bottom right of your screen, you'll see a new green icon: that's WAMP in action. If you can't see the icon straight away, you may need to click the arrow to see it (as shown in Figure 1-5).

Figure 1-5. The WAMP icon may in fact be hidden by default and can be shown by clicking the arrow.

You can click the Customize link, which was made available when you clicked the arrow, and then change the WAMP option to "Show icon and notifications". This will give you much better access to it in the future: you won't need to use the arrow to see it, it'll always be visible. Check out Figure 1-6 to see the icon customization screen.

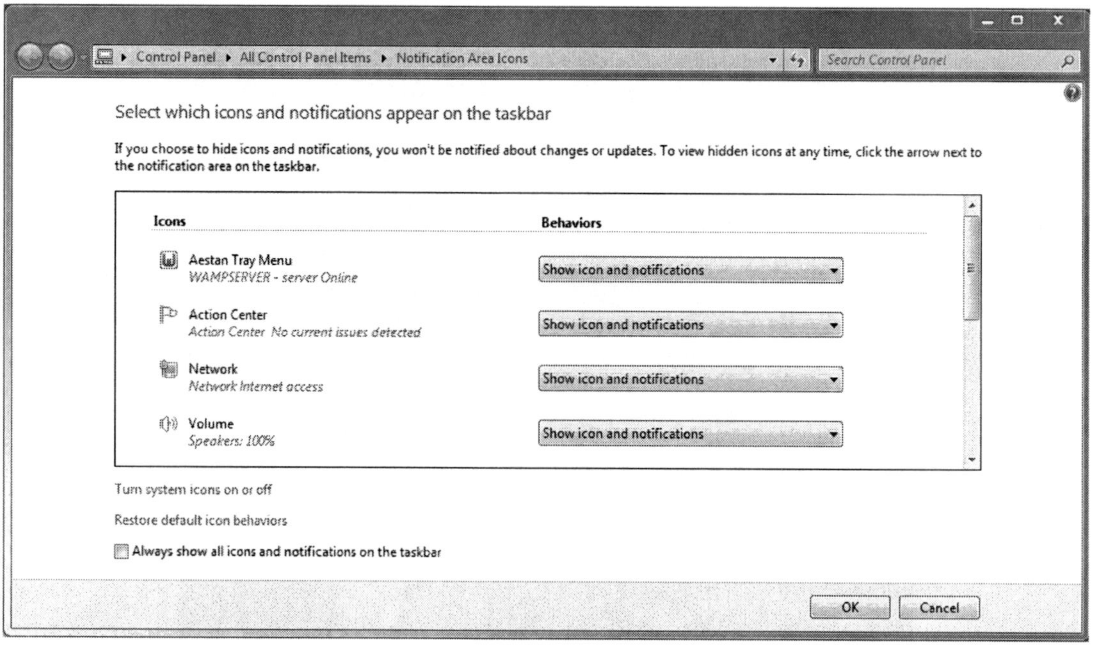

Figure 1-6. Customization options available for the icons in the tray. Set this to "Show icon and notifications" so they'll always be on display.

Examining the WAMP options

Now that you've made the status icon a lot easier to access, it's time to see what happens when you click it (see Figure 1-7). There are a lot of useful options here, one of which is the localhost option. This will take you to the default dashboard page supplied by WAMP—if you can navigate to this page and it displays something, you know everything is working correctly. If you just see a broken page when clicking localhost, it could mean a multitude of things. The most common reason for this page not displaying, however, is that the server isn't online. To determine this, click the icon on the bottom right; if you see a link at the bottom that reads "Put online," your services are offline. Give that link a click, and the server will be online.

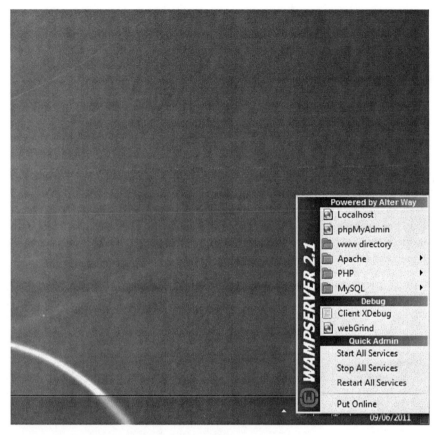

Figure 1-7. The menu that is opened when you click the WAMP icon

If that still doesn't fix the problem, and you've viewed a site over a local network before, then you may need to edit your hosts file. This file contains references to addresses used locally on your machine, that point to different IP addresses, which are normally different users machines over a network. For example, testsite.localhost could be pointing to 192.168.1.20 on your local network, which is in fact a developers machine in your office. The easiest way to edit this file is to use Notepad. When opening Notepad, be sure to right click it and use 'Run as Administrator', otherwise you won't be able to save the file. Now, head into 'File > open...' and navigate to:

C: > Windows > System32 > drivers > etc

Once you arrive here it may seem as though there are no files, but don't worry, just change the dropdown next to the filename box from Text Documents to all, then you should see a number of files. The one we're after is called hosts. Don't be thrown by the fact It doesn't have a file extension, that's just how this file exists on the file system. So even though it's a text file, don't feel like you need to give it a file extension. Once you have the file open, ensure the following line:

127.0.0.1   localhost

You'll need to make sure that line doesn't have an '#' preceding, it because that means it's commented out, and we don't want that now do we? If that's the case in your file, then uncomment it by removing the '#', and that should fix the problem. However if you've never even heard of a hosts file before, then you won't need to edit this file at all and WAMP should just work straight away which is great.

There are many other reasons why WAMP fails to start, which can stem from it being blocked in the firewall settings, to a rogue anti-virus system being overly protective or a lot more. In these times Google is most definitely your friend, if you put in your symptoms then someone else will have had the same problems and will be able to help you. Failing that, you can always ask me (hey@chrisdkemper.co.uk) and I'll do my best to get you up and running. With that out of the way, let's get back to the Localhost option.

The Localhost option is available in the menu. When clicked, it will take you to the site that is currently configured to run from localhost itself. If you're working with a clean installation, then you will see the screen shown in Figure 1-8. This screen shows you which extensions are currently loaded in Apache, as well as giving you some links to useful tools like phpMyAdmin and sqlbuddy. The most important role of this page is to show that everything is working. Given that the page requires Apache and PHP to run, if you can see it then everything is running smoothly!

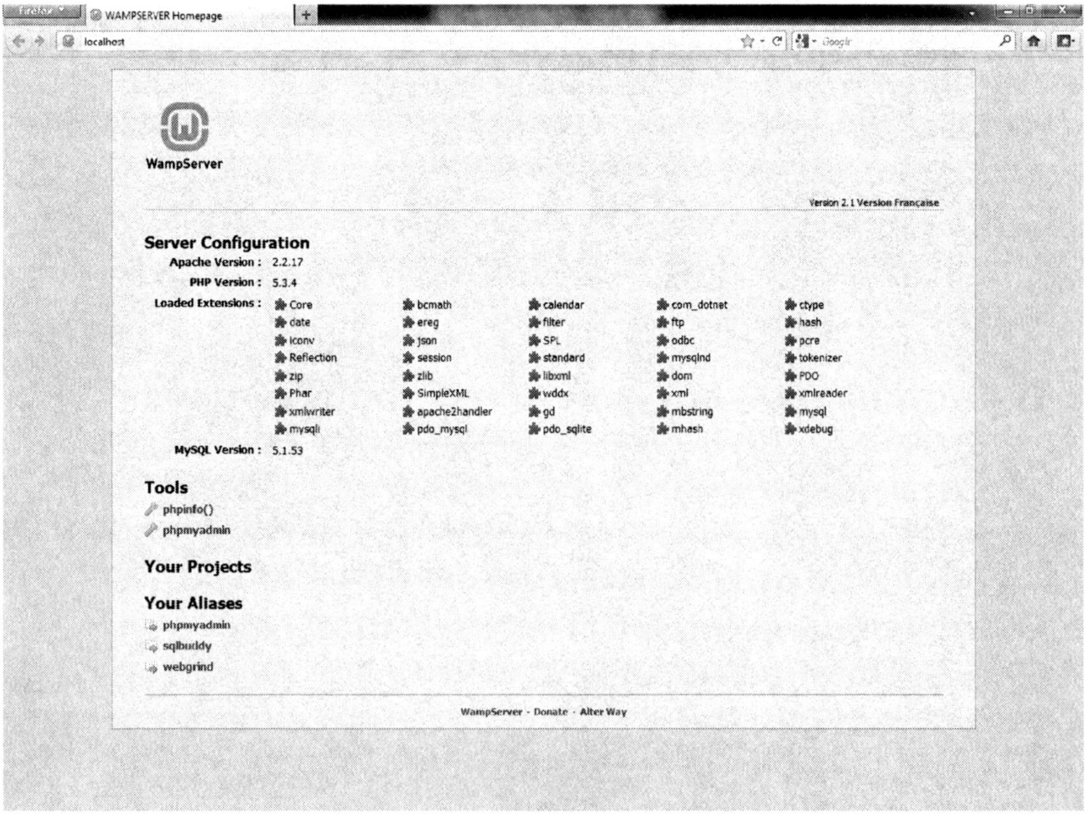

Figure 1-8. Default page for the localhost address, which also shows that WAMP is functioning correctly

If you want to test a website you've made using PHP and/or MySQL, put it in the www directory in your WAMP folder. However, there's a link for this in the popup menu. If you were to put a website into this directory, you would be able to view it by navigating to the file or folder, preceded by the localhost address. For example, if you had a website called `test` and inside you had a file named index.php, you would view that file by going to `http://localhost/test/index.php`, or `http://localhost/test`.

Another great link from this menu is phpMyAdmin, which is a handy web app for managing your databases. Here, you can modify an existing database, or add any amount of new ones. You can also change user information and other settings, but for a basic environment, you won't need to alter any of these settings. When it comes to accessing the database, it's worth noting that your database host is *localhost*, the account is *root*, and a password isn't set by default. If you ever need to install a fresh copy of Wordpress or Drupal or any other package, you'll need that information to connect to the database.

All in all, WAMP is a pretty good package to use, nice and easy to install, and the menu helps you access some good locations quickly. My only gripe is the lack of support for editing hosts or creating virtual hosts. Although I haven't mentioned it yet, you would need to edit your hosts/virtual hosts files to create something like `http://dev.example.com/`, which would be your local development version of `http://example.com`, which will be running on your machine. If you just used the default that came with the WAMP installation, it would mean you would end up having `http://localhost/example`. This may not seem that bad, but having a lot of sites running through it can be very confusing. Other than the hosts issue, WAMP gets two thumbs up from me. Huzzah!

Mac

When it comes to installing on a Mac, you have a couple of options. By default, Macs come with a built-in web server, which you can use for basic websites. To enable it, head into System Preferences ➤ Sharing. You'll then see the Sharing window (see Figure 1-9). By clicking the link for your web page, you open up a default page that is already in the system.

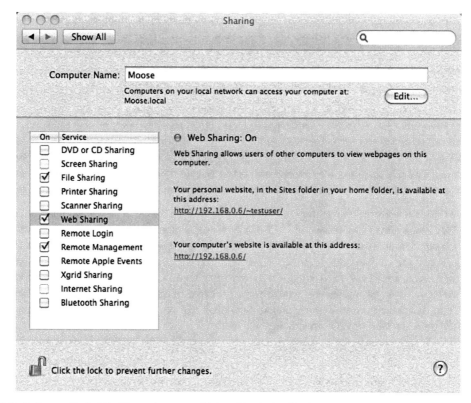

Figure 1-9. Setting up the built-in Mac web server which resides in the Sharing section of System Preferences

If you want to look at this site, or add more sites into the folder, you can do so by going from your home directory on your Mac to the Sites folder. If you open up a new Finder window, by default there will be a link to your home directory in the sidebar; this is the directory with a tiny house next to it. Once you're inside your home folder, the Sites folder should be visible. Inside this folder you'll see the files used to create the default website, which are simply an HTML file and an images directory.

This is a very limited server, however, and you don't get the luxuries of phpMyAdmin, or even PHP out of the box. You can install these manually, but it takes a lot of configuration to do so. To remedy that problem and make the installation a lot more painless, there is a package you should install that will add all of this in. This particular package is known as Mac, Apache, MySQL, and PHP (MAMP). Although MAMP is highly recommended, there are other options out there as well, including XAMPP for Mac, which will do the same things MAMP does. However because of its highly regarded status, in this chapter I'll show you how to set up MAMP.

Getting the package

The first thing you'll see when you head over to www.mamp.info is a download link for MAMP, and an option to buy MAMP Pro. I'll go into more detail about MAMP Pro later, but for now, download the regular version of MAMP. Once it's downloaded, you'll be presented with the standard install options for most Mac applications (see Figure 1-10). First, you'll want to drag the MAMP folder into your applications folder. (Don't worry about MAMP Pro right now. I'll get to that a little later on.) Once that's done, you can move onto setting up MAMP.

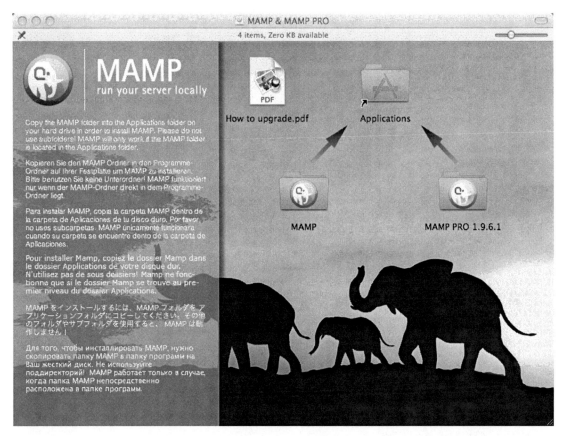

Figure 1-10. The installation package received after opening the file downloaded from the MAMP website

Setting up

Once you've downloaded MAMP, head into it by opening up a new Finder window by pressing Cmd+tab until you reach Finder, then Cmd+N to open up a new window, which by default will take you to your home directory. You can also open up a new Finder window by right-clicking on the Finder icon on your dock and selecting New Finder Window. From your home directory, navigate to Applications, then MAMP (Figure 1-11).

Figure 1-11. Once you install MAMP, this folder houses the htdocs folder, where all the sites are stored, as well as configuration files used by MAMP itself.

1. The first thing you'll want to do is install the widget by double-clicking the Mamp Control.wdgt file, which will launch the Dashboard view where you can choose where to put the new widget and whether or not to keep it. I'd advise installing it because it comes in quite handy and saves you having to open the MAMP application every time you want to use it.

2. Now, using either the widget or double-clicking the app, you need to start the services. Once you do so, navigate to the start page (see Figure 1-12 to see how this looks). This page displays some useful information, including your MySQL login information. You also get links to phpMyAdmin, SQLiteManager, FAQ, phpinfo, and much more. The only link you'll use here, for the moment, is phpMyAdmin, which gives you the ability to manage any databases you have installed locally.

3. One thing you don't have, however, is a link to your sites folder. If you installed the widget earlier, you'll already have seen this folder; if you have not, head on over to Applications ➤ MAMP ➤ htdocs as in Figure 1-11.

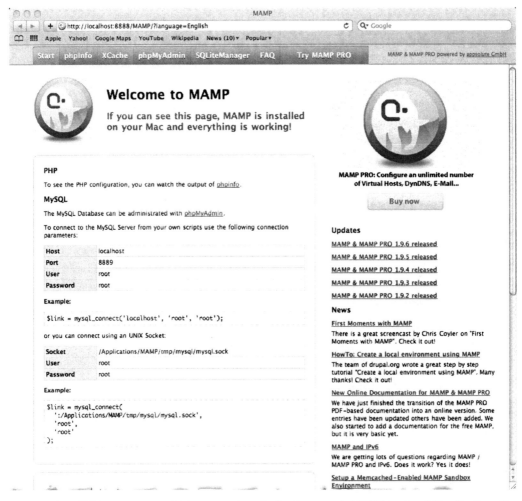

Figure 1-12. The MAMP startup page which opens automatically when you start MAMP, or by clicking the Open Start Page button. It shows the configuration needed for MySQL, supplies links to SQLiteManager and phpMyAdmin, and shows that MAMP is working correctly.

You can put any website that's running HTML, PHP, and MySQL, or any mix of the three into this folder, and you'll be able to navigate to it using `http://localhost:8888/website-name`. Notice the *8888* in the URL (if you've been following along from the start of the chapter, you won't have seen this before). It refers to the port which Apache is running on. The reason this is included is to allow the default web server that comes with Mac to run alongside MAMP without causing any problems. You can, of course, change this to the default ports, thus removing the 8888, by going into Preferences ➤ Ports, then clicking the "Set to default Apache and MySQL ports" button. If you make that choice, then you should be aware that the default Mac server won't work alongside MAMP while it's running. That's all you need to get set up on a basic level. But now I want to tell you about the benefits of MAMP Pro.

MAMP Pro

MAMP Pro offers some pretty cool features that you can get for a neat price of around $59 that is totally worth it if you're going to be using this on a day-to-day basis. MAMP Pro has a built-in option whereby you can add a new site to the htdocs directory and then give it a unique address on your system. For example, instead of `http://localhost/example` you could have `http://dev.example.com/` or `http://example.local`, or anything you'd like to call it. There are a lot of benefits of using this method, many of which are organizational, since having a lot of sites coming from the localhost domain would be rather hard to handle. It may also be required for some sites to ensure certain bits of code work correctly.

You can, of course, make these changes manually, but that requires editing hosts file (best achieved by editing in Terminal) and some of the config files of MAMP, which can be quite daunting for some people. Plus, if you really are one of those people who doesn't ever want to touch the command line, this program could save you a lot of headaches.

If that's convinced you to give it a try, open up the .dmg file you downloaded from the MAMP website and drag the MAMP Pro directory into Applications and you're ready to go. If you forget you have Pro in there, and you open up MAMP by mistake, don't worry, it'll prompt you that Pro's there and will offer to open it for you, because it's nice like that.

One word of warning, though: you can give MAMP Pro a try via the trial that is built right into the installer (how cool is that?!). If you then open MAMP rather than MAMP Pro, however, and bypass the prompt it gives you to open Pro (see Figure 1-13), it will not work correctly. Another slight negative is that the widget you installed at the start will no longer work, so you'll always have to have the application open; you can always minimize it, which is what I do. If you decide Pro isn't working out for you, and you're fine with editing the files manually to create new local domains for yourself, then be sure to run the MAMP uninstaller located in the MAMP Pro directory in Applications; as I mentioned earlier, MAMP won't run properly if it knows Pro is around. (I think it's scared of it or something.)

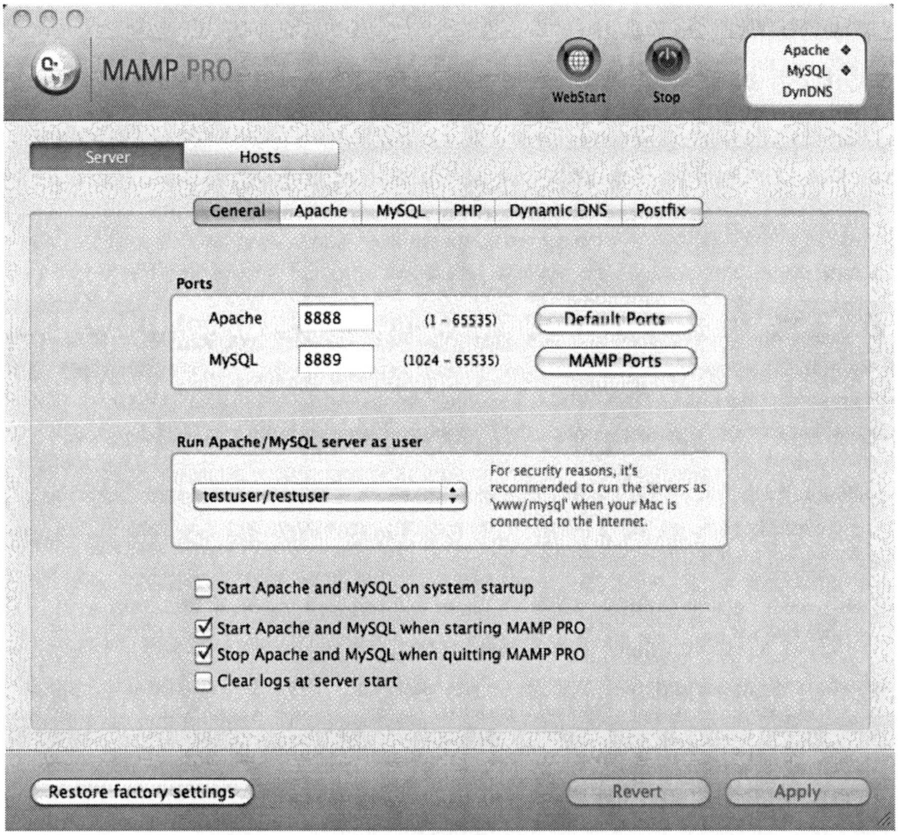

Figure 1-13. Here you see the MAMP Pro start screen which has a lot more configuration options than regular old MAMP. You can easily configure the port settings from this screen, as well as configuring startup options for Apache and MySQL.

Ubuntu

For those of you who are already hardcore enough to be using Ubuntu (or maybe just using an old laptop and this is what you have to deal with), never fear, I'll get you set up! With Windows and Mac, you have a couple of options about which package to download, any of which makes it a lot easier to install Apache, MySQL, and PHP and have them configured correctly, Ubuntu, however, doesn't give you that luxury. There are a couple of methods to get you set up, either by entering a few commands into Terminal (don't worry, it's easy) or doing it through the Package manager. Since I'm a nice guy and I want to cover all the bases, I'll run you through both.

Package manager

In the latest version of Ubuntu (11.10), for some reason the Synaptic Package Manager wasn't included by default as it had been for all previous releases of Ubuntu. This application allows for the easy installation of a whole load of applications which would otherwise need to be installed by other means. You'll need this for the majority of the processes in this book, so before you can proceed, Synaptic Package Manager will have to be installed. To install this application and all the other fancy software, you'll need full admin access to your machine. If you're working on a network of some kind and you don't have full admin access, you may need to ask one of the network techies or whoever administers the network to install the software for you. You'll need to dive into Terminal here to install the Synaptic Package Manager,which you can open by pressing the Dash button in the sidebar; in the search field, type in `Terminal`, then when it comes up, launch it with a click. With the Terminal window open, type in the command `sudo apt-get install synaptic` and hit enter. When you do so you'll be asked to enter your password. This is required to complete the installation. You may notice that when you type nothing comes up on the screen. This is normal, so just type in your password and hit enter. When the command runs, you'll be asked if you're fine with the installation taking up space on your machine; just type `Y` here and hit enter. Once the installation is complete, you'll be able to open the Synaptic Package Manager by hitting the Dash button, searching for `Synaptic`, and clicking it when the search finds it.

This should also work on any older or newer versions without a problem. In older versions of Ubuntu the package manager can be found by going to System ➤ Administration ➤ Synaptic package manager.

With the package manager open, it's time to get installing. Here you're going to install the same environment as shown on both Mac and Windows; you're looking for PHP (in this case PHP5), Apache, and MySQL, and for the sake of consistency we'll throw in phpMyAdmin as well.

1. To get started, type `php5` into the search bar (Figure 1-14). Then click on the check box next to where you can see php5, hit "Mark for installation", then click mark.

2. You'll want to do the same for apache2, MySQL-server, and phpMyAdmin.

3. Once you have them all marked for installation, click the apply arrow and it'll start the downloading process.

4. For the most part you'll just see files downloading, but you'll also get hit with a couple of prompts during this process, one of which will require you to select a root password for MySQL. Since this is just a local machine, the password should be something simple, such as "root" or "password". I've opted for "root", but feel free to use any password you like, as long as you can remember it. Let it be a warning that if you do forget the password, you don't get the luxury of having it e-mailed to you, and you can't change it once it's been set. Also, if you choose to have a basic password and then connect to an open wi-fi connection, or anything where outside users can get access, your data could be easily accessible to someone who knows a little about hacking. If this machine is going to be a production server and will have public access, I'd advise using a stronger password with a mix of characters, numbers, and symbols.

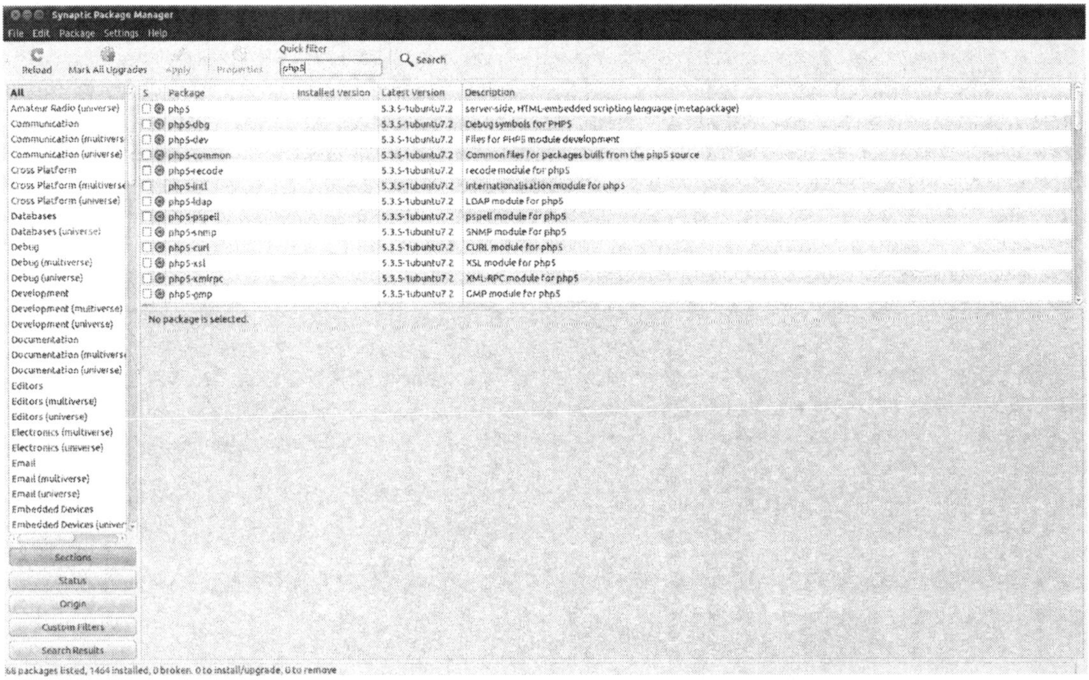

Figure 1-14. The package manager allows for easy installation of a number of different applications.

5. The only other prompt you'll be shown will be one advising you to reconfigure your server, and it'll prompt you with two options. Go ahead and hit apache2, and continue. Once the installation has finished, you're good to go.

6. To test that it's all working, head on over to `http://localhost/` and you should see the default Apache page with a nice big "It works!" on the screen. Now go to `http://localhost/phpmyadmin` and enter the information you specified during the installation. If everything has worked out you should see phpMyAdmin doing what it does best, showing you your MySQL databases. Yay!

Unfortunately, you won't get a nice menu like you do when you install WAMP for Windows, but that doesn't matter. Navigating to phpMyAdmin and localhost couldn't be simpler. You may be wondering, "Where do my sites live?" This is, of course, a great question. As part of the installation process, a folder called "www" has been created, which you can find by accessing your File Systemdirectory by) selecting Home folder in the dock, and selecting File System from the left-hand side then navigate to var ➤ www. All the sites you want to show on the web server should be included in this folder, just as on Windows.

Terminal method

If you're feeling a bit more hardcore, you can always install the LAMP server using good old Terminal (and you'll appreciate my `apt-get` pun after you're finished). To get started, open up a Terminal window by going into Dash again, and search for *Terminal*. When it shows up, just click it to open it. If you think you'll be using Terminal a lot, it could be worth pinning it to the sidebar by right-clicking its icon and selecting "Keep in launcher", which means it'll always be readily available.

Installing everything you need via Terminal is actually quite simple. The recommended way to install a LAMP Server is to use a `tasksel` command, but that doesn't come preinstalled, so you need to get that installed first using

    sudo apt-get install tasksel

The shortened version of "substitute user do", *sudo* basically means do *x* with another user's privileges, normally the root or super user. Without using `sudo`, you can run into file permission errors of all sorts. Next, `apt-get` is a command that handles the installation of software, and `tasksel` is what you want to install. Just enter that command and you're ready to go!

Once you enter the command you'll be asked for your password. If you can't see anything when you're typing, don't worry. This is a standard feature in the command line to prevent people seeing how long your password is. Once you've typed in your invisible password, you'll be prompted to confirm if it's all right to add *X* amount of space to the file system. Just type **Y** and hit enter. After that, let the install process do its stuff and you're done! `tasksel` is a way of installing certain common packages needed; you can see a full list of these by entering `sudo tasksel` into Terminal and hitting enter (or if you'd rather not do that, look at Figure 1-15 to see what the menu looks like).

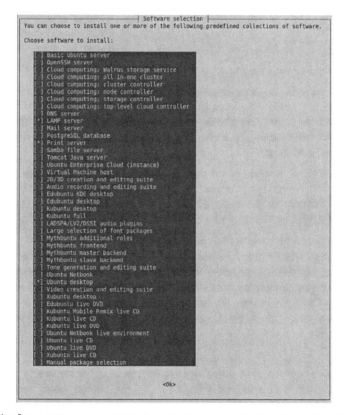

Figure 1-15. The `Tasksel` installation menu, which allows for the easy installation of a number of applications (we're only after the LAMP server, however).

Since you know what you want to install, you can specify the package in Terminal without opening the menu, so just enter this into your Terminal window:

```
sudo tasksel install lamp-server
```

The only difference between this command and the previous one, of course, is what you're installing: in this case, `lamp-server`. Also, you're now using `tasksel` instead of `apt-get`. You'll be asked for your admin password again, then you'll see the Terminal window change into a progress bar, until you get a prompt asking you for your MySQL root password. If you know this machine is going to be available only to you, then feel free to make the password something simple, such as "root" or "password". However, if you are going to be accessing wireless networks, or any other network where your machine will be visible to others, it may be advisable to use a slightly more complex password to stop people touching your data. Just don't forget it, though; you won't be able to get it back if you do. Once you've decided on your password, just wait for the rest of the files to download and you're done! If you head over to `http://localhost` you'll see everything has worked correctly. However, you haven't installed phpMyAdmin yet, so let's do that now! Go back to Terminal and type this command:

```
sudo apt-get install phpmyadmin
```

You'll again be asked for your admin password and whether you're OK with downloading X amount of data for the installation. You'll then be prompted to indicate which web server you'd like it to be configured for; just select apache2 and continue on. The final prompt you'll see will ask you to configure phpMyAdmin (see Figure 1-16), just click Yes and you'll be almost ready to go.

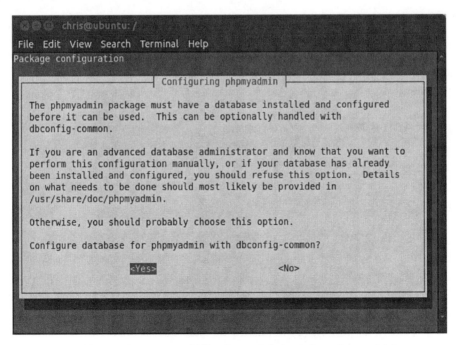

Figure 1-16. The prompt asking whether or not you'd like phpmyadmin to configure its own database

There are a couple of changes you need to make before everything will work correctly. First of all, you need to edit the file, apache.conf. To do this, head back to Terminal and type in

```
sudo gedit /etc/apache2/apache2.conf
```

This will bring up a text window. Scroll down to the bottom of the screen, then include the following (just like in Figure 1-17):

```
# Include phpmyadmin
include /etc/phpmyadmin/apache.conf
```

This tells Apache where to find phpMyAdmin, otherwise it just won't work with it. Save the file and close the window. Now you just need to run one more command and you'll be ready to go.

```
sudo /etc/init.d/apache2 restart
```

This command restarts Apache, complete with a working link to phpMyAdmin. To test that everything worked OK, head over to http://localhost/phpmyadmin and you should see the phpMyAdmin screen. That's everything you need, all set up.

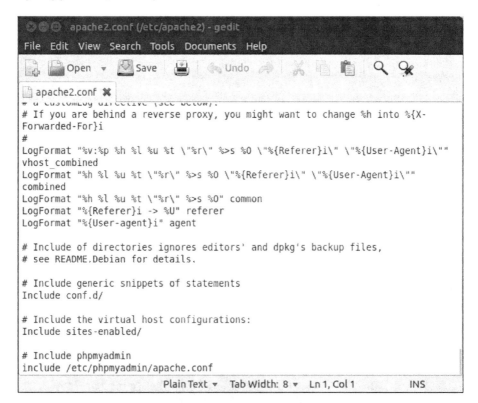

Figure 1-17. The apache2.conf, including the reference to phpmyadmin to allow it to work

Summary

So that's it. You're all set up! You're ready to be unleashed into the world of creating websites, knowing you're capable of running anything the world can throw at you (provided its' PHP and/or MySQL, of course). Although these walkthroughs have all been written using the latest releases at the time of writing, you should still be able to use all the steps I've mentioned with previous versions without any problems, so don't be afraid to use these instructions if you're running an older version of an OS I've mentioned here.

Now that you're ready to display a website, it's time to get into the nitty-gritty of keeping your site backed up using source control.

Chapter 2

In the Beginning There Were Just Files

Everyone has been there at some point: that moment when you think "Oh no! Where is the original version of that file?!" Whether the client decided, "Actually, I don't like those changes I asked you to make—it was better the way it was," or you made that assumption yourself, sometimes new functionality you're working on just doesn't work out. If you're just working with plain old files, the time to re-create those original files could take just as long as the new work took. Surely there's a better way to get around such problems? Don't worry; it's time to meet your new best friend, version control.

If you have no idea what I'm talking about, you've come to the right place. Even if you *do* know what I'm talking about, you've still come to the right place. I'm going to teach you what version control *really* is, and why it can make your life a lot easier. (In some cases it can really save your bacon.) If you already know a little something about version control, I'll teach you some things you didn't know, and maybe even improve your workflow a bit, which is always good!

I'll start with a definition of version control. Once that's out of the way, it'll be time for a history lesson. I'll show you how things used to be, and why you're a lot better off now than you were in the 1970s. I'll also tell you about how things have progressed, right up to some of the leaders in the market at the moment.

So, let's gets started, shall we?

What is version control?

Although I'll use the term *version control* a lot throughout the book, it's also known as *revision control* and *source control*, both of which are types of software configuration management (SCM).

If you were to type "define: Version control" into that popular search engine beginning with a G, it would give you this:

> **Noun**: The task of keeping a software system consisting of many versions and configurations well organized.

Although that *is* correct, that's not really what I'm aiming to teach you about here. When I mention a version control system (or VCS hereafter), I'm referring to the management of files. This is either on a local or remote basis, which allows you to do the following: update, commit (which adds it the repository, so it's safe and if need be you can go back to it), delete, comment on, and revert to any previous version of a file, or files you've committed. So basically, if you commit it, you can revert back to it at a later date if you need to. Pretty cool, eh?

If you want another way to think about it, imagine when you're using Photoshop, or any other software with an undo function, and you reach the point when you've hit undo one too many times, and you're out of history states. How frustrating and annoying is that? Well, with a VCS you have every iteration of your file, or files, right from version 1 to however many versions you end up with. Every time you add or update a file, it goes to the next version, so everything is safe and backed up. When making any kind of change or update, you have the option to add a comment with that change. This can come in really useful when trying to find where a new feature was introduced, or just to generally keep track of what your changes did.

To use an example: if you're trying to code something new, and for whatever reason everything goes wrong and you lose your work, you don't have to panic. It's all backed up in the repository, and if you've been good with your commits, each change will have a comment associated with it, so you can pinpoint the exact revision you need to go back to.

You can also reclaim accidentally deleted files (or intentionally deleted files), too. If you update your code and it sees that a file is missing, it'll replace it (that is, if you haven't told it to delete said file, of course). That's how powerful version control is. If you weren't using a VCS, you didn't have the files backed up in some way, and you made a big mistake, it would be pretty much the same as flattening a PhotoShop document, hitting Save, then closing the program: there's nothing you could do to go back. It only takes losing your code once to convert you into a VCS lover.

Oh, and did I mention, VCS also allows multiple people to work on the same code, at the same time? That's right, and it will merge all the changes together so you won't get your work overwritten. That's another of the great benefits of VCS and how powerful it can be. Of course there is *a lot* more to it than that; this is just a taste to get you excited about managing your files. I'll get into the cool things you can do with the big VCS players available at the moment, but that's for later.

The earlier version control solutions

As I said earlier, it's always good to learn about the history of a new topic, even if it's just to see how much better things are now than they were back in the day, or more accurately, the 1970s. I'll take you through the very first systems of version control, show you a couple of pros and cons, then we'll get to the good stuff, the current big players in the market.

SCCS

Source Code Control System (SCCS) is definitely worth mentioning because it was the first VCS. It was released way back in 1972 by a gentleman working at Bell Labs, named Marc J. Rochkind. SCCS was mainly geared toward versioning text files and software and was written in a programming language called SNOBOL (String Oriented Symbolic Language) which was the main language used by Bell Labs between 1962 and 1967. Rochkind later rewrote it in C (a different programming language) which greatly improved its speed and allowed it to be used on UNIX. SCCS later became the dominant VCS for UNIX, which it remained for a number of years, until the release of the Revision Control System. Although it's considered obsolete now, it was still a great help to other developers and helped lead to newer and better systems.

RCS

Revision Control System (RCS) came along in 1982. It was released as a free alternative to SCCS, which was still quite popular. Rather than working with a full repository (like some of the more modern systems), RCS gave each file its own repository, which was an RCS file. This, as you can imagine, had limitations. It did, however, let you create a branch for a file you were working on. This meant you could, in a sense, make a copy of the file within the system and then make changes to it.

The downside to this was that the naming conventions for the branches were quite terrible. For example, a file could be in version 2.4, a branch of that file would be 2.4.1, and any revisions on that branch would be 2.4.1.7—as you can see, this wasn't the best of systems. You can still see RCS used in some Linux distributions, and at the time of this writing, it's still maintained under the GNU Project and is in version 5.8.

> **Note** *A quick word about branches: if you're working away in the main repository, or trunk, and you decide to make some major changes or try something new, you need to create a branch from the main code of the repository to experiment with the new changes. The changes in the branch don't affect the main code at all; you're free to make any changes you'd like, without worrying. In newer versioning systems, such as Subversion, Mercurial, and Git, as well as many others, the branches themselves are also versioned. This keeps the changes you've made backed up, and if you like, the branches can also be shared with other developers for collaborative purposes. If you think the code you've just written is top notch, you can merge it into the main codebase, or if you'd rather just destroy the branch, that's fine too. The changes will be forgotten and nothing will have changed.*

PVCS

Polytron Version Control System (PVCS) was released in 1985 and was a commercial product that changed hands many times, sitting finally with Silver Lake Partners. It was also a more advanced version of RCS. As well as being able to make changes and branch files, PVCS could be configured to allow multiple users to work on the same files. It didn't have a native merging system, unfortunately, so if multiple users were working on a file, the chronological second person to commit a change would create a branch of the file alongside the original. This could result in many different versions of any particular file which, as you can imagine, would be quite hard to work with.

By today's standards, PVCS would be considered outdated, but it's still supported for those who choose to use it and it is now a proprietary version control system.

CVS

When Concurrent Version System (CVS) was launched in 1990, that's when things started to change. This system had a central storage repository with capabilities to allow files to be worked with on different machines, and then pushed to the central repository.

CVS had also improved on some of the techniques used by RCS; you could now branch out directories in single branches, rather than only being able to branch single files. It also added support for merging, so if multiple users had been collaborating on the same file, this allowed them to collate any changes together. That being said, the merging and branching capabilities were somewhat limited and didn't always work as well as desired, which led to some people being off put by the fear of potentially losing work due to poor merges or branching. Another disadvantage of CVS was its inability to track changes to directories or file names, so if you needed to change a folder name or location, it would result in an error in the repository.

CVS is considered an outdated means of version control and most people using it are encouraged to migrate to a new system. If you're one of those people, then head on over to Chapter 15 and I'll show you how to migrate to a better system.

ClearCase

When ClearCase launched in 1992, it made some serious changes in how version control was handled. Unlike previous systems, ClearCase actually integrates into your operating system, to make the versioning experience a lot more seamless. In 2003, IBM bought ClearCase, and they still maintain it. Having a seamless versioning process isn't simple; there's a lot of complexity in there. Whether it's creating configuration specs or configuring your internal network, ClearCase is not simple to set up and isn't really designed for use by the average Joe looking to manage one or two websites. If you do happen to be part of a large company with a couple of network engineers at your disposal, then you could still take advantage of the many options available to you from ClearCase, including automated software builds, a nearly automated merging system, branching, distributed builds, a fast extensive database, and a whole lot more.

Of course, all of this functionality isn't cheap. IBM won't disclose a cost on their website; as you can imagine, that can't be good. Additionally, ClearCase isn't quick to set up. If you do decide to go down this path, you'll be a looking a long setup time—not a couple of hours, more like a couple of months! Setting up all of those network protocols and configuration specs takes a long time for your network engineers. Just make sure they don't do all that work on old machines; ClearCase is quite resource intensive, and if it crashes, you'll know about it. Despite all that, though, ClearCase is still one of the market leaders, and is used by many corporations all over the world. It seems all those negatives are worth it if you have the money and the resources.

VSS

Don't let the fact that Visual SourceSafe (VSS) was released in 1994 make you think it was an improvement on previous systems, because it wasn't. Straight off the bat it used a locked repository—so, basically local only—which means no coding with your friends using this. You could live with that to begin with because in its early development it was created for all systems. But after the initial developers (One Tree Software) were bought out by Microsoft, all development on other platforms ceased and it became Windows-only.

Although not the best of options, it's not all bad. VSS was GUI (graphical user interface) only, so no tampering with the command line for you. That was one of the reasons for its adoption and use for managing source code. (Or, who knows? It could have had something to do with the fact that it was bundled with Microsoft products such as Visual Studio.) Those who did choose to use it would also have the luxury of managing any kind of file, but don't let that fool you. It was quite unstable when it came to files that weren't text based, so images, exe files, and anything like that wouldn't work so well.

If you wanted to look into some nice branching with VSS, think again. You could branch out and make changes, but it was by no means nice. The branches themselves would often become corrupt, and the changes created in the branch would be lost. It would also update the branched file when the trunk was updating, which made the branch useless. Branching support in VSS may as well have been nonexistent. If you did manage to get a branch working, you wouldn't have an easy job getting those changes back into the main repository; merging was highly integrated into checking in new changes, so examining changes and making sure you only had good code being committed was a real challenge, to say the least. It was a lot easier to take a manual copy of the file you wanted to branch and work on it independently, cutting out the branching process altogether.

I could write a book on the negatives of VSS, and it would use the word *slow* a lot, because pretty much any feature it has either doesn't work very well, or does so very, very slowly. It was also notorious for becoming corrupted, and in most cases checks for this would need to be done very regularly. That is, of course, if it hadn't already worked itself into a mess by having poor time zone support, using a database over 5GB (which Microsoft recommends you do not exceed), or crashing Visual Studio, causing you to lose work. (Microsoft has published an article on how to remove VSS integration).

Another problem with VSS was the way the checkout system worked. If you checked out a file, it would be marked as locked in the repository, meaning nobody else could edit it. If someone else were to try and check out the file, you would see a message telling you it was locked, and therefore you couldn't check it out. This caused huge problems if the user were to forget to check the file back in, as nobody else could work on it. Also, if the user were to leave the company, or go away on holiday, the checked out file would be locked indefinitely. As I said, I could write a book on it.

All these negatives seem to have gotten back to Microsoft because the final release of VSS was way back in 2005, and it won't be supported from 2017. Rather than trying to improve the existing product, Microsoft has started again with a new one, Team Foundation Server, which looks to resolve the issues of VSS with a complete overhaul.

Perforce

Perforce (P4) is a beast. It's like the younger brother of ClearCase, but not as beefy. Don't let that fool you, though; it has a fair few bells and whistles of its own to shout about. First of all, it's available on all platforms, which is always a good start. It has a lot of GUIs at its disposal, including one for merging and diffing (that is, a way of finding differences between multiple versions of a file, such as your local copy of a file, and the most recent revision which you need to download.

> *Note: You would most likely need to diff a file when multiple people are collaborating on the same file. This would potentially result in each contributor changing a different part of the file, so you couldn't just take one person's version of the file, as some changes would be missed. To get around this problem, you would perform a diff on the multiple versions of the file, which would highlight any differences between the versions. From that, you could take the changes from each to create a unified file, containing changes from each version of the file. It also gives you the opportunity to remove unwanted changes that have been added.*

Perforce also had a GUI for viewing the history of a file, which can make navigating versions of a file a lot easier. Before you get too excited, it's not all perfect. One of the drawbacks of Perforce is how it manages branches. Instead of using metadata as the newer systems do, it uses directories, which can make managing branches a little complicated. However, having a Software Development Kit (SDK) and an Application Programming Interface (API) allows for some great integration with third-party applications, such as issue tracking software. This can make it rather useful and a good foundation to build a project on. At least that was the case in the mid 1990s when it was released.

P4 also has the capability to have an RSS feed for all the updates you do. That could come in quite handy if you were maintaining a project and needed to be kept up to date with changes from those maintaining the code for it.

It can be argued that using a central repository isn't the best of options, but as of May 2010, Perforce is licensed to more than 320,000 users at 5,000 organizations, which is a nice statistic to have alongside your company name.

AccuRev

Not a lot of positive things can said about AccuRev since it was released in 2002. The general consensus is that it's slow and overly complex for what it does. For example, files can exist in a multitude of states, unlike other systems which may only allow three. It's also a proprietary system, so you have to pay for all of this glory. You may get the impression that because you pay for it, you could use it on large projects—that isn't actually the case. Due to the file storage system, it actually gets slower to use when you have a bigger project, and it uses a lot of disk space to do what it does.

It also seems to use strange terminology for its processes. For example, *branches* are called *streams*, which seems to have just helped confuse the developers who use it. Why reinvent the wheel? If you do get a little stuck and want to have a look online for some help, don't bother—all you'll find is a whole load of negative reviews and very limited resources. Despite being limited to small projects, however, AccuRev is rather a solid system, with a decent branching system that actually worked. It also comes with a built-in issue tracking system, which is pretty awesome. It also comes with a rather slow, clunky user interface (UI), which makes the whole system that little bit harder to use. One positive thing it brought to the table is that it helped users move away from CVS and ClearCase, which is always a good thing.

BitKeeper

BitKeeper is another system where you don't work from one central repository, but from your own local one. This means all changes, commits, and such are made to your local repository, otherwise known as a *distributed system*. It really hit it big in 2002 when its community version was chosen as the versioning tool for Linux kernel development. This sparked a somewhat heated debate between developers, some even refusing to use it altogether because they refused to adopt a proprietary system for controlling the code of the Linux kernel, a hugely open-source project. This went on until 2005, when BitMover (the developers of BitKeeper) decided to change its pricing structure and remove the free version.

The community edition was slightly limited in its use anyway, due to how the licensing worked. It could only be used for open-source projects and the developers of a project couldn't be working on the advancement of another VCS while using BitKeeper. So basically, if you were working with BitKeeper, you couldn't be working to improve CVS, AccuRev, or another VCS. In addition to that, even after you'd finished a project using the open source license for BitKeeper, you couldn't contribute to the development of another VCS for a whole year after the project had finished. How crazy is that? Also, BitKeeper required certain metadata to be stored on servers operated by them, which made it pretty much impossible for anyone to use this edition of BitKeeper without BitKeeper themselves knowing about it.

After a change in policy in 2005, the BitKeeper license allowed developers to work on an open source alternative to BitKeeper, which led to the development of Git, which you'll learn about shortly.

Summary

In the 1970s you had little to no branching, poor multiuser support, and nonexistent workflows. Now though, you have multi-user support included out of the box, the option for centralized repositories for improved security and much better workflows, the ability to work on multiple machines with little to no effort, and all that using free and open source systems.

There is also a huge amount of resources to take the strain out of setting things up or even determining where to host repositories. It's even possible to migrate between systems to allow for growth, or to make the switch from a centralized to a distributed versioning system, which you could never have dreamed of with the limited systems of the 1970s and early 1980s.

By looking at these old systems, you've seen how things used to be. Terrible folder structures, terrible merges, and other terrible things were a reality of some historic version control systems. I could hook you up with a copy of RCS, and you could create nice branches with crazy version names. You could try PVCS if you wanted to go back to not being able to merge your changes and conflicts, resulting in new branches. But these systems aren't going to make your life easier! So, what will?

Well, I have left a few key players out of this list—three, to be precise: Git, Subversion (SVN), and Mercurial. These systems have amassed a huge user base, and are used throughout the web industry by novices and pros alike. Thanks to this, they are seen as the leaders in the field, which means the support for them cannot be matched. In the coming chapters you'll learn everything you need to know about these systems, where they came from, and how they work—without any "terrible" in sight! For now, just be happy that these older systems are behind you and you're moving onto bigger and better things.

Chapter 3

Meet the Current Players in the Game: SVN, Git, and Mercurial

Here's a brief rundown of how this chapter is going to work. First of all, I'll explain why Subversion (SVN), Git, and Mercurial are so awesome and all the things they do best. Then I'll introduce each one individually, and describe what they do and how they do it (sounds a bit like a version control dating game!). Finally, I'll show you how to get each one set up on Windows, Mac, and Ubuntu. I'll be keeping this format—following the SVN, Git, and Mercurial layout—in later chapters. This holds true for improving workflow right up to creating a server, and everything in between. In each case, I'll cover SVN, Git, and Mercurial; I don't have any favorites here.

The differences between then and now

As you may remember from Chapter 1, I've already gone through a brief history of version control, starting way back with SCCS in 1972. This one started everything by being the first version control system (VCS); things really have come a long way.

There are a few products you need to be aware of to help make sense of the main players as I introduce them, the first of which is Concurrent Versions System (CVS). As already explained, CVS is a centralized system which was released in 1986. It did a good job for the time, but It was by no means perfect. The good thing about its flaws was that they led to the development of Apache Subversion (SVN), which is one of the systems you're about to learn a lot about.

The two other systems you're going to be learning about, Mercurial and Git, both stemmed from the same time. Back in 2005, BitKeeper withdrew its free version from the market, meaning there was no longer an open source distributed control system out there—thus both Mercurial and Git were born!

An introduction to the lead players: SVN, Git, and Mercurial

Now it's time to really get into the swing of things, and get to know these systems a little better. At the moment they are all just names, without any relation or context. To remedy that, I'll dive straight in at the deep end and explain the differences between the applications and why that matters.

What's the difference between them and why should I care?

The main difference between these three systems is that two of them are distributed systems and the other, SVN, is a centralized system. Which means you have the repository either on your machine (distributed) or in one central (and in most cases, remote) location (centralized). That's the essence of it on a very basic level; I'll be going into more detail about each one very soon.

Using a centralized system allows for better adoption because the learning curve is significantly less than its non-centralized competitors. The code is checked out of the repository, you make a few changes, maybe even add some files, then you check for updates and, provided there aren't any conflicts, push the code back in. Simple. Although distributed systems can take a bit of getting used to, the benefits of taking the time to do so can be huge. They allow you to have more control over your revisions, a great speed increase, and great scalability. Each of the systems discussed here has its own pros and cons, which I'll be addressing soon enough; you can decide which one suits your needs best.

Apache Subversion (SVN)

Apache Subversion first appeared on the scene in October 2000 after it was funded and developed by CollabNet, Inc. It's a centralized version control system, so if you ever commit/update files, they always originate from the same central location. It means you can always collaborate with other developers, even those in remote locations. Since SVN usually runs over HTTP, it's easy for most people to use since HTTP is a standard protocol and is allowed on most firewall setups. SVN comes with built-in merging tools for those times when people have been working in the same place in a file. It tries its best to merge the two versions of the file together, but if it can't resolve the conflict itself, it gives the option to you. When a conflict does come up, you can sort it out using a multitude of methods and programs, which I'll go over in a lot more detail later on in the book.

Apache Subversion is a bit of a mouthful if you're talking about it on a daily basis, so it was given the shortened name of SVN after the command used to control it. (I think it's a lot more catchy, don't you?) During development, its developers would use SVN to keep a history of web pages, documents, source code, and a lot more. This, of course, means the developers had enough confidence in it to use it while it was still being developed.

In November 2009, Subversion was accepted into Apache Incubator, which is the first step for open source projects to become a fully-fledged Apache Software Foundation project. In February 2010, it became just that, an Apache Software Foundation project.

Subversion was initially built to improve on the flaws of CVS, including the lack of support for moving directories, no symbolic versioning, no atomic commits, and a whole lot of other problems. SVN totally left CVS in the dust with its awesome feature set. One great feature was true atomic commits, which basically means either the whole commit completes, or nothing is comitted. True atomic commits work this way to help stop repositories from becoming corrupted due to incomplete data. Other features include being able to rename/copy/move/remove files while still keeping the full version history, and the ability to version symbolic links and have space-efficient binary-diff features, which give you more accurate versioning of binary files. Also included are branching support, commit messages, HTTP integration, and a whole lot more.

All these features, and the fact it's all open source, has led to SVN's wide adoption by a large number of companies, including Django, Ruby, Free BSD, PHP, Tigris.org, and whole lot more. Its simplicity of use has resulted in wide adoption between web agencies, developers, and designers alike.

SVN, of course, isn't all positive news; like anything, it has its downsides, one of which is its speed. If you're working with a remote repository and you need to commit your files and you happen to be using a slow Internet connection, you'll be waiting a long time. Of course this isn't SVN's fault, but since you always have to push remotely, it may discourage those with poor connections from committing, which is kind of against what versioning is trying to achieve. It's also fair to say that SVN's merging abilities aren't that great. If the merge isn't handled correctly (for example, if the file is not cleared of the additional code generated), then this can cause problems. In some cases (rare, but it can still happen), this can lead to the whole file being classed as a conflict, resulting in the file containing a duplicate of itself. To avoid such problems, it's always a good idea to ensure all conflicts are handled correctly.

Although there are other, older systems on the market that provide a centralized system to work with (such as ClearCase or Perforce), SVN is definitely the leader in the field. Although it does have some negatives, its ease of use and wide support with third-party applications make it a great product.

Mercurial

Mercurial first came into being in April 2005 after the free version of BitKeeper was removed from the market, so developer Matt Mackall decided to write an open-source version and called it Mercurial. Its Terminal command always starts with hg—those of you who remember school chemistry will know that HG is the chemical symbol for Mercury. (Clever, eh?).

Unlike the previously mentioned SVN, Mercurial is a distributed version control system, so if you push changes to your repository, it goes to your local machine. This does, however, give you a huge speed increase because you're not constantly pushing to a remote server (although it can be set up that way). If you are committing to a location on a network or a remote location, Mercurial can be set up to work with SSH. This is very similar to the standard HTTP protocol, but can be more secure. It can also be an alternative if you are on a locked-down network and the HTTP ports have been closed for whatever reason.

Mercurial is built primarily using the Python programming language, which gives it great cross-platform compatibility. This probably makes you think it's a command-line tool (which it is, mostly); however, there are graphical tools available for those of you who don't want to touch Terminal. You can also find these lovely GUIs (graphical user interfaces) on most modern operating systems (Windows, Mac, Linux), as well as the command line tools, of course!

Another of Mercurial's nifty features is the ability to export the changes you've done to a file and have another user import them. You may be saying to yourself, "Why would I want to do that?" Let me give you an example. If you're working on a very closed network, and you have no easy way to get access to a remote repository, you could export your changes to a file, and e-mail them to another member of the team outside of the office so they can push the files for you. Exporting the code also gives the full history and the user information. So even if someone else were to commit the code for you, it would still be under your name. You could also use this method if the project you were working on required each new bit of code to be reviewed and approved by a member of the team before it was committed. You could export your changes and e-mail them over and have the code reviewed that way, before committing it.

All these fancy features have led to its use by a large number of products, including Adium, Mozilla, Netbeans, Vim, Growl, and a lot, lot more. This doesn't even include the large number of designers and developers who have chosen to manage their own code with this great versioning tool.

Git

Git emerged around April 2005, and as you may remember from the previous section, that's also when Mercurial's development kicked off. As with Mercurial, Git was created to fill the void when BitKeeper's free version was pulled. It was created by Linus Torvalds, who also initialized Linux kernel development, which meant it was going to be good! As well as filling a void in the version control market, it was also created to manage the source code used for Linux kernel development, Torvalds' other project.

Development on the project started on the April 3, it was publicly announced on the April 6, and began self hosting on April 7, so within four days, Git was using it own system to host its source code. Now that is an impressive turnaround. Between April 7 and its 1.0 public release on December 21, Git was used for the Linux kernel 2.6.12 release, a huge milestone in its popularity.

After the 1.0 release, and a lot complex development, Torvalds passed the project on to Junio Hamano, who had been a large contributor to the project. He still maintains the project today!

If you're British, you may have a problem with the name of this version control system: the word *git* is British slang for a person who is a deliberate and cunning nuisance. Here's a quote from Torvalds himself: "I'm an egotistical bastard, and I name all my projects after myself. First Linux, now Git." I think that says it all.

Like Mercurial, Git is a distributed version control system with a difference: this one is *fast*. Git was built for speed and security. It was also built for rapid branching, with the type of development in mind in mind where you should be branching for different features, then merging back into the main repository. It's also scalable: you can have a huge project and see no slowdown in speed. (Tests done by Mozilla can confirm this). The speed increase comes from the fact that it is a local repository first and foremost; you can see a noticeable speed increase accessing a local repository against a remote one.

Git also has a nifty feature known as Git stash. Although it may sound like some kind of sketchy shoplifter, Git stash is a pretty awesome feature. It allows you to take your current code version and stash it away, leaving you with what you had after your last commit. Say you're busy working away on some new features, but you're not ready to commit them yet and all of a sudden the boss comes in saying this bug needs to be fixed asap. Normally, you'd need to either copy the files away, quickly finish what you were doing, or commit some shoddy half-finished code. Not with Git stash. This bad boy takes whatever changes you had made, and stashes them away for you. This leaves you with the newest version from the repository, so you can fix the bug and commit it into the main code base. Then, once you're ready to continue working on it, just bring back your code from the stash, and you'll be back where you were before the pesky bug came along. You can also have multiple stashes, so you can have them from multiple projects or simply from different times. From there, you can decide whether you want to just discard the stash, or use it; it's up to you. Now that's a powerful tool!

Although Git's local use is somewhat impressive, when it comes to remote use it's a little harder to set up. To access a remote Git server you need to have SSH keys for both your local machine and the remote one. This is why some people are put off its adoption, due to the complexity of its initial setup and the learning curve to use it. To help make the learning process a little less painful, there are a number of services out there which make working with Git and remote Git repositories a lot easier. A service called GitHub is one of the more popular options when it comes to working with remote repositories. It includes easy-to-understand instructions to set up a server using their service and then gain access to it, as well as a number of other guides for setting up and using Git. With great services like GitHub and great books like this one to help get started, there's no reason why you shouldn't give it a try.

Where to install and usr/local

Before we dive into installing things, we need to take a brief look at where software packages install themselves, and why you should care about it. The first question that always comes to mind when installing anything is "Does it matter where it goes?". Depending on what it is you're installing, you may not actually have to care, but for the sake of what's coming in this chapter, I'll assume you do.

To make this a little more clear, let's talk a little bit about Mac OS X and Linux. Sadly, Windows doesn't use a UNIX file system, so these rules don't apply to it. Let's start with Mac. In most cases, if you install a new application, you'll put it into the main Applications folder. If you created a new user, that user will be able to see the same applications because the main folder is shared with all users. What if you want to keep an application all to yourself? This is where usr/local comes into play. usr/local loosely translates to your user account on your Mac or Linux machine. Anything in your own user account is only for your eyes. This includes any software you've installed, files, or anything like that.

When you perform system upgrades or install new software, by default the new software will go into the global install directory. This means that not only is it available to all users on the system, but it's not always safe from unwanted changes. If you spent a nice amount of time configuring and working with a particular application, but then all of a sudden a system update came in for that application, any changes you had made would be overwritten, which of course would be terrible! This happens because whenever a system update comes in, any changes the system needs to make will take priority over your local changes. If you had a configuration file in an application, and the system update included an update to that config file, the system update would overwrite it without question. It would be like your files having a tough man contest with Chuck Norris, they just won't win. This is why usr/local is so useful: no matter what system updates you install, they won't touch anything in your user directory, so your precious files and applications will be safe.

You can achieve this on a Mac by creating an Applications folder in your home directory. Then, your Mac will know that you want to have your own applications just for you, and it'll make the newly created folder work just like the older one. You'll even get the same logo and everything!

This, of course, isn't required for installation; in most cases everything will work just fine if you install it in the default location. However, it's advisable to install software you'll rely on on a day-to-day basis in usr/local, just in case a software update comes and wipes it out, in which case any configuration you had made would be lost. Unless you had a backup, you wouldn't be able to get it back very easily.

Those of you who have to use Windows don't have the luxury of usr/local or even choosing whether or not a program is for just one user or not. Unless the particular program that you're installing has the option to just install for the current user, then you're out of luck. You can, of course, use admin privileges to choose who can use which programs, but you don't have the option to have your own version of a program installed on the system. That, sadly, is just how Windows works.

Compiling software

A program or application will always have been compiled in some way for you to use on your system. *Compile* is really just a fancy word for *build*, so when you compile an application, you're building an application you can run from its source code. The source code can be dependent on the system the final application will run on, such as Visual Basic for Windows, or Cocoa for Mac. As for Ubuntu, it doesn't have a unique language specific to it, but Python and C or C++ are common languages to use. You can, of course, have some shared languages across multiple OSs, such as C++ and Java. However, you would need to make changes to how the code is compiled to allow it to work on different systems, the same way .exe files won't work on a Mac. So far, I've been discussing things that have been precompiled. This is especially noticeable on a Mac because in most cases you will just drag a single file to your Applications folder. While navigating around the Internet, you may or may not have seen "compile from source" kicking about when you go to download a new program. This is another option when you want to use a program and you simply build your own version from the source code. It can seem a little scary to some people, but when you understand how the different stages work it becomes a lot easier.

Although you may never do it yourself, it's always good to know how compiling works and the different uses you can get out of it. Of course it may not always be as easy as just downloading some source code and magically turning it into an application. Sometimes said application will have dependencies in order for it to work correctly, which would involve you compiling and installing those as well. These commands won't work on Windows machines, however, as software is compiled totally differently in Windows than on Mac or Linux. This has to do with the way the operating system is constructed; to allow applications to be easily compiled, additional software and configuration would be required.

If you were to download an application's source code, you would normally have to route through the install file to see the best way to compile it. However, it basically comes down to the following stages:

1. First of all, you'd get into the directory of your lovely bit of source code which you would have gotten from the applications website, from a friend or colleague, or even written yourself. Once in there, you'd look for the configuration file, which is included in the folder. The configuration file is like a guest in a posh hotel. It comes into your system, checks to make sure you have all the right amenities, and, if you don't have something it needs, it lets you know that if you don't provide it, it won't be happy. So if the application has any dependencies, or anything like that, this script will tell you about it. This script can come in the form of a configure file with no extension, a file with an .sh extension which has the same name as the application, or a number of other names. If you're unsure which file it is, check out the README or INSTALL files which will usually have no extension. Inside that file it gives the name of the configuration file, and all the dependencies the application has, which can come in quite useful.

    When you find out which of the files is the configure file, open up a Terminal window and ensure you're in the same directory as the configure file, then run `./configure`.

    If you are missing a library it needs or an application it depends on then the configuration will fail, and will continue to fail until you get the needed components.

2. Once the configuration stage is complete, now comes the big part: it's time to actually compile the code. The compiling process adds in any links it needs, finds where certain things are installed on the system, and does all the hard work. If your configuration went without a hitch, you may still run into problems at this stage. This can be for any number of reasons, but if something is going to go wrong, it'll go wrong here. The command uses a `make` file in the directory, which contains all the needed commands and magic to create the application. When you're ready to take the plunge, while in Terminal run this command in the root of the application directory:

    `make`

3. If it goes without any errors, then you're close to being finished. If it does have errors, however, they need to be addressed and fixed before the application will compile. You may need to download a new version of an application, or even an additional library.

    Once `make` has successfully run, the next stage moves the compiled application to the `usr/local` directory to keep it safe from software updates and everything we've been through previously. To move that application into `usr/local/bin`, run this command in Terminal:

    `make install`

    You may get errors when doing this, for example, if the application has insufficient privileges to create new directories and such. These can be alleviated by using `sudo` at the start of the command. This will run it with admin privileges, so it can do what it needs to do without being questioned.

4. Once the application is in the correct place, it's time to clean up after the install, just in case it's made a mess in the application (to pursue the hotel analogy). To initiate the cleaning process, run this command in Terminal:

    `make clean`

Once the cleaner has finished doing its job your theoretical application is compiled and ready for use. When it comes down to it, the processes for compiling your own application aren't that bad. Plus, by compiling the code yourself, you get a lot more control over some of the configuration options, and you also have the option to choose where the application will live once it's been compiled. This will be usr/local by default.

If doing this isn't your bag, there are things called package managers, which do pretty much all of this work for you. They're pretty nifty, and if you've worked with Ubuntu before, you will already be familiar with apt-get, which is Ubuntu's standard package manager. You can also get a multitude of them for a Mac, but poor old Windows gets nothing of the sort. If you're on Windows, then you'll just have to put up with good old .exe files where all the hard work has been done for you.

If you want to go down the compiling road on Windows there are a few options available. A good one is to look into Visual Studio, which has a lot of functionality built in, including the ability to compile applications. It's not as simple as clicking a compile button or anything like that, but it is possible. If you want to take the compiling in Terminal route, you'll need to install Cygwin, which is a set of emulation tools which allow for UNIX-based actions to be performed on a Windows system. Among other things, Cygwin gives you a new Terminal window, which you can use to perform UNIX commands such as make and configure which, using the previous steps, allows you to compile applications.

For the sake of Windows-only applications, there are other methods you can use to run them on non-Windows systems. For Ubuntu users, there is an application known as Wine is not an emulator (WINE) which allows for the use of Windows applications on a UNIX-based machine. You can also use OS emulating software like Virtual Box to run a full Windows OS on your machine. It just depends on your needs, really.

The process of SVN and setting it up

We've talked a little about SVN, but now it's time to get into how it works. As was mentioned previously, SVN is a centralized system, so you have one central repository. The first step is to create the repository that your code will sit in. This will either be on your local network, a remote server, or third-party service that offers repository hosting. This is, however, still classified as a remote repository, it just happens to be hosted on a server you don't fully control. Once your repository is created, you then do a "checkout" of the code to a folder on your local machine. This is a copy of the remote code, which you can make changes to as need be, without affecting the code in the repository.

Having one main repository allows for multiple people to take a copy of the same code base and collaborate on the same code project. Now that there is a local version of the repository on your machine, you can make any needed changes to it, including adding new files. Any number of files can be added to the repository by using a number of methods, but until those changes are pushed to the main repository they are only available to you. Once you have made any needed changes to the code or added any new files, you would then "commit" the code to the repository. When you commit any files, whether they are existing or new, you get the option to add a message. These can come in very, very useful when you come to revert a file and wonder why it was committed in the first place. There is always the option to use a message with no meaning or relevance at all, such as on http://whatthecommit.com; however, that doesn't help at all. Having useful commit messages is an asset to anybody using version control, and getting into the habit of using them should be learned as early as possible. Once your message has been added, the code will be merged with the existing code in the repository. If, however, SVN detects that someone else has made a change to a file you're about to commit, it will stop it and tell you to update to the latest version of the code. This, of course, means you check for any changes to the central repository compared to your local version. If it detects that you need to download new files, or new versions of files, it will do that for you. If you do add new files and they are successfully committed, from now on, any user that updates from the repository will get the new files. Although putting it into words can make it seem complicated, it's actually quite simple. Have a look at Figure 3-1 to see it in a nice visual format.

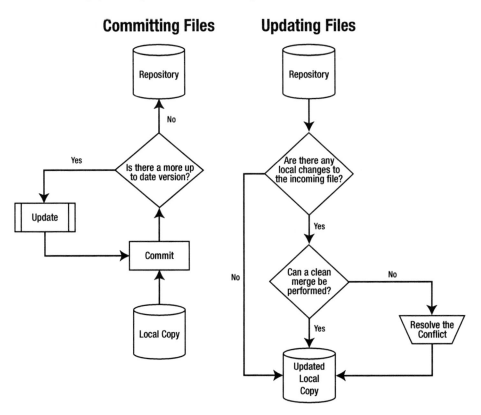

Figure 3-1. The processes used when updating and committing files

Of course, that only handles pushing updates and new files. What If something goes wrong and you need to get back a previous version of a file your working on? Well, you can revert your local version of a file to the version currently in the repository, or an even older version than the current one.

All of these actions can easily be managed with a SVN GUI on any of the main operating systems. In most cases updating, committing, and reverting can be done by one or two clicks of a button, which makes it very simple to use and manage, and also explains why so many designers and low-end developers like it for its simplicity and ease of use.

Setting up on Windows

It's time to install SVN onto good old Windows 7. First of all, head on over to http://sourceforge.net/projects/win32svn/ and download the latest version of the code by hitting the nice green download button. Once the file is on your machine, run it by double-clicking it. When it's open you should see what's pictured in Figure 3-2.

Figure 3-2. The first installation screen for the Subversion application

Go through the installation as a normal process. You'll be asked to accept a license agreement and whether you agree to allow the system to download some information to complete the setup. Once the installation is finished, you'll get another of those annoying Windows prompts that asks for permission from you before it makes any changes to accept before the installation can finish. Once the installer has finished doing its work it means Subversion should be installed on your system. To make sure it is working correctly, open up a new Terminal window. There are a number of ways to do this; the fastest is to press Start, type cmd into the search box and press enter, which will launch the application. Alternatively, you can access the application by pressing Start and going to All Programs ➤ Accessories ➤ Command Prompt or by pressing Windows+R, which will open the run prompt. To open a command prompt from this dialog, simply type cmd and click ok and you'll open a command prompt window.

Once it's open, type svn and you should see what's in Figure 3-3.

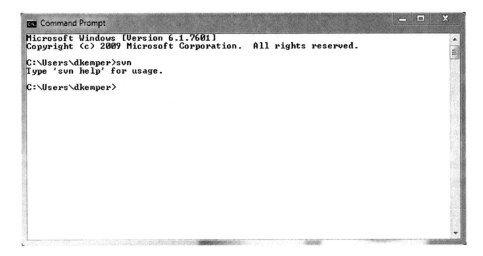

Figure 3-3. The Windows command prompt showing the output from the svn command

Once you know that SVN is installed on the system, that's all you need for now. Pretty simple! Now it's time to do the same thing again, but this time on a Mac.

Setting up on Mac

Any modern Mac system will have SVN installed by default, which is great! But because I'm going with the whole "New is *always* better!" philosophy, you really always want to update the current version of SVN to the latest version. Updating your SVN client can also fix some errors you can get when working with some repositories. A commonly seen error is

```
svn: This client is too old to work with working copy
```

By upgrading the version of SVN on the Mac OS, you avoid this message, and end up with a shiny new version of SVN. Although there are a lot of ways to install Subversion on Mac, the easiest way is through a package manager called Homebrew. Before you can install Homebrew, however, you need to install a few other things, one of which is called Xcode.

Installing Xcode

One place Xcode can be found is on the Mac OS X installation DVD, so if you have your DVD kicking around I'd advise grabbing it. If you take this approach, you will be running an old version of the software, so if you do have the ability to download an updated version, it would be advisable to read on. The most recent version of Xcode requires Mac OS X Lion to run, so if you're working with an older version of OS X you'll need to stick with the DVD approach, as an older copy of the software is hard to come by.

If you don't have an installation DVD to hand, never fear; you can head over to http://developer.apple.com and download Xcode there. You will need to go to the Member Center and sign in with your Apple ID. It won't cost you anything; you just need to finish the registration and you'll be given access. Once inside, you'll want to go into either the iOS dev center or the Mac dev center—it

43

doesn't matter which one. Once you're in a dev center you will need to download the SDK of the section you're in, which comes bundled with Xcode. Before you start the download, be warned: it's *huge*, at least 4.5GB, so it'll take a while to download. If you don't to go through the Apple developer registration you can download Xcode for free straight from the Mac app store. However doing it this way won't make the download any smaller—it's still over 4GB. If you need to take the downloading route it may be worthwhile to look for that DVD one last time, or ask someone you know if you can borrow theirs. Otherwise, you'll be sitting for at least an hour, maybe more, depending on your Internet connection, waiting for this beast to download.

If you managed to locate an installation DVD, throw it into the drive. Once it's in, open up the Optional Installs folder and run Xcode. This will launch you into a normal application process. If the storage on your Mac is a little limited, feel free to uncheck the option boxes when you have the option to do so. All you need to install are the essential components, which you cannot uncheck. I'd advise grabbing a coffee or something while this setup does its stuff, otherwise you could be watching a progress bar for around 20 minutes, depending on your system. Once it's finished, Xcode is installed and you're ready to move on!

Installing Homebrew

Once Xcode is installed, you're finally ready to install Homebrew. A package manager for use on Mac OS X, it works in a similar way to apt-get on an Ubuntu machine. Let's get it installed, shall we? Open up a Terminal window by typing Terminal into Spotlight and hitting enter when it comes up. Once it's open, enter the following command:

```
ruby -e "$(curl -fsSL https://raw.github.com/gist/323731)"
```

First of all you'll be told to hit enter to proceed with the installation. You'll then receive a warning about improper use of the sudo command. After that, you'll be prompted for your password. When you enter your password, you won't be able to see what you're typing. This is normal, so don't let it phase you. When the setup is finished, if you happened to have skipped the first step, you'll get a prompt at the end of the installation, asking you to install Xcode. If, however, Xcode was already installed before the Homebrew installation, then you won't see the message. Homebrew is installed and ready to go, but before you go installing a new version of SVN, it's good to look at a bit of information about the version that is currently installed.

Getting the right version of SVN

You can find out the version by entering the following command into Terminal:

```
svn --version
```

At the very top of the output for this command, you'll see the version number for the current svn version you have installed. Another command you need to use is this:

```
which svn
```

This simply returns where the current version is installed which, if you haven't made any updates, will be

```
/usr/bin/svn
```

Now that you have that out of the way, you need to install the new and updated version via Homebrew. To do so, while still in Terminal, enter this command:

```
brew install subversion
```

This will install Subversion and all its required packages for you. Don't worry if it seems to pause for a while during the installation; just wait it out and it'll finish eventually (it took around 7 minutes to install on my machine). Once the installation is complete, you'll have a shiny new version of SVN, but if you were to do which svn in Terminal again, you'd see the path still remains as follows:

```
/usr/bin/svn
```

This isn't what you want. Homebrew always compiles applications in usr/local, so what's the problem? The system doesn't know which version of SVN to use, so it's sticking with the core version. You can change this, however, by modifying an existing file or creating a new one if it doesn't already exist.

The file in question is called the .bash_profile file. This is a config file which can tell your system a couple of things, including which editor to use in Terminal, and what we're interested in, the locations in which to look for applications, which is in the form of the PATH variable. By default, if you run a command in Terminal or in a program, it will look in /usr/bin, rather than the version in your user account usr/local.

By editing this file, you're able to tell the system to look in the local directory first when trying to run applications, and therefore to use your version of SVN and not the system version. You may have noticed that in your home directory you cannot see a .bash_profile file,. This is because it's a hidden file, and by default those are, well, hidden. Although there are a few methods to show hidden files and edit them, I'm not going to show you how to do that. What you're going to do is simply open the file, make a change, and get out of there.

The first thing you need to do is open up a Terminal window, which you can do by searching for Terminal in spotlight. You can access Spotlight by hitting the magnifying glass in the top right corner, or by hitting Cmd+Space to launch it (unless you have changed the default shortcut). When it's open, type in Terminal, and hit enter once it pops up.

Once you have Terminal open, you need to type in the following:

```
touch .bash_profile
```

This command does a couple of things. If there wasn't a .bash_profile file on your Mac (which by default, there won't be) it will create an empty file for you with that name. If you do have that file already, it'll simply update the time it was last altered and not make any other changes.

Now that you know the file exists, you need to edit it. While still in your Terminal window, type the following command:

```
open -a TextEdit .bash_profile
```

This command calls to open .bash_profile, but by using the -a operator, you are able specify a program to use. In this instance, you should specify it to be TextEdit, a nice and easy text editing program built into the Mac OS. Once you hit enter, you'll see a TextEdit window appear, and if you've just created the

`.bash_profile` file via Terminal, it'll be blank. This is what you want. Now, while the file is open, enter the following line of code:

```
export PATH=/usr/local/bin:/usr/local/sbin:$PATH
```

This command is quite simple once you understand it. The first part, export, is there to ensure this line will be available on every new Terminal session. Without it, the command would only last while Terminal was open; once it closed it would be ignored. In the next bit you are specifying your own version of PATH. You then give the install path you're using; so, /usr/local/bin is one path, and the other is /usr/local/sbin. They are joined by the colon (":"), which is just like adding another item to the list of possible locations for software. The last part is the $PATH part. This simply adds any other previously defined paths to the end of the queue, so that if the first locations don't have the command that it's looking for, the system will look in the default locations.

Once that command is in TextEdit, simply save it via File ➤ Save, or Cmd+S. Then you need to use the following command in Terminal:

```
source .bash_profile
```

After that, your paths should be sorted out. To confirm this, in Terminal type which svn. This time you should see

```
/usr/local/bin/svn
```

There you are. You now have an updated version of SVN, located in usr/local/bin. Grab yourself a beer and pat yourself on the back. Good job!

Setting up on Ubuntu

It's Ubuntu time! We'll be going through two different methods of installing SVN on Ubuntu, using the package manager, and the more challenging but sexy option, compiling SVN from source. Let's get cracking. We'll start with the package manager.

Installing via the package manager

On the latest version of Ubuntu (11.10), the Unity desktop replaced the standard GNOME one which, meant, among other things, that the package manager wasn't installed by default. You'll be using this a lot, so to install it you need to use a line of code within Terminal. To reach a Terminal window in Unity, hit the dash button, which will open up an overlay of sorts and, among other things, contains a search box. Within the search box just type in Terminal, then double-click the application to launch it. With it open, type in the following to install it:

```
sudo apt-get install synaptic
```

You'll be prompted for your password here because of the sudo command. which is fine. Just type it in and press enter. When typing your password there won't be anything visual on the screen to indicate the typing. This is normal, so don't worry

After the installation has completed, Synaptic will live in the same place it used to, which is System ➤ Administration ➤ Synaptic package manager.

When you try to open it, you'll be asked for your password. Once you enter it, type subversion into the Quick filter text field, and you'll see what we have in Figure 3-4.

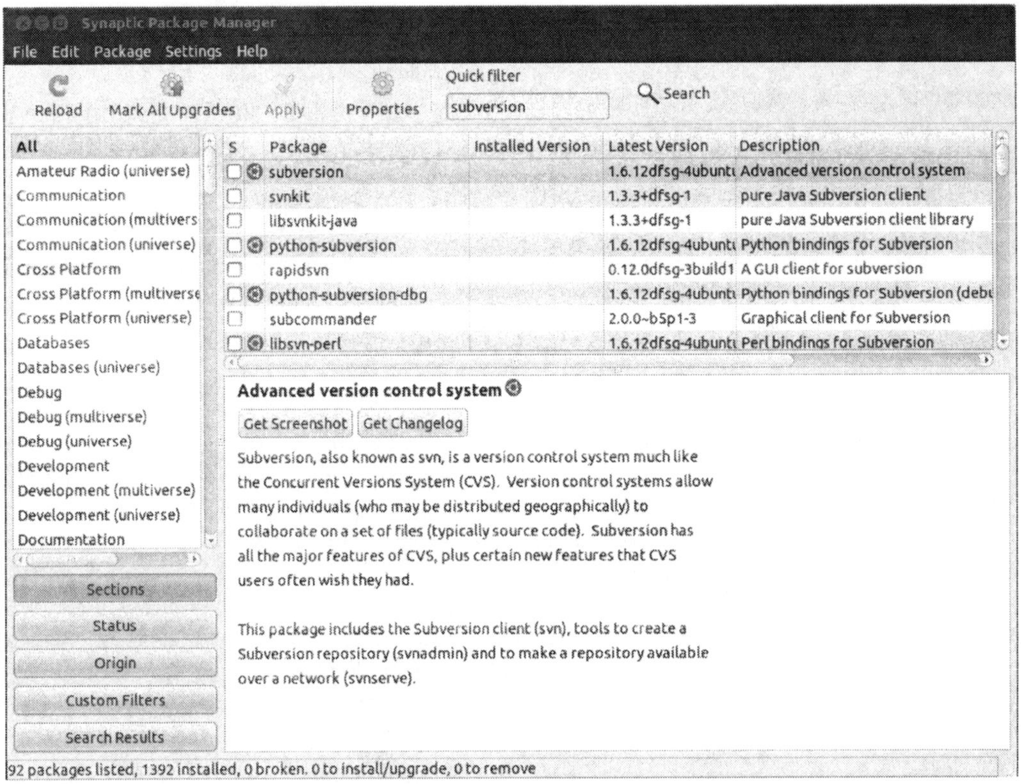

Figure 3-4. The Synaptic Package Manager showing the results after searching for Subversion

Click the check box to the left of the subversion option, then hit "Mark for installation". You'll get a prompt mentioning you need to install another package (libsvn1) to get Subversion to work. Just hit Mark to approve this and it'll be automatically marked for installation. Since that's all you want to install on this run, simply hit Apply and you'll be ready to go.

SVN is now installed. If you want to confirm it's working correctly, you can open up a Terminal window by hitting the Dash button and in the search field typing Terminal. In older versions of Ubuntu, Terminal can be found here: Applications ➤ Accessories ➤ Terminal.

Once it's open, type in svn, then hit enter. Terminal should then display the following message:

```
type 'svn help' for usage.
```

This shows SVN is working just fine, which is great!

Building from source

Now for the slightly harder version: compiling Subversion from source. Although it's more difficult than using a package manger, it's still easily doable, and offers these benefits: it keeps this version safe from future updates, and gives you total control over what packages are used. So it's time to developer suit up, and dive straight in.

First of all, you need to go and get the source code, so you have something to compile. Head over to http://subversion.apache.org/download/, which is the download page for the source code of SVN. You should aim to download the "Best available version", which is shown at the top of the page. You can then click on that to take you to download links for that version. Take note of the file name of the latest version, or better yet, copy the link location to the clipboard by right-clicking it and hitting "Copy link location". Be sure to select the .tar.gz version of the source code, to ensure the unpacking command you'll be using will work. The reason you need the URL is that you'll be downloading it via Terminal, so it'll be easier if you have the full link to the file. You'll also be using the Terminal for the full compiling process because it allows you to compile the applications using the process I talked about earlier. With that said, open Terminal up by searching for it in Dash and hitting enter, or on older systems by going to Applications ➤ Accessories ➤ Terminal.

The first thing you want to do is download the source code using the link you've just gotten from the Subversion website. You need to type wget, which will do the actual downloading of the file. Next you need the URL of the file. You can paste it into the Terminal window by pressing Shift+Ctrl+V because the regular paste shortcut won't work as expected. Once you have entered that in the Terminal window it should look something like this:

```
wget http://mirror.ox.ac.uk/sites/rsync.apache.org/subversion/subversion-1.7.2.tar.gz
```

The only difference you may see is that the version you're downloading may be newer than the version I'm using or you've selected a different download mirror, which can be done at the top of the downloads page. This command simply downloads that file to the directory you're currently in, and if it's a fresh new Terminal window, that'll be the home directory, which is shown via the ~ next to your username. Once the file is downloaded, you need to unpack the file, which you can do with the following command:

```
tar -xzvf subversion-1.7.2.tar.gz
```

Once it's unpacked, you need to cd (change directory) into the new directory that has been created. It'll have the same name as the file you just unpacked, only without the file extension. In this case, my folder is called subversion-1.6.17. To save from typing the full name, you can type subversion, or even su, then the tab key, which will autocomplete the name for you. The command should look something like this:

```
cd /subversion-1.7.2/
```

Now you're in the source code directory, it's time to start the compiling process. As mentioned above, the first thing you'd normally need to do is configure the installation. However if you tried to run this

```
./configure
```

you'd get an error, and the compiling process would fail. This is because Subversion requires a few additional packages to get it to run, and of course, you need to get those before it'll work. So let's get those now, shall we? Run the following command which will install the needed packages to get SVN installed correctly:

```
sudo apt-get install libapr1-dev libaprutil1-dev
```

As with any sudo command, you'll need to enter your password, and you'll need to confirm that you're OK with the installation taking up X amount of space on your machine. Once everything is finished, that should be all you need to install SVN, so let's run ./configure again, but this time, there won't be any errors.

You'll notice a lot is output while this is running and the script is looking around your system like a dog looking for scraps on the floor; it won't miss a thing. If you look closely at the output, you'll see Check for x a lot, then either a yes, or a no. It should be mostly yes's, but if something isn't there you'll be told via an error.

There is yet another complexity we have to deal with before compiling Subversion, which is for a package called neon. You could go ahead and compile SVN without neon; however, if you tried to check out a remote repository, you would get this error: "svn: E170000: Unrecognized URL scheme for http://address-of-remote-server" which, of course, would be a big problem. You need to compile neon from source, just like we're doing here. However, neon has no dependencies, so the process is a lot simpler.

To get the latest source code, head over to www.webdav.org/neon/, where the latest package can be downloaded which, as of this writing, is version 0.29.6. If you want to take the full Terminal approach, get the URL for the file by right-clicking and selecting Copy link address to store the location on the clipboard. As this is just a straight compile, you can run through these commands in one block, to make life a lot easier:

```
wget http://www.webdav.org/neon/neon-0.29.6.tar.gz
tar -xzvf neon-0.29.6.tar.gz
cd neon-0.29.6/
./configure
make
sudo make install
sudo make install clean
```

Now that you have neon compiled, you can go ahead with the compilation of Subversion, so just run ./configure again and it should run as expected. Once the "configure dog" has finished looking for scraps you can go through the next stage of the compiling process. Now you need to make the installation. This does the majority of the building for you, but it can take a while, so go grab a brew while it does its job. To run this, just type

```
make
```

After an age, this will complete. Now you just have a few more stages and SVN will be compiled. Huzzah! Now you need to move the application into usr/local from where it is now. To do that you just run the following:

```
sudo make install
```

The sudo has been included in this case to get over the file permission errors you may encounter when moving the application over. Including the sudo ensures the install will just run and you won't hit any errors.

The final stage is the cleanup after the installation. To do this, use the following code. It'll remove any temporary or unneeded files that were created during the installation. Just enter this and you should be all ready!

```
Sudo make install clean
```

That should be everything—all finished! As a final step, just type in svn into the open Terminal window. If you get "Type 'svn help' for usage" then everything is hunky dory, which is just what you want!

That should be everything you need to have SVN running on your machine. I still haven't mentioned how all this can work for you, so it's time for a bit of a walkthrough on how to work with SVN using a real application.

Using a real application to work with SVN

Although I'll go into detail about many more of the programs you can use with Subversion in Chapter 5, for now I will walk you through svnX on a Mac. svnX is a free application for managing SVN repositories on Mac OS X, which is why I've chosen to use it. But enough about what it is, let's see it in action!

First of all, you'll need a repository to work with, so I've done something nice and set one up using a third-party service called Beanstalk which allows the hosting of SVN and Git repositories online. (In addition to that, it also offers a whole other set of features, which I'll discuss in greater depth in a later chapter.) Now you have a repository to use, you need the program. If you're working on Windows, you can still get a good understanding of how SVN works by reading along. But never fear, I'll take you through the best programs to use on Windows in Chapter 5.

Getting the application

First of all, you need the application. The best way to get it is to just type svnX into Google; the top result should be a link to the svnX project which is now hosted on Google code. On the left of the page, you should see a download link for the latest version of the program. At the time of this writing, that was version 1.3, so my download link said the following:

```
svnX 1.3.dmg
```

When the file has finished downloading, open it up and you'll get the svnX program, with a few other help files. Although you don't have to, I would recommend creating an Applications folder in your home directory (if you haven't already) and dragging the svnX application into that folder. This means that this application and any others in that directory will only be available to the current user, and not all users. This keeps all your settings to yourself, and avoids any problems with two users on the same machine using the application. Anyway, regardless of whether you've dragged svnX into this Applications folder or the main application folder, double-click it to get started. When you open the application, you'll see what's shown in Figure 3-5. This basically boils down to two main things: repositories and checked-out versions of those repositories, or local copies of the repository.

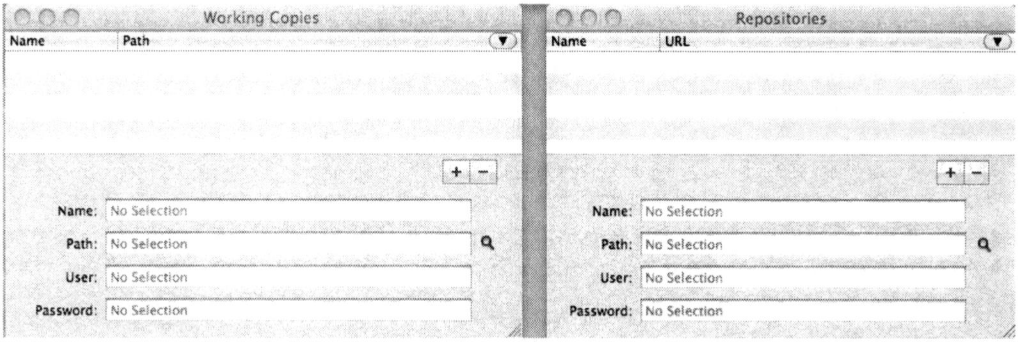

Figure 3-5. The two main panels within svnX, the Working Copies and Repositories panes. These control the local and remote repositories that are references in the application, and are very important if you use the application frequently.

Creating a new repository

You can also create local versions that you've checked out using another method. Then svnX can be used to manage the repository with that pane. In this example, I'll be creating a new repository, so open the Repository pane in the application, either by clicking it to make it the active pane in the application, or by pressing Cmd+Shift+R to open it if it's not open. Once you have the pane selected, click the plus arrow; this will create a new repository in the list. It will also insert some dummy information into the bottom of the dialog. See Figure 3-6.

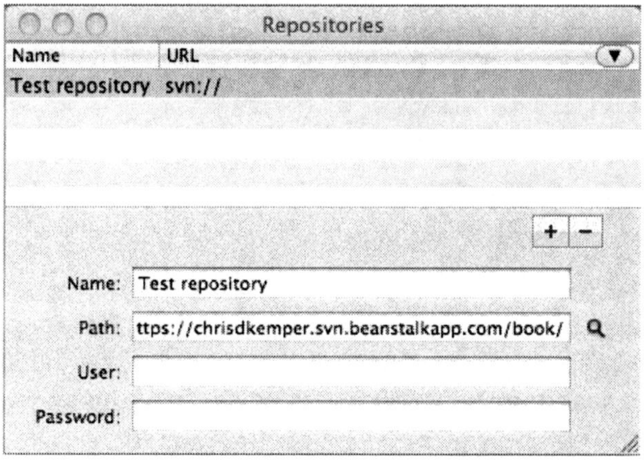

Figure 3-6. The Repositories pane with a new repository having been added to it

This is where my previous generosity will pay off: using Beanstalk, I have been able to create a repository with anonymous read access. This means you can check it out, but you can't commit anything. Inside the repository, there is a basic Wordpress install with a custom theme, so this repository may mimic one you have yourself, or one you may have once I make you a master of version control. This repository, even though it's read-only, will be enough to get an understanding of how the basic processes work, so let's get started!

Understanding basic processes

In the new dialog, there are two fields you need to be concerned with at this time. The first is the name. This is just a label for the repository, so you can make it anything relevant you like. The next is the path field, which is the actual link to the repository:

```
https://chrisdkemper.svn.beanstalkapp.com/book/trunk
```

That's all you need to access this particular repository. In most other cases, you will need to add in a username and password in the fields below to gain access, but because this is an anonymous repository, you don't need them.

Once you've entered the required information, double-click the new item you added. This will open up a new dialog, which is a view of the actual repository. (See Figure 3-7.) You get a lot of options in the view, but at this moment in time, you only want one: checkout.

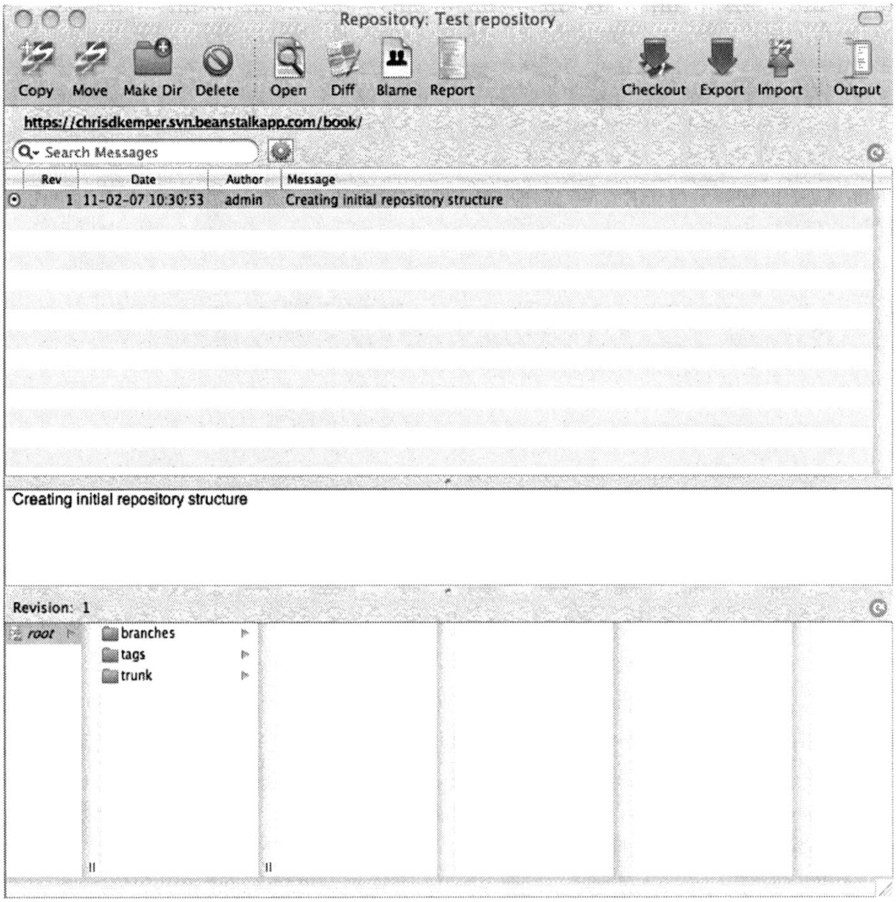

Figure 3-7. The repository view within svnX which allows you to browse the repository and view the files within it

Clicking the checkout button will open up a file explorer, which gives you a choice of where you'd like to place the checkout. I'd suggest putting the checkout in your htdocs directory. This will get you in the habit of doing it for future coding projects. If you have the standard MAMP installation, then you will need to go to Applications ➤ MAMP ➤ htdocs. This will make it a lot easier to set up any needed Vhosts for the projects.

Once you have selected a directory to house the checked out repository, you'll notice a new link created in the local copies pane of svnX. Click on the new link you have created and it will open up a new window, which is where all the main action happens. See Figure 3-8.

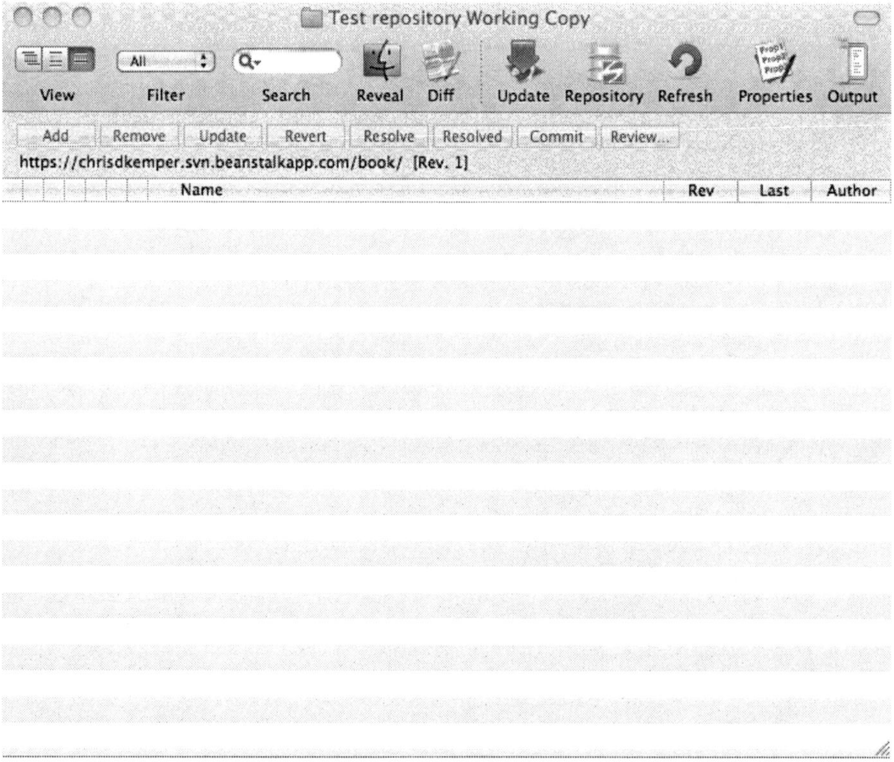

Figure 3-8. A window used for managing a working copy of a remote repository. Any changes to files will show up in this window, which will allow them to be handled accordingly.

This pane shows the current state of your local version of the repository, so any changes you've made to files or any new files detected in the local version will show up in here.

Since this is a Wordpress blog, let's assume you want to make some changes to it. Navigate into the theme and make a change to the style.css file, no matter what the change is, save the file, and navigate back to svnX. You will see the style.css file in the project svn pane, which indicates that it's been changed in some way. You'll notice that to the left of the file there is an M. This means that version of the file on your local machine has been modified, and is different to the version in the repository and needs to be committed. This will be same with any file that you edit in the local copy of the repository that is currently under version control, but what about new files?

No matter what you're working on, you'll always need to add new files to the repository. Whether it's a new plug-in for Wordpress, an Internet Explorer–specific style sheet, or simply some new images, they will need to be added. If you add a new file to the local copy, you will see this reflected in svnX, by the file name showing up in blue in the project pane, with a ? to the left. If you've added a new folder into the repository, you will see the folder name with a ? to the left, but you won't see any files inside the folder. Once you add the folder, you will then see all files inside the folder listed, as well as the folder itself with an A to the left. (See Figure 3-9.) These files are now ready to commit to the repository.

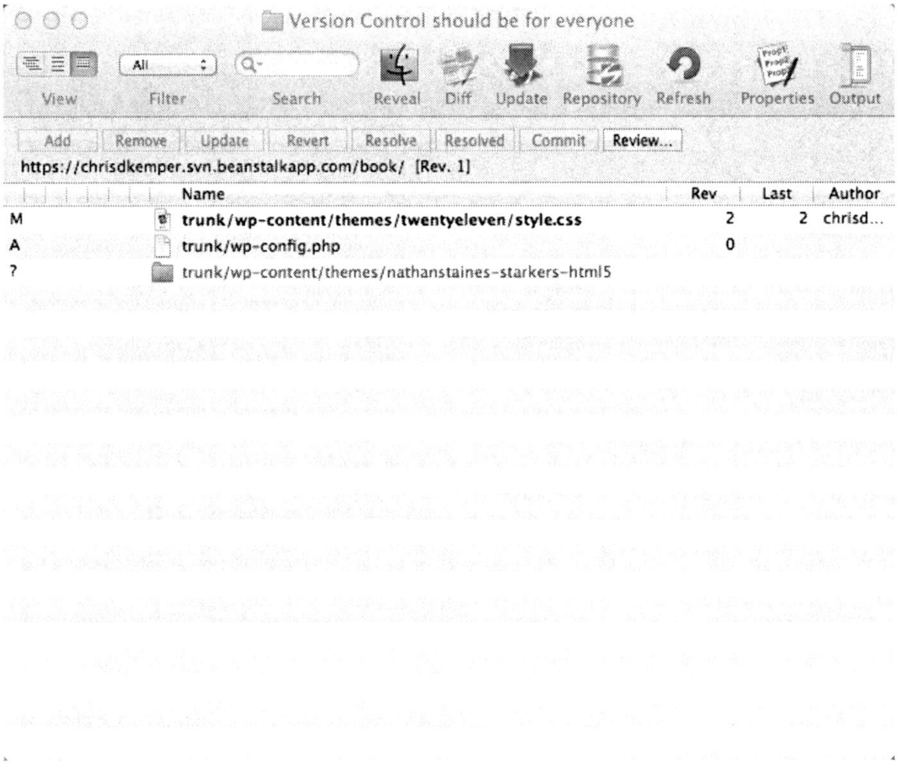

Figure 3-9. Multiple files in svnX

After new files are changed or added, you will select the files you wish to commit by clicking them, or by using Command-click, or Shift-click to select multiple files. When dealing with folders, if you try to commit a file within a newly added folder, without committing the folder itself, you will get an error. This, of course, makes sense, because if you were able commit files within a folder, without committing the folder, where would the files live? Once you have the files selected, and you've made sure to include any new folders, then you're ready to hit Commit and send the files to the repository. It is worth noting, that if you have a new folder with items inside it, committing just the folder will not add the items within it to the repository.

You will need to either include both the files and folders in one go, or commit the folder, then commit all the items inside it.

When you do commit new changes, you will then be prompted to add a message to accompany the commit. These can be both useful and useless, but I'll mention that later on. Once you add a message (or not, it's optional) then you are adding new changes to the repository, which anybody else using the same one will be able to download! Unfortunately, you can't do this with the example repository because it is read-only, but if this were a normal repository where you had full write access, then you would be pushing files, which is awesome!

So that's a basic overview of how SVN does its job and how you'd go about adding new files to a repository. Don't fret if you still have some questions about the workings of SVN. I'll be going into a lot more detail about its workflows and functions in Chapter 5. With all that said, it's time to move on to setting up Mercurial.

How Mercurial does the job and getting it set up

As already mentioned, Mercurial is a distributed version control system built primarily using the Python programming language. As with any distributed versioning system, the repository sits primarily on your local machine, but you can, of course, use a remote or networked repository if that's required. Creating a repository is a rather simple process, and can be done simply with one command in Terminal or a press of a button in a GUI. Once your repository is created, you just need to add some files to it; these could be source code, documents, text files, or any particular type of file. Once you have the files in your new repository ready for your initial commit, you just need to add them to the repository, which is just as simple as creating one in the first place. It can be done with the press of a button or a simple Terminal command. Once your files are added, the last step is to commit them, and once they've been committed they're now being versioned by Mercurial, and they get to feel its awesome versioning love.

There is another way you can create a repository using Mercurial, which is to clone an existing one, such as the one given on the Mercurial website at http://selenic.com/repo/hello. When you use a remote repository, there is an additional step for sending it the files. You still need to add any new files, and you still need to commit them to your local repository, but after that, you need to push those files to the remote server. This is a great method of working because it means you can do a lot of commits yourself to keep your code versioned, but you only push to the remote repository when you're all finished. Also, when you do, all the previous changes you've made are pushed as well, so you never lose any of your changes and everything stays versioned!

Mercurial also gives you the ability to build rather complex or very simple workflows. It can accommodate a lone user working on a linear basis, with the code staying only on their machine or, at the opposite end of the scale, a hugely complex workflow with supervisors vetting code, different working versions, and a boatload more.

So that's Mercurial's basic workflow sorted out. Let's get it set up, shall we?

Setting up on Windows

As always, start the installation process with Windows. The first thing you need to do is head over to http://mercurial.selenic.com/. Once you hit the landing page, don't be tempted to click on the download link. Just below the button, you'll see three links: Mac OS X, Windows, and other. Click the Windows link and you'll be taken to a download page. See Figure 3-10.

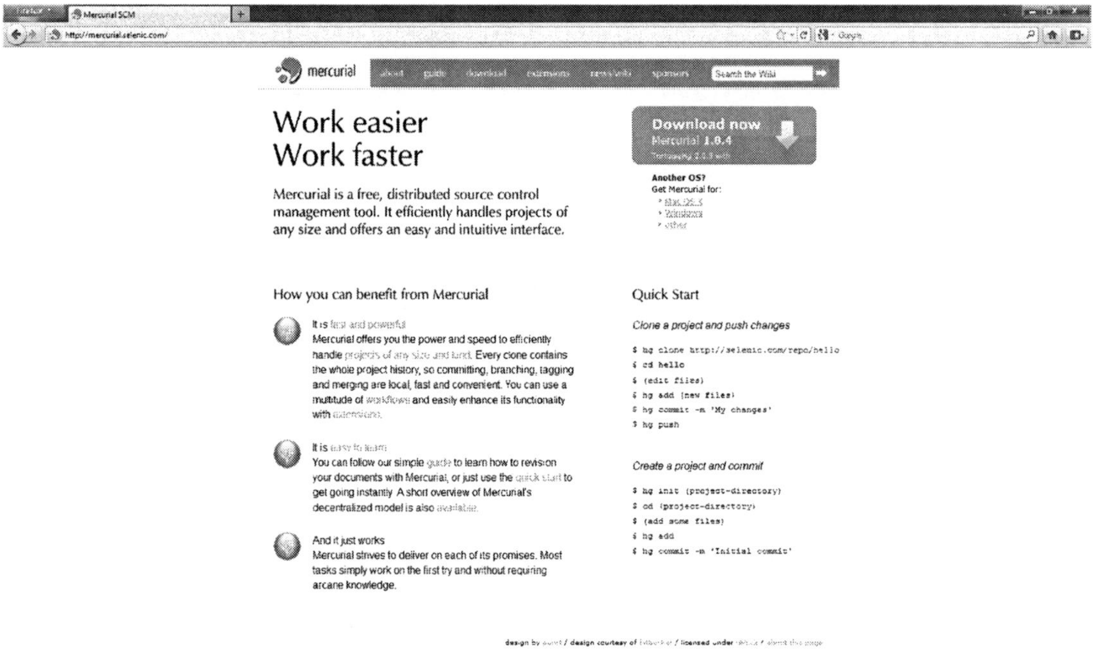

Figure 3-10. The homepage of Mercurial, which allows you to download the software and, if you'd like, clone a test repository

The reason you aren't using the direct link on the site is because this installs a GUI editor with Mercurial bundled with it. Installing just Mercurial gives you the freedom to pick any GUI you'd like, without being tied to any one in particular. It also gives you integration with the Windows Command prompt, which you don't get when you just install the GUIs.

On the downloads page, you'll see a whole number of packages; at the time of this writing I had seven Windows download packages. The one you're looking to download this time is Mercurial 1.8.4 MSI installer - x86 Windows - requires admin rights. The version number may change, but this is the version you're after. The reason for choosing this one is that it'll work on both 64-bit and 32-bit systems because it's a 32-bit package. If you do know you have a 64-bit system, and would prefer to use that version, feel free to download the x64 version of the installer. The MSI package also comes bundled with Python, so there's no need to manually install it.

Once the package has been downloaded, simply run it like any other program. The installation process is very simple, and requires no information to be entered, you just need to agree to the terms and let it do the work. You will see the screen outlined in Figure 3-11 which asks you if you'd like to install all of the components. Leave all of these as they are because this does a lot of nice things for you, including offering some good help documents and integration directly into the command line.

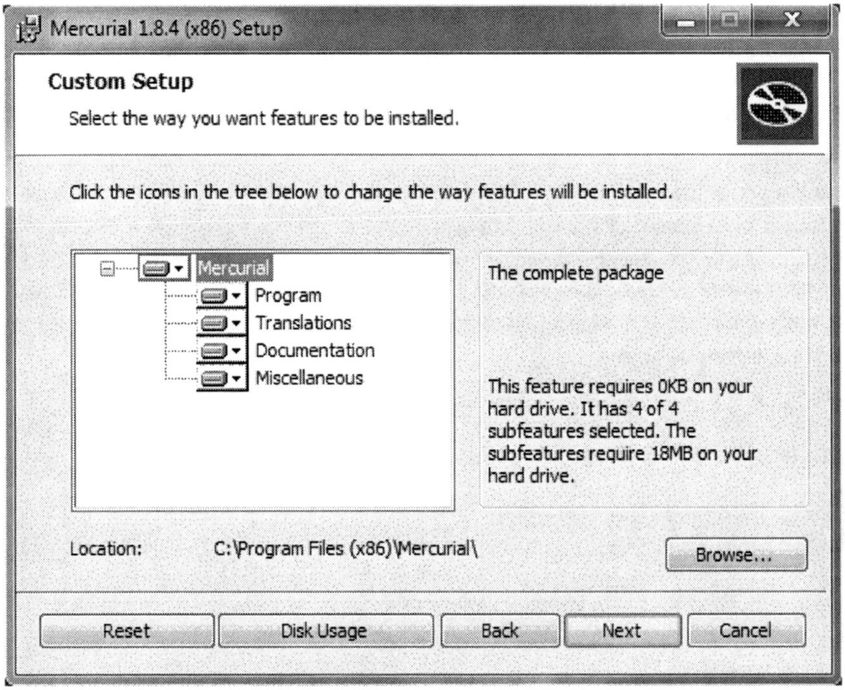

Figure 3-11. Custom setup screen for component information

Once the installation has completed, you need to make sure everything is set up correctly. To do so, you need a command-line window. I've already shown you the easiest way to achieve this, which is to type cmd into the search field within the start menu and press enter.

Once you have the window open, via this method or any other method, type in hg and press enter. This should bring up a large chunk of help text and all the commands that can be used with Mercurial. If you see you something different, then you may need to install Mercurial again.

With Mercurial successfully installed, there is one final step that needs to be added in, which is the configuration of the global user credentials for all newly created repositories. On a Windows system, the configuration file lives within your user account directory: C:\Users\<account>\Mercurial.ini on Windows 7 and C:\Documents and Settings\<account>\Mercurial.ini on pre-Windows 7 systems. If the file doesn't exist, you'll need to create it. With the file open, enter the following lines:

```
[ui]
username = Chris Kemper <hey@chrisdkemper.co.uk>
```

57

You'll just exchange my information above with your information. This sets the default for the user account used when performing commits, which makes the commits more specific to you, and allows other users to contact you.

Setting up on Mac

As with the Windows installation, you need to head over to http://mercurial.selenic.com/ to download Mercurial. Unlike the Windows installation, you can go ahead and click the big blue download link to download it. If you were to go onto the downloads page for the sake of curiosity, you would only see two download options: one for Mac OS X 10.5 and one for OS X 10.6 (in other words, Leopard or Snow Leopard).

If you happened to download the file from the downloads page, then you'll end up with a zip file, which you'll need to unzip by double-clicking it before you continue. This will give you a directory with the same name as the zip, containing a .mpkg file with the same name as the directory. Now that you have that file, you can start the installation by double-clicking it. If you hit the big blue button I mentioned first off then you'll have already gotten to this stage, because the button gives you the .mpkg file for your particular flavor of Leopard: Regular or Snow.

You'll notice that during the installation, it says this:

```
This package installs the hg executable in /usr/local/bin
```

See Figure 3-12.

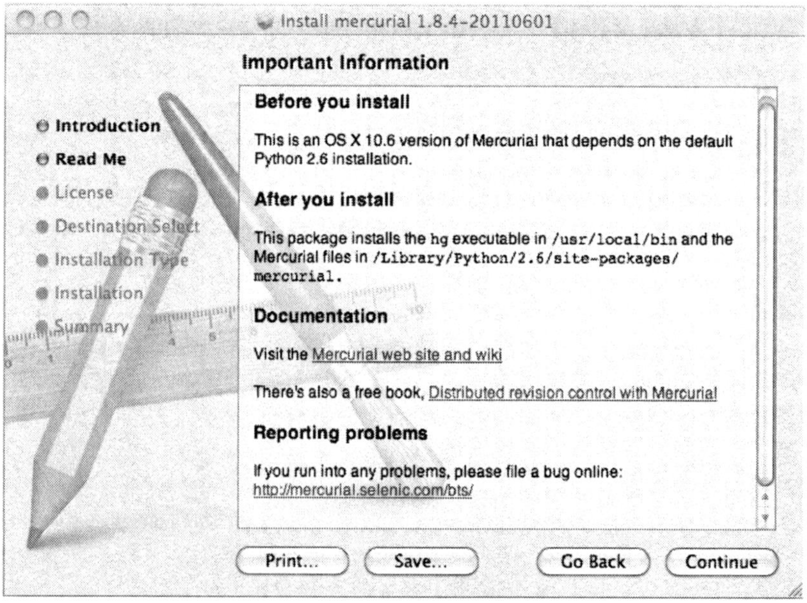

Figure 3-12. This is the second screen within the Mercurial installation which informs the person installing the application where it's going to live on the system, which is /usr/local/bin.

As you can see, it's installing in /usr/local/bin, which is exactly what you want. The rest of the installation process is quite simple, and as per usual you will be asked for your admin password at the end of the process. Once the process has completed, you'll need to open up another Terminal window to check that everything is working correctly. Once it's open, type in:

    hg

Then, hit enter. This should give you the Mercurial help menu and basic command list. Don't worry about those too much though. I'll be discussing them in a lot more detail in the Terminal chapter later.

You now need to do one final step, which is setting up the default username used for commits in your Mercurial repositories. To achieve this you either need to edit an existing file or create it if it doesn't already exist. The file lives inside your user directory with the name .hgrc. If it already exists, just add the following lines to the bottom of the file, otherwise the file will be blank and you can just insert these lines and save the file.

    [ui]
    username = Chris Kemper <hey@chrisdkemper.co.uk>

As previously mentioned, this ensures that each commit you make has a name and e-mail address associated with it, which is more helpful for you, and anybody else you work with, so just replace my information with yours, and you'll be ready to go.

Setting up on Ubuntu

We'll start of with the easiest way to install Mercurial on Ubuntu, which is through the package manager. As usual, you need to search for Mercurial, and you'll need to select the top hit in the list and mark it for installation. Have a look at Figure 3-13 to see what you'll get when you search for Mercurial.

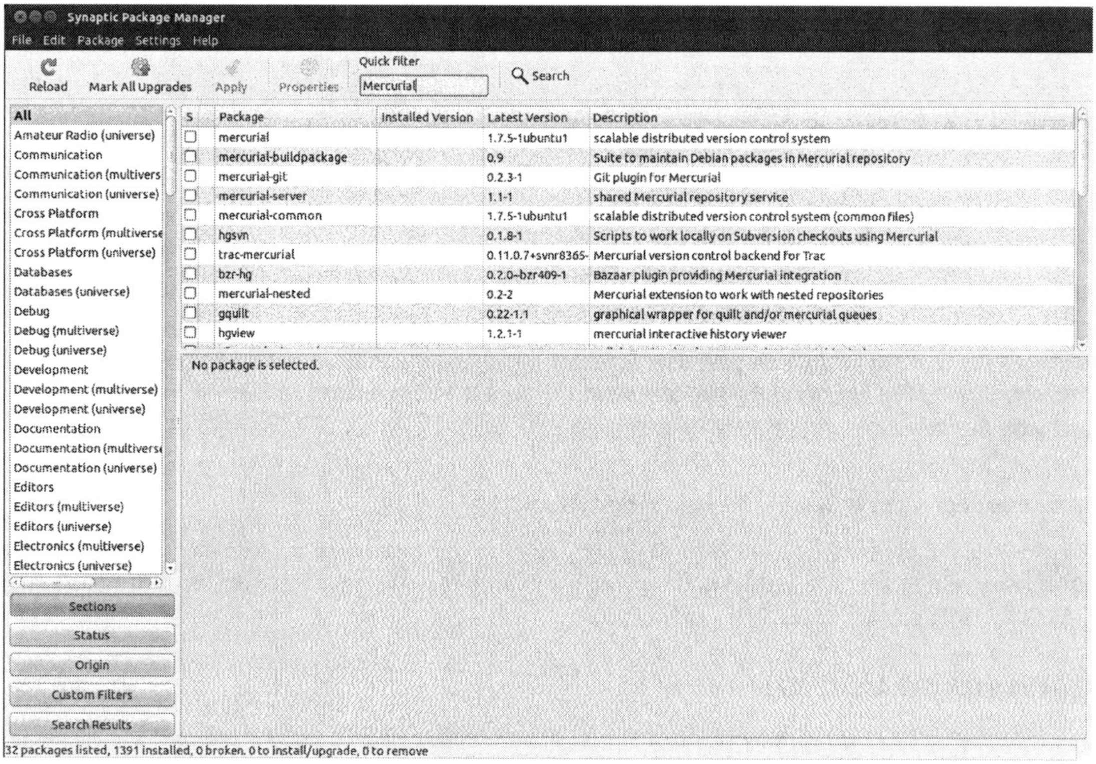

Figure 3-13. The Synaptic Package Manager after searching for Mercurial

Once you've clicked apply and installed everything you're ready to go! To check that everything is working correctly, you'll need to open up another Terminal window. Once it's open, type in

    hg

Once you hit enter you should see the Mercurial help menu, just as in the Mac install. That's it for installing Mercurial via package manager: nice and easy.

With hg installed you need to do a little configuration in the .hgrc file, which is located in your home directory. If it doesn't exist yet, just create it and add the following lines to the file:

    [ui]
    username = Chris Kemper <hey@chrisdkemper.co.uk>

This sets up all of the default user information for all commits in the repositories you create on your machine, so just replace my information with yours and you'll be set. This ensures there's a name to each commit and allows others to contact you if need be.

Compiling from source

Time to check out the building from source option again. Let's get straight into it, shall we? If you don't already have a Terminal window open, get one ready, as you'll need it very soon. Before you can do anything, you need the source files for Mercurial You can grab the latest version by heading to `http://mercurial.selenic.com/release/`.

This is a list of all the source releases for Mercurial, so just grab the latest one from the list—in my case that is Mercurial-1.9. Make a note of the file name, because you won't be downloading it the traditional way. This will be all Terminal, baby, so make sure you have one of those bad lads open. It may be advisable for you to get the URL of the latest version, to save you typing it in later. The easiest way to do that is to right-click the latest version and hit copy link location. This will copy the full URL of the file to the clipboard, which will save you typing it. Clever, eh?

The first thing to do is create a folder to house Mercurial while you compile it, so go ahead and make a directory. You can do this by using the following command while in Terminal:

    mkdir mercurial-test

The `mkdir` command simply creates a directory in your current location on the system, and if that's a fresh Terminal window then you'll be in your home directory. I've specified my folder name to be `mercurial-test`, but you can call the folder anything you like. Once you hit enter that'll be your directory. You can use `ls` command in Terminal to see a list of files and directories, and you should see your newly created directory in there, chilling with the other directories, looking cool. Now that you know it's been created correctly, `cd` into it and get ready for the Mercurial compiling magic to begin.

First thing you're going to do is download the source code you need for the installation. Remember that file name I told you to make a note of? If you don't, if you no longer have the path available in your clipboard, head back to `http://mercurial.selenic.com/release/` and get the path of the latest version. Once you have it, you're ready to download the source code. To do this, you need to run a command called `wget`, which will download a file you tell it to. In this case it's a `tar.gz` file. This means your command will be `wget` and then the url of the file. Mine looked like this:

    wget http://mercurial.selenic.com/release/mercurial-1.9.tar.gz

Once you have `wget` in, hit Shift+Ctrl+V to paste the URL from your clipboard into the Terminal window, as the normal paste function (Ctrl+V) will show up as ^V, which isn't any use to you. Once the file has finished downloading, you can do another `ls` which will show you a Mercurial `.tar.gz` file, which is great. Now you need to unpack it. To do so, run the following command:

    tar -zxvf mercurial-1.9.tar.gz

This will unarchive the `tar.gz` file for you into a directory which has the same name as the file you just unpacked, minus the file name. If your file name is slightly different than mine, you can type tar -zxvf and press Tab, which will tab through all the files in the directory, so you don't have to type the name in. Once that's finished unpacking, you want to head into the directory, so `cd` into it. Now that you have the source code unpacked, all that's left is to get started with the good stuff: compiling it. Since Mercurial is built using

61

Python, the first step is to ensure Python is installed on the system. To do this, enter python into your Terminal window. See Figure 3-14.

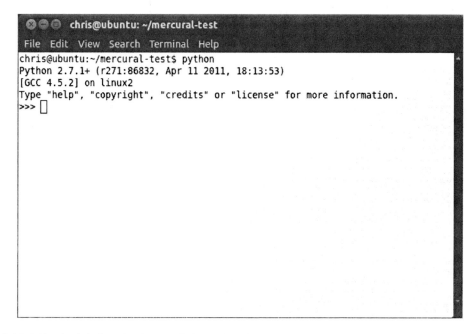

Figure 3-14. A Terminal window showing that Python is installed on the system as the Python console has launched after typing in python and hitting enter

If it's installed, you'll now be in a Python command line, but you don't actually want to be in here—you just wanted to know that Python was installed. To get out of this mode, simply press Ctrl+Z. This will exit the Python Terminal and get you back to regular old Terminal. The Ctrl+Z command is actually quite powerful; it will quit any process you're running in Terminal (it's nice to know if something isn't responding, or you don't need it to finish doing what it's doing). Now that you know Python is running, you need to install a package before you can compile Mercurial: python-dev. You can apt-get this without a problem. Enter the following to get it installed:

```
sudo apt-get install python-dev
```

As always with sudo you'll be asked for your password, and you'll also be asked if the installer downloads some files to your machine. Just hit Y and wait for it to do its job. Since that's all you need, all that's left to do is compile this bad boy, but since it's built in Python you only need to run one command to do the whole thing. That excellent command is

```
sudo python setup.sh install
```

The sudo is needed here to ensure the installer doesn't run into any permission issues along the way, which it would if you didn't use it. Once it finishes its lovely work, that's Mercurial installed on the system—which you can test using hg in the Terminal window, and if you do which hg you will see it's having a lovely time in usr/local/bin with SVN. Now you have Mercurial installed in usr/local and it's safe from any OS updates that come to the system. Considering you only ran a few commands, it's not that difficult. Here are all the commands you've run, in one block:

```
mkdir mercurial-test
cd mercurial-test
wget http://mercurial.selenic.com/release/mercurial-1.9.tar.gz
tar -zxvf mercurial-1.9.tar.gz
cd mercurial-1.9
python
sudo apt-get install python-dev
sudo python setup.py install
hg
```

For the sake of a few commands and a little bit of time in Terminal, you've gained ultimate control over your Mercurial installation and protected it from any system updates which may change its files. There's one more step with the setup on Mercurial, which is setting up some default user information for the commits that will be done within the repositories on your local system. This ensures there's a name to all of your commits, and, if needed, your e-mail address is available for others to contact you. All of this takes place within a file called .hgrc which lives within your user directory. If it doesn't exist, just create an empty file, then either add these lines to the existing file or the newly created blank file:

```
[ui]
username = Chris Kemper <hey@chrisdkemper.co.uk>
```

This just tells Mercurial the username for you on the system; just replace my information with yours, save the file, and you're all set.

Now that Mercurial is set up and working, it's time to move onto its good friend, Git, so let's dive straight in and start working on getting Git installed!

How Git is a little bit different

Now for the final player in our little version control game. Don't think that coming last in my list here is a bad thing, though, because it isn't. Git is a great piece of kit to use to version your files, although it can be a little hard to come to grips with. Never fear, though. I'm here to make it as painless as possible for you. Now, on to how Git works.

Depending on whether you're working alone, or in a team, you'll make a different first step when it comes to getting started. If you're working in a team you'll be using some kind of remote or shared repository and to get started you'll "clone" that repository to your local machine so you can contribute to it. If you're working by yourself and you want to create a new repository you'll initialize one in the folder you want it to be in, and that'll be it. Once you have your repository set up, you'll work away as normal until you want or need to push some changes.

First of all, you need to add any new files you've worked on that weren't under version control. Once you've got them added, you then need to commit those files into the repository. If you're working locally, that's all you need to do. If you're working on a remote repository, however, you have an additional step.

When you commit files, regardless of whether your repository is remote or not, it pushes the files into the local repository, so you'll always maintain a local repository and you can keep committing and adding files to it. If you are working on a shared or remote repository, you'll need to push those files out to the remote repository. This takes all the changes you've committed since the last update you did from the remote repository, and sends them right back up.

The main difference between Git and Mercurial, is that you can be up and running with Mercurial within a few minutes, whereas with Git, you have a bit more configuration to do, namely in the form of SSH keys. They sound a lot more complicated that they are, and I'll make sure it stays that way. I'll show you how to install Git in the easiest possible way, so don't worry about it. Let's just get started.

Setting up on Windows

Until recently, installing Git on a Windows machine was challenging to say the least. Since it was initially created for Linux use, the dependencies have caused it to install unreliably on a Windows machine. Not anymore, though!

Using msysgit

To install Git, you're going to be using a package called msysgit, which you can download from Google code at http://code.google.com/p/msysgit/downloads/list.

The first thing you need to do is download the latest full version of the application. If you check out Figure 3-16 you'll find the list of applications you'll expect to see when you visit the previously mentioned link. The file you're after is the full version; in my case the file was Git-1.7.6-preview20110708.exe. Your file may be a little different in name, but it should have a description along the lines of "Full installer for official Git". To download the file, first double-click it, which will take you to a new screen. This will have a few bits of information on it, the most important of which is the file name. Double-clicking the file name will download the file to your local machine. (See Figure 3-15.)

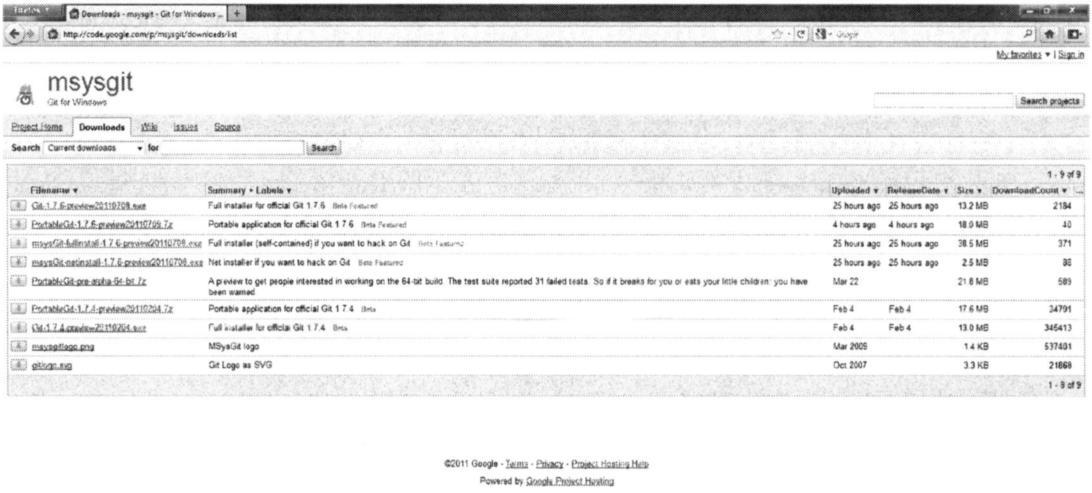

Figure 3-15. The download page for msysgit hosted on Google code, which shows all the available versions of the application available to download

Once you have the application downloaded, double-click it to get it launched. Of course you'll get one of those lovely Windows prompts to ask for permission to make changes, unless you've gotten sick of them by now and turned them off, that is.

Installing Git

The first couple of screens in the installation are somewhat standard, the first is telling you what your installing, and the second informs you that the software is under the GNU public license, so if you wanted to, you could make changes to it.

The next screen is again another familiar one, which asks where you would like to install the application, you can leave this as is, there's no real need to change the location, unless you would prefer to do so for whatever reason.

On the following screen, you will be asked what you would like the menu item to be called. The default is Git, and I'd suggest leaving that as it is. The next option (see Figure 3-16) in the installer is a lot of check boxes which ask if you want desktop items or shortcut items created. Again, I would suggest leaving these as default. There are options you can choose to check or not—Git bash here and Git GUI here—which would add those options to your right-click menu for use when navigating through your file structure. These can come in quite handy, especially if you want your repositories set up in deep menu trees. These are unchecked by default and I'd suggest checking them because it can make your life easier. They are

65

optional, though, and it won't affect Git's inner workings at all if you decide not to use them, so don't feel like you need to.

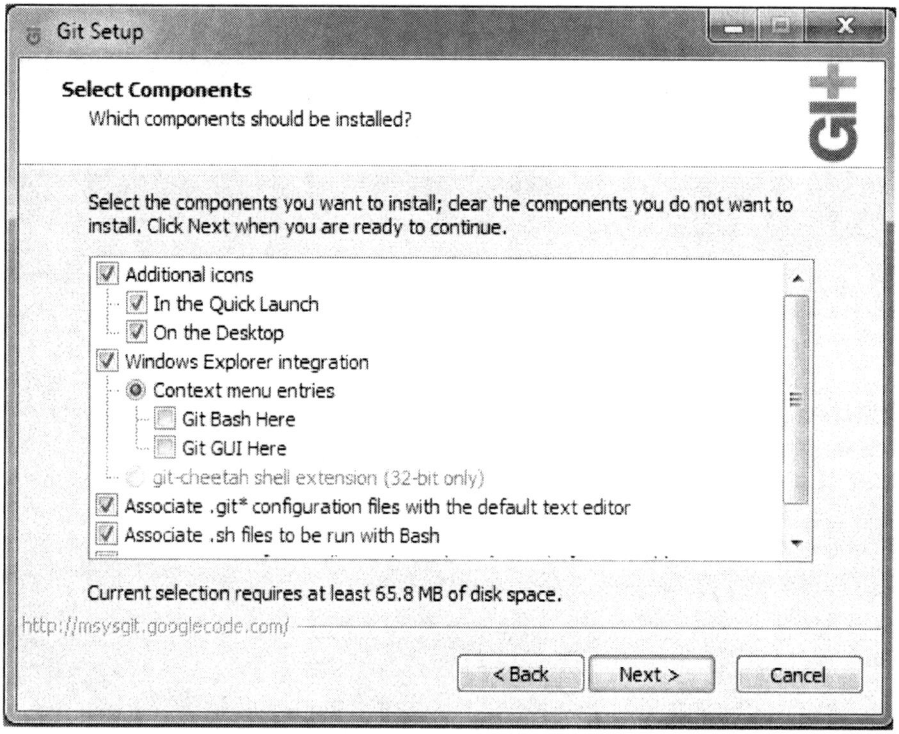

Figure 3-16. A screen within the msysgit installation which asks whether or not some optional components should be installed. The components here are contextual menu options for Git GUI and Git Bash.

The next screen is one to take note of, which you can see in Figure 3-17. You get three options here: the default option specifies that you will only use Git bash for interacting with Git on a command-line level. The second will allow you to interact with Git via a Cygwin prompt. This basically gives the Windows prompt some Unix command line–type abilities. The third and final option is to add a boatload of Unix tools to your PATH variable, so the Unix tools will be used in place of the default Windows ones. The installer does put a warning about this in RED, so you should take notice of it (if someone has taken time to write something in red, you need to take notice of it). To make sure you have a nice happy installation, stick with the first option, which gives you a nice Terminal window to use for Git, which is all you need.

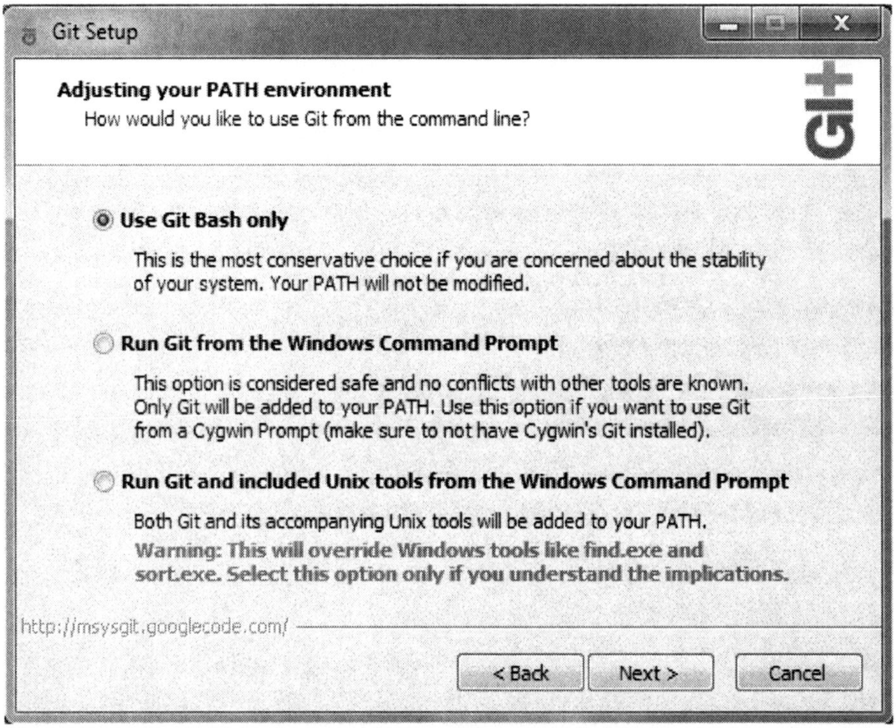

Figure 3-17. The three potential installation options for the Git Bash part application

The next stage of the installation basically addresses how line breaks and new lines are treated when working on multiplatform projects (see Figure 3-18). Each OS has its own way of determining when a new line starts, and keeping option 1 selected will convert the other ways to initiate a new line, into the Windows way, and back again when you commit code. This is the best option for a Windows install, so that's the option you'll be using.

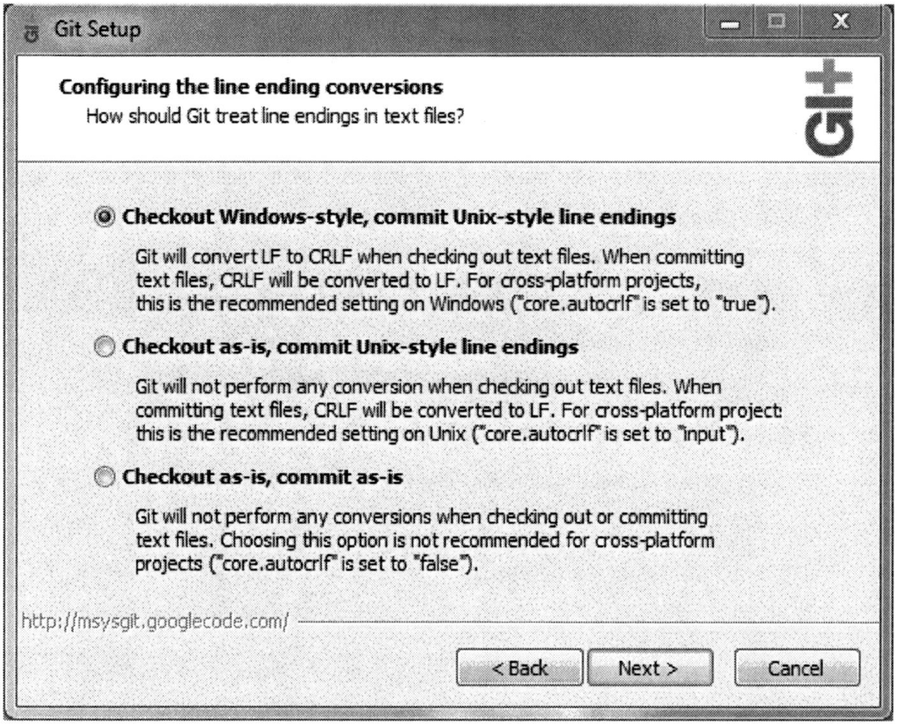

Figure 3-18. The different options available for how Git Bash will treat repositories when performing checkouts

The only other stages after that are the usual copying over of files from the installer and the final screen asking if you'd like to read the README file. I'd advise unchecking this and hitting finish, that is unless you want to read a very long document about Git, in which case keep the box checked.

The setup has done two main things: it's installed a simple GUI to work with Git and it's also installed a stand-alone Terminal client for use with Git. You'll be working with both of these in the latter chapters of the book, but there will be an in-depth look at them both in Chapter 5. There is, however, one final thing to do, and that is set up a name and e-mail address for yourself so that Git knows who you are.

Identifying yourself in Git

To let Git know who you are, set a global name and e-mail address for yourself that will be included in all commits. This is so you can identify who's done what, or who to blame if something has gone wrong. To do this, open up Git Bash which is one of the programs you just installed. When you open it up, it looks like what's in Figure 3-19 (if you haven't seen it before, this what a Terminal window looks like). For now you only need to enter two basic commands, so let's get right into it.

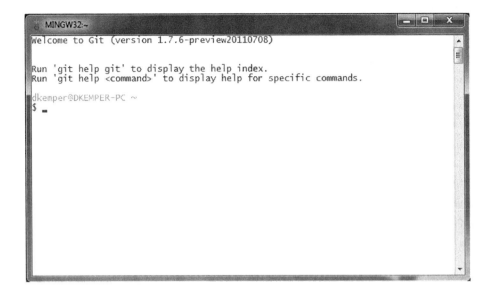

Figure 3-19. Git Bash doing its thing and displaying some generic git help output above the actual prompt within the window, which is indicated by the $

With Git Bash open, you first want to configure the user name, which is the user's actual name, not a username. In my case, of course, that's "Chris Kemper," so in the following command substitute your name for mine, unless you're either called Chris Kemper, or you think my name is awesome.

```
git config --global user.name "Chris Kemper"
```

Once you hit enter, you won't see any form of acknowledgment. In this case, silence is golden, so if nothing comes up, then nothing has gone wrong. You then need to do a similar command for the user's e-mail address, which for me is "hey@chrisdkemper.co.uk" (and, yes, that is my real e-mail address; feel free to send me nice comments, but if they're mean, I'll just mark you as spam). Same goes with the previous example: substitute your details for mine, in the following command:

```
git config --global user.email "hey@chrisdkemper.co.uk"
```

Once you hit enter, you won't see a success or fail message, but if you entered the above you'll be fine. You can, of course, change any of these values once they have been set by running the needed command again.

If you're curious to see if the information has saved correctly, just like I was, there is a command you can run. If you look at Figure 3-20, you'll see my output for the same command. The magic command is as follows:

```
git config --list
```

This will output a lot of stuff you don't need to worry about, but at the bottom of the list are two things you should care about: the name and e-mail address of your lovely self.

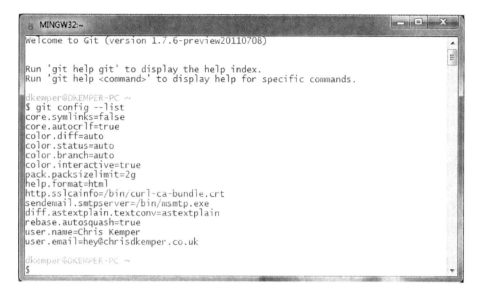

Figure 3-20. The output from the Git Bash window after inputting "git config --list"

As it stands, you are only set up to run local Git projects on your machine. You'll notice the keyword "local" in that last sentence. There is another step to allow access to remote Git servers, which involves SSH keys. I'll go into more detail about remote repositories and SSH keys in another chapter. Now, though, it's time to do it all again, but on a Mac. Let's get started!

Setting up on Mac

To kick off the installation of Git on the Mac OS you need to open up a browser, and head over to the Git website at http://git-scm.com/. Once there, navigate to the Mac download link which is in the lovely red box on the site's homepage. This will take you to a Google code page which hosts all the current and previous versions of Git for Mac. You want to download the latest version which has *i386* and *Leopard* in the name; this will work regardless of whether you have a 32- or 64-bit system. When writing this, my latest version of this file was git-1.7.5.4-i386-leopard.dmg. To start the download, double click the file name. This will take you to another screen containing another file name link. Clicking this link will start the download.

Before you go any further with the installation, it's worth mentioning that if you followed along installing Homebrew to upgrade SVN, and you installed Xcode 4 from the app store, then you will already have a version of Git installed. That setup, however, installed it into usr/bin, which you don't want. Running the installer you just downloaded will install the latest version to /usr/local/bin, which will be much better in the long run.

Another point worth mentioning is that you can actually install Git via Homebrew if you've now gotten a taste for the command line after upgrading SVN. If you'd rather take that approach, then you can enter the following into Terminal, which will install the latest version of Git via Homebrew:

brew install git

This will give you the same effect as installing it via the package you just downloaded; it all depends on your preference. For those of you who'd rather download it the old-fashioned way, then we'll crack on and get started.

To kick off the installation, double-click the .dmg you just downloaded, if it hasn't already opened itself. Inside, you will find a .pkg file. Double-click that to start the installation. You don't really get anything to configure during the install, just keep clicking Next and enter your password when asked for it.

When the installation is finished then that's nearly it. You do need to enter a name and e-mail address for the user using Git, that is, you. To do this, open up a Terminal window via your favorite method, then, to enter a name for yourself, enter the following command, replacing my name with yours:

```
git config --global user.name "Chris Kemper"
```

This attaches a name to any commits you make from this account on your machine, so if anything goes wrong, whoever is looking to fix it will know who caused the problem. The next thing you need to add in is an e-mail address, just as before, replace my info with yours (and yes, that is my e-mail address, so send me nice things):

```
git config --global user.email "hey@chrisdkemper.co.uk"
```

Now that's all set, you can review the information you've put in by typing the following:

```
git config --list
```

You'll then see the information you entered above. If you ever need to change any of the information for whatever reason, just run the above commands again and it'll overwrite the current record, quick sharp.

No matter whether you used Homebrew or the package you downloaded to install Git, after entering the user information that's all you need for now. I'll go into a lot more depth on how to work with repositories a little later on, but for now it's time to go through installing this lean, mean, version-controlling machine on Ubuntu.

Setting up on Ubuntu

As always, you have two options when it comes to installing on Ubuntu: the package manager or the compiling route. First of all, head into the package manager, then, once it's open, do a search for Git. You'll see Git as the first option that comes up. Do the usual and mark it for installation. Once that's done you'll have what's in Figure 3-21, then just hit apply as usual and you're almost ready to go.

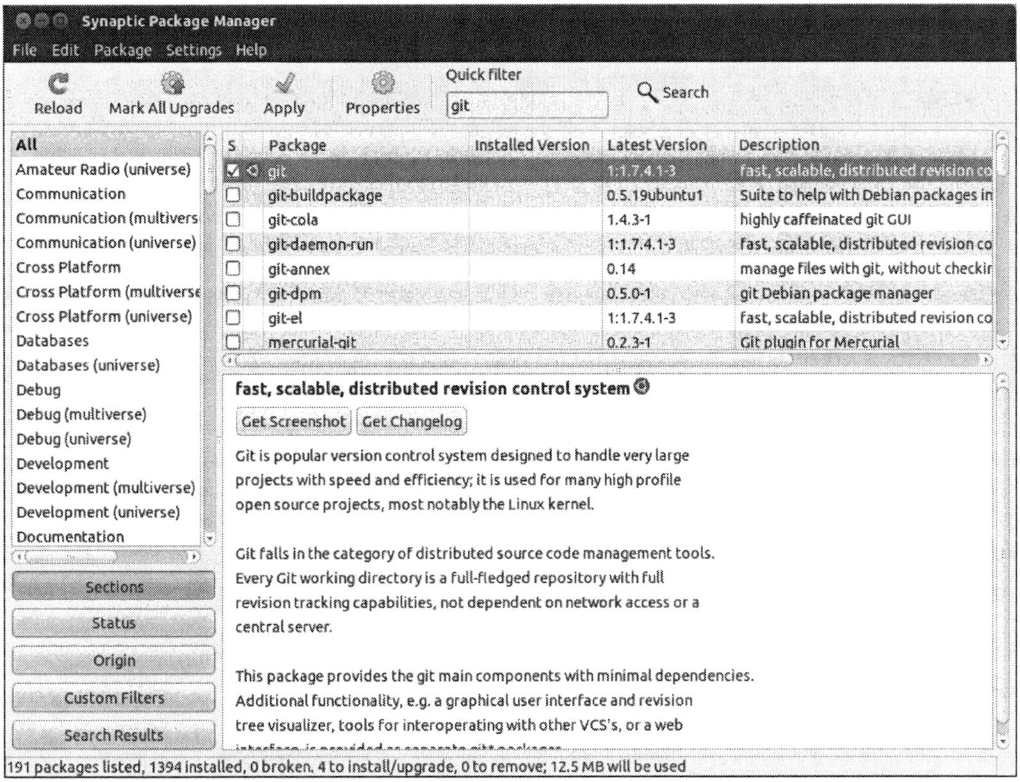

Figure 3-21. The Synaptic Package Manager atter inputting git

That's it, all installed! To make sure, just open up a Terminal window and type in:

    git

Once you hit enter you'll see the help menu for the git command, and you'll notice it is quite big compared to the others you've seen, but I'll get into this a lot more later in the book. To finish the install you need to enter some information while you're in Terminal, first of which is your name. This is used when you commit any code, so others looking at commits will know who wrote the code, or who to blame if something goes wrong (just kidding!). To do this, just replace my lovely name with yours in the following command:

    git config --global user.name "Chris Kemper"

With that done you now need to add an e-mail address for the same reason as the name, although with an e-mail address entered it means people can send you a nice e-mail when something goes wrong. Just like before, replace my e-mail with yours. The command is:

    git config --global user.email "hey@chrisdkemper.co.uk"

That's all the core info you need now. If you need to update any of that information, just enter the command again and it'll overwrite what's already in the system. You can also review the information Git has stored at any time by entering this in Terminal:

```
git config --list
```

This will give you a list of the information stored, but since you've only entered a name and an e-mail address, that's what it'll show.

That's all you need as far as setting up from the package manager is concerned. Give yourself a pat on the back. Now, though, it's time to compile this bad lad from source.

Compiling from source

First things first. You need some source code before you can compile it, so head over to the Git website at http://git-scm.com/ and click the source link, which is located under Tux the penguin. The link will download the latest source code straight away, so that solves that problem. Depending on your browser configuration, the file should be in the Downloads folder, so open up Terminal and cd straight to the folder where it downloaded to. First of all, you need to unarchive it, which you can do by entering the following command:

```
tar xvfj filename
```

This command will unarchive the file to a directory with the same name, minus the extension, so just replace the file name with the file you've just downloaded and you're in business. Next up, cd in the new directory and get ready to start the fun stuff, and by that I mean the compiling and installing. This is actually a rather simple process. First of all you need to run ./configure, which does all the major legwork and looks around the system to make sure everything it needs is there. The next stage is to run make; this does the actual compiling of the application. Once that's finished, you're nearly done. Enter sudo make install, which will move the application to the correct location, which is usr/local/. The sudo is needed to make sure no file permission errors come up, which they would do if you didn't use it. Now the final stage is to clean up any mess the installer left, which you can do by running make clean which will remove any temporary files and such created by the installation.

Now that Git has compiled successfully, you just need to add a couple of bits of information before we can call it day. These are your name and your e-mail address. This allows Git to track who has made which changes to make it easier to fix bugs, or to play the blame game when something is broken. To add this information in is quite simple: just replace my info with yours in the commands below, and you be all set and ready to go.

```
git config --global user.name "Chris Kemper"
git config --global user.email "hey@chrisdkemper.co.uk"
```

No matter which route you came down, that's everything you need to have Git installed on your Ubuntu system. Great stuff!

Summary

You've done it! No matter how you went about installing them, or which operating system it was on, you now have working versions of SVN, Mercurial, and Git on your machine. I showed you the different methods you can use to install the packages, some being harder than others, but when it came down to it, they weren't actually that bad. There is, of course, a lot more work to be done, but now we're all on the same page. It can only get better from here. So give yourself a pat on the back and grab a beer, you've gotten the tricky stuff out of the way. Now all that's left is to master version control so your projects won't know what hit them!

Chapter 4

The Benefits of Version Control

Now that you've got all your systems installed, it's time to look at the benefits you gain from version control. In this chapter I will cover some of the terms mentioned in previous chapters in more detail.

Having a backup of your files

The main benefit of version control is having a backup of your files. I don't think anybody would argue with you if you wanted to say that having a backup of your files is a good idea. It seems to be somewhat common practice now: everyone backs up their work. No matter what you're working on, or what you're using, you always want to keep some kind of backup—or you will wish you had kept some kind of backup when things take that horrible turn for the worse and files get lost.

Naming conventions

Back in the dark ages, before anybody had any methods of version control, backups would be done according to the naming convention of the file. I can't tell you the number of times I've had documents called *x-final-final-thisisthefinal* or something very close to that. I think if anybody has dealt with this method before they'll soon realize that trying to work out which is which is a real pain. To get rid of some of this confusion, some of us would opt for version naming files, such as *file-v1* or *file-v5*. This is fine in the early stages, but there may come a time where you have 12 different versions of a file with different version numbers, something like Figure 4-1.

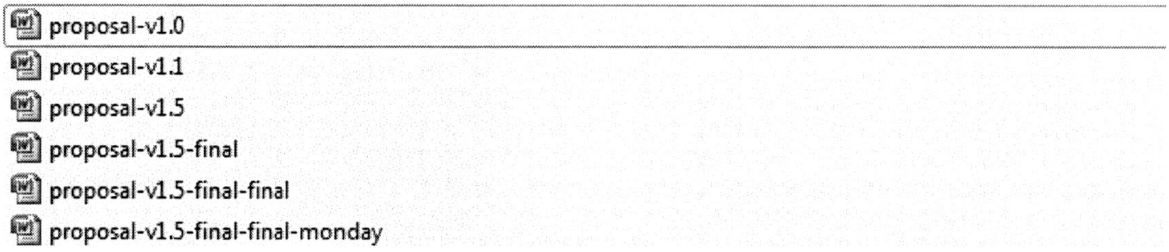

proposal-v1.0

proposal-v1.1

proposal-v1.5

proposal-v1.5-final

proposal-v1.5-final-final

proposal-v1.5-final-final-monday

Figure 4-1. This shows a list of documents which have been named according to their version number, in some cases, with words such as "final" and "monday", which are really confusing for another person looking at the files, or even for the creator coming back to the files after a period of time.

This system did have its flaws, like the fact that it looks messy, or that editing a previous version meant you had to pretty much open every version of the document to find what you wanted. Even then, you had to copy the changes back into the most recent file and then make another version of it. Despite all that effort, it did work, and for some of us it worked fine. Those of us who used that method were definitely a lot better off than the ones who chose to live dangerously and not have a backup at all or rely on the undo states in the document's own program.

USB drives

Some people will also choose to have two versions of a particular file, one on a USB drive and one on their local machine. I used this method for a while, especially when I was working at college. I'd have all my work on my memory stick, and then transfer it to my home computer as a backup. This was going just peachy until I lost my memory stick, and I hadn't backed up to my PC for a good while, mainly out of laziness; as you can imagine, I was done for. If that memory stick had included important documents or some important code files I needed for work, I'd have been screwed. With the files gone, I'd have to re-create them from scratch or from an early backup, which, no matter how you look at it, sucks.

External hard drives

You could also go down the route of backing up your whole machine to an external hard drive every day. That in itself is fine, but it can leave you in a somewhat sticky predicament. If you did want to go back to a version of a file from a couple of days ago, you would have no real indication of what changes you had made since then or if the older version of the file would even be of any use, since backups like that are done weekly at best, if you happen to remember (for those who like to have a constant backup, daily or two-daily schedules are often common). Unless you opt for the daily/two-daily option, this method of having a backup for your files is better suited for archived work that you can't get rid of but you don't really want to keep on your machine, or just to make sure you have everything backed up somewhere. If that hard drive were to malfunction on you, you'd be lost.

Dropbox

In this modern age, when cloud computing is all the rage, we have some nice options for backing up files now. One of these is Dropbox. For those of you who have been living under a technological rock, Dropbox is a service that allows you to share your files across multiple machines nearly instantly. It also contains a hidden gem: a form of source control built right in. You can log into your Dropbox, go into a file and see the previous versions of it. You can also revert back to an older version of the file if something has gone seriously wrong. But before you go and put everything you've worked on into Dropbox, I must warn you that it isn't perfect by any means. I'll go into a lot more detail about Dropbox, its features, and my referral code for it a bit later in the book. For now, though, if you want keep your files safe, Dropbox is a good solution.

Backup summary

So now we come to version control as a backup method. No matter which path you choose to take, whether it's Git, Mercurial, SVN, or even another version control system, version control can give you a huge amount of control over the backing up of your code. Even with your code safely in a repository, it's also worth thinking about keeping your repository backed up, just to be doubly sure your code is safe. If you decide to set up camp on your own server, all decent hosting companies have a backup option, which will mean your previous files will be backed up on a daily basis. So, unless something goes majorly wrong on the hosting company's end, your files will be safe and won't be going anywhere. If you decide to go the third-party service route, they will ensure your code is correctly backed up, it may cost you a little extra, but it's worth it!

Collaborative projects

It's safe to say that a *huge* perk of version control is the ability work on a collaborative project with other users, without having to worry about who's working on what. If we gaze back into the past again, before all of this fancy stuff, working with someone else on a project wasn't exactly easy.

If you were that way inclined, you may have set up a server, and given both of you access to the same area; whoever was working on a file could potentially change the file extension of that file to append their name, such as file-Chris, or gone with the whole *v1*, *v2* approach to ensure files weren't overridden. This method would work, but it still meant you couldn't work on the same files.

You may have also delved into the e-mailing files method of collaborative working. Although this method did work, if you had a huge e-mail conversation going on, it got really confusing really fast. Even though you would no doubt be sending the same files, or even the same site back and forth, unless you always replaced the version you had, you still needed to rename the folder/file you were working on to make sure it didn't get overritten, which led to the same kind of problems you've seen already. The perk of this method was if you did happen to delete a file, it was still around, although the same can't be said for FTP.

If you were working in an office environment and you had to work collaboratively on projects, you would need to be really careful when it came to working with files. To give you an example: say you have an office with five people and today, Janis and Dave need to work on the same files on a shared system.

Janis shouts over to Dave and says she'll be working on the index.html file on the shared server to make some changes. Dave doesn't respond because he has his headphones on, but Janet assumes he heard. Little does she know, Dave has just spent the last few hours making changes to that file straight onto the shared area. He then decides he's all done and hits Save. Janet, who has the version of the file before Dave made his changes, saves her changes which then completely erase the changes Dave had just made. Everyone will have had something like this happen and it's painful when you're the one who has to redo your changes. This problem could have been avoided by using a renaming convention I mentioned earlier, or by using a VCS.

Whether you decide on a centralized system or a distributed system, working on collaborative projects couldn't be easier. SVN, Git, and Mercurial all have built-in merge tools, and the option to use external tools to fix problems. No matter which one you decide to go with, or even if you decide to use a different one, they all have the ability to allow you to work with others on your projects without worrying, although it's safe to say some are better at it than others. (I'm talking to you, CVS.)

The ability to work on different machines

If you told me that you've never ever wanted to work on the same file on two different machines, I would say you were lying (in the nicest possible way, of course). Whether it's to add in a new idea you have, or to make that urgent bug fix the boss has asked you to make, everyone at some point has needed to change a file from a different location. Most of the time, the two main locations will be at work and at home, with the potential for a third, most likely offsite, like a café or a bar. If you're one of those people who has an FTP area that can be accessed from all of these locations, then you may be allright if your boss suddenly says "I need this change right now, can you get the file to me?". If you were lucky enough to preempt this request by placing the file on FTP already, you'd be safe. But what if you didn't? Most of us would simply have to say "The file is at work" or "I'll go make the change from the office now" or the good old "Can it wait till tomorrow?"

It's fair to say that you may not have had access to an FTP service before version control, so a more likely method to work on a file from a new location would be to e-mail the file to yourself. Failing that, there's always the good old memory stick option, which is a good method for times like this. But say you make your changes at home and save everything, but just as you're about to put it on the memory stick, or mail it back to yourself, someone knocks at the door, your cat jumps on you, the roast burns, or any other distraction arises. The next day when you go back to work you have the horrible realization that the most recent version of the file you need is sitting on your computer at home.

You can, of course, pay for a service to allow you to use a work computer from home, which would give you instant access to those files, and you wouldn't need to worry about e-mailing files or anything like that. An example of software like this would be pcAnywhere from Symantec, which will set you back around $199 (for that kind of cash, I'd rather send an e-mail). You may, however, be provided with a similar method from your work place which involves some kind of FTP or file server, which would be gravy, but doesn't always happen.

When it comes down to it, working on multiple machines is possible, but it's never perfect, which is why a VCS is so useful. If you're using a remote repository, you can create multiple copies of it and keep that one location constantly updated, so you can commit your files from home and update them again once you're at work. Simple. You can have multiple clones of a repository, which can span across operating systems, machines, or even countries. Have a look at Figure 4-2 for a visual of this. Using any of the versioning methods I've previously mentioned would help you avoid the need to e-mail yourself files or rely on a memory stick ever again. (For most files, that is; but more on that later.)

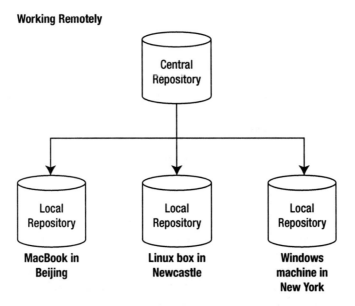

Working Remotely

Figure 4-2. This shows how the repository can be cloned and used on multiple locations, over multiple machines and operating systems.

A full history of changes

Being able to maintain the full history of a project is priceless for many reasons, especially for keeping your files (yes, you've guessed it) backed up. Whether you make the mistake of deleting a file, need to go back to a previous version, or just want to know what's changed, these are all possible with a full history of changes.

Safety from deleted files

In more ways than one, having a backup of your files is a key and important part of versioning your files. As soon as you commit a file, it's safe! That can come in more useful than you can imagine. Let's go back to the memory stick example I used earlier: if you delete a file from one of those bad lads, then it's gone, vanished. That is, of course, unless you have some kind of backup, but in most cases, that backup will be really old, which pretty much makes it useless. If you have a file versioned, however, and you delete it, you can always get it back. You may need to get it from a previous change set, or simply "update" your local version to that of the repository and it'll restore the deleted file(s). More than once I've needed to reclaim a deleted file because I'd accidentally deleted it, or simply lost it in my file system (I used to be a bit clumsy when using my graphics tablet to navigate my machine). No matter what the need, being able to recover your deleted files is a huge advantage of versioning your files, generally using version control.

Going back to a previous version

Inevitably when you're working on a file the time comes when you make a mistake and it's time to play the press-undo-oodles-of-times game. That is fine if this is a recent change, but what if you need to go way back? Unless you've been renaming your files or keeping versions, getting an older version back is nigh impossible. This is why having a full history is so important. If you keep committing your code frequently, then you can have an indispensible resource while working with documents or code. If you did need to revert back to a previous version, for whatever reason, then it's as easy as pie. You can simply browse the repository and find the version you'd like to go back to, and then revert. Simple.

Checking for differences between files

You do have other options besides just reverting. Another spiffing feature you can get from using version control is the ability to diff between files. This, of course, is telling the difference between two or more files; in version-control terms, it refers to being able to check for differences between different versions of a file. So if you make some changes to a file and you want to see how it differs with the latest version in the repository, you can run a diff between the two files. You can also check for changes between different versions of the files, so you can decide what you need to do with the files, whether it's reverting or committing them. This would be especially useful if you've been made aware of a bug in some code and you need to get the version of the file before the bug was added in. You can run a diff against your current version and a few different versions to see which will be the best version to revert to.

Dealing with indecisive clients

Let's put this into a client situation, shall we? You've slaved away creating a beautiful layout for a client, who then gives you a boatload of amends to do. To keep the client happy you go ahead and make the needed changes (hopefully they're not utterly frivolous, such as the client's nephew likes cats, so they want cats in the design). Once the changes have been made, the client says those horrible words: "I liked it better the way it was." This, of course, would mean going through various files and putting the changes back to normal, which could take just as long as it took to make the new changes. If, however, your code is versioned, you can just revert the working copy back to the way it was before any changes were started with a few clicks—easy. You also get to keep the changes you made; they'll still be in the repository somewhere, so If the client then decides they liked something from the changes and want it added back in, you can have a peek at the amended version in the repository, check out the file, make the needed additions, then put it back into the repository. This means a happier client because the changes were done quickly, and a happier you because you don't need to waste any time reverting changes back manually, [was something accidentally deleted here?]

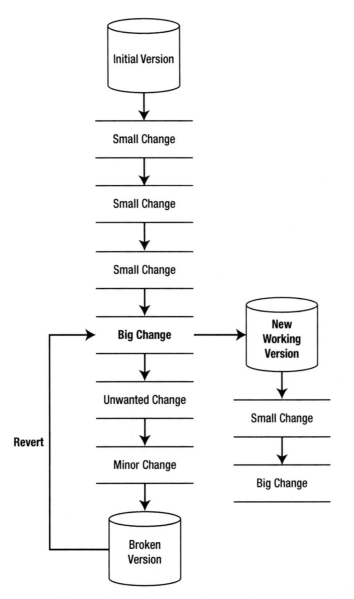

Figure 4-3. The history can be useful by enabling you to revert back to a previous version, use that as the new latest version of the file, and then make changes to it.

Comments

As I've mentioned before, comments are a huge part of version control. Any commit, no matter how big or small, can have a comment attached to it (or not, of course, since comments are optional). It's always advisable to add a comment, though, no matter what you're committing, because it comes in handy when you need to look up versions for whatever reason.

One of the better uses for comments is to track version changes. If you're committing a significant update, then you can add details about which changes have been made. This can include any bug fixes that have been made, new features that have been added, or even features that were removed.

Using comments to deal with bugs

In the days before version control if, god forbid, a bug came into your code, what would you do? Depending on the update, you might have made a backup and labelled the original file slightly differently so the change could be reverted. What if you didn't have that backup, though? It would be a frantic 10, 15, or 20 minutes, maybe even an hour, while the bug was fixed. Depending on whether said bug was obviously noticeable on the website, you may also have had the boss breathing down your neck to get it done faster. This, of course, adds up to wasted time, and most likely a lot of stress.

Let's go through the same scenario again, but with a version control system in place. The new feature is pushed to the site, but with it comes a bug that takes down one of the pages. Since you don't want to attempt to fix the bug while it's online, you simply need to revert to the previous version, which means, yep, you've got it, no bug anymore. This, of course, can go down without anybody being any the wiser; even if someone does notice, as long as you notice it just as quickly, by the time they refresh to double-check that the bug is still there, it will already have been fixed, thanks to a speedy revert.

Although sometimes you're lucky enough to catch bugs like that straight away, sometimes a bug has been sitting in code for a long, long time and just hasn't surfaced. In those cases, commenting really comes in useful. If you make a habit of making good comments, it makes looking at the history of a file a whole lot easier. You can go through the commits of the file and see which version it is you need to revert to. However, this is impossible if you use useless comments. When committing changes several times in a day, it's tempting to simply not put a comment, or something so vague it's of no use. (If you want to get ideas for some useless comments, check out http://whatthecommit.com.) You could go down the humorous route when working with friends or close colleagues to make them laugh, but when it comes to actually needing your previous versions, pointless comments are as useful as a chocolate fireguard.

Figure 4-4. One of the many commit messages you can generate from http://whatthecommit.com which is terribly vague; if you came back to it in the future, you would have no idea what actually got changed lin the commit, based on the message.

The drawbacks of e-mail

You may be thinking, wait a minute, I can just e-mail my files to anybody I'm working with. This will allow me to send the file, but also allow me to add comments, à la a message, and I'll have all the previous versions that I've sent and received in my inbox. Sounds like a bulletproof system to me—oh wait, I'm lying. It's as bulletproof as a plastic bag, or fire. (I know there was no need to add the fire, but it just makes it sound a little more dangerous.) If you do choose to manage your collaboration of files by using e-mail then in all honesty it could be made to work, if you make sure to tell the other people when you won't be working on the files so they can safely do so. To do that you might have to tweet or text the other people, however, because they might not be cool enough to have e-mail sync'd to a device. (Kind of like when e-mail was first introduced: you'd send someone a funny chain mail, then text them with something like "Dude, just sent you an awesome e-mail, did you read it yet?!") Let's assume you're working with some tech savvy folk who all have their e-mail downloaded to a lovely desktop mail service. You hear that bing or beep, or see that notification, so you know it's time to do your share of the work. You can check out the reply in the e-mail to see what kind of work has been done, and download the file. By now though, the file will most likely have some insane file name, because everyone will be downloading it to the same place so it'll have a load of (1)(2)'s in the file name. Even if you try and keep it clean, one person will just save it as is, due to time problems, then everyone will get a little lazy, until you end up with something like

```
File-test(1) Mondays-meeting(1)(2)-final.doc
```

That's just if you're working with a single file. What if you're working with a full website? Each time you need to send it around you'll need to zip up the site. After a while, work will only continue on a few files, so only those will be sent around. But maybe after that, a change will be made to a different file, but the person making the change forgets to send said file over with their update, so everyone else gets errors, and for whatever reason you can't get ahold of the needed file, so work stops till the guy or gal wakes up from their power nap or gets round to reading their e-mail.

Don't get me started on files getting overwritten; working over e-mail pretty much encourages this because there's only ever one up-to-date version of the files, so it's bound to happen. Although the previous version of the file will be kicking around in the e-mail trail somewhere, what if that file was only included from like five e-mails ago? Going back to that version would mean redoing some work, which everyone hates doing, especially if it could have been avoided.

Despite all this, the e-mail system does work, and it does keep your files backed up to a secure server, especially if you're using Gmail. (Who isn't these days?) This, however, doesn't account at all for human error. What if you've just pulled a huge stint working on a project, but you pass out at your desk and wake up ten minutes before you go. You need to get into your e-mail, reply to the massive file, attach the new file, write a little about what you did, and head out. But when you get to the next place you realize you've made a change to a different file, and you didn't attach it to the e-mail, or mention it at all. At this point, you're officially, without the use of a better word, fudged. This, however, can all be avoided by using source control. Whenever any commits are done, you can always check which files you've changed on your local machine, then you can be sure to include any needed files in the commit. Plus there's no more messaging the other guys to make sure they're not working on the files. Version control pretty much encourages collaboration, and because of merging tools, it couldn't be any easier. Plus, the file names never change, so no messy log file names. Good, eh?

Giving clients confidence in you

Let's put this into a more modern example, shall we? The number of people freelancing is growing more and more as years go by. A key part of freelancing is having the ability to go into a new client's office and do the job you've been hired to do with little to no help or training. Since you are charging for your services as a freelancer, employers tend to expect some things from you, and one of those is an understanding and knowledge of the workings of version control.

Although some employers may help you out with such things, some employers may not consider hiring you again: it seems unprofessional not to have knowledge of source control. For the sake of a good example, let's say you, as a freelancer, get hired by a specialist company to do some design work. Going in, you may be thinking you don't need to worry about source control because you only do design work, but this particular client would like some of the designing to be done in browser, a somewhat standard request these days. Although your skills are limited, you're still able to deal with the request and start working. Before you get onto the coding stage of the design, the client asks you to check out one of their Mercurial repositories to code the site on top of. Due to your lack of knowledge on source control, you are left having to ask the client how to go about checking out the repository and how to commit code, or even what that is.

Even if the client is helpful and teaches you quite a lot, it can still be a little damaging to your reputation. This could have all be avoided by doing some prior research on version control, or even on the company itself to see if they make the system they use publically available. In most cases, a company will heavily stand by its version control system, which will have been chosen for a very specific reason. Having knowledge of the main players in the version control game, and even the processes and inner workings of each one, can be greatly helpful when moving from client to client. The less they need to assist you in setting up, the better.

A slight downside to working freelance is that, although a client may initially ask you to come into the office to work, it's not uncommon for you to be able to work from home once the project and what's expected of you have been established. If you have an opportunity to work away from the office but the project requires knowledge of version control and you are unable to work with their system, you will be required to come back into the office to work. Even if the client teaches you about their system, they may feel a little uneasy allowing you remote access to their precious code when you have limited knowledge of the system protecting it!

Giving your clients confidence in you really comes down to knowing at least a little about the various parts of the industry you work in. In our case, that's having the knowledge of at the least the basics of the common versioning systems and, at the very, very least, what those systems are. You can also gain bonus points for having this knowledge from clients who wouldn't expect you to have it—for example, if you are a designer doing some work for a development agency but you know how to work with their versioning system. Knowing the deal about versioning systems also allows you certain perks, such as working remotely, and gives you a positive reputation for knowing your stuff within the industry and having knowledge on something you don't necessarily specialize in.

Working on projects and files

There are, of course, a lot of social benefits to using version control, but more important are the benefits that inpact your day-to-day workflow and help keep your files safe and your project running smoothly. These help both when working solo on a project and if you're working as part of a team, with the added bonus of enabling you to keep up good development practices by ensuring that your code is fully versioned and therefore backed up.

Going local

Using any versioning system is better than nothing, but if you happen to choose one of the distributed members of the version control family then there are an additional couple of benefitcs. As you know from previous chapters, having a distributed system means that the repository containing all the file changes is stored locally rather than in a central location (centralized). The benefit of this is the increase in speed for performing actions, since no remote calls are needed. This means all commits, merges, and more are achieved a whole lot faster *and* you can set up a remote repository, to get all the benefits of sharing the code with others, too!

Merging

One of the biggest and best features of version control is the ability to merge changes. At its most basic level, merging comes into its own when multiple users work on the same file at the same time. Say two people, Dave and Jenny, are working on the same CSS file. Dave is adding his changes at the top of the file, adding in some new font rules, something like this:

```css
h1,
h2,
h3,
h4,
h5,
h6 {
    font-weight: bold;
    margin: 10px 0;
}
h1 {
    font-size: 1.538em;
}
h2 {
    font-size: 1.385em;
}
h3 {
    font-size: 1.231em;
}
h4 {
    font-size: 1.154em;
}
h5,
h6 {
    font-size: 1.077em;
}
```

Unknown to Dave, Jenny has also been making some changes to the same file, but at the end of it. Let's say for comparison's sake that Jenny's changes are more structural, like so:

```css
/* Dashboard */
#dashboard .dashboard-region div.block h2 {
    background: #E0E0D8;
}
#dashboard div.block h2 {
    margin: 0;
    font-size: 1em;
    padding: 3px 10px;
}
#dashboard div.block div.content {
    padding: 10px 5px 5px 5px;
}
#dashboard div.block div.content ul.menu {
```

```
   margin-left: 20px;
}
#dashboard .dashboard-region .block {
   border: #ccc 1px solid;
}
```

Now, if these guys both started working from the same version of the file at the same time, they'd both, of course, need to push their changes. If nobody else has made any changes to the most recent copy of the file In the repository, then whoever commits first will be able to do so without any problems. Let's say Jenny managed to get in there first. Now if Dave went to commit, he would first have to update his local version, and upon doing so, both sets of changes would be merged together into one file. Collaborating at its finest!

This, of course, can work for any number of people working on the same files at the same time, and it makes collaboration a lot easier when working in teams. Sometimes, though, the merge fails for some reason, and the file is left in a conflicted state. This can happen for a number of reasons, but the most common is that people have been working on the same lines in the same file, maybe even on the same styles if it was a CSS file. When this happens, there are a lot of ways to solve it—there's a full chapter on this later on in which I will go into it in a lot more detail.

The main thing to take away here is that it's possible to work on the same file at the same time as someone else without having to tell them to wait till you're finished, or wait for them to e-mail you their version of the file. If you happen to be working on different parts of the file then in most cases you can just update your version of the file, get the new changes, and everything will be fine. It's not always as simple as that, however, and if you've been working in the same area of a file as someone else, or changed the same things in your version, the file will be conflicted when it is updated to the latest version. I'll go over this in a lot more detail in a later chapter; just know that if your file gets conflicted, it can be solved easily enough.

Branching

Yet another bitchin' feature of version control is *branching*. It's one of the best features of version control, and it's even better with distributed systems. When you create a new branch on your code, it's like mixing paint: you wouldn't want to just mix all your paint straight away, because if the color is wrong, there's no going back. Instead, you take a bit of blank paper and do your mixing there. If you decide, wow, that color is amazing, you can make the mix straight in your paint. Otherwise, you can just discard the paper and forget you ever wanted to use that other color. This, in essence, is branching.

Working on new features

When you want to work on a new feature in your code, you can create a branch and perform all the changes you want in the branch, without it affecting any of your existing code. If you like the feature, it can be merged into the main code base without a problem. If you hate the feature, you can discard it, just like that. You can also develop on a branch once it has been created, so the initial idea can be developed before you decide what to do with it.

Using branches as project states

Although branching is great for testing out new or experimental features, it also comes in really useful for creating certain states of a project. For example, the project you are working on could have a development state and a release state, with the release state being the client-facing, stable side of the project, and the development being the improvements and bug fixes. In cases like this, it's very common for the release state of the branch to see no activity for a long time, because all development is done in the development branch to ensure the client-facing project doesn't break.

Now what if a bug is discovered in the release state? You can't merge the development branch in yet as it contains too many unfinished changes, which would cause way more problems, and you don't want to just work on the live version because that could cause other problems. In this instance, you would create a branch of the current stable version of the code, which would allow for the bug to be fixed and tested in an isolated environment without causing any other problems. You could, of course, do this on the live version of the files, but if anything is accidentally pushed, it could cause major problems. With the bug fix tested, the branch can be merged back into the release branch with the development branch remaining intact.

You can use branching easily enough for keeping a project in certain states, for developing new features or even for fixing bugs. It can also be used for creating workflows for teams, to allow for certain users to only push to certain branches, ensuring all changes are reviewed by another user before going live, and a whole lot more. If you were a project manager, you might wish to review certain code changes before they went live, which is possible using branches. You could have a development branch, as described in the previous example, but that branch would actually be a branch of the review version of the code. This means that changes from the development version could be pushed to the review version before being pushed to the live version. Although this is overly complex for the majority of users, it can be necessary for some companies to ensure all code is reviewed and handled correctly. You can see this represented in Figure 4-5, which makes it easier to digest.

Branching can be quite simple and quite complex at the same time; it all depends on how you'd like to use it. Some people couldn't live without the flexibility of branching and the ability it gives you to work on a new feature or test something new, without causing any issues to existing code. It can also be used in great depth to create complex workflows to ensure no untested code goes live or for something as simple as fixing a bug. For this exact reason, there's a full chapter dedicated to branching later on in the book. I'll go through everything you need to know about branching and really get into why it's awesome!

Branching

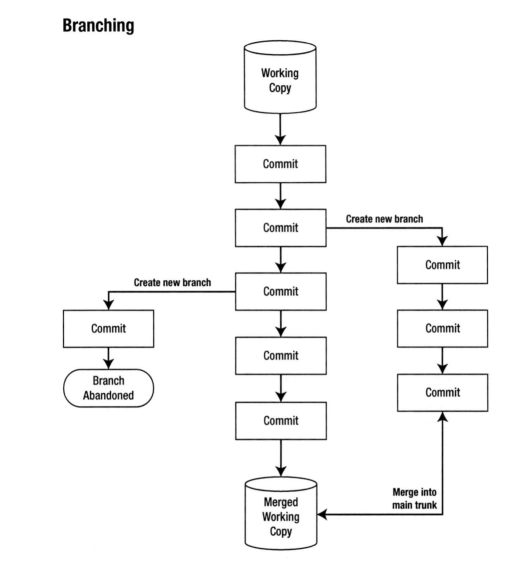

Figure 4-5. The process of branching from the main trunk of a repository, either merging it back into trunk, or abandoning the branch completely

Bridging

This benefit is a little more complex than some of the others, but it's a benefit all the same. *Bridging* very literally means bridging between two systems, such as Git and SVN. If you are primarily using a system such as SVN to control your code, then you don't get the benefits of distributed version control such as a personal repository for your code. Using a bridge, it's possible for you to use Git to version your own local code, getting all the benefits from it, and then using the bridge to push the code into the SVN repository. In theory this seems very simple, but it is quite complicated to accomplish easily. First of all, you need to know the terminal commands for both Git and SVN and have knowledge of how the bridge works to use it correctly. There also isn't just a standard option when using, in this instance, a git-svn bridge; there are a few options out there, such as git-svn-bridge or actually using the git-svn feature built into Git. The latter is a system built into Git which allows it to understand SVN commands and work with them accordingly, using commands such as `git svn co http://repository`, whereas the former is an independent package you can install which runs a different set of commands in the form of `git bridgesvn co http://repository`. As you can already see, bridging has a number of complexities, but its benefits are amazing if you can tame the bridging-beast.

That, of course, just deals with SVN and Git. There are a number of other bridges available that allow for communication between Mercurial and Git and SVN and Mercurial. The last two examples are third-party applications developed to allow for communication between the systems in terms of checking out repositories and pushing or pulling changes.

Bridges are great if you want to get the best of both worlds, when you can't necessarily change the primary versioning system you use, which allows you to keep the original system, while taking advantage of the benefits of the new one. It isn't for the faint of heart, though; bridging is an all-Terminal deal and requires knowledge of both systems. If you're working with a bridge on a larger repository, it's possible to see slow-downs when working performing commands on the repository itself. While using a bridged system you're unable to fully take advantage of either system, as they need to be slightly limited to ensure the systems can communicate correctly. For example, in the Git-SVN bridge, the way you have to commit changes means you cannot perform regular branching because SVN just wouldn't understand them and would freak out. This means any branches you do make have to be rebased (i.e., the branches merged into the original in a linear fashion, as if all the commits had been performed without the branch) which is extra work, but if you don't do it, it can cause major problems with your SVN repository. You also shouldn't use a bridge to learn a new versioning system because of the limitations of the bridged system; above all else, it'll teach bad habits when it comes to using the new system in its entirety. If you have enough knowledge of both the systems involved in the bridge, then working with it is an awesome idea; you get the benefits of the new system and you won't pick up any bad habits from using it because you already know better.

Summary

I've given you a lot of reasons for version control, and I think it's safe to say that if you code without using version control at all then, as Mr T would say, "You're a crazy fool!" We've already been through SVN, Git, and Mercurial, and you get all the benefits I've described from each of them, although the extra speed of a local repository is only seen in distributed systems. s You also get a full history of all your changes (including the option to restore files you accidentally deletes) and the ability to collaborate on group projects. You also get the ability to create coding branches and the joy of adding comments to code commits. You can also work on a range of different platforms, machines, and locations, and even mix different versioning types together, thanks to bridges. Given all that, it's safe to say that the benefits are huge, and if you haven't already picked a versioning method to use, I'd advise picking one and getting your code versioned ASAP. With that said, it's time to move on to taking a tour of some of the most popular version control GUIs. So let's get to it, shall we?

Chapter 5

I Don't Like Terminal; Which Programs Can I Use?

In this chapter, you're going to be having a tour of some of the more popular version control clients. I'll go through how to use them and why they're awesome. I'm following the same order as in the previous chapter, starting with SVN and then breaking it down by operating system. After that, I'll do the same with Mercurial and finally Git. This chapter helps cement the theory I've been talking about so far and gets you into the programs, or may even convert you from one program to another. Let's get started.

SVN

There are a load of great applications for managing your SVN repositories on the operating systems covered so far, some more popular than others. Let's dive straight in so you can get to know these applications a little better and see if switching to one of them could save you time by improving your workflow.

Windows

First, as always, is Windows, where I'll talk about two great clients. They both take different approaches to managing repositories. In addition to working independently, they can also be combined to help with certain situations, or you may fall in love with one of them. The first program you look at is TortoiseSVN.

TortoiseSVN

TortoiseSVN is the most popular windows SVN client by a long way. If you try to find a different program to use, you'll probably come across someone asking why you're not using Tortoise. Although Tortoise isn't the only option (others are available), it has a brilliant reputation. Without further ado, let's get it installed and ready to go.

Installation

To download the latest version, head over to http://tortoisesvn.net/downloads.html, where you can find the latest stable version of the program. Notice the two big blue buttons on the page, one for the 32-bit version and one for the 64-bit version. You need to make sure to download the correct version for your system; otherwise, the setup will fail, and you'll have to go get the other version. Once you've downloaded your version, you can run the installation: keep to all the defaults, and you'll be fine. When the installation has completed, you're asked to restart your machine. Now you have some lovely new options when you right-click your mouse (see Figure 5-1).

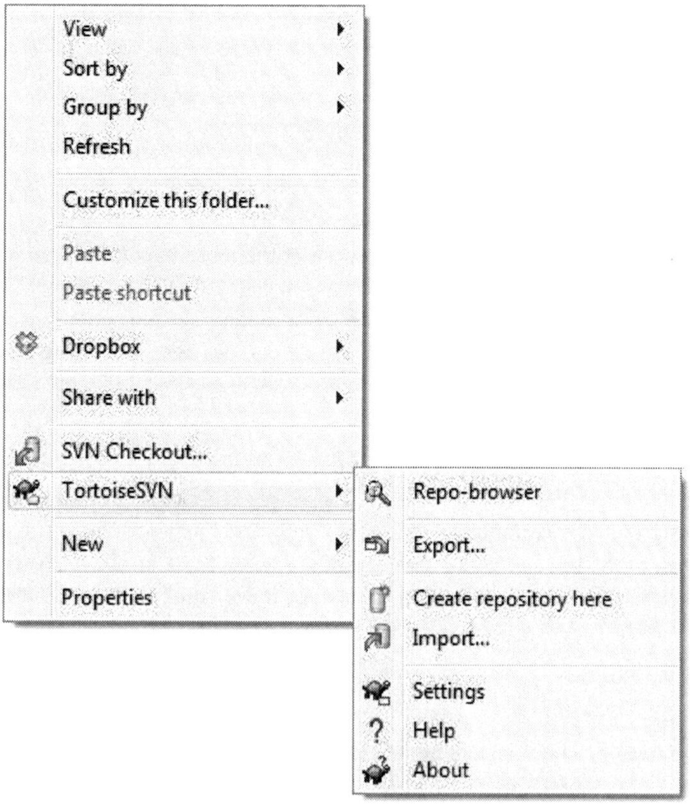

Figure 5-1. New options when you right-click the desktop after installing TortoiseSVN

This menu controls the majority of the SVN activities you do on your computer. It's a very powerful menu that gives you a lot of control over your files.

Checking out a repository

Since for now you're working with external repositories, the SVN Checkout option is the first place you go. Note that, for the link to work, you need to right-click a folder. If you try to perform a checkout without selecting one, you'll get an invalid directory error. Figure 5-2 shows the dialog in action. Once the dialog is open, you can navigate to a different folder on the system by clicking the double dots to the right of theCheckout directory field. This brings up a standard file explorer window where you can navigate through your filo cyotcm and even create new folders if need be.

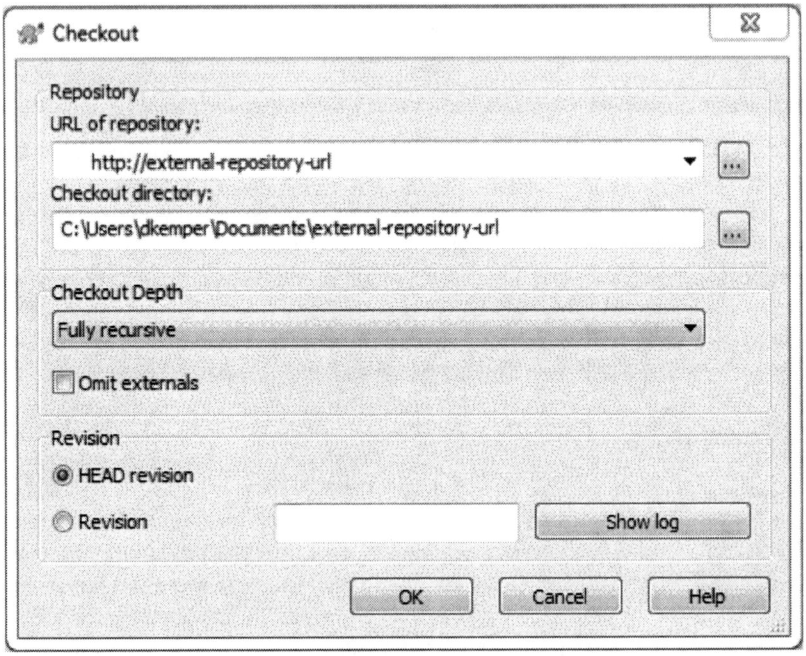

Figure 5-2. SVN Checkout dialog box

The only other thing you need in order to check out your repository is the URL, or where it lives in the big wide world. This can, of course, be a network address or an external address, as long as it's a valid repository. If you try to use an invalid URL, you'll be hit with an error, something like the one shown in Figure 5-3.

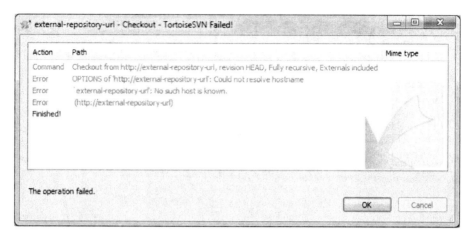

Figure 5-3. An example error message that results from checking out a repository from an invalid URL

When you have a valid URL, you can browse the repository by using the other double-dot browse button to the right of the URL of repository field. Depending on how the repository is set up, you may need to log in before you can gain access to it or even check it out. Once you've entered the needed information, you can gain access to it to either view it or check it out. If you do decide to look at the repository, you're viewing the most up-to-date version in the repository. That is, unless you make a change to the Checkout Depth option below the text fields. This option allows you to check out a certain repository number, rather than the most up-to-date version. If you enter a revision number and then decide to browse the repository, it'll be the version relating to the revision number, rather than the newest version.

Checking out a revision

Checking out a certain revision can be useful if you have a standard base install you like to use for projects, such as a WordPress or Drupal installation; you can then check out that version and start from there. If you're wanting to use a certain revision number as a new starting point, then you'd be better off exporting said repository, which you can easily do. The reason for using an export rather than checking out a version number is that when you export the repository, it has no repository information included—it's literally just the files, allowing you to completely start again. If you check out an earlier version of the repository, it's still linked to that repository, so if you want to start a new project, having it link to the previous repository wouldn't be very useful. It would retain all the history of the previous project, which isn't very relevant to the new project. While you're checking out a new repository, just have the URL and everything ready, and the checkout will be fine. You can click the revision number at upper right as a quick link to change the revision number of the repository you're looking at. When you're on the correct revision number, right-click the very top folder on the left side, and then click Export. You get a file prompt to ask you where you'd like to put the export—and that's it.

Update/commit/add

Once you have a working repository, you get to do the three main version control actions: updating, committing, and adding. To help you with controlling your code, you'll have noticed the icons on your files and folders within a repository. On a basic level, if it's a green checkmark, then it's fine; if it's a red exclamation mark, then you've made a change to the file; and if it doesn't have an icon, then it's not in the repository. You can add any new files by right-clicking the new file, going into the TortoiseSVN menu, and clicking Add. Doing so, adds a new + icon to the file, which signifies that it's been added but yet not committed. You can commit a single file again by accessing the TortoiseSVN menu and then clicking Commit. However, to ensure that you don't miss any files, I'd advise going to the top level of the repository and doing your committing from there. You also see any newly added files there, so you can commit and add your new files from one screen (see Figure 5-4).

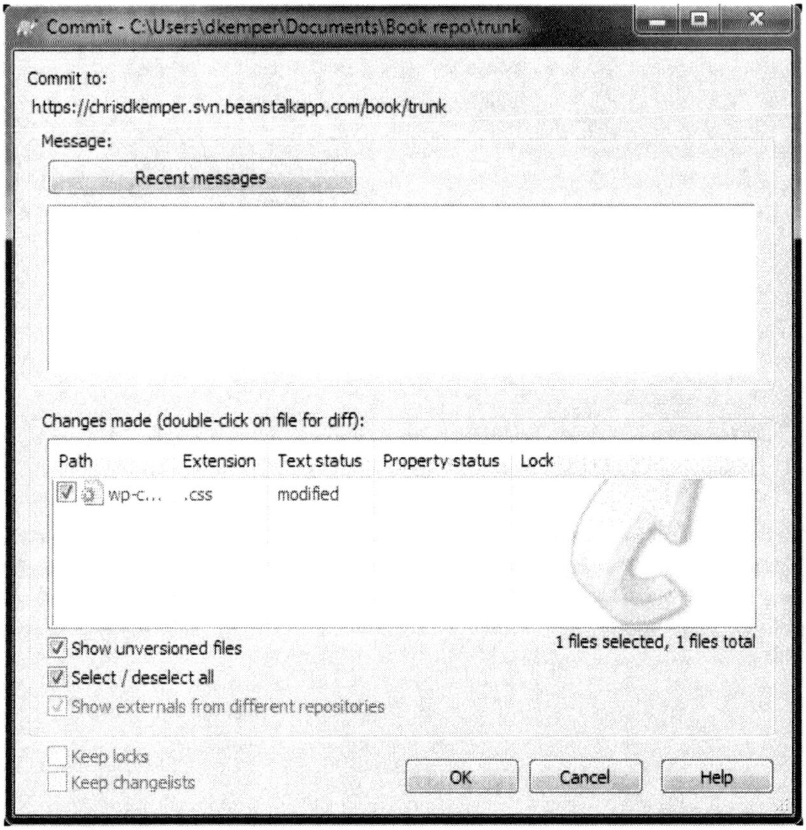

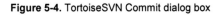

Figure 5-4. TortoiseSVN Commit dialog box

The same goes for updating: you can run the update by right-clicking any file or folder in the repository and clicking Update. This runs the update from the repository on the file or folder you've clicked. If you're working on one particular section, and you're constantly updating/committing those changes, then it may be easier for you to work on the files/folders themselves. Otherwise, it may be easier to run all commits and updates from the main repository folder, to ensure that no updates, changes, or new files are missed.

Ignoring files

The Ignore command can be very useful when you're working with development sites. If you ignore a file that is ready to be committed, TortoiseSVN removes it and prevents it from appearing when you look up changed files. Ignore can be useful for files created by some editors or for folders that include server-generated files or uploaded files.

The Ignore command works by adding the files you ignore to a folder; then, when you do updates and commits, the added files aren't listed, which ensures that you don't commit them. This can be useful when you have to deal with certain editors or applications that produce files that are specific to them but nobody else would have any need for; an example of this is the `.project` files created by Aptana and Eclipse.

You can access this option by right-clicking a file/folder in a checked-out project or local copy, choosing the TortoiseSVN option, and going into Delete and add to ignore list. In this option, you can choose to ignore that one particular file or folder; and if it's an individual file you've clicked, you can choose to ignore all files of that extension, identified by `*.extension`. This is useful for removing the `.project` files I mentioned earlier. After a file or folder is ignored, it's deleted from the repository, which makes it unversioned. Once the ignored file is committed, which deletes it on everyone else's local repositories, then that file is ignored on everyone else's machine (just something to bear in mind). If you change your mind and would rather the file was in SVN again, follow the same steps, but this time you're presented with a "Remove from ignore list" option; select that option, and it'll be a normal file again.

Repository browser

If you've been following along from the beginning, then you've already seen the repository browser. As you can imagine, it does in fact allow you to browse repositories. If you use the repository browser while you right-click a local repository, then you default to viewing that repository. If you use it on a regular folder that isn't a repository, then you get the option to enter a URL of a repository to view—pretty sweet. You still get the same options you did previously; if you click the button in the upper-right corner, you can change repository versions, as you could before. You can also check out said repository by right-clicking a folder on the left side of the window and clicking Export. If you've checked out a repository from here before, you're familiar with this.

One of the best bits of functionality with using the repository viewer is the change log, which you can access by right-clicking any file or folder and clicking Show Log. This view (see Figure 5-5) allows you to see all commits for that particular file or all changes in the folder you clicked. It also gives you dates and the message that accompanied each commit. In the bottom of the pane, you can also see the other files that were included in the commit. This can come in handy if you're trying to work out where bugs originated: you can see what other files were included, which can imply they're linked.

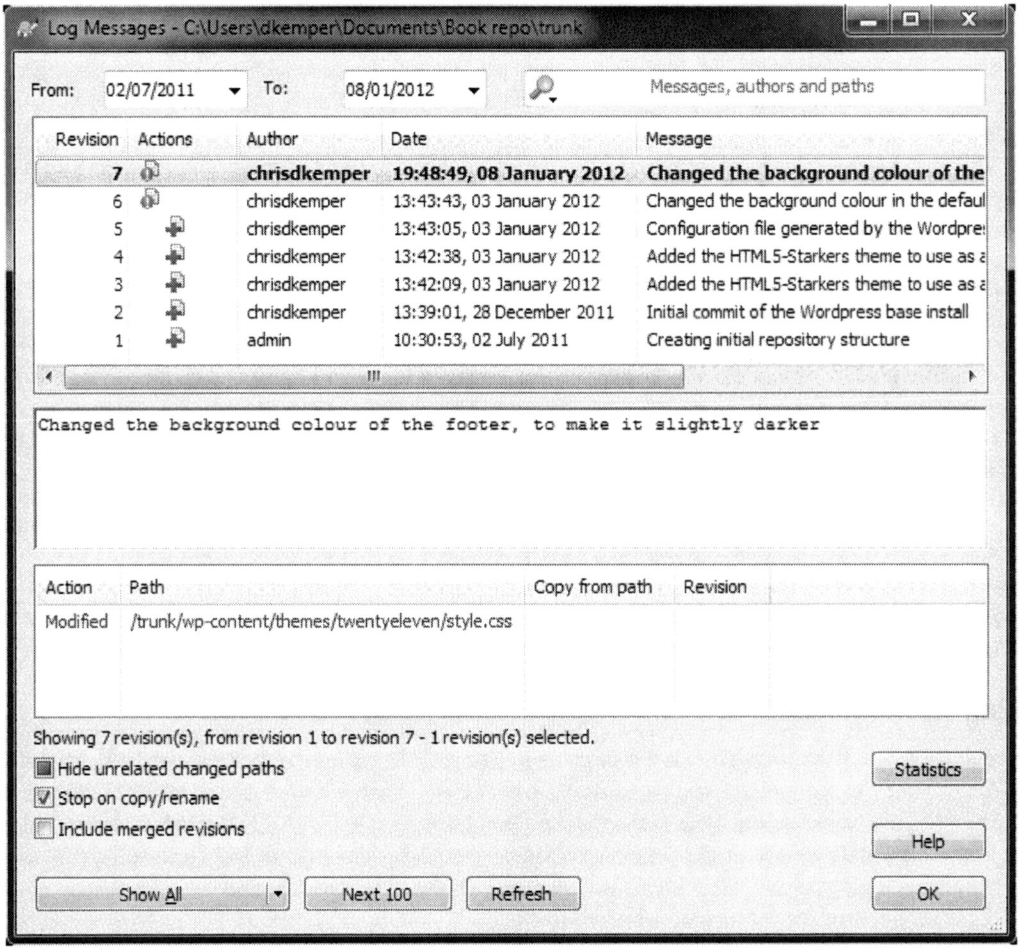

Figure 5-5. Log Messages dialog box in the repository browser

You get a few standard options you would expect to have, including Delete, Rename, Save/Save As, and Open. When you use any of these functions, the repository browser makes the changes in the most recent revision. If you were to go back a revision, the changes would be as they were before.

You also have the option to move files while in the repository browser, which you can do using drag and drop. You can also drag files into the left folder structure; this can be useful if you need to move a file up a folder or two. This works the same with any other changes, if you move anything in the repository, it's as it was in a previous revision, so you can always undo the changes.

Import

The import facility is mainly for importing folder structures or files into a repository. It has the same effect as using the Add function in a checked-out repository, where you copy the needed files into the local repository and then add the new files. The import approach is primarily for use with a repository that hasn't been checked out before, perhaps to import a new feature, or maybe when a new person commits code for the first time.

It's worth noting that if you right-click a folder to import it, the folder itself isn't imported, but the files in it are. So if you have a folder called mytheme that contains two CSS files, and you try to import the folder, TortoiseSVN imports the two CSS files in the folder but not the folder itself. You need a folder in a folder if you actually want to import the folder. Slightly annoying, but you can make it work with a little effort.

Creating a repository

A nice perk of using TortoiseSVN is that you can create local repositories. This can be great if you want a test repository that you can play with and add some changes to, or you need to get used to working with version control. First, you need to create a new folder to use as a repository, ensure that it's empty, go into the TortoiseSVN menu, and click Create Repository. This command does all the hard work for you—there you have it, a repository! This isn't all, though; you now need to check out this repository before you can use it.

To check out the newly created repository, as usual, create another new folder and do an SVN checkout; this time, though, start the repository path with file:// which points the path to your local machine. By doing this, you can use the browse button to navigate to your newly created repository. Now you have a sexy local repository that you can use to use for fun and games, or, more , likely, code.

Checking for modifications

The Working Copy dialog may be one the most-used panes in TortoiseSVN. It shows you all changes that have been made in the project you're currently working on. That includes added files, conflicted files, changed files, the whole works. You can access it by right-clicking either the folder that contains the local copy of the repository or any of the files/folders inside the folder; then, go to the TortoiseSVN menu and click "Check for modifications." This brings up the dialog shown in Figure 5-6, and it's likely to stay open on your machine when you're committing files frequently.

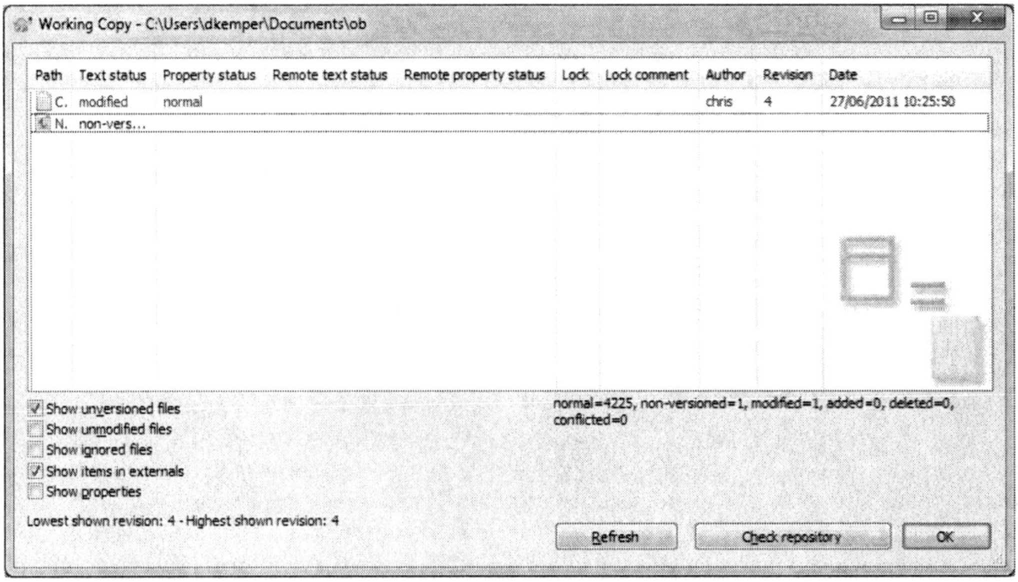

Figure 5-6. Checking for modifications

For any files or folders included in this dialog, you see their current state, whether that's nonversioned, changed, or conflicted. You also have the ability to right-click a single file or select multiple files in the pane and right-click them to get a familiar menu for managing commits and adding new files. You can also click the "Check repository" button to see if you have any updates to download; then you can compare those files to your local version before updating, which can be useful if you can tell a conflict is coming.

You can control which files are visible by changing the check boxes at lower left. These can come in handy for navigating a long list of files; you can also show ignored files, just in case a file was ignored by mistake.

At lower right in the window, you can see stats for the current version of the window, including how many of the various types of file you have. This can be handy if you've unchecked some of the boxes at the lower left and certain files aren't showing, or you're plain curious; either is fine.

Relocate

This command is one you won't use very often, or even at all. You can access the Relocate command from the TortoiseSVN menu when you right-click the main repository folder, and it allows you to change the URL of the repository you're working with. By this I mean that if, for some reason, your repository has moved, this option ensures that all the updating and general workings of the repository still work correctly. In most cases, repositories never move, unless for some reason the server they're located on changes its IP address, the repository is renamed, the protocol changes (e.g. from http:// to https://), or the repository is moved on the server. This command is around to ensure that everything still works if something does change.

To use it, select the Relocate option from the TortoiseSVN menu, and you're served up with a dialog box that has the current URL for the repository and a text field to enter a new repository. You can also browse the repository you're changing by using the familiar three-dot browse button. Once you have the repository you want to change, click OK, and you move on to the next stage of the process.

As you'd expect when doing something of this nature, the next screen is a big warning, explaining to you that you only need to do this if the repository URL has changed, and that if you have specified an incorrect URL or anything like that, your local copy can be corrupted. Be extra careful when making this choice. If you're confident that you have the correct repository, click Yes. Otherwise, click No; as you'd hope, no changes are made. If you click Yes, then Relocate will do its work and inform you when it's finished.

Revert

Unless you work without ever making errors, you have to revert changes every once in a while. Reverting is pretty much going back to the newest version of a file that's in the repository, or to a specific version if you know what its version number is. In most cases, you need to revert if you break something or generally fudge things up. You may also need to revert sometimes when you find out someone else has already done what you're working on, and if you committed your changes it would cause a conflict of epic proportions. I've found myself in that situation before: I copied any new changes I knew I'd made, reverted, put my changes back into the new file, and committed. The reason you revert rather than updating is to avoid the epic conflict, since reverting replaces your version of the file with the most recent version.

To use this sometimes extremely useful feature, get into the TortoiseSVN menu on the file you want to revert, and click the Revert link. You can do this on any file or folder, but nothing happens unless you've changed files in the folder. I advise doing it on the file you want to revert, though: in the Revert dialog you don't get to see file names, so it's difficult to select specific files. When you have the file, make sure it's checked, click OK, and that's it—the file is reverted, nice and easy.

TortoiseSVN Summary

In a nutshell, that is TortoiseSVN. It's a very good application, and if you're on Windows I advise checking it out, just to see what all the fuss is about. Having the contextual menu can come in handy when you're working with large projects, or even small ones. Plus, it can be used alongside any other SVN applications you want to install, without anything breaking; that means you can use it in conjunction with other programs or application plug-ins, which is always a good thing.

Syncro SVN Client

Another offering from the SVN GUI family for Windows is Syncro SVN, and it's a nice piece of kit too. Sadly, this application isn't free; if you want to use it forever, you need to shell out $99. When I was writing this, they did have a sale on, so the price was $59. Of course, Syncro does have a try-before-you-buy scheme in the form of a 30-day evaluation license. You can get one by signing up on the site, which is www.syncrosvnclient.com/. As a minimum, you only need an e-mail address to sign up, and your key is mailed pretty much straight away. You can also download a copy of the software from the site. A good thing about the evaluation is that the software isn't limited at all, so you get a proper feel for how the application works and whether you should consider paying the cash for it.

Installation

Once you have the program downloaded, the installation process isn't anything special; there are no specific changes you need to make, just the usual "allowing the setup to change the files on your computer" dialog that you're used to seeing by now. You don't need to enter any license information at this stage; that's done when you open the application for the first time. Without a license of some kind, you won't be able to open the program.

A great plus with having a windowed application is getting to use keyboard shortcuts. Although TortoiseSVN is a great application, having to always go through a menu to do anything can become annoying. Syncro is full of keyboard shortcuts (you can find a full list at Options ➤ Preferences ➤ Menu Shortcut Keys) for all the common tasks you run, such as updating, committing, and adding, as well as some slightly less used but still very useful functions.

Synchronize

This is a particularly useful command in this lovely little program. It consolidates all the changes that need to be made or updated with both the repository and the local version. You can access this action by clicking the button that looks like a circle made up of a blue arrow going into a folder, and a black one going into a database. You can see this particular icon second from the left in Figure 5-7. This shows you any changes that are set to update from the repository and puts them in the modified screen so you can see what'll be updated when you update. This can make the process of merging and managing conflicts a lot easier in the long run because you have a lot more control over the merging process; and you know what you'll get with your next update, without having to update.

Working copy sections

This section of the application can be very useful for managing your local copy of a repository. In it, you can flick between five sections to manage your files: All Files, Modified, Incoming, Outgoing, and Conflicts. Between them, you can manage any state your files are in, whether those files are unversioned, ready to be updated, or a view of the local copy as a whole.

The Modified section may be the most useful when you're making a lot of changes, because it covers unversioned files and those you've changed that need to commit. In this section, you also see files modified in the repository—in other words, files other people have committed that you need to update.

Another feature of Syncro is its right-click menu. You can access it throughout the application, but it's useful in the working copy sections; plus, if the action has a keyboard shortcut associated with it, the menu shows that right next the action, which is pretty cool. You can see an example of the modified view in Figure 5-7.

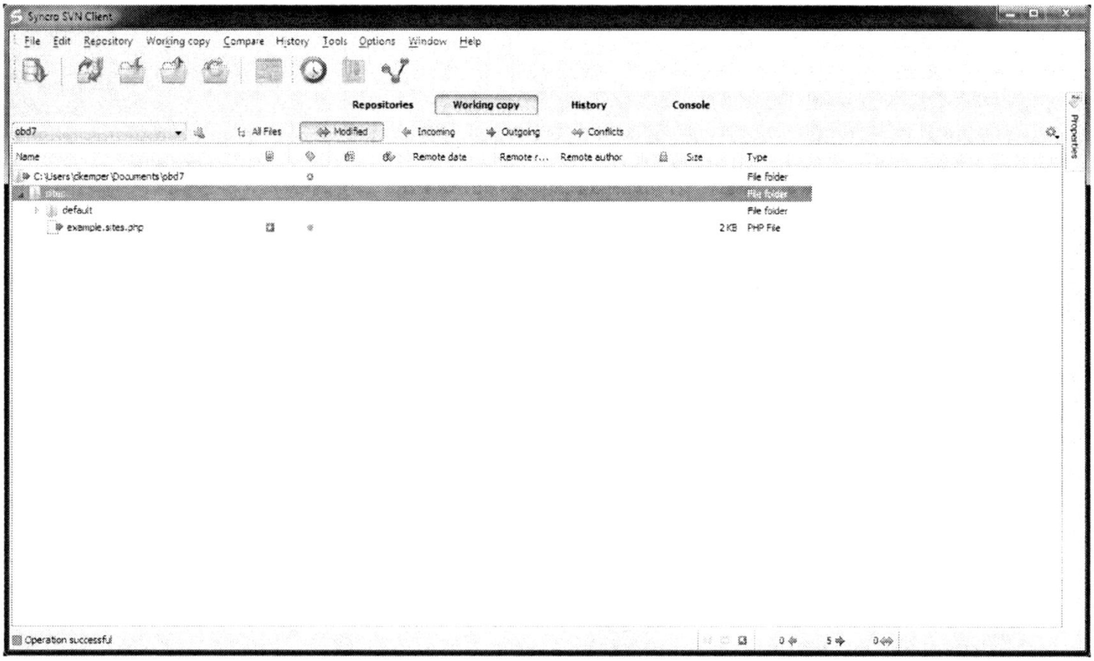

Figure 5-7. The Modified view in the working copy section

The Outgoing section is similar to the Modified section; they both show changes that have been done by you, but as the name suggests, Outgoing includes only changes done by you—no server changes. It also includes unversioned files, so you can be sure to add them and not forget. Unlike some other applications, it shows you the full directory structure that the new files lives in, which can occasionally be useful to make sure you're adding the correct files.

Update/committing/adding

Thanks to all of its crossover menus and specialized buttons, Syncro makes it easy to manage the basic actions of your files. No matter which section you're currently in, you can right-click to access an action menu for managing the files selected at the time of the right-click. This covers a lot of the actions you can do in Syncro, but in this instance I'm referring to updating, committing, and adding files. For instance, from the working copy sections, you can see any incoming changes; you can right-click one of those files that is ready to be updated and choose Update, and you're fine.

If you have a lot of files to update or commit, using the dedicated controls may be better for you. Next to the Synchronize button are the "Update all," "Commit all," and Refresh buttons, respectively. As their names suggest, they control the dedicated actions. If you need to update your whole project, you can do so by clicking the "Update all" button. The same goes for committing: if you have a lot of files to commit, clicking "Commit all" brings up a dialog showing all new and changes files on the system that need to committed. You get the option to add a message to accompany your commit, as usual, and below you can see all the files that can be committed. By default, the files to be added are unchecked; to commit a file, select the check box next to its name, and you're ready to rock and roll.

The Refresh button simply refreshes the application to scan for any potential new files in the system. This process generally needs to be done when you know you've added a few new files into the local copy but the application hasn't picked them up yet. Give the Refresh button a whirl, and if the files are in the local copy, they'll get picked up.

As I've mentioned a few times before, you get keyboard shortcuts with Syncro, and a lot of them. A couple of commonly used shortcuts involves the basic processes: updating, adding, and so on. You trigger the Update command by pressing Ctrl+U when you have a specific file open. And if you want to update the whole working copy, add a Shift into the mix to get Ctrl+Shift+U—you're up to date, easy as pie. If you want to add a new file to the repository, select it with your mouse, press Ctrl+Alt+V, and Syncro adds the file for you without an issue. The Refresh action has a very familiar shortcut key, in the form of F5, which is the default key for refreshing various browser versions such as Firefox and Internet Explorer. You can also run the Synchronize action by pressing a simple command: Ctrl+Shift+S.

History

The History tab is fantastic. With it, you can see every commit that has ever been made in the repository (if you want to), including any commit messages and affected files. As you may have noticed from the label, you get into the History tab by clicking it. By default, you see the 50 most recent revisions of the repository, but you can always get more by clicking one of the two blue arrows just under the tabs: one shows the next 50 revisions, the other shows all of them. Although being able to browse History in an easy-to-use format is good, you can also right-click any revision to update to, revert to, or check out from the selected revision, which can be really useful when it comes to debugging issues.

If that wasn't enough, you also get a snazzy search to use to help you filter your revisions even more. The search itself looks through anything, so you can put in a date, a comment, or a user's name. The only downside is that if you want to search all revisions, you need to have clicked the All Revisions button; otherwise, you just search the revisions you've loaded, which makes sense but may catch you out—so be careful.

Compare

This option can be remarkably useful either before updating or when you're looking for that crucial change that worked back when you made it but now has broken everything. Although you can access this option while highlighting any file and clicking the Compare button (Ctrl+Alt+C), this by default checks for differences between the version you've highlighted and the most recent version; you can see an example in Figure 5-8. Doing this opens a new pane at the bottom of the window, which I like to refer to as a *diffing window*, because that's what it does: it shows differences. This remains on your screen until you close it using the X at upper-right; if you need it around, you can change its size as you would a normal window by grabbing the edge and making it a bit bigger or smaller.

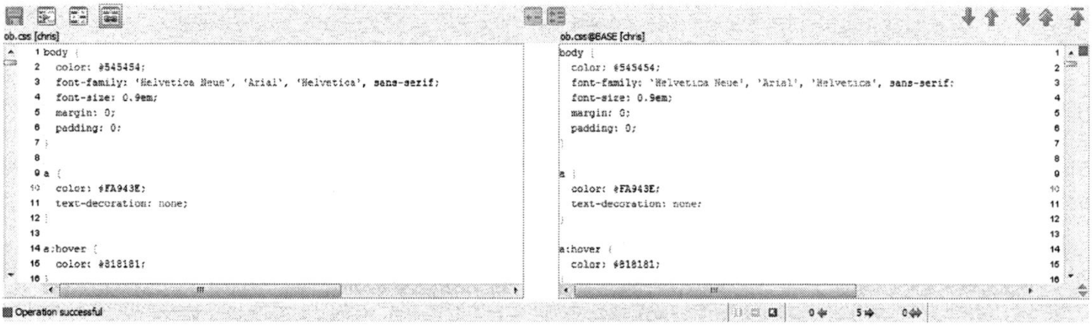

Figure 5-8. The diff pane in Syncro SVN. You can navigate differences between two versions of a file, such as its base and working copy versions.

This by itself isn't so great, but what *is* great is when you combine this with the History tab: it's a winning combination, like ice and cream (everyone likes ice cream, or at least appreciates that the two are a great pair). To unlock this brilliant potential, right-click a file and select one of the options under "Compare with." I personally prefer Revision (Ctrl+Alt+R) because you get to pick the revision you'd like, which is always better than one of the predetermined choices. Doing this takes you to the History tab again, but this time you have the diffing window open and ready so you can compare the file you just clicked with any of the listed revisions; double-click the revision in question, and Syncro refreshes the diffing window to reflect the changes. The differences in the file are indicated by lines to the right of the scrollbar; these show changes in either file, and when you get to one, the window helps identify which changes have moved/been added in a nice and easy way.

You can also navigate between the differences by using the blue arrows at upper-right in the window, which can be useful if the file is overly large or there are a lot of differences. These commands also include shortcuts, which again are handy. To navigate to the next change, press Ctrl+Shift+period (.); and to go to a previous change, use Ctrl+Shift+Comma (,). You can use the arrows, but keyboard shortcuts are much cooler.

Show annotations

Although I've said this a lot, this one really is a cool feature that isn't found often with versioning apps. The "Show annotations" button allows you to see not only what changes were made in a file, but also who made them and what message they entered when committing this revision. This is done on a per-file basis and can be accessed by pressing Ctrl+Shift+A, right-clicking the file and selecting "Show annotations," or clicking the big "Show annotations" button. Any of the options lands you in the same dialog, which is shown in Figure 5-9.

Figure 5-9. The History view lets you easily browse through past revisions of a file. You can see the Annotations View by selecting the desired option on the right side of the dialog.

From the options, you can choose between revisions numbers, all versions, and even dates, so you have a lot of control here. Once you've chosen your filtering method, click OK and you're ready to go. This opens the History pane again, but this time with a new sidebar that shows all the changes and a new editor window that shows the contents of the files. To help this process along, these windows all work together: if you click or move around in one, it's reflected in the others. If you click a line in the editor window, Syncro highlights the other changes made in the file in that revision in the same window; it shows the revision, user, and number of lines in the right sidebar; and it shows comments and additional files above. This is a great way of tracking down where files got changes, who changed them, and what comments were left.

Checking out and local copies

You would expect that with any versioning application, you get the option to check out a new repository or rig the GUI up to an existing local copy, and Syncro is no exception. The button to check out a new local copy is the first button you see in the app, in the upper-left corner; the keyboard shortcut Ctrl+Alt+O makes it even easier. Using the button, the keyboard shortcut, or the option from the Repository menu brings up a dialog that lets you input a destination for the repository on your local system.

Once you've selected a destination for the repository, put in the location where the repository current lives and which revision you'd like (which will most likely be HEAD, a.k.a. newest), and then you're set. You do have the option to specify which Subversion version you want the local copy to be. This only applies if you're using an older/newer version of Subversion to house your repositories. If you're not sure of the version, double-check whoever set up the repositories; or if that was you, check your SVN version. Otherwise, leave it as the most recent version. When all the options are in place, click OK, and the checkout process begins. Once it's done, you can access the repository you checked out from the drop-down below the Checkout button; this changes all the options in the application to that repository.

If you already have the repository checked out, whether from the command line or from another application, you can add it into Syncro without a problem. To do this, you need to use the wrench or spanner icon to the right of the Repository drop-down. This opens a new window that allows you to manage the repositories listed in the app. You get options to reorder repositories as well as remove or edit them. To add a new local copy, click the Add button; this opens a further dialog that asks for a name for the repository and where it's located on the system, which you can find by either using a file browser by clicking the folder icon, or typing the path. Once you have this confirmed, click OK to be brought back to the previous screen. Now, when you return to the main application, the newly added repository is available in the drop-down menu. Excellent.

Export

Another standard feature in versioning GUIs is the ability to export repositories without having to go all command-line to do it. This is no different for Syncro, which as it down to a couple of clicks. If you're getting into this whole shortcut malarkey, then you won't be disappointed: you can use Ctrl+Shift+X to access the Export dialog, or select Export from the Repository option on the main menu. Either way, you end up with the dialog shown in Figure 5-10.

Figure 5-10. The Export dialog box

You get very similar options to the ones you see when you're checking out a new repository; you need to know where the repository lives now, where you want it to live, and which revision number you'd like to check out. You can specify a revision number by selecting the Other radio button and entering a number to check out. If you're unsure of the revision number but you have the repository URL in place, then you can click the History button that gives you access to all the previous revisions with comments, to make the choice easier. Just double-click the revision you want, and the dialog auto-completes the revision number for you.

Once you've entered all you need to, leave the rest to Syncro. You see the progress of the export at the bottom of the window: Syncro displays which file(s) it's currently exporting. When it's done, the message reads "Operation successful"; that means if you go to the directory where you specified that the code should live, it'll be ready for you.

Cleanup

Sometimes, when you're working with a repository, something happens that causes you to need to clean up the repository before you can take any further action. This can be due to commits or updates not completing for some reason, a big merge, trying to add a file that is already in the repository, or a multitude of other situations. Regardless of why it happens, you may need to run a cleanup, and again, Syncro has you covered. Sadly, this time there isn't a keyboard shortcut to take advantage of, but you can access the option from the main menu under "Working copy," which is just as good. When you click the link, you see the page loading; a message at lower left says "Cleaning up" and then Refreshing. If everything is fine, you should then see the familiar "Operation complete." And that's how you do SVN cleanup in Syncro!

Syncro summary

If you're working on Windows and you do a lot of Subversion work, then this app is a great piece of kit if you don't mind paying the cash for it. In addition to a nice clean interface and easy-to-use controls, it also boasts some pretty cool features, especially "Show annotations." With the addition of keyboard shortcuts to help increase productivity, Syncro can be used alongside other applications to create a great SVN workflow, and anybody using SVN on Windows should at least take it for a spin. What do you have to lose? Plus, it's free to try.

Mac

From the Windows side of things, it's time to head straight into the Mac and look at how they do things Mac style. A lot of options are available when it comes to SVN GUIs on the Mac, but to cover them all would be plain crazy. To get around this, let's look through some of the cooler and better-known applications, starting with the lovely Versions.

Versions

One thing Versions has over many other clients is that it's damned good-looking. Take a look at the web site (http://versionsapp.com/) to see for yourself. However, Versions isn't just good-looking: it's also got a cracking set of features. As anybody knows these days, beauty isn't free, and Versions is no exception; however, you can get a 30-day free trial to win you over, and if you want to take the plunge and buy it, it'll only cost you $59 (which really isn't bad). If you pay for Versions, you'll be using an award-winning and widely used bit of software. Some of its better-known users include Disney, Apple, NASA, Nintendo, Blizzard, and a load more, so clearly you'll know you've purchased a quality product.

Installation

As with most Mac applications, the installation needed is rather minimal. First head over to `http://versionsapp.com/` to download the trial version of the application or, if you'd like, buy it straight away. Either option leaves you with a Zip file that you need to double-click to open. At this stage the Versions application is available to you, so drag it into your `Applications` folder, and you're all set.

Let's dive right in and get to know Versions and its features a little better.

Checking out and local copies

First, you need a repository to manage. When you open Versions, it makes this easy for you by putting some buttons in the middle of the screen (see Figure 5-11). To check out a new repository, click the New Repository Bookmark option, which prompts you for a name for the repository, its URL, and any login information you need to connect. Once this information has been correctly entered, you're taken back to the main Versions window.

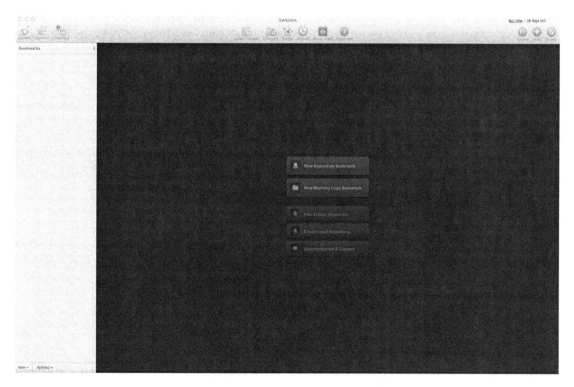

Figure 5-11. The Versions welcome screen

You've just created a bookmark for the repository, so what you're seeing on screen is the repository as it currently stands. This does come in handy, but right now you want to check it out; so, select the folder you would like to check out, which is either the root of the repository or one of the subfolders, such as Trunk. Once it's selected, you have two options: either click the Checkout button at upper left, or right-click the item and click Checkout. Each option takes you to the same location, which is a dialog asking you to name a location where the checked-out code should live. Choose a name and location and click OK, and the checkout process begins. While you're deciding on a location for your code, if you find yourself with a very small window, click the arrow next to the Name field to expand the window to reveal the full file browser.

When the process is finished, your checkout is complete. Now, what if your repositories are checked out already from other applications or from Terminal? Don't worry, Versions has that covered too!

If you click some free space on the bookmarks bar (left sidebar), you get the same screen you had when you first started the application, only this time you want the New Working Copy Bookmark button. When you click it, you get a file browser again; all you need to do is find where your repository is stored, and click OK. You don't see the file browser when you first see the dialog, but click the folder icon to see the usual browser. After you've click OK, that's it—the repository is ready for Versions to work with. Notice that you have both a folder and another icon above it. The folder is the working copy on your machine, while the icon above is a repository bookmark: if you click that, it opens the remote repository. This is handy if you ever need to check versions of files with the most up-to-date data. You don't need to put anything else in; Versions covers that for you.

Versions also has another little trick up its sleeve, in the form of drag-and-drop support. This allows you to simply drag and drop your local copies into Versions without having to go through the process of adding a new bookmark for everyone—and you can also drag more than one at once. So if you're trying out Versions but you already have a load of repositories checked out, no problem: drag them all into the bookmarks bar, and they're in the application, ready to use.

Timeline

Once you have your code in Versions, it's time to take a tour of some of the features at your disposal. Timeline is the leftmost tab in the main pane of the app, and it can be pretty useful for tracking back changes that have occurred in different revisions. While in this tab, you're able to see any files changed in the revision, their path, and any comments associated with the commit. A useful part of this view are the sticky date headers: if you're scrolling through a lengthy commit, you can always see the date the commit occurred, and on the right end of the bar, you can see how many commits happened on this day and the total changes. Figure 5-12 shows a rather large commit; you can see that the date has stayed at the top of the screen.

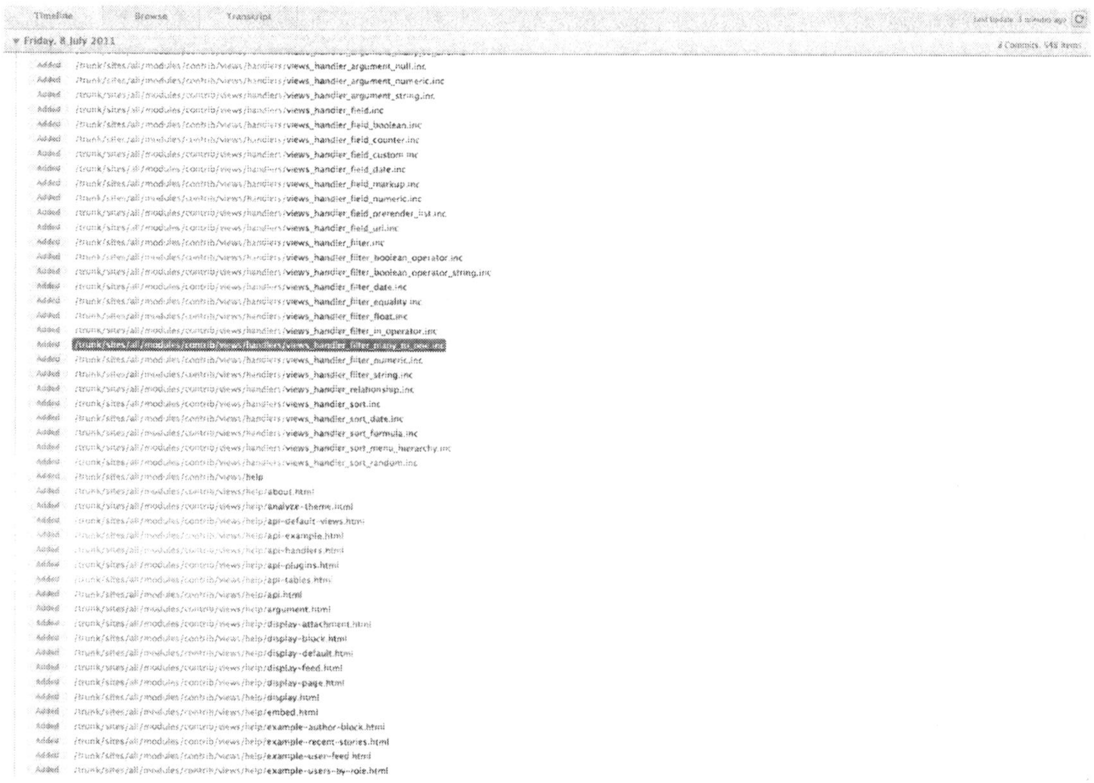

Figure 5-12. Timeline view of a large commit

You can also hide certain updates if they're of no relevance to you by using the Hide link at the top of the particular commit you'd like to hide. This won't remove updates from other users, so you can remove them without worrying that they'll be removed for someone else.

While you're in the Timeline tab, you can also click any of the files to see what was changed. Doing this opens a change-viewing application that I go into a little later. The process of seeing changes that were done in certain commits can be extremely useful when it comes to debugging code, especially if you know the date when a commit was done, but not which one it was.

It's also worth noting that by default not all changes are loaded, as you may have a huge repository. But if you need to show more than the current number, click "Load more" at the bottom of the screen to load another selection into the interface. A slight annoyance with this view is the lack of filtering options: if you want to look at changes from a few months ago, you can end up scrolling for a long time. There are ways to get around that, though, as I'll discuss soon enough.

Browse tab

It's time to move into the tab that controls the majority of the actions in Versions: the Browse tab, which allows you to view all the files in the repository and interact with them. While in the Browse tab, you have two main views to choose from: All and Changed. You can switch between the views via the control at upper left in the main browse window.

In the All window, as you can imagine, you see all the files in the current repository, including the ones that have changed. The Changed window, however, shows all changed and new files, so it's easier to see all the changes you've made and to ensure that all the new files get committed. There's an example of the Changed part of the Browse window in Figure 5-13.

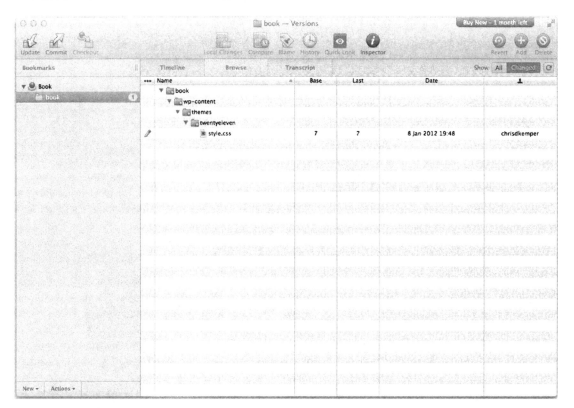

Figure 5-13. A changed file in the Changed version of the Browse view. You can tell it's a changed file thanks to the pencil icon to the left of the file.

You'll most likely find yourself switching between these two views quite a lot to get the best view of the files you're working with. To make it easier, both sections also include file-status icons that overlay the files and folders to show their current status: these include unversioned, changed, newly added, deleted, and conflicted. That covers how to view your files, but not how to manage them. This can be accomplished in two ways: either by using the substantial right-click menu you have access to in either of the windows, or by using the buttons in the upper-left corner of the screen.

Both of these options depend on you having a file or folder selected for them to work (especially the right-click menu); otherwise, they are inaccessible or, in the case of the upper-left buttons, grayed out. With committing, it's always a good idea to commit from the root of the repository to ensure that no files are missed when you run the commit; you see a dialog that shows the files that will be included in the commit. However, this doesn't include any unversioned files, which in some applications are listed here with the opportunity to commit, so it's always a good idea to double-check the Changed view to ensure that no files still need to be added before committing. If you run the commit on an individual file, then if that file has changes, as usual you get the option to add a comment and then commit the file. That can be useful if you want to have a comment dedicated to that one file, rather than one long comment explaining the changes in multiple files. If you try to commit a file that has no changes associated with it, then you're given an error and the commit process is aborted.

Add/commit/update

Updating files works on the same basis: you can update from the root of the repository or on an individual file. With updates, though, it's generally a good idea to always update from the root; otherwise, some files you have been working on may be left out of the update, and that can lead to hefty conflicts down the line.

As you may have noticed, adding doesn't get its own button at left, but it does get one next to the Revert and Delete icons in the upper-right corner. You can also add files and folders by using the right-click menu. If you add a folder that has files in it, the contained items are also added; this saves you having to do that yourself. All you need to do to add a folder full of items is to right-click the folder and then click Add, or ensure that it's highlighted and click the Add button at upper right. Once that's done, you can commit that folder by itself or commit the root folder of the repository. Adding files is as easy as that—either a right-click or a button click, and your file or folder is added without a problem.

Transcript

The third and final tab that can be viewed is the Transcript tab. This shows all actions that have happened on your local machine; if files were added or deleted, or if you performed an update, commit, cleanup, or anything of that nature, it's listed here. This allows you to keep tabs on any changes you've made with a little more detail, since it gives exact times, files affected, and actions undertaken. It can come in handy if you need to double-check some more specific details against one of your commits. Really, though, you probably won't spend any time in this section, since the History tab shows all you need to know in a format that's easier to use.

Creating a repository

Versions also lets you create local repositories for getting to grips with Subversion or for versioning your files on a local system. To achieve this, all you need to do is either click some of the blank space in the bookmark bar to take you to the creation screen, and then click "Create local repository"; or click New at the bottom of the bar and then click the link with same name. You're prompted with a window to specify where the repository lives on the system; when you've decided on a place, click OK, and the repository is created. You get into creating repositories in more detail a little later, but for the sake of managing your code, you can create an empty repository that you can then check out and add files to using the methods explained earlier.

Show History

This little feature pretty much does what it says on the tin: it gives you the history of the file or folder you use it on, which is pretty cool. When you open the tool, it shows you who made the commit, the date, and the comment associated with the commit, as you can see in Figure 5-14. You also see any files included in the commit at the bottom of the screen, including the paths of the files in case you need to check them out for the sake of fixing bugs or whatever else. While you step through the revisions of a file you can also select a file in the bottom section of the dialog and click the Show Changes button to see what actually changed in the commit. This also works for images: if an image has been updated, then Versions opens both versions for you to compare, using preview windows by default. There are ways to make this easier, which are discussed in Chapter 8.

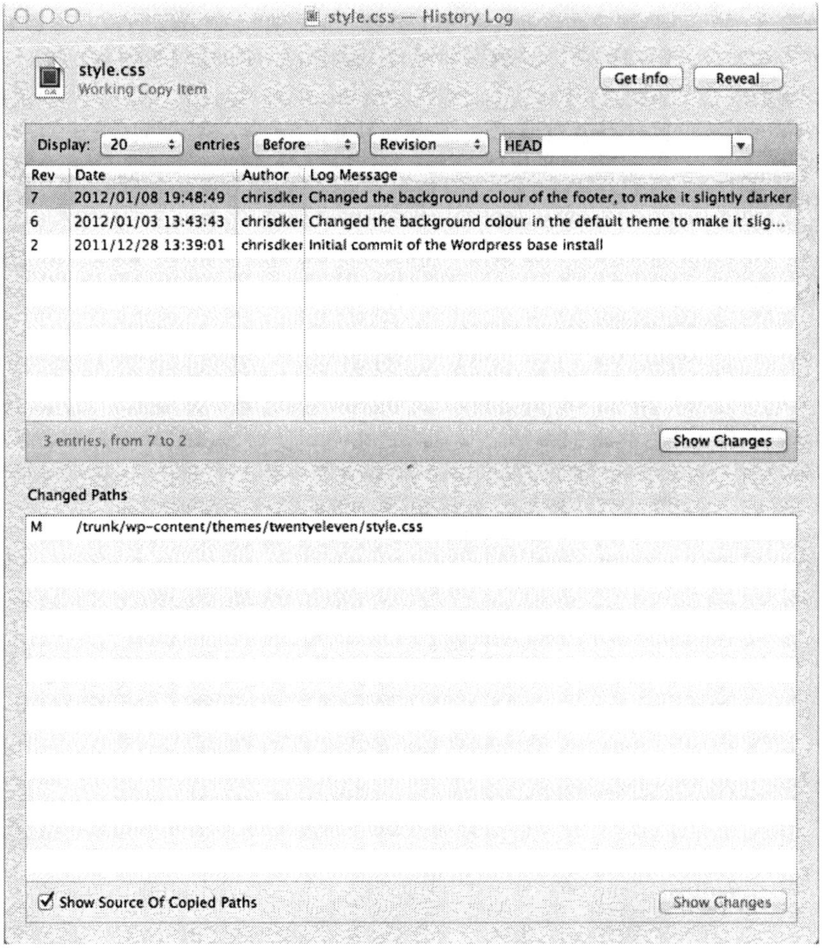

Figure 5-14. Past revision of the `style.css` file, including the date of the commit, the author, and the comment associated with it

You can access the History window in two easy ways. The first is to select a file or folder in the Browse tab and then click the History button illustrated by the clock-face icon. Another way to access the History dialog is to right-click a file or folder and then select Show History from the right-click menu, which brings you to the same location.

Compare Differences

This option can come in very handy when you're trying to debug issues in code or find out what happened to certain bits of code. Compare Differences allows you to see all changes between any two revisions in the systems. If you want to, you can go as far as using the first and most recent revisions, which shows you all the differences between the two files. This feature comes into its own when you're debugging features that used to work but no longer work, and you don't know why; you can look back at the revisions that affected the file responsible and examine the changes between the two files. This can be extremely useful, and I've used it many times to fix those bugs that hide until around an hour before launch time.

To access this wonderful feature, you need to find the file on which to compare changes, right-click it, and click "Compare changes." This brings up a dialog similar to the one used for Show History. It has the same basic features, and you can see comments and other files associated the commits; however, this time you have two columns. Using both columns, you need to find the versions of the file to compare. If the revision you need doesn't appear, you can adjust the number shown via the drop-downs at the top of each column. Once you've selected the revisions to compare, click Compare, and you see a file-comparison program. You learn more about managing conflicts in Chapter 8.

Blame

This is a feature in a lot of SVN clients, because it's a standard Subversion feature, but Versions does it in a nice, minimal way. Blame in itself displays a file on a line-by-line basis and shows who is responsible for each line, so you can Blame them for problems. Again, as with a few Versions features, Blame has both a button and a right-click menu entry. Depending on which is easier, either select the file and use the button at the top of the screen, or right-click a file and choose Blame (see Figure 5-15).

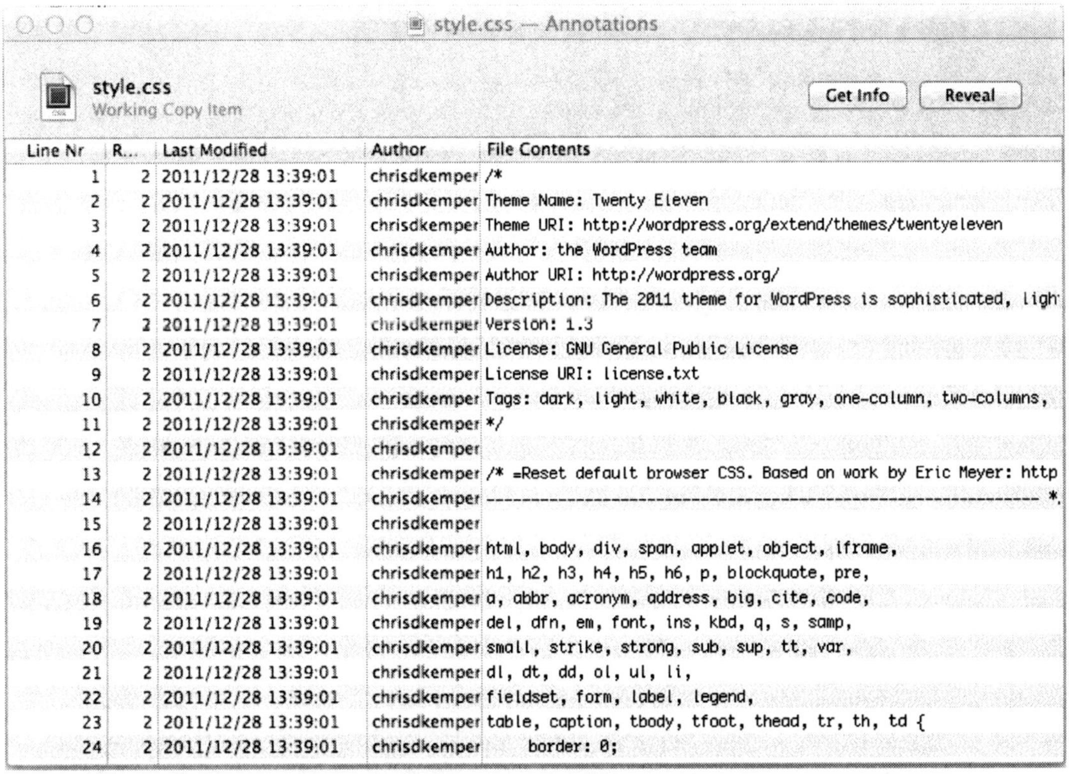

Line Nr	R...	Last Modified	Author	File Contents
1	2	2011/12/28 13:39:01	chrisdkemper	/*
2	2	2011/12/28 13:39:01	chrisdkemper	Theme Name: Twenty Eleven
3	2	2011/12/28 13:39:01	chrisdkemper	Theme URI: http://wordpress.org/extend/themes/twentyeleven
4	2	2011/12/28 13:39:01	chrisdkemper	Author: the WordPress team
5	2	2011/12/28 13:39:01	chrisdkemper	Author URI: http://wordpress.org/
6	2	2011/12/28 13:39:01	chrisdkemper	Description: The 2011 theme for WordPress is sophisticated, ligh
7	2	2011/12/28 13:39:01	chrisdkemper	Version: 1.3
8	2	2011/12/28 13:39:01	chrisdkemper	License: GNU General Public License
9	2	2011/12/28 13:39:01	chrisdkemper	License URI: license.txt
10	2	2011/12/28 13:39:01	chrisdkemper	Tags: dark, light, white, black, gray, one-column, two-columns,
11	2	2011/12/28 13:39:01	chrisdkemper	*/
12	2	2011/12/28 13:39:01	chrisdkemper	
13	2	2011/12/28 13:39:01	chrisdkemper	/* =Reset default browser CSS. Based on work by Eric Meyer: http
14	2	2011/12/28 13:39:01	chrisdkemper	-- *.
15	2	2011/12/28 13:39:01	chrisdkemper	
16	2	2011/12/28 13:39:01	chrisdkemper	html, body, div, span, applet, object, iframe,
17	2	2011/12/28 13:39:01	chrisdkemper	h1, h2, h3, h4, h5, h6, p, blockquote, pre,
18	2	2011/12/28 13:39:01	chrisdkemper	a, abbr, acronym, address, big, cite, code,
19	2	2011/12/28 13:39:01	chrisdkemper	del, dfn, em, font, ins, kbd, q, s, samp,
20	2	2011/12/28 13:39:01	chrisdkemper	small, strike, strong, sub, sup, tt, var,
21	2	2011/12/28 13:39:01	chrisdkemper	dl, dt, dd, ol, ul, li,
22	2	2011/12/28 13:39:01	chrisdkemper	fieldset, form, label, legend,
23	2	2011/12/28 13:39:01	chrisdkemper	table, caption, tbody, tfoot, thead, tr, th, td {
24	2	2011/12/28 13:39:01	chrisdkemper	border: 0;

Figure 5-15. Blame view of the `style.css` file. The line-by-line breakdown of the file shows the author, the revision when each line was added, and the date it was committed.

You can also see which revision the line is from and when it was changed, so if you notice something wrong, you can use some of the other tools mentioned to dig a little deeper. In a nutshell, that's Blame. It can be more useful with scripts, as you may sometimes wonder, "Why did they do it like that?!" Now you can open Blame on the file and ask the correct person why they did it that way, which can save a few headaches and prevent wasted time.

Versions summary

That's Versions and its cracking features. Some of these can't be understood without looking at it for yourself, so if you're looking for a new program to manage your repository, check out Versions. It does what it does very well, and it looks good at the same time. You may say the price is more than you're willing to pay, but if it saves you five or ten minutes a day, that'll quickly mount up to a lot of saved time, which I think can justify the cost.

Although I have a lot of positive things to say about Versions, it does have a couple of negatives. For starters, Versions has no support for merging files that don't use SVN's own functions. Second, the company behind Versions (Sofa) has been acquired by Facebook, which means that its future development and improvements are a little cloudy. This may be a huge deal breaker for you, so it's something to bear in mind; but if you aren't going to be doing a lot of merges, then I can't recommend Versions enough.

Cornerstone

This is another attractive application offering in the Mac-SVN market, and it's a good-looking one as well. Cornerstone boasts a wide feature set, but one of its best has to be its merging capabilities, which give it a better all-round score as an application to suit all SVN scenarios.

Installation

You can get two versions of Cornerstone: a 14-day free trial or the full version, which costs $39. You can even get it on the Mac App Store. If you go the latter route, then buying the application downloads and installs it for you in one step. If you'd rather buy the application directly from Zennaware (the creators of the app), or you'd like to use the 14-day free trial, either can be obtained from the web site www.zennaware.com/cornerstone/. The file you download is a .dmg file, which when opened gives you the application and a shortcut to your Applications folder. Drag Cornerstone into the shortcut, and you're all done.

Adding a repository

As with most of the applications you've looked at, adding working copies and remotely accessing repositories are standard features. When you open the application for the first time, you see a screen with two buttons prompting you to add a repository or a working copy, as shown in Figure 5-16.

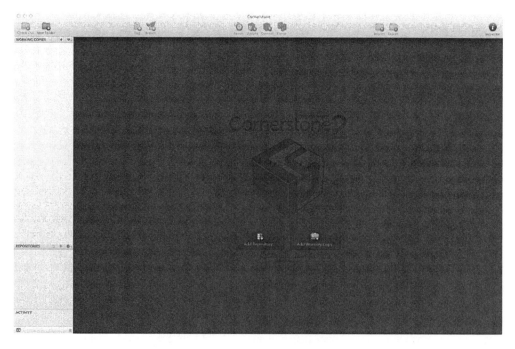

Figure 5-16. The Cornerstone welcome screen

Let's go with the repository for now to keep the consistency going. When you click that button, a new dialog opens. By default, you're sent to the HTTP server option, and then you're prompted for all the usual information: the location of the repository, a name for it, and login credentials if they're required. Options are also available to switch this into Cloud Service, File Repository, or SVN Server mode, if that happens to be where your server is located. The cloud service is a direct link to one of Cornerstone's partner's (CollabNet) hosting service, Codesion. You touch on what Codesion does in Chapter 11, but for now all you need to know is that it's a third-party service that can be used to host SVN repositories. The Cloud Service option therefore allows you to connect straight to your Codesion account with a great deal of ease.

The File Repository option is used when a repository has been created locally on your machine. In this tab you're asked to locate the repository and give it a nickname, as easy as that. You can also create a local repository using Cornerstone: go into the Create a New Repository tab, and specify where you want the repository to live and what you would like it to be called in the Where and "Create as" fields, respectively. The final option, SVN Server, is similar to the HTTP server in its configuration, but instead of being http://, the repository has an svn:// address; other than that, the information needed is the sane.

Once you've entered the required information and Cornerstone has been able to establish a connection to the repository, the repository then loads on the screen and is available for you to browse as you've done before using other applications. You can now also see the repository you just created, linked in the lower-left corner in the Repositories section of the sidebar. This means you can view the repository in this manner whenever you'd like by clicking this item. It's also possible to add more repositories to that section by either clicking the plus icon or choosing File ➤ Add Repository.

Checking out a repository

Although you can browse the repository, it's not really any use to you in this form, so you need to check it out to your machine. This can be done in a few ways. The easiest and most convenient is to use the Checkout icon at upper-left in the application, which is available when you have no items selected in the repository you're viewing or a folder is selected. Be warned, though: if you select a folder and proceed to check it out, Cornerstone only checks out that particular folder, so it's advisable to either have nothing selected so the whole repository is checked out or, if applicable, select the root folder and check that out.

The other method of checking out files is found in the Working Copy menu with the name Check Out Working Copy. The same rules apply for this option as earlier: if you select a single file, then the option is grayed out, and if you have any folder other than the root selected, only that folder is checked out.

Once you've decided on a method, clicking either option brings up a new dialog that asks for a location to store the repository once it's checked out, and what to call the repository. You can also choose to open the newly checked-out repository in Finder after the operation is complete by selecting that option from the When Complete drop-down. In the Additional Options section of the dialog, you get the option to choose a specific option to check out; it defaults to the most recent revision, but you can change the value if needed.

Another option available lets you choose which version of SVN to check the repository out of. Leave this as the most recent version unless for whatever reason the project the repository is being used with has a specific version requirement. Along with this, you can also specify the depth of the checkout. By default it's set to check out all files and folders in the repository, but you can change it to "Immediate files and folders only" (the first level in the specified folder or checkout); "Immediate files only," which is the same as the previous option but without folders; just the folder selected; or no contents.

The final option lets you choose whether any SVN externals included in the repository are checked out as well. This is selected by default, and unless an external repository included is huge, I would leave this option checked. SVN externals are references to either other parts of a repository or different repositories entirely. They can come in handy if you keep adding a certain set of files to every project you work on; you can put them all in one repository and set it as an external in the main repository.

Once you're satisfied with the configuration of the checkout, click that all-important Check Out button to start the process. When it's completed, you're shown the same view as previously, only this time you see a new item in the Working Copy section of the sidebar rather than in the Repository section.

Adding repositories

You may have some repositories already checked out on your machine that you would like to add into Cornerstone, which is easy to do. There are two ways to add a new working copy, both of which are similar to the steps taken with repositories. The first is to use the plus icon in the Working Copy section. Clicking this button opens a Browse window that you can use to locate the repository in your local file system; then click Add, and the local copy is added into the application. The same action can also be triggered from the menu by choosing File ➤ Add Working Copy, or by dragging and dropping local copies from Finder straight into the application. The latter also works with multiple items, so it can save a bit of time if you want to add multiple working copies into Cornerstone.

Managing repositories with views

Now that you have a working copy to work with, it's time to go through some of the basic functions of managing a repository. To simplify this, and to make the whole application easier to navigate, Cornerstone has seven different sections to show files in different versioned states. The default option is All, which displays all the files in one screen, no matter what state they're in. Then next screen to notice is Changed, which as its name suggests shows any changes you have made to the working copy; if you've changed a file or two, and they need to be committed, they appear here. This view also shows any unversioned files or other files you've added that need that initial commit to the repository.

The Modified view shows the same thing as the Changed view, but it doesn't include the newly added or unversioned files. It can come in handy to filter out all other unneeded files when you're working on the same files in quick succession. It's also useful when you're working on styling changes or something of that nature, when only one or two files are changed; it saves having to deal with any other files. The next view is the Conflicted view; this is a shortcut to allow you to see any conflicted files in your working copy.

The Unversioned view displays files that, as the name suggests, are yet to be added into the repository. However, the view doesn't show you the files when you've added them and they're ready to committed for the first time. While you're in this view, if you add one of the files (or all them, by selecting them all), then the file is removed from the view. If you add all the files or add the only file in the view, then you're redirected to the All view without any unversioned files to show (which aren't useful).

Adding files

You can add files using a few methods. To make life easier, Cornerstone has a big Add button at the bottom of the panel, which you can click to add the file. However, to add a folder, there is a slight change. If you only want to add the folder itself, clicking the button with the folder selected is fine; but if you want to add the folder and its contents, click and hold the Add button to get the option "Add to working copy with contents," which does as it suggests. Easy. You can also add files by using the main menu and choosing "Working copy" ➤ "Add to working copy." There is also an option just below, for folders, which allows you to add the folder, and the contents of the folder in one go; if you use the first option on a folder, then only the folder itself is added and not the contents.

With the menu options, you'll also notice the handy keyboard shortcuts Cmd+D and Cmd+Shift+D, which add the item to the working copy and add to the working copy with contents, respectively. These commands work across any of the different sections, so if commit them to memory they can speed up working with Cornerstone on a regular basis. If that isn't enough, files can also be added with ease by right-clicking the file or folder you want to add and clicking "Add to working copy." Adding a folder in this fashion results in the folder being added but not its contents, so you need to dive into the folder and add the contents via this method or any other previously mentioned method.

Locked files

The last item in the menu of the repository view, Locked, isn't actually a view and is instead an option. You can select it to be either on or off. When a file is locked, by default it isn't shown so you don't interact with it in the application. This option is around in case the file is locked by mistake. With it selected, you will only be able to see the locked files within your repository, all of the others will be hidden, so bear that in mind if you're wondering why you have no visible files.

Updating

The immediate option that is available when updating your local copy is the Update button in the top center of the application. To update the whole local copy to the latest available version, be sure no items are selected in the view, and click the button. You can also use the button to update a specific file or folder by highlighting it with a click and then clicking the Update button.

Using the main menu to update your local copy can have its advantages because you also have the option to update to a certain revision as well as to the latest working version. The menu item launches a dialog that the button doesn't. It also has a keyboard shortcut associated with it: Shift+Cmd+U. In the dialog, you can browse the latest commits that have been done on the file or folder you have selected, and you can even search commit comments to make the process easier. This is mainly used when you don't want to update to the very latest version of the file, but to one or more commits before. If you run the update on a file which has an older version than its current revision, then the file remains unchanged.

Conflict management

Cornerstone also has some ability in the conflict-merging department. When you get a conflict, you can use the buttons at the bottom of the main window to compare the file with certain versions of the file, such as the base (most recent change before the conflict) and head (the latest version of the file). Doing so brings up a new window that looks similar to any other file-diffing tool and shows the changes side by side. An example is shown in Figure 5-17.

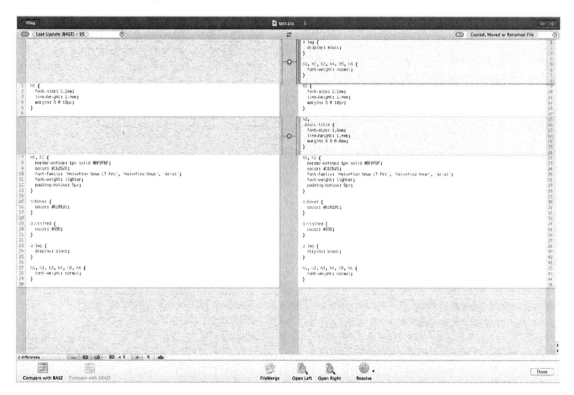

Figure 5-17. Comparing the base and working copy revisions of a file in Cornerstone

With this tool, you can look for differences between the two files, which are shown as blocks of code. The side of the window they're on controls the color in which they're highlighted. For example, In Figure 5-17, some code on the right side of the window has green highlights; this is because the right side is treated as though it's the more up-to-date file. Therefore the text in green is seen as a new addition to the file and is highlighted. If you swap the positions of the files by using the arrows in the top-center of the window or the option in the Compare menu (Cmd+>), then that same text is highlighted in red. The text being present on the left side and not the right implies that it has been deleted from the right-side file, and it's therefore marked as red.

When a conflict occurs in the file, markers in the middle column allow you to remove the text from the comparison, therefore deleting it from the file. Clicking one of the arrows—or crosses, if you have already clicked one of these, —it toggles the removal or replacement of a change. If you remove all the changes, you can then save the file as a singular file by either choosing File ➤ Save or clicking Done in the lower-right corner, which prompts you to save the file or abandon all of the changes you've made thus far and deal with the conflict later. Once that has been completed, you can open the file from the application or from Finder to double-check whether any conflicts remain; if not, you can safely mark the file as resolved.

This in its basic form is a way of managing conflicts using Cornerstone itself, but in some instances the conflicts need to edited manually or you need more control over managing the annoying conflict. For these cases, Cornerstone lets you use third-party applications; if you don't have any others installed, at the very least you have FileMerge at your disposal to handle conflicts. You can compare the changes with FileMerge by choosing Compare ➤ Compare using FileMerge; this launches FileMerge and allows you to amend the conflict as you'd like. Then you can save the file and resolve it in Cornerstone, nice and easy.

In some cases you may have a tool you'd prefer to use to compare differences between files or manage conflicts, such as Kaleidoscope. You can select which program you'd like to use by choosing Cornerstone ➤ Preferences and selecting an application from the "External compare tool" drop-down.

Branch merging

A great feature of Cornerstone is its ability to manage the merging or branches back into trunk. To achieve this it has four different methods of merging:

- Synchronize branch
- Reintegrate branch
- Cherry pick changes
- Advanced merge

Each option caters to a specific case, and some can be more useful than others. To see these options, just click the Merge button in the main toolbar of the application.

Synchronize branch

This merging method allows you to check the changes you've made into the trunk at various points that suit you. It'll merge the changes back into trunk, but still keep the branch active, so you can continue push to it. This allows you to ensure the branch doesn't get too outdated against the main codebase, and also allows you to periodically check that the code you are writing is merging correctly back into trunk. Within this view you have a Merge from field, and an Options dropdown. The Merge from field allows you to select the location of the branch you'd like to merge, through a variety of methods. The button within the Merge from field will offer you a number of options, such as suggested branch paths based on your repository, as well as a number of different URL options, such as an absolute URL or one relative to the server. As soon as you select a branch, Cornerstone begins performing a test merge, the results of which can be seen in the dialog below. This allows you to see if the merge will work correctly, and will also show all the files within the branch. Since it's best practice to make sure your working copy is up to date before you attempt any branch merges, Cornerstone shows if you have modified files in your working copy that haven't been committed, and gives you options to either Commit or Revert them. It also checks to see whether or not updates are available and gives an option to Update, if required.

Once everything is up to date and committed, it's time to start the merging process. If the dry run that has been automatically run has been successful then you can just hit the Merge Changes button to start the process. You can still perform the merge if the dry run fails, you'll just have to cope with the reason it failed manually, after the merge has taken place. When you hit the Merge Changes button, you'll be taken back to the main view within Cornerstone while the merge takes place. Everything just needs to be checked and committed, and then you're done!

Reintegrate branch

This way of merging works pretty much the same way as synchronizing does; however, performing a reintegrate merge will close the branch after it's complete, meaning changes can no longer be pushed to the branch. The view gives you the same options as the previous one, allowing you to select a branch in the Merge from field, and select various options from the Options dropdown. It'll also perform a dry run for you and prompt you to update your repository or commit files as needed.

Cherry pick changes

Cherry picking changes is rather clever, and allows you to select certain revisions from the branch to merge back into the trunk, which can be really useful when you have a bug fix branch or you want to roll out certain features from a feature branch. The branch is selected in the same way as the previous merging methods using the Merge from field. In addition, the Cherry Pick Changes view also has a Revisions field, which gives you two buttons, one to either select None, All Revisions, or Other and one to launch the revision selection dialog (which is also launched by selecting Other from the previous option) which allows you to select multiple revisions, and filter them by message or author. It also informs you whether or not the revisions have been merged previously using Synchronize Branch, which helps avoid merging in revisions that now already exist in trunk (although you can merge them anyway, if you want to). Once the specific revisions are selected, Cornerstone begins performing a dry run again, and you can perform the merge in the same way as the previous views.

Advanced merge

The Advanced Merge view offers something a little different than the other merge options: the ability to compare and merge two branches into a third. On a basic level, the view contains the same options as the others. It'll still perform the dry run and prompt you to ensure your working copy is up to date, but there are also two new fields, Compare and Against. These two fields work in the same way as the Merge from field and allow you to select branches in the same way. Once you're happy with the way things are set up, just hit the Merge Changes button, and the two branches will be merged into trunk.

Timeline

A lovely feature of Cornerstone is its Timeline, which lets you see all the commits made for a particular file, with each one's date and comments. You can also compare different versions in the Timeline by clicking the first one to select it and then Cmd-clicking a second. You can run the Timeline tool on a folder in the same manner; however, clicking different commits in the Timeline doesn't open anything in the window, as the folder can have had any number of changes in that commit.

To view the Timeline for a given file, you can either use the Timeline option at lower right or go to View ➤ Timeline (Cmd+3). If you have only one file open, then the file that corresponds to the commit you have selected is displayed in the left side of the window, where you can read it as needed. As soon as a second file is selected, then any differences between the two files are made apparent thanks to red highlighting for removed text and green for added text. In this case, there is no option to change the revisions around, so the colors are an accurate representation of the file in its current state; this makes it useful for finding the origination of an issue or simply checking the difference between the two versions. You can also open the same two files in the application you've specified as your external compare tool by clicking its log at the bottom of the screen. This option is accompanied by additional options to open each of the files using your default editor for that kind of file.

Log

The log in Cornerstone is another useful feature. It gives you a simple way of viewing all the changes that have been committed for a file or folder. While browsing the log, you can see other files that were included in the commit, as well as any comments included with the commit. Another bonus with the log is the ability to update the version of the file on which you ran the log. For example, let's assume that you're working on a file that you aren't ready to update to the latest version, due to potential conflicts or another reason; you want to update it to one or two commits before the latest one. In the log, you can read the comments associated with a commit and any files along with it, and if that commit is newer than the revision of the file being logged, then an option becomes available to update the file to that revision.

After you've updated the file to the specified version, it gains a Working Version label next to the revision number, so you know that this particular revision is the one being used in your local copy. In addition, you can search on Message, Author, or file to whittle down the potentially long list of revisions to a more usable size, which can help when you're working on complex projects and you need to update to an old revision.

Cornerstone summary

All in all, Cornerstone is a useful application with a huge number of features, and it's easy enough to be used by anyone at any level of expertise with versioning files. That's not to say it's perfect; like all things it does have issues, but these are relatively small. For example, if you drag a working copy into the application, Cornerstone makes no attempt to create the repository bookmark for you, so you need to do that manually every time. Although that is only a small issue, it can be a little annoying when you have to work with lots of repositories.

That aside, the application is great. You should take it out for a trial for its ease of use alone, and the fact it has branch-merging support is a huge bonus. The latter is in relation to merging branches back into the main trunk of an SVN repository. Cornerstone has a wizard to make this process easier, and you can perform test runs on the merges, which comes in handy.

Unix

Now it's time to head into the Linux world and explore the applications you can use with SVN to help you avoid using the command line. Although users of Ubuntu and other Linux distributions are generically seen as coders, some people would rather use a GUI for managing SVN repositories. If you're one of those people, then I recommend that you take a look at this section. Let's get straight into it by exploring RabbitVCS.

RabbitVCS

If you've ever had the pleasure of using TortoiseSVN on a Windows machine, then you have some familiarity with how Rabbit works; and those of you who haven't will find it a pleasure to use. Rabbit integrates straight into the Nautilus file manager, which is the default in Ubuntu and other Linux distributions using the GNOME desktop environment. I could go into more detail about it, but that's not what you're here for. If you're interested in reading more about Nautilus, you can always check out the official web site (http://live.gnome.org/Nautilus) or the Wikipedia page (http://en.wikipedia.org/wiki/Nautilus_(file_manager)) to find out anything you need to know.

Installation

Due to Ubuntu updating to Unity, installing RabbitVCS isn't as easy as is it should be; however, it can still be easily achieved. The first thing you need to do is add the Rabbit code repository into Synaptic, to make sure you always get the most up-to-date content; to do so, go to Settings ➤ Repositories ➤ Other Software. Here are all the software sources applications that can be installed and updated from. You need to add a new one, so click the Add button, enter the following, and click "Add source":

    ppa:rabbitvcs/ppa

Now, go back into the main Synaptic window and refresh all the packages using the button at upper left. After everything has updated itself, perform a search for RabbitVCS, and you should see the six options shown in Figure 5-18.

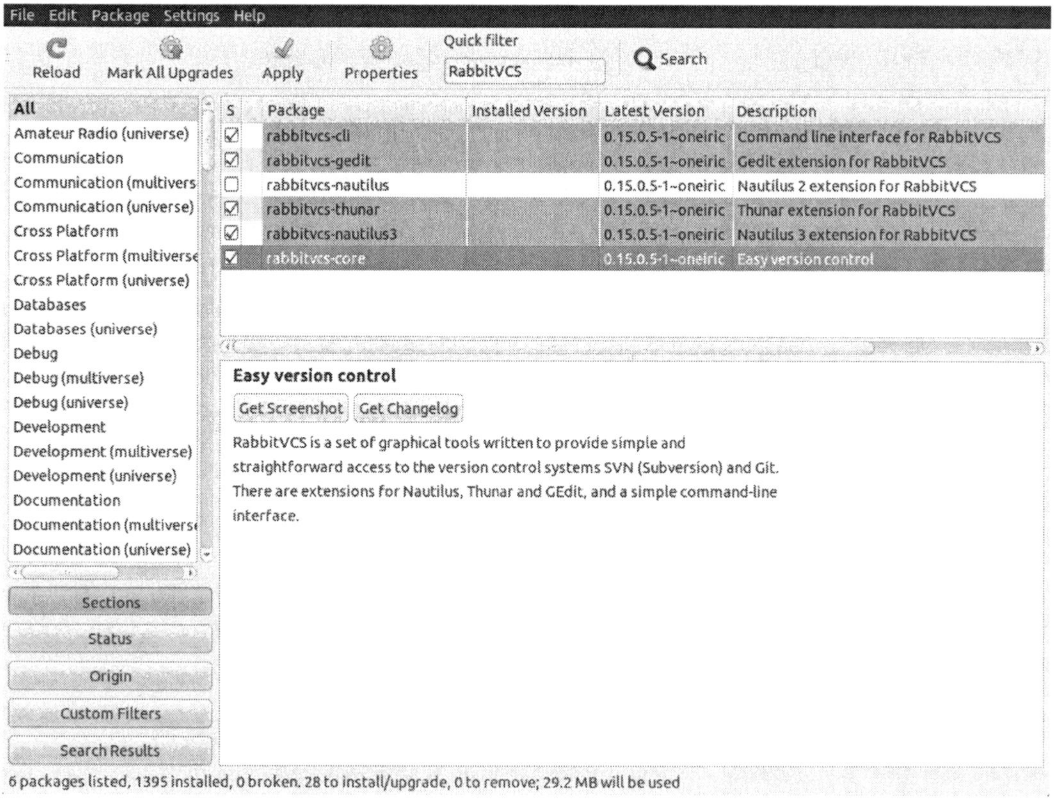

Figure 5-18. Searching for RabbitVCS after adding the new software repository

If you're using Unity, select all the packages selected in Figure 5-18; otherwise, select `rabbitvcs-nautilus`, not `rabbitvcs-nautilus3`, because the new version is for use in Unity only. You also need to select `rabbitvcs-core` first, because the other packages depend on it, and you get an error if it isn't already marked for installation.

With everything installed, you need to log out and back in before the changes takes effect. After that, when you right-click a file or folder in the file browser, you're presented with two new menu options. The one you're concerned with is RabbitVCS SVN, which as you imagine controls all the SVN interactions that take place on your local system.

Checking out a repository

First things first: you need to check out a repository. Right-click either a folder or the blank space in the file manager, and then choose RabbitVCS SVN ➤ Checkout. This option opens the dialog shown in Figure 5-19, which allows you to specify a repository URL and the location where you would like to house the repository.

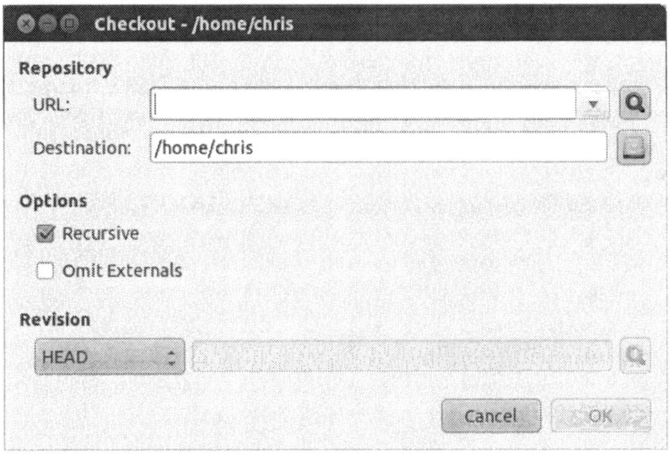

Figure 5-19. The Checkout dialog box in RabbitVCS

What you clicked to launch the menu dictates the default value in the Destination field. If you clicked a folder, that folder is the default location; however, if you clicked blank space, then the folder you're currently in is the default value. Either way, if you aren't happy with the default location, it can always be changed by manually amending the destination or by using the file browser to navigate to the desired location.

Once you're happy with the information in this dialog, click OK. The next dialog asks you for authentication if it's required. With that information in place, click OK again, and the repository begins checking itself out.

Managing basic controls

Rabbit makes the process of managing the basic controls of your repository a breeze. While in an SVN repository, you'll notice a couple of changes to the right-click menu and to the files and folders in the repository. First, each file and folder now gets a badge on top of it to show its current status. As a guide, if it has a tick, then everything is fine with that file: it's versioned, and nothing has changed. If a file has a red exclamation mark, then that file has been changed and needs to be committed or reverted; and if a folder has the same icon, then a change exists in that folder. Any unversioned files are indicated by a blue question-mark icon, and once they have been added, this icon is replaced with a plus sign.

When the time comes that you get a conflict, the file will again get an exclamation mark on top of it; however, this time it's in a triangle closely resembling a warning symbol. Also, if you have a folder full of changes but one of those changes happens to be a conflict, then the hazard exclamation mark is shown on the folder, since it's the most important issue in the file.

Updating and committing

Rabbit adds quick links for the Update and Commit commands to make performing those actions that little bit easier. This means updating is a really easy task. All you need to do is right-click a folder and choose Update, or do the same on an individual file. This brings up the Update dialog, which downloads all changes that apply from the repository and performs the update, just like that.

Committing your changes is just as easy. The same process goes: you can run the Commit command at the root of the repository or on a per-file or -folder basis, whichever applies in the situation. You can also right-click empty space and select Commit, which performs a commit on the folder you're currently in and its subfolders.

When you run the Commit command, it launches a dialog (shown in Figure 5-20) that allows you to add a message to accompany the commit you're doing, as well as select which files you want to commit via check boxes in the lower half of the dialog.

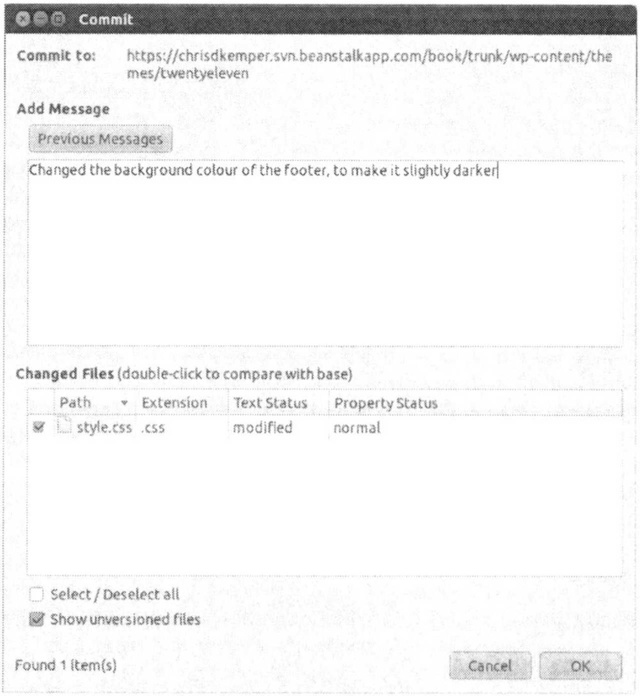

Figure 5-20. The Commit dialog in Rabbit, showing the files committed and a text area for a commit message

If you want to commit an unversioned file, to avoid adding it and then doing a commit, cut out the middle man and commit the unversioned file directly by right-clicking and choosing Commit. If the file is included in a folder you're committing, check the option for it in the bottom half of the screen, and it's added for you.

If you want to add the file without committing it straight away, you can do that too. Right-click the file you want to add, and then head into RabbitVCS SVN ➤ Add. When you click that, a dialog opens to confirm the addition of the file; click OK, the file is added, and that's that. You can also perform this action on multiple files by right-clicking them and choosing the same option.

If you add an unversioned directory using either the commit method or the manual add method, any files in the folder are added as well, with no way to specify otherwise. If you think "Haha! I'll go in the folder and add the files there," that won't work. The contents folder isn't associated with the repository you're in, in the eyes of Rabbit. You can see this quickly by the Git option being available on the right-click menu again and by there being no Add option in the Rabbit VCS menu.

Check for Modifications

To access this window, right-click any file, folder, or empty space in a repository in the file browser, and choose RabbitVCS ➤ Check for Modifications. In this window, you can see the path, status, and, if applicable, the extension of the file. While in the window, you can also perform certain actions on the file by right-clicking; sadly, though, you can't commit from the window, which makes it a little less wonderful.

It's a great window to have open when you're working on a project that you commit to or update from on a regular basis. It shows you any changes that have been made in your local copy of the repository in one window, and by selecting a different tab you can see which updates are available from the repository, without having to update.

Repository Browser

Rabbit also comes with a basic Repository Browser window, which allows you to browse the repository from your local machine. You can launch the Repository Browser by right-clicking any file, folder, or empty space in a local copy and choosing RabbitVCS SVN ➤ Repository Browser. Once it's open, you can see the repository in its most recent revision and browse through your files and folders. Sadly, that's it, but you can look at a different revision of the repository by shifting the HEAD drop-down to Number and entering your specified revision number. To look at the repository view, check out Figure 5-21.

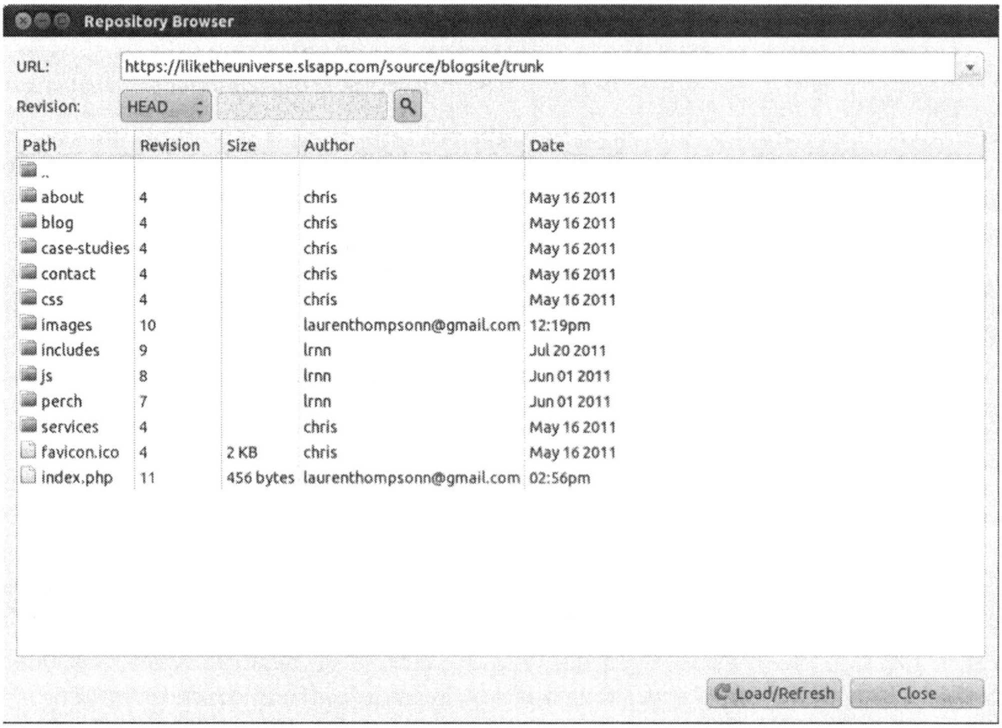

Figure 5-21. Repository browser view in RabbitVCS

Ignore

There will be a time when you want to ignore a file from your repository to prevent it from being committed, for whatever reason. Rabbit has this covered, plus it's easy as pie. To add a file to the Ignore list, right-click it and choose RabbitVCS SVN ➤ "Add to ignore list" ➤ "filename"; or you can ignore all files with the same extension as the file you click by selecting the * option below the file name. Now, if you try to commit this file, it simply isn't listed in the list of files available to commit.

If you suddenly have a change of heart and decide "Oh, I actually want to commit that file," then you can remove the file from the svn:ignore list easily enough. To rectify the Ignore mistake, you have a couple of choices. First, you can right-click the folder that contains the ignored file, and choose RabbitVCS SVN ➤ Properties. This opens a dialog that contains any ignored files in that particular folder, listed showing the Name, Value, Reserved, and Status. Of these, only two matter—Value and Status—because the name for any ignored files is svn:ignore. The Value and Status are the file name and the status of the file before it was ignored, respectively. To remove the file from this list and therefore allow it to be committed again, right-click the file and select "Delete property." That's that.

You can achieve this same effect by going through the same process but, instead of right-clicking the folder containing the changes, going into that folder and right-clicking some empty space; then choose RabbitVCS SVN ➤ Properties, and follow the same steps.

Creating a repository

In some circumstances, such as wanting to play with version control on your local machine, you need to create a repository to work with. This is simple with Rabbit and only takes a few clicks via the familiar RabbitVCS right-click menu. First create an empty folder to house your new repository, and make sure it's not in any other existing working copy. Open right-click menu, and choose "Create repository here." That's it! You have a repository that you can check out and add files to. However, I suggest committing three folders—trunk, tags, and branches—which are the main folders used in any SVN repository.

If you check out a repository that is located on your local machine, instead of specifying a URL, put in the path to the repository on your local system. It's checked out as if it were a remote repository.

Log

There always comes a time when you need to look at previous changes to a specific file to see who's changed what, or to look at the comments associated with the commit so you can try to understand what they were thinking. Whatever the case, you can review the log of commits for a file or folder in the working copy with ease by right-clicking it and choosing RabbitVCS ➤ Show log. This launches a new dialog that contains by default the last 100 instances that particular file was used in; in the case of folders, it also shows activity from inside it.

If you simply want to review the entire log for the repository without filtering it by a particular file or folder, you can do that too. Rather than clicking a file or folder, right-click an empty area in the file browser and select the same option. This time all commits in the working copy are shown, regardless of where they occurred.

In this dialog there are a lot of number ways you can visually compare differences between revisions, which you can access by right-clicking a particular revision. If you use one of the "View diff against" options, it shows the differences in gedit, the default text-editing application on Ubuntu. This is a quick and easy-to-use comparison, but it doesn't work so well for large commits.

You can also make the diff more specific, which can be useful if a large amount of data was committed at once. To do so, select a commit in the main window; then, in the lower-left portion of the dialog, select a specific file, right-click it, and select either "View diff against previous revision" or "Compare with previous revision."

Another option available in the Log dialog is "Show changes against previous revision." Selecting this option from the right-click menu brings up a new dialog that shows you which files were changed between the two revisions. If you select "View unified diff" from the "More actions" menu, it launches an external comparison tool so you can see the differences in a visual way. Let's look at those in a bit more detail.

Conflict management

Rabbit doesn't have any tools to manage conflicts, which is where Meld comes in. Meld is a program that handles all the diffing that Rabbit can throw at it. It comes installed with Rabbit automatically, which makes life easier. When a conflict does come in, such as from an update, a dialog opens by default, asking what you would like to do with the conflict (see Figure 5-22). Four options are available: Cancel, Accept Mine, Accept Theirs, and Manage Manually. Cancel takes you out of the process, which allows you to manage the conflict yourself (strangely labeled, I know). Accept Theirs and Accept Mine take the remote version or the local version, respectively, as the correct version. The last option, Manage Manually, is terribly labeled, because it launches Meld, which you can use to manage the conflict in the application. There is also a check box under these options that automatically marks the file as resolved when the changes are committed, which can speed up the editing process in some cases. With the box unchecked, you need to mark the file as resolved yourself once the needed changes have been made.

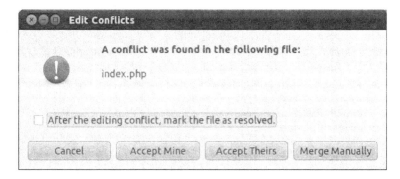

Figure 5-22. Edit Conflicts dialog with the four possible action options

Editing conflicts

With Meld, editing conflicts is as easy as pie. It mainly comes down to the ability to edit both files right there in the editor and still have them compared to each other. The left file is your version of the conflicted file, and the right is the latest version of the file causing the conflict; any changes you make are then saved to their respective files.

With the two files side by side, the conflicted areas are highlighted in red to make them easier to identify. Once a conflict is identified, there are a few options available to manage it, the easiest of which is to copy any required code from the right side (a.k.a. the latest revision) and paste it to the left side as required. There are also arrows between the two files, one pointing at each file; clicking an arrow takes the change from that file and copies it to the other file to resolve the conflict.

After you've made the needed changes, make sure the left file is selected, and click Save; or close the application, and you're asked if you would like to save the changes. That's it. If you selected the check box to resolve the file after saving, then you're all set and you can commit the file without a problem. If you didn't check the box, then resolving the file is as easy as right-clicking it and choosing RabbitVCS SVN ➤ "Mark as resolved." A dialog opens with the file selected: click OK, and you're ready to commit the file again.

RabbitVCS summary

All in all, RabbitVCS is great, you can happily use it by itself to manage the needs of any repository. It has support for most features and works at a nice speed, plus it's free. It's basic in some respects, such as code comparisons and options available when viewing a remote repository, but nonetheless, if you're working with one of its supported systems, RabbitVCS is worth looking at. You can use it in conjunction with other applications, or even a bit of Terminal use, but the fact that it sits in the right-click menu gives it an edge. If you want to look into Rabbit a little more, head on over to `www.rabbitvcs.org/` to learn more about it.

SVN Summary

You've been through a lot of applications so far, covering Windows right through to Ubuntu. You have TortoiseSVN and Syncro on Windows, Cornerstone and Versions on the Mac, and RabbitVCS on Ubuntu. TortoiseSVN is a great application, and even if you want to use another application for your management, it never does any harm to have it installed; its context menu integration allows for quick updates, commits, and checkouts—and best of all, it's free. Syncro offers a number of benefits, including its diffing tools and the fact it's a windowed application, which keeps all the actions in one place that is easy to navigate and use. If you're more of a heavy user, it can be worth getting a trial o Syncro and taking it for a spin to really appreciate its features.

Both Cornerstone and Versions for the Mac are great applications to use, and if you're a regular SVN user, then either will suit you for day-to-day use. The real difference in these two applications comes down to dealing with branches: Versions has little to no support for it, and Cornerstone has a helpful wizard that can make the process a lot easier. For me, Cornerstone has the edge as an application; little things like Cornerstone's logs and merging tools make it a pleasure to use. It's a little slow at times compared to Versions, but I'd happily take that for the extra features Cornerstone brings to the table.

On Ubuntu, you have RabbitVCS, which is also a great application and works well. All its actions are performed relatively easily, and it has the right-click menu integration I love from TortoiseSVN. Its developers are always looking to improve it, but right now it's a cracking application you can use to manage any of your SVN needs.

Mercurial

Now that you've looked at the options available for SVN, it's time to go down the Mercurial road and tour some of the applications available across platforms. Compared to SVN and Git, there are slightly fewer applications you can use; however, let's have a look at those that are available and how to use them to manage your repositories.

Windows

Managing your Mercurial goodness can be achieved just as easily on Windows as it can on any other operating system. Let's go through how to achieve this using the wonderful application TortoiseHg. This section goes through how to perform the necessary actions to allow for the management of any Mercurial repository you happen to be working with.

TortoiseHg

As you may have put together from the name, this application is brought to you by the same guys and gals who are responsible for TortoiseSVN, so right there you know it's going to be along the same lines and have the same level of quality. Let's see if that expectation holds true.

Installation and integration

Before you can accomplish anything with TortoiseHg, you need to get hold of it. Head straight over to http://tortoisehg.bitbucket.org/, which is the home of the application and all its various versions. The site has one of those big, clever Download buttons that can detect which version of the file you need; click it to start your download.

When the file has finished downloading and you're ready to install, go ahead and run the file with a double-click. The process is simple enough; leave all the default settings while you go through the pages of the installer. You're prompted to allow the installer to download from the Internet, but other than that there shouldn't be any problems.

After the installer has finished, you now have a new item in your right-click menu: the TortoiseHg menu. You can perform all the actions necessary to maintain your Mercurial repositories from the comfort of the right-click menu.

Configuring TortoiseHg

Although you can go ahead and use TortoiseHg as it is now, to make collaborating with others easier, you should do some configuration. Right-click some whitespace in a Windows Explorer window, and then head into TortoiseHg and click Global Settings. Go to the Commit page, and set a username for the main user on the system, which no doubt you or someone you're helping set up. Setting the username here saves TortoiseHg from having to ask for it when you commit or update, which gets old fast; it saves time to set it once here.

While in the Global Settings dialog, go back into the main TortoiseHg settings and look at the drop-downs for the Three-way Merge Tool and Visual Diff Tool. KDiff3 is included with the installer, so if you have no other alternates, you can select this one; or leave it as it to let TortoiseHg take care of the merges and diffs. There are other options available, which I go over in Chapter 8, but you can always come back and change your mind later.

Cloning a repository

For the times when you need to work with an external repository, TortoiseHg has your back by making the process a piece of cake. First, create a folder to house the repository clone, and then right-click the newly created folder. In the right-click menu, choose TortoiseHg ➤ Clone to launch the Clone new dialog. In this window, it can be as simple as entering the remote location in the Source field and where it is located on your system in the Destination field.

Also in the dialog is an Options drop-down, which lets you perform other actions while cloning the repository. The simplest of these is the ability to clone to a certain revision number that you can specify by selecting the "Clone to revision" check box and entering the preferred number. Another option is the ability to not update the new working directory after the clone has completed. This option is most useful when you're cloning a repository that is being used by someone else, potentially in a workflow environment, when you want that repository's changes, not the most recent ones.

Add/Commit/Update

Managing the day-to-day use of a Mercurial repository using TortoiseHg is easy enough, but if you've had the pleasure of using TortoiseSVN before and compare the two, Hg (in my opinion) is a substandard second. It's not difficult to use, but it seems a lot clunkier than its SVN equivalent.

However, it still performs simple tasks very well and keeps you out of the command line. The easiest action to perform on your files is a commit, and it's right there in the right-click menu. A simple click of the Hg Commit link takes you into a Commit window; however, if the file you're committing doesn't need to be committed, you get a lovely error saying "No files found for this operation." Provided the file/folder you're committing needs to be committed, then you need to add a message to go along with the commit, and you're set. In the Commit window you also see the change that was made to the file and the other files included with this commit.

In addition to committing, the right-click menu also gives you the options to add, revert, rename, forget, and remove a file or folder. The Add option, as it says, allows you to add files that are currently unversioned—easy enough. If you try to add a file that is already versioned, though, you get an error you've seen before: "No files found for this operation." You see this a lot in TortoiseHg.

The Rename option lets you rename a file in the proper Mercurial fashion. If you renamed the file normally, it would be seen as a new file, not as the old one with a different name. Although that is the case, TortoiseHg also has an option to help you if you rename a file the regular way. Right-click any blank part of the Files window, go into TortoiseHg, and then click Guess Renames. This little guy is handy, and with the click of a button it scans the files in the folder you're in to see if there are any matches with unversioned files and files in the current working copy. If you find the correct match after clicking Find Renames, click Accept All Matches, and the file is renamed as if you used the Mercurial method. Nice, eh?

The Remove and Forget options are somewhat similar in how they work; both commands mark the file to be deleted in the next commit. Forget, however, goes a step further and deletes the file there and then. It's worth mentioning that deleting a file doesn't remove its history: it stops any future changes from being tracked on the file.

Thus far, you've covered adding, committing, and updating, but you've missed pulling. This is because you can't pull from the right-click menu—it has to be done from within the Workbench, as you see in a moment.

Revision History

Revision History allows you to look at the previous changes and commits to a file you specify. To get into the Revision History window, right-click a file, choose TortoiseHg, and click Revision History, which opens a window with all the changes for the specified file. You can navigate the changes in the top half of the pane and see how the file was changed in the lower section. Figure 5-23 shows an example.

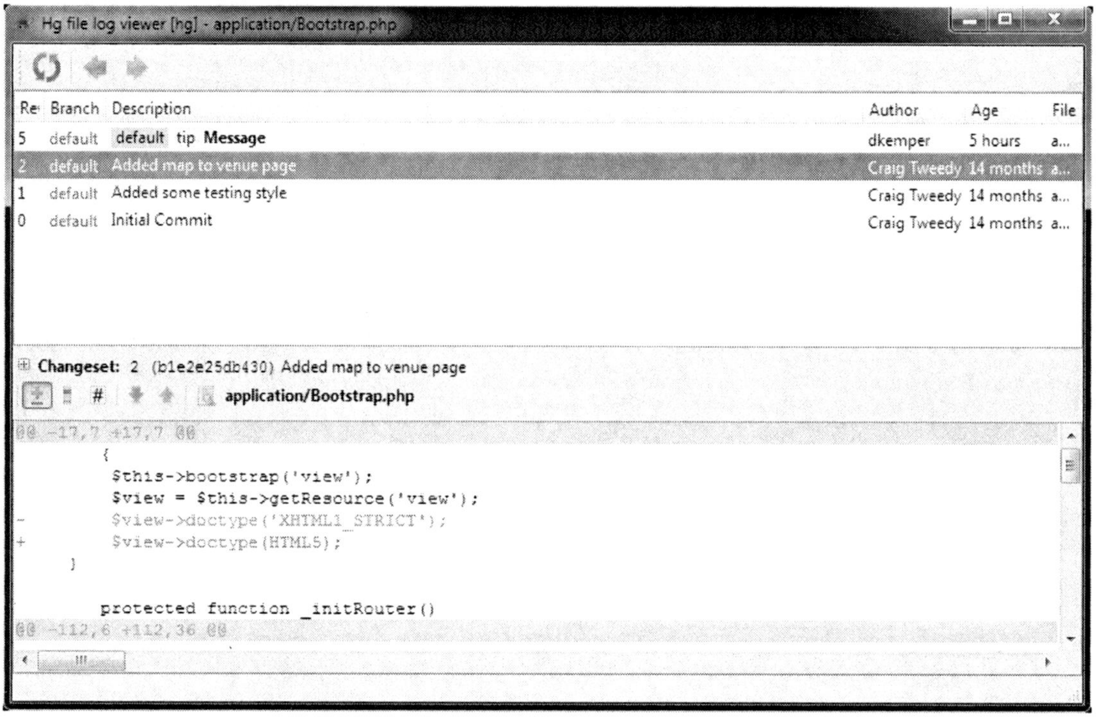

Figure 5-23. The Revision History window in action

The default view selected when viewing the previous changes is the unified diff view, represented by the button with a + symbol above a –. This view only shows changes that have been made, and nothing else; any new additions are highlighted with green, and any removed items are highlighted in red, to make looking through the versions even easier.

You can use a couple of different views to look at the changes in each revision. The next button shows the file as it would be, but with the changes highlighted so you can see where they happen in the file. The final view, represented by the # button, shows essentially what the previous view did; however, it includes the revision numbers so you can see which revision the changes were made in; this can be helpful from time to time.

Hg Workbench

If you open Revision History on a folder, then you see a different view: the Hg Workbench. This pane controls a lot of Mercurial actions and is easily the most-used window in TortoiseHg, so let's get to know it a little better.

You can get to the Hg Workbench by right-clicking any bit of white space available and choosing Hg Workbench or, as previously mentioned, by right-clicking a folder in the repository and clicking Revision History in the TortoiseHg menu.

The first thing to mention about this pane is that if multiple Mercurial projects have used the Workbench before, they all appear on the left side of the window; this lets you switch between them as you need to by double-clicking the one you'd like to switch to. Switching between the views also opens tabs for each one above the list of changes, which can be used for easy switching. You can see the Workbench by checking out Figure 5-24.

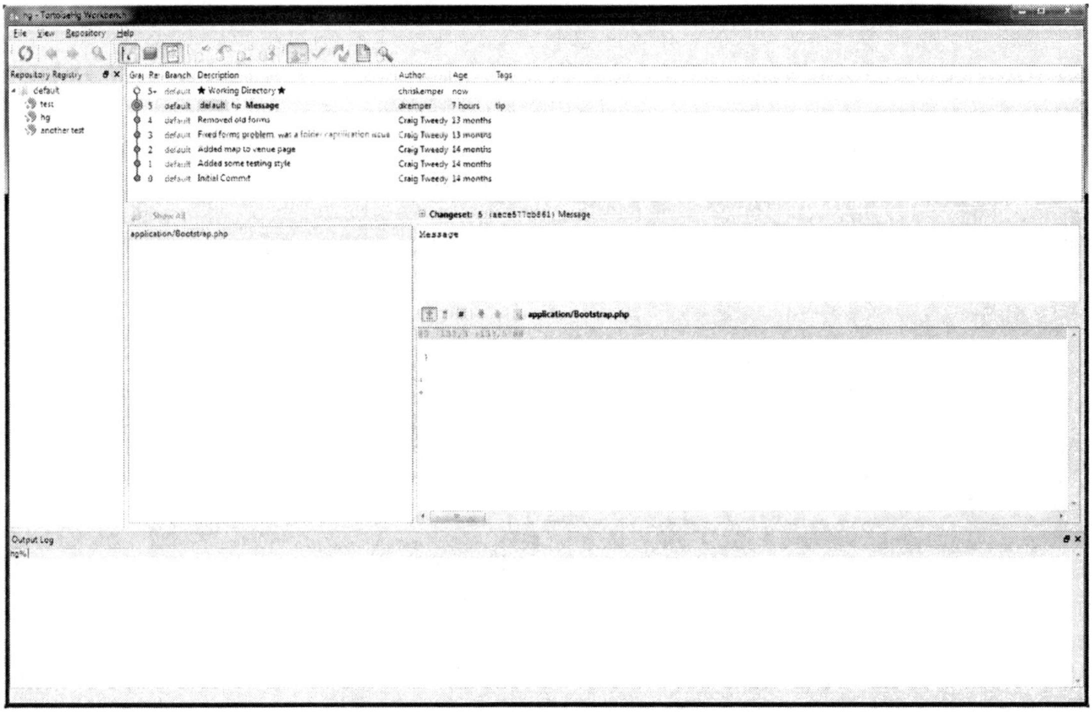

Figure 5-24. TortoiseHg Workbench, with the Repository Registry on the left

In Figure 5-24, you can see that I have three projects open: hg, test, and another test (very original names, I know). You also see that my friend Craig Tweedy has been busy with commits on this particular project—nearly all the revisions have been authored by him.

As I mentioned before, *a lot* happens in this view, and it can be a stand-alone application by itself, so let's chop it into bits starting with the left side. In the Figure 5-24 example, the far-left column is the Repository Registry, which as I've mentioned before is a list of all the repositories that have used the Workbench; so if you create a new repository, it won't appear here by default. You can add a new repository by right-clicking one of the folders in the menu and clicking Add Repository, which opens a new window allowing you to navigate to the repository and select it in your file system.

You can also group the repositories in the Repository Registry with different folders, but the default is only one: the default folder. You can rename a group by double-clicking it and add new group by right-clicking a folder and selecting New Group. Easy. You can then simply drag the repositories between the groups as you see fit. This may come in handy when you're working on work and personal projects on the same machine.

If you need to change the position of the Repository Registry, you have some control in the Workbench. You can easily move it in the application by clicking its name at the top of the pane and dragging it around; you'll soon find out where it can and can't go. If this doesn't cut it for you, then you can always pop it out of the Workbench entirely by clicking the Expansion button (which looks like two windows behind each other) or double-clicking the name itself. With it in this state, you can drag it anywhere on your computer screen or even back into the application.

If you want the window to go away for now, you can do that too. Either click the X at the top of the pane, or toggle the Repository button in the main navigation. You can also achieve the same effect by choosing View ➤ Show Repository Registry or by using the shortcut Shift+Ctrl+O. The latter three options can be used to toggle the visibility of the pane fairly easily, so if you feel bad about getting rid of it, you can easily get it back.

Output Log

The Output Log is another pane whose visibility you can toggle easily by clicking the Log button on the main navigation, choosing View ➤ Show Output Log, or pressing Ctrl+L. Although removing the pane from view gives you some extra room, it's better to lose some of the room than to have this bad lad disabled. Any action you perform, all the commands you use, and the results of each command are displayed in the log, so if you get any funky errors, you can use the output to help with debugging. Or, if you keep watching the commands, you may even learn a few of them if the time comes when you decide to jump into Terminal. Notice the % used before every command, like this one, for example:

```
% hg rollback --repository C:\Users\dkemper\Documents\hg –verbose
```

This command rolled back my changes to the last version I had pulled from the remote repository, but the % is irrelevant in that command; it represents a Terminal link, the same as $ whenever you see a Unix command. It helps you find out which commands control which actions, which as I can say can be useful if you want to make the switch to a more text-based version control existence.

Another great bonus with the Output Log is the ability to run Mercurial Terminal commands right in the pane. At the very bottom of the window you see hg%; clicking next to it lets you run any Mercurial command in the Workbench by simply typing **hg** followed by the command, which is pretty awesome. Although I haven't touched on Terminal commands yet (don't worry, I will), knowing this is here will benefit you some in way using TortoiseHg while knowing the Terminal commands needed to perform certain actions, like committing, adding or pulling. You may be running a status command, pulling code, or practicing commands in an environment where you can easily find out the correct command, if you happen to have gotten mixed up. This allows for the best of both worlds and lets you use Terminal in the instances where you can perform the action faster in code than in the application.

Pull/Push changes

The Pull and Push commands are used pretty often when collaborating with others, or if you want to regularly push updates to a remote repository. Either way, the Workbench gives you two Pull commands, and two Push commands to work with: one for checking for changes to pull or push, and the other to perform the action. Before I go into this any further, I need to say that if you create a repository on your local machine, you don't need to pull or push your code: committing it is all you have to do. That is, unless you have a remote repository set up for backup purposes, in which cases listen up as I go through pulling and pushing.

The advantage of performing the check before doing the action is that you can preempt potential problems such as hefty conflicts. With the pull check, you can also see exactly what was changed, and then you don't have to update until you've made the needed changes. All you need to do to initiate this is click the button on the left with an arrow going into an outline of a box, which is the 8th button along in Figure 5-25 if you're unsure on which one it is. Figure 5-25 shows what happens when new changes come in, including the choice to either accept the changes or reject them.

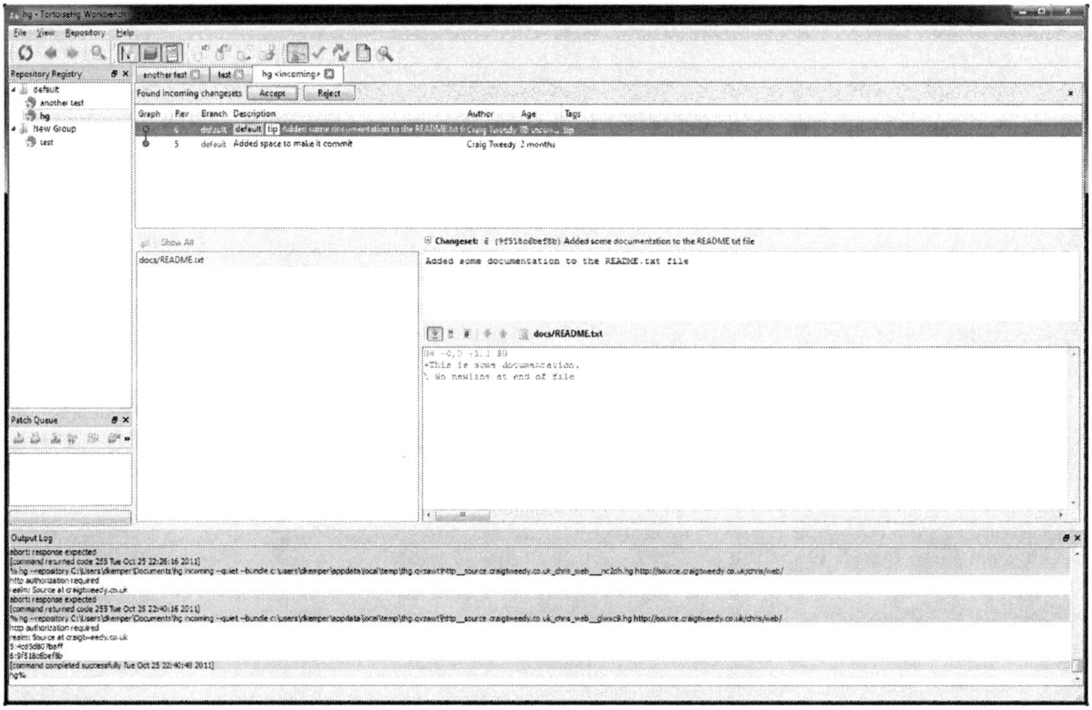

Figure 5-25. Incoming changes shown in Workbench, with the option to accept or reject

Accepting the changes takes the same form as pulling the update directly, so if you were to reject them right now and not pull the changes, you can. Use the button to the right of the current one will pull the latest changes, without asking whether or not you want to accept them. Once you have the new changes pulled down, you need to update the latest version of your code to coincide with the newly pulled code, which you can do by right-clicking the latest revision and clicking Update. Unless an update is actually available, you can't click the Update button in the dialog: if it's grayed out, then there is nothing to update.

With pushing, the process is exactly the same when it comes to checking for changes to go out. When you click the "Check for outgoing changes" button (which is the opposite of the pull button: an arrow going up into the outline of a box), you see the output shown in Figure 5-26, with the option to push or cancel the changes.

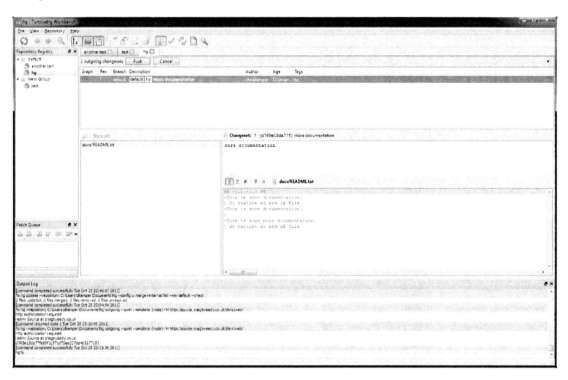

Figure 5-26. Outgoing changes with the option to push or cancel

Clicking the Push button sends the changes out to the remote repository, and Cancel cancels the process and allows for more changes to made before the new changes are pushed. This process also gives you the chance to review all the changes before they're pushed, to make sure everything is as it should be. With the pull check, pushing the changes directly without checking for changes doesn't prompt you to accept the push and does it with the click of one button.

A slight annoyance with the push process is that if you haven't already committed your changes from outside the Workbench, then when you try to push changes, it'll say the push was completed, but not push any changes. If you check the Output Log, you see that no changes were found, but the command completed successfully. So, if you know you have files to push, but they don't appear in the Output Log, then you need to go back and commit them. Situations like these are made a lot easier by keeping the Output Log open at all times, because when you perform actions, you can see how many files are affected—if any.

Synchronize

This option, represented by the two green arrows going around in a circle, allows you to synchronize your local working copy with a remote one by means of pulling and pushing. If you've cloned a remote repository, rather than creating a new one on your local machine, then the information used to clone the repository is the default in the Synchronize window.

If that's not the case, the options are blank so you can specify any remote location you want to interact with by selecting the connection type you need from the drop-down: Local, SSH, HTTP, or HTTPS. The remote options all give you different boxes to fill in to build up a full URL, starting with the domain name, then the port, and finally the path. The Local option—which you can use for a backup repository in something like Dropbox, or a network share—sadly doesn't give you any help, so you need to either type the path yourself or copy and paste it from a file explorer window.

Notice that this pane duplicates the four buttons responsible for performing the actions I was just talking about, as well as a couple of others. The new additions are "Email outgoing change sets" (the envelope with the arrow on it), Unbundle (the floppy disc going into the repository symbol), and a big Cancel button.

> **Note** *In some cases, such as when connectivity isn't great or other technical issues such as firewalls stop direct access to a remote repository, the time may come for a bundle. A bundle is really just a big patch file, with the patch file being a particular commit that is sent to another use in code rather than through a commit or update. A bundle is essentially the same thing, except it contains several different change sets, not only one or two. To go back to your connectivity problem, if you can't pull or push new updates, you can mail a bundle to another user you're collaborating with, have them unbundle the changes, and then have them push the remote repository. The same goes with changes needed by the user with connectivity problems: they can unbundle the changes, merge them, and then carry on working as before.*

The "Email outgoing change sets for remote repository" option ties in well with bundles. Although this option needs to be properly configured before it'll work (you need to set the required SMTP configuration in the global settings), when you open it you have a few options for how to send the changes to the user. Two of the options involve using bundles and patches, respectively; the receiving user applies those files to their local version to see the changes.

Another option sends the changes in the form of a Git format patch, which in essence works the same as a Mercurial bundle. The last option is to include the update in plain text, but include no Hg headers. This option is only used when someone needs to send changes to themselves and there is only one change set; otherwise, any other commit information or comments would be lost, and the changes would come up as one new change set, which doesn't help anybody.

The last option on the graphical button side of things is the ability to unbundle, which opens a file explorer window and gives you the option to find the bundle file on your local file system and apply it. Once the bundle has been applied, you can work with it the same way you would any other changes being pulled from a remote location.

This leaves only three more possible choices in the Synchronize window: the Post Pull button, the Options button, and the Target check box. Clicking Post Pull opens a small dialog with a number of options, two radio buttons (None and Update), and a check box. The radio buttons indicate whether you would like to update the local file system straight after pulling new files, or if you would rather leave them as they are and perform the update manually. If you're new to Mercurial, I would definitely select Update here, as it saves you having to remember to update your repository after pulling new changes (which can sometimes cause huge headaches if you forget).

The check box is another potential post-pull action: it tries to automatically resolve merge conflicts where possible, which is another great thing to have enabled if you're new to Mercurial. It saves you having to merge new change sets together if, for example, you've made more commits than the remote changes being pulled, and the remote changes need to be merged into your local copy before they can be used. Selecting the check box performs this task for you automatically; it only prompts you for attention if something goes majorly wrong and you need to sort out a beefy conflict.

The Options button also gives you some extra settings you can enable when performing push and pull actions in your repository, including forcing a pull/push, allowing the push of a new branch, and emitting debug output. Most of these can be enabled without a problem, but I advise leaving all them disabled unless you have a specific reason for enabling them—especially the force pull/push option, because doing that has the potential to cause monster problems with your repository.

The last option available is the Target check box, which, when checked, allows you to specify where the new changes are applied. By default, this is the most recent change set in the main branch of the code. However, you can use this option to direct the update into a specific branch. I haven't gone over branches yet, but don't worry, I will.

Commit/Revision Details

These two views are mostly used in the Workbench, partly because they're linked. The Commit view, which is represented by the tick icon, is responsible for committing changes. You can easily reach this view by clicking the * Working Directory * option at the top of the change set view, which shows you the files that need to be committed via the Commit view. Clicking any of the previous revisions in this list then sends you into the Revision Details view, which shows all the previous commits, the files included in them, and what specifically in each file was changed.

Committing files in Workbench is pretty easy, although on first glace you may not immediately notice where the Commit button is (I didn't, anyway) due to it being way over on the right. To commit files, select the modified files to be committed from the list on the left, add a commit message in the large empty space just to the right of the list, and click Commit. It's as easy as that! The Commit view also shows the changes made to the file you've selected in the left menu via the bottom of the pane; this can be handy as a reference point, to double-check that everything that should have been changed, has been.

Manifest

This view in the Workbench is used as a reference point for viewing all the previous changes made to tracked files in the repository; in addition, this view lets you see the full file in all the change sets, which gives you a much greater understanding of how the file has changed. It's easy enough to access this view: click the icon that looks like a piece of paper with the top-right corner folded, and you're presented with a Widows Explorer–like view of the files and folders in the repository. If you have the * Working Directory * option selected in the change set viewer, and you have uncommitted changes, then you can access an additional couple of options when viewing a file. The leftmost option (the plus above the minus) shows just changes in relation to the previous change set, in an easy-to-see view. It also lets you navigate between these differences with the arrows, which are grayed out if you're any change set other than the most recent one or if you have no changes in your working copy.

If you browse back through the previous change sets, it only shows you what the file looks like as a whole, which isn't all that useful if you want to see which changes have been made. The one thing the Manifest view does supply is a quick link to the Shelve tool via one of its buttons.

Shelve

This is one of those commands that you either use all the time or pretty much never use at all. It comes into play when you've been working on some changes locally but, because whatever is being worked on isn't complete or ready for testing, you have yet to commit it. This is all fine and well until a client calls, gently informing you that a bug has been found and if possible they would like you to look at it. This loosely translates to "STOP WHAT YOU'RE DOING AND FIX MY WEB SITE!!" in most cases. Now you have a problem because you're working on the files the bug occurred in, but you can't just delete your changes. What do you do? This is when you use the Shelve option. In the Repository menu, clicking Shelve opens the Shelve dialog.

This dialog is useful only when you have uncommitted changes or if you have a shelf you want to inspect. If you open it with no changes, you'll most likely click around a bit and think, "What does this even do?" Luckily, Figure 5-27 shows what the Shelve dialog looks like with a couple of changed files, so you can see it for yourself.

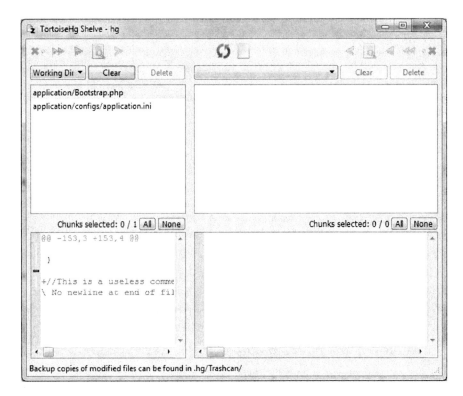

Figure 5-27. The Shelve dialog with a couple of changed files

Any files that have changes in them appear in the upper-left section of dialog, with the changes relating to the selected file appearing in the section below. The right side of the dialog is the equivalent of the left side, but for shelves rather than the working copy of the repository. In Figure 5-27, notice that the right side looks grayed out and unusable: that's because you need to create a new shelf by clicking the New Shelf button, which is next to Refresh. This opens a new dialog where you can specify a name for the shelf; the default name is useful, though, as it contains the current revision and the time and date when the shelf was created. Once you have a name, the right side looks a lot more useable, which is what you want.

Adding items to and removing them from the selected shelf is easy: move files between either the shelf or the current working copy by using the arrows above each side. You may need to squint to notice the active state of the buttons, as they're a very pale color, but clicking the single arrow moves the selected file to the other side, and the double one moves all files over.

When you're happy with the changes you've made, close the dialog, and the changes have already been made. If you've shelved all the current changes in the working copy, a quick refresh shows that you're working with a clean working copy, ready to work on the lovely client's bug. As soon as the bug has been squashed, open the dialog again, select the shelf where you stored the information from the drop-down on the right side, and reverse the steps, and the changes are in your working copy again. It's also possible to move changes from shelf to shelf: select the desired shelf from the drop-down on the left, and then do the same on the right. Easy.

Purge

The Purge tool, located in the Repository menu, is just as harsh as it sounds. When you select it from the menu, it launches a dialog that gives you the ability to remove any unnecessary folders in the repository. This process includes removing empty folders, clearing .hg/trash, and deleting unknown files. It also, luckily, includes an option to exclude files that start with .hg, which is a good thing, since you kind of need those. This tool is useful when you want to double-check that a repository is as clean as can be; so if you want to nuke those unwanted files in your repository, Purge is the tool for you.

Rollback/Undo

This tool is for those "Oh no, I didn't mean to commit that!" moments when you want undo what you just did and go back. Undo lives in the Revision menu, and when you click it, it gives you the simple choice shown in Figure 5-28.

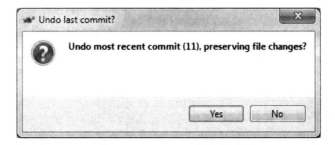

Figure 5-28. The "Undo last commit?" dialog box, which lets you choose whether to retract a previous commit

Although the commit number may be different, you're prompted for the same choice. Although the Yes and No options seem like the only options, they're not. If you wish to get out of there without making any changes, click the X at upper right, and no changes are made. The question at hand is whether you want to keep the data that was committed. Selecting Yes puts the working copy in the state it was in before the commit; the changes are still present as they were, so you have the option to commit the same files again. Selecting No is the more brutal option: any changes you made are deleted, so click No with care, or you may lose some very important changes without thinking.

TortoiseHg summary

If you're on Windows and using Mercurial, TortoiseHg is the ideal choice as a GUI to work alongside your development on various projects. The way it works can take a bit of getting used to, such as having to do some actions in Workbench and others from the right-click menu. When you get past that, it really is a powerful application, and it's updated all the time. If you're on Windows, you don't have an excuse for not giving it a try. It's free and relatively easy to use; what can go wrong?

Mac

When it comes to Mac-based Mercurial apps, there isn't much on offer; however, there are a few decent up-and-comers and a few well-established apps that can help you when manage your Mercurial repositories. Let's get right into it with MacHg.

MacHg

This is a good new application in the Mac-Mercurial thing, but that doesn't mean it's any less of an app. At this current moment, MacHg hasn't made a 1.0 release and is therefore still considered to be in Beta by some standards. An upside is that MacHg is open-source, which other than being awesome also means the application is free. You get this great app without having to fork out any dough, and for a free application it's nice looking and very easy to use.

The MacHg package is a one-window application, so there's no Finder integration or anything like that, although it can be argued that keeping all the controls in one place can make things a lot easier to manage. In the application, you can create repositories, work with repositories already on your system, clone remote ones, and more. It's also possible to clone existing repositories and perform all the basic actions as well—everything you need, with no hassle.

Installing MacHg

Unfortunately, this application isn't in the Mac App Store yet, but that doesn't stop you from enjoying its goodness. To get a copy, head over to the web site http://jasonfharris.com/machg/ and go to the downloads page, where there is a nice big blue button you can use to download the latest version of MacHg. The file you download is a zipped version of the application: unzip it, drag the application into your Applications folder, and you're ready to go.

Tour of the application

In the main window of MacHg you have three main views to play with: Browse, Differences, and History. You can easily switch between them by using the controls at upper left in the application window. A great feature is that they also have shortcut keys assigned to them: Cmd+1 for the Browser view, Cmd+2 for the History view, and Cmd+3 for the Differences view.

Browser view (shown in Figure 5-29) is a Finder-like screen that allows you navigate through the selected local-repository's files.

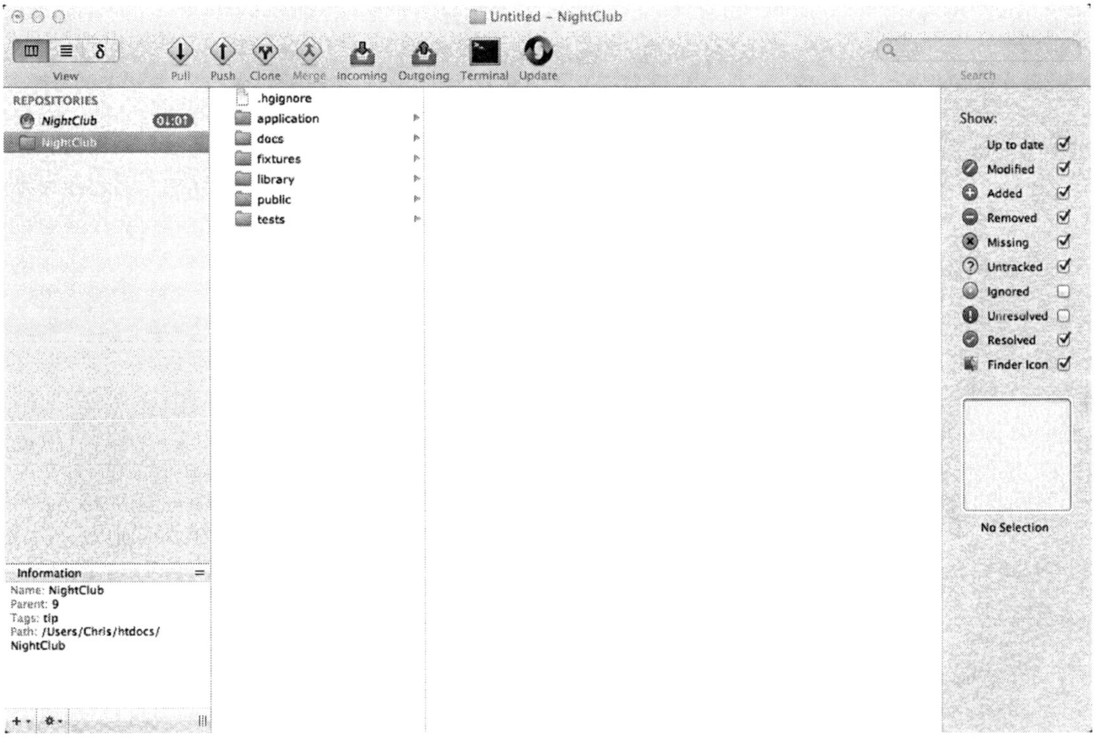

Figure 5-29. Navigating using a Finder-like screen

If you want to view the files in a remote repository, then you have to look at another application, or you can clone it, which you get to later. On the right side of the Browser view are a number of check boxes with icons next to them. These let you filter the Browse view, focus on the key files you need to target, and remove unneeded ones, such as up-to-date files.

These check boxes allow for very easy filtering to ensure that you know what's happening with your files. When a file is in modified, untracked, added, or any other state, the relevant icon appears next to it to make the change easily noticeable. In addition, if multiple files with different statuses are in the same folder, the icons also show up next to the folder, which gives you a visual indication that files in the folder need attention.

In this view, the right-click menu is very much your friend. It allows you to perform any desired action on a file or files, including committing, renaming, untracking (deleting), opening with a certain program, and a lot more.

The lovely History view, as its name suggests, lets you see the history of the repository you're currently viewing; it also gives you easy access to all history, including branches. It's easy to move through the changes and see what has been committed in this particular change set, as well as who made a change, when they changed it, and what they said about the change. In Figure 5-30, you can see that Craig Tweedy has been rather busy making a lot of changes, and in the selected item I've been adding documentation to the README.TXT file.

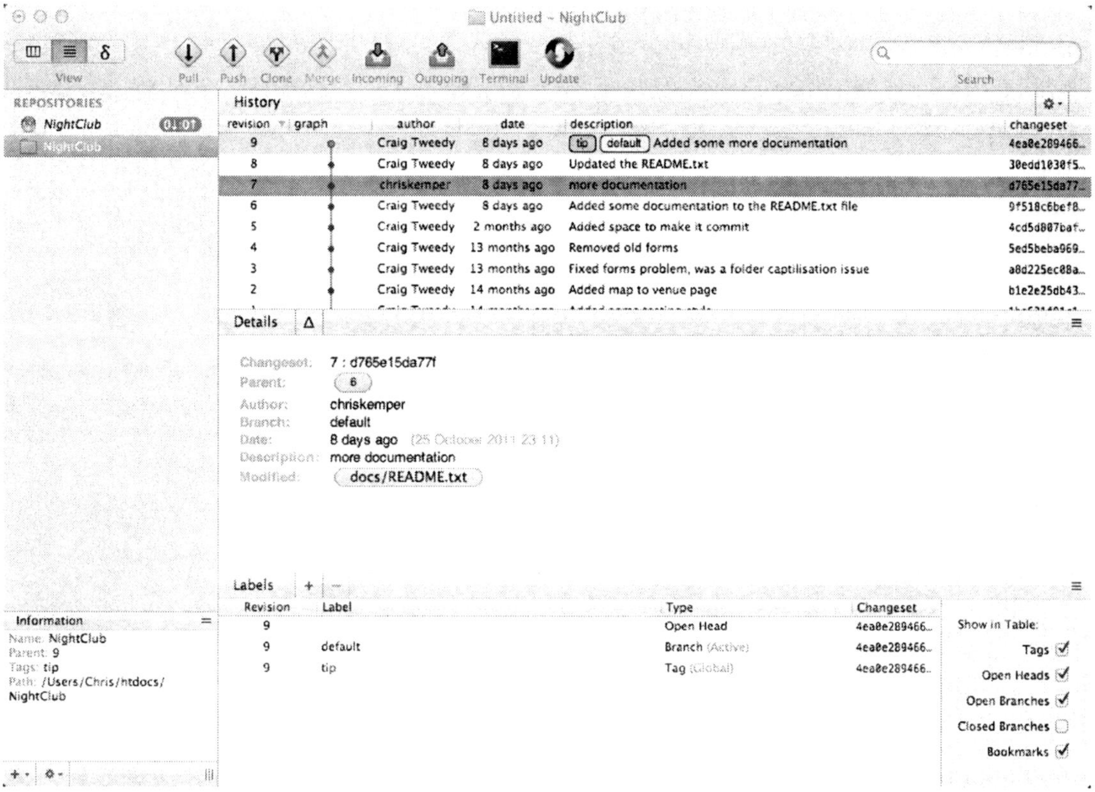

Figure 5-30. The complete history of the repository, with the modifier's name (Chris Kemper and Craig Tweedy) visible next to each change

One key action that can be performed in the History view is reverting your code to a previous change set with just a few clicks. Maybe a branch needs to be created at a point before another feature has been implemented, a bug needs to be fixed, or any other reason. To update back to a working copy to a previous revision, right-click the desired revision and select Update Repository to Revision. You're asked via a check box if you want to delete all the current changes in the working copy. If you have changes you don't mind discarding, then go ahead and check the box; otherwise, click Update, and that's it.

Notice that the selected revision is now pink, showing that it's the parent repository for any changes made to the working copy. Now you can make any needed changes to this revision, and when you're finished, the changes can be committed. This creates a new branch of the repository that can easily been seen in the History view: the graph branches out a new section on the normally straight line.

When you get to this stage, the easiest way to merge the revisions is to right-click where the branch's most recent commit is and select Merge Revision. You're prompted to confirm this, and the merge is partly complete. Now you need to go back to the Browser view, make sure all the changes are fine, and commit them. When the changes are committed, the merge is complete. It's good to remember that when you merge branches, the process is never finalized until the changes have been committed to create one new, merged change set.

The Differences view is a combination of the other two with a bit of a twist. In it, you can compare differences between change sets, which looks like two versions of the History view side by side. In addition, the bottom half of the screen takes the form of the Browse view, allowing you to see how the repository has changed between the two versions. This is made a lot easier thanks to the filtering options being brought along too.

The left side of the view is considered the base view, so the revision selected on the right is compared with the revision on the left. You can use this to determine which files were added and modified between the selected revisions, which can be a useful tool. Just be wary that if you use a more recent revision for the base, and select an older as the comparison, it may say that some files were deleted, when in fact they just hadn't been added yet. Although this view can be very handy when you're comparing changes, other than that it doesn't have many uses. You can't perform any useful actions in it—it's merely around as a reference point.

Adding new repositories

MacHg makes creating new repositories as easy as possible by having some cool tools, including drag-and-drop functionality. If you've been working on a project without version control (tut tut) for a while, but have now decided you want to hook it up to a Mercurial repository, MacHg has your back. Drag the root folder of the project straight into the left sidebar of MacHg, and MacHg will realize you want to create a new repository in this location containing these files. You're asked for a short name for the project; this is a reference name that is displayed on the left side with the other repositories.

That's all you need for now, because the location has already been entered thanks to the drag-and-drop action. Confirm that all is correct, and click Create Repository; doing so creates a new repository, ready for action. In MacHg, you see all the files in the repository, but currently they aren't being tracked by the repository, which isn't good. Add all the files to the repository by selecting them (or selected files, if you don't want to version everything), and then choose Action ➤ Add (Track) Selected Files to get them all ready to be committed.

The last stage of the process is to do an initial commit of the files by choosing Action ➤ "Commit all files." You're prompted for a commit message, which in most cases is something along the lines of "Initial commit," because that's what it is. From now on, any changes made to those files will be tracked, and they can then be fully managed by Mercurial.

Creating an empty repository

If you would like to create an empty repository with no files in it, that's fine too, and it can be done in MacHg. Choose Repository ➤ "Add local repository," and a dialog asks for a short name for the repository and a location for it in your system. This is the same dialog you see if you create a new repository by dragging a folder into MacHg, but without the location being filled in for you. With the repository created, it's the same as in the previous example: all that's needed now are files to track.

If you already have a few Mercurial repositories kicking about, but you fancy taking MacHg for a spin, it has your back here, too. All you need to do is take the folder containing the repository, drag it into the sidebar of MacHg, and that's it. No prompts for a short name or location—it picks up all the data from the folder name. Now that the repository is in MacHg, you can use it as you would expect to, with access to the history of the file and so on.

What if you want to add a remote server, so you can clone the repository and work on it locally? That's possible too. The easiest way to accomplish this is to right-click the repository bar in the application and select "Add server repository." In the dialog that opens, the first thing requested is a Short Name, which as you know is a reference to be used when the repository is shown in the sidebar. The other information required is a repository URL and any access information required to access the repository. Once all this information is in, MacHg displays a globe icon with either a tick or an X on it, depending on whether it can access the repository with the details provided. If you see an X, you may need to double-check the information you entered; otherwise, click Add Server, and that's that.

Buttons

MacHg does a good job of making its buttons easy to understand, thanks to their appropriate labels and, more important, thanks to the names of the commands underneath. Each of the processes has been designed to make it as simple as possible, and because the commands are named appropriately, you always know what you're doing without having to click a button and hope.

Pulling

The left-most button is the Pull command, which as it suggests pulls in any changes form the remote repository, if the repository happens to be using a remote repository. When the button is clicked, you're prompted for a confirmation of which server to pull from. This is autoselected for you if you have originally cloned the repository from a remote server; otherwise, you can select a remote repository from the drop-down in the prompt. There are also a few advanced options available, which can make your pull requests more specific and therefore more useful. You can run a remote command, run an SSH command, pull to a specific revision, and so on. The best option to select is Update After Pull, as this automatically updates your local copy after the pull with the latest changes.

Once you've selected everything you need, click Pull to start the whole process. You're asked if you want to pull via a confirmation prompt; if you're happy, click Pull again, and you're off. A new dialog pops up after the pull has completed, showing any output from the request such as logs, confirmation messages, and changed files.

Push

As opposed to Pull, the Push button pushes all the commit changes in the repository to the remote server. Before you think about clicking this button, ensure that your working copy of the code has no modified files, unresolved conflicts, or anything of that nature; otherwise, the push will fail. Once that's out of the way, give the Push button a click to start the process. The next dialog you meet is the same one used by the pull process, but with some different command options. There is an option to allow the push to force, so if you have changes in your local repository, they're pushed regardless. Use this command with care, because it has the potential to ruin the repository and ruin other users' code in the process.

As with the Pull command, once you've selected the server and any options, there is a final confirmation dialog after you click Push. MacHg then does its stuff, and any errors and output are delivered in the form of prompts and the log window.

Clone

Cloning is a very common action in MacHg, mainly because it's so easy to do. The most common time to clone a repository is when you've referenced a remote repository and you want to make a local clone of it so you can begin making changes to it locally. To do this, you have to create a server repository, which I went over a little while ago. If you already have one set up, great; otherwise, you need to create one for this to work.

Provided everything is well and good, select the server repository from the left menu, and then click the good old Clone button. Doing so launches a new dialog that looks a little different than the previous ones but is the same. All that's needed is the short name and the location to store the clone repository; click Clone, and that's it. The new cloned repository appears on the left side, so it can be used exactly the same as any other repository.

It's also possible to clone a local repository the same way. Select it from the left navigation, click the Clone button, and enter a short name and a location, and that's all you need. When everything has finished, you can use the cloned repository as usual—plus you can use the original as a parent, which gives you the option to pull and push changes between the two.

Merge

This button is active only when a merge is required in the repository that is currently selected, which keeps from it being used by mistake. When it's available, the window used for merging changes is extremely easy to use. In Figure 5-31, you can see the list of revisions; the branch that has been created is shown by the graph and creating a new line.

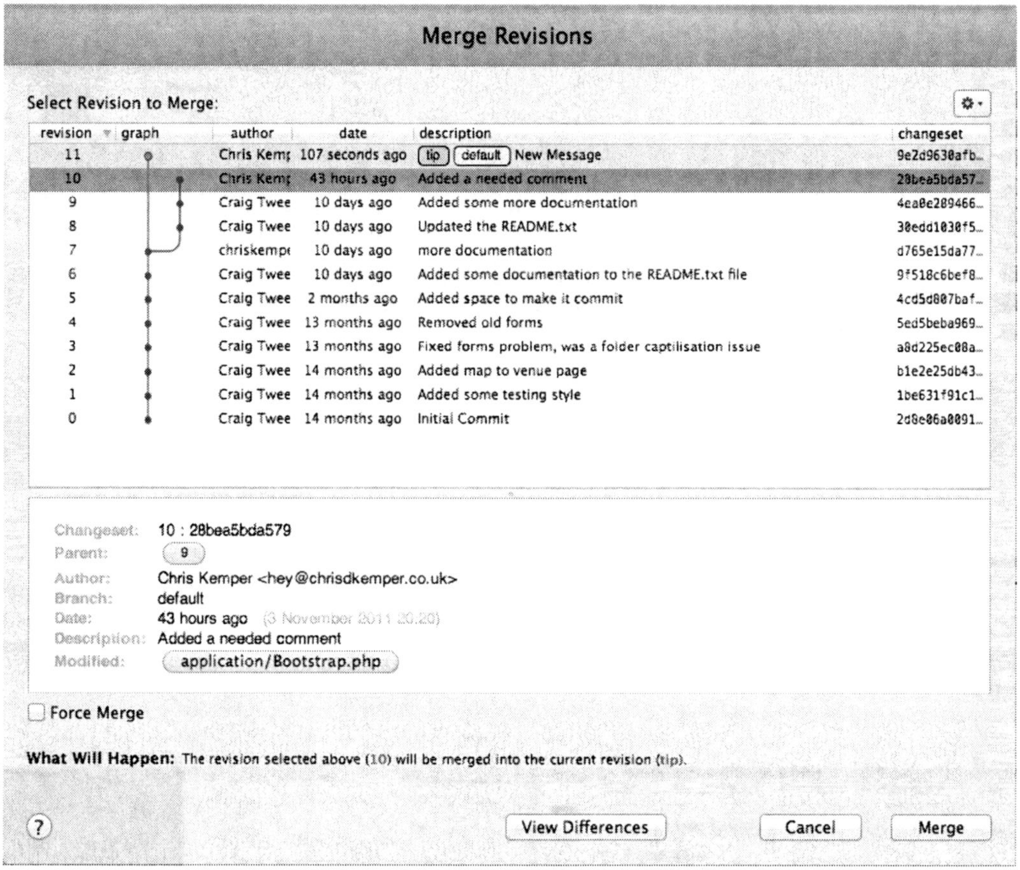

Figure 5-31. A list of revisions with a clearly visible branch in the Merge Revisions view

To merge the changes, pick the last change on the branch and then click Merge. The Merge button is also disabled if you select a change that isn't applicable for merging, which makes things a lot easier. After you click the Merge button, any conflicts are shown with your change-comparison tool; and after the conflicts are resolved and the application is closed, the merge is partially complete. The final stage is to commit any outstanding changes; then the merge is complete.

Incoming/Outgoing

These two actions work the same way, just in their own respective directions, by checking whether changes are available to pull down or if changes need to pushed out. When you click one of these buttons, you're prompted to select the remote server to use for the check, but in instances of cloned repositories, this is preselected. After you double-check the information, click OK, and away it goes. A dialog pops up after the request is complete, showing any changes that need to be pushed/pulled or reporting that no changes are available for pushing or pulling. This is a great way to make sure all changes have in fact been pushed out to the server and to know when an update is required.

Terminal

This button comes in handy for those who like to dabble in both the command line and a GUI, because its sole purpose is to open a Terminal window that is automatically set to the location of the repository. This means you can run any commands straight away without having to change directories or locate the project from within Terminal. It also has no effect on MacHg: any changes you make in Terminal are picked up without a problem, so you can have the best of both worlds.

Update

The Update command is useful in MacHg and lets you complete a few actions from within the dialog that launches when it's clicked. If you recall the History view from a few pages back, the Update button allows you to update the current project to a specific revision. This means you can go back to a previous version of the code in a couple of clicks. In addition to this feature, the Update button also lets you update to more recent changes that have been brought down from pull requests, since pulling changes down doesn't have any real effect until the working copy is updated to use them.

Updating to a past revision or updating to the most recent set of changes is easy. First, select the desired version from the list: the most recent revisions are at the top, and they're in descending order as you go down. Once you've selected the desired revision, click the Update button. You're then asked whether you want to continue, and a check box lets you select whether to delete modified files. Clicking Update again confirms the request, and the repository is updated as needed. A dialog shows which changes actually occur.

Toolbar customization

Although these are the buttons included on the menu bar by default, they aren't the only ones available. If you right-click the button toolbar and select Customize Toolbar, a new dialog opens, showing the additional items that can be placed on the toolbar. This dialog also allows you to reorder items and remove items from the toolbar, to make it the way you want it. Some of the buttons you can include are Commit, Commit All, Add, Remove, Diff, Print, and so on. This is a great feature of MacHg: it helps you create an application that works for you and remove options that won't be used to free up space for desired items.

MacHg summary

In a nutshell, that is MacHg. It's a great, free application that has a lot of potential and will continue to improve. It's also been optimized for use with Lion, which makes it a lot faster and more responsive in its everyday use. The developer behind the project, Jason Harris, is very active on answering support queries and is always taking suggestions about potential improvements, which is always a good thing. If you use Mercurial on a Mac, or even if you're a Terminal user, get the application from http://jasonfharris.com/machg/ and give it a try. You won't regret it!

SourceTree

This application is another bit of great work from the guys over at Atlassian (The JIRA/Bitbucket guys); they're certainly kept the standards high with this one. SourceTree is an impressive application with the ability to manage Mercurial and Git repositories through one app. It also boasts a huge set of features and is very easy to use. When you first work with SourceTree, you're asked to allow access to the configuration files for both Git and Mercurial to ensure that all the features of SourceTree work. There's no reason to disallow this, because it makes sure all the information in your commits is up to date and enables additional features in SourceTree.

Installing SourceTree

You can install SourceTree in a number of ways, the easiest of which is through the Mac App Store: search for the application, and download it. Easy. You can go direct, which requires you to head over to http://sourcetreeapp.com/ and click the Download link. This launches a download of a .dmg file containing the application; when the download is complete, open the .dmg file and then drag the app into the provided Applications folder shortcut, and the app is ready to run. This works for now, but to take advantage of SourceTree after the evaluation period, you need to register for a free account. You're prompted for this when your evaluation expires, so follow the links, sign up for the account, and you're all set.

Managing/Creating repositories

You manage both remote and local repositories in the Bookmarks view, which keeps your repositories in an easy-to-view format. Each repository also shows how many files are ready to be pulled, pushed, and committed, providing an overview of all your repositories in one go. To get to the Bookmarks view, press Cmd+B, and you see all the bookmarks you've created; or, if you haven't created any yet, this is the first thing you see. Drag-and-drop functionality plays a big a part in using SourceTree and how easy it is to use. To add a local repository, drag the folder into the Bookmarks view: SourceTree works out which repository type it is and adds it to the list.

You can also create brand-new repositories using SourceTree. In the Bookmarks window, click the "Add repository" button and then "Create repository." Now, all you need to do is select the repository type (Git or Mercurial) and a location for it on your system, and the repository is created for you.

Integration

SourceTree also has great integration with GitHub and Bitbucket. Clicking the Hosted Projects button lets you enter your account information for both GitHub and Bitbucket and see all the repositories you've created on each service. Then, double-clicking one of your repositories starts the cloning process so you have a local copy. In addition, you can create repositories for these services right in SourceTree: click Create New Repository and give the repository a name, and it's created for you straight away. Once it's created, you can clone it to your local machine and get started using it. Although this is a great feature, there are slight issues with authentication, and sometimes it won't accept your details—even if they're entered correctly, it may still ask you for them, but putting them in correctly enough times works.

The integration with Bitbucket and GitHub also has another useful feature. Go to the project page for a repository you want to clone and drag the URL of the page from the browser address bar into the Bookmarks window, and the repository is cloned for you. All you need to do then is enter the desired name and location for it on your system.

Cloning a repository

There are instances where you need to clone a repository that isn't hosted on GitHub or Bitbucket, which is fine too. Click the "Add repository" button to open a dialog in which you enter the URL of the repository in the first field. Then you need to pick a place for the cloned repository to live on your system. SourceTree also attempts to connect to the repository, to ensure that it's valid; if authentication is requested for the repository, you're prompted to enter the login credentials. Once everything is as you need it, click the Clone button, and SourceTree takes care of the rest.

It's also possible to organize the repositories using various folders. This is done by clicking the "New folder" option on the toolbar. All that's needed is a name for the group, and it's created. Then you can add repositories to it by dragging and dropping.

Views

Day-to-day running of repositories is all managed in one window, which you launch by double-clicking the desired repository in the Bookmarks window. You can easily switch between the views by clicking the icons at upper left or by pressing Cmd+1, 2, or 3, depending on which view is required. This window is created by a main navigation toolbar across the top of the application and lists branches, tags, remotes, and shelved items. The main content of the window changes depending on the view you're in at the time.

File Status view

This is where the majority of the action happens, and this is the default view when you're managing a repository. In File Status view, you can see the different file types in your repository and what actions need to be taken. The left drop-down menu lets you change the way the files are displayed, with either a flat view, where all the files are listed; a tree view, where it's easier to see folder structures; or a column view, which mimics the Finder column view.

The next drop-down is the most important one: it allows you to filter the results by different types, ranging from all file states to untracked files or even conflicted files. This makes it a lot easier to target the specific files you're after and to make sure no files are missed.

Selecting a file on the left side of the screen causes the right side of the window to change. For changed and conflicted files, the differences are shown; for untracked files, the entire file is shown; and so on. With modified files, it's also possible to launch an external tool to make viewing the changes even easier; the tool defaults to FileMerge, but you can change it by going into SourceTree's preferences. Figure 5-32 shows File Status view in action.

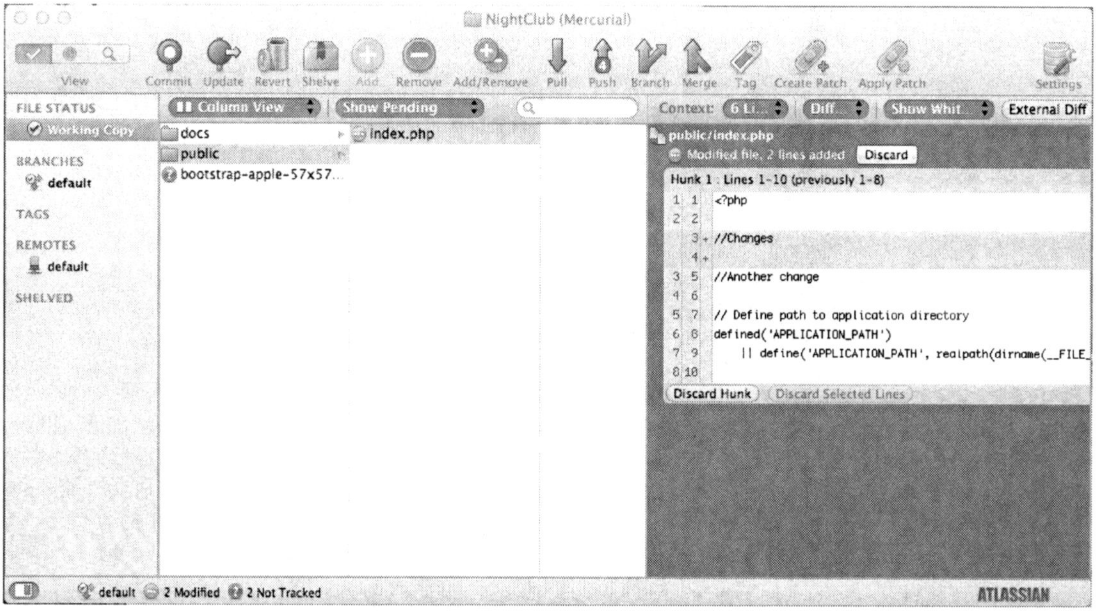

Figure 5-32. File Status view in SourceTree

Log view

Log view is the best way in SourceTree to view the history of your repositories, including what was changed, when it was changed, and who changed it. The graph on the left lets you see easily when branches happened and, if they have been merged back into the main system, when they were merged.

When you select a past revision from the list, the bottom half of the screen changes accordingly, allowing you to see all the changes in that revision, the files affected, and who made the commit. The comments associated with each commit are included as well, which makes it easier to find the specific version you're looking for. If you want to revert your local repository to that version, double-click it and confirm the prompt.

Search view

The comprehensive search features in the Search view let you easily find the commits you're looking for. The powerful search allows you to search commit messages, files, and more. Then, any commits including the string searched for are brought up in the lower panel, where you can examine the changes and take a closer look at what was included in the commit.

It's also possible to search for a specific user, to see all their commits and pinpoint all the changes they've made throughout the course of the project. To do this, select User from the Search drop-down menu. In addition, you can limit a search between specific dates, which makes pinpointing a specific change even easier. The date-limiting works on a normal search, too.

Basic actions

Performing all the basic actions in SourceTree couldn't be easier. All the major and commonly used actions have their own buttons on the main toolbar to make it much more convenient to perform them. The AddRemove action is one that comes in very handy. It marks any untracked files to be added and marks any removed files to be deleted—like a two-for-one special. You can also click the button without selecting any files, which makes the process a lot easier. In addition, you can run the Add and Remove actions separately: select the desired files, and click the corresponding button for the action you want to perform.

Committing these changes is easy too. One click of the Commit button launches a dialog showing the list of files changed and the changes that occurred in the files. This is useful when you're composing your commit messages, as you can refer to the changes that have occurred and make the commit messages more specific and therefore useful.

Pulling, pushing, and updating

A perk of using SourceTree when you need to push changes is its ability to detect them. If SourceTree detects any changes that need to be pushed, it displays the number of changes that are to be pushed as a badge right on top of the Push icon. This allows you to only push changes when necessary; plus, with the number there at all times, it's a lot harder to forget about them. When the time comes to make a push to the server, the process couldn't be easier. Click the Push button, make sure all the changes you need to push are present, and then click OK. The changes are pushed to the remote server.

As far as pulling goes, the process is easy. SourceTree periodically checks the remote server to see if there are any updates to be pulled, and if it detects any, it shows the number in a badge on the Pull icon. Although this does work, it's better to check for changes to pull manually by clicking the Pull button, regardless of whether it has a badge on it. When the button is clicked, any changes that are due to be pulled appear in the dialog that is launched, as well as the comments associated with the commits.

When changes are pulled in, you're given the option to set an Action after Pull, which, as the name suggests, is an action to be performed after the pull has been completed. Although a few options are available, the two main choices are None and Update. Selecting None pulls the changes down from the server but makes no changes to your local files, whereas Update updates the local copy of the repository with the pulled changes. When you've decided on an action, click OK, and the changes are pulled down from the server.

In the event that you keep this set to None to manage all changes yourself, you can perform an update easily by, you've guessed it, clicking the Update button. To update to the latest changes, select the top revision from the list and then click OK; your local repository is updated with the remote changes. The Update dialog also lets you update the working copy to a previous revision: select the desired one from the list and click OK, and the working copy is updated as needed.

SourceTree summary

SourceTree is an application that is packed with features, especially its integration with Bitbucket and GitHub. In addition, it's easy to use, and it's free. Although it does have some issues with its integration, thanks to authentication issues, it's still packing features that other applications can learn something from.

A huge plus is the fact you can manage both Git and Mercurial repositories in one application. Thanks to both systems being Distributed Version Control Systems, the processes they use and the way they go about managing the repositories are nearly the same. This means no matter which type of repository, Git or Mercurial, the application can be used the same way, which makes life a lot easier. If you want to give it a try for yourself, either head over to www.sourcetreeapp.com/ to download a copy, or search for SourceTree on the Mac App Store.

Mercurial summary

You've been through a number of applications here: TortoiseHg, MacHg, and SourceTree, to be exact. Each of these applications is worthy to be used and has no real disadvantages. All the applications are free to use and are under constant development, which means you're seeing bug fixes and better features all the time. SourceTree's integration with third-party applications does give it somewhat the edge, but the others are also great to use and work just fine. I like MacHg because of how easy it is to use and the fact that it only contains what it needs, but that's just me; any of the applications will be fine for you.

Git

It's time to move into the world of Git GUI applications for our favorite three operating systems. You go through how to use some of the main contenders in this field so you can get up and running with your own Git repositories as quickly as possible. I know you're bound to be excited, so let's dive in with some cracking Git applications for Windows.

Windows

Although there are options available if you want to use Git on Windows, it's safe to say that they aren't as good as some of the other offerings on different operating systems. I'll go through a few of the best ones. For those of you who would rather avoid Terminal, there's something here to keep you happy, so let's get started.

Git GUI

This application comes bundled with the Git installation you went through a few couple of chapters back, which gives the initial impression that it isn't that good, and that assumption is somewhat correct (sorry, Git GUI!). Although it can be argued that it's not the best application in the Git arsenal, it does save you from using Terminal, which for a few of you is what you want to hear.

First things first: it's time to create a repository on your local system. Open the Git GUI program from the Start menu. If it's installed in the default location, it should be under Start ➤ All Programs ➤ Git ➤ Git GUI, which opens the first screen in the application. Upon first opening it, you see three options: Create New Repository, Clone Existing Repository, and Open Existing Repository. This screen also contains any recent repositories that have been opened in the application, which makes accessing your previous repositories a lot easier.

Depending on whether the context menu shortcuts were added during the installation, it's also possible to launch the application using a right-click shortcut. If you navigate into an existing repository and right-click a file or folder, you get a Launch Git GUI option that takes you straight into the management screen for that repository. The option is also present when you right-click any file or folder in the system; however, if it's not a repository, you're presented with the same screen you would see if the application was accessed from the Start menu.

Creating a new repository

Creating a new repository only takes a couple of steps. First, click the link for Create New Repository, which brings up a dialog asking for a location for the repository. The easiest way to choose the location for the repository is to click the Browse button, which lets you navigate through your system and pick the best spot. You can also possible create additional folders in this view. Once you're happy with the location, click Create to initialize the repository and launch the next window of Git GUI, where all the main action happens.

Adding an existing repository

For cases when you already have a Git repository on your system, and you want to manage it, Git GUI is easy to deal with. From the start screen, select Open Existing Repository to launch a dialog similar the one used when creating a new repository. Well, really, it's exactly the same, except the text is a little different. This time, locate the repository on your system, select it, and click Open to get started managing it using Git GUI.

Cloning an existing repository

Cloning an existing repository is as easy as the other methods, but you click the Clone Existing Repository link to get started. This screen is slightly different to the others you've seen because there are two fields that need information before the repository can be cloned. The first field is the location of the repository to be cloned; this can be either a local repository or a remote one. In the case of a remote repository, copy its URL into the first field, and for now that's all that's needed. Underneath is the familiar field that asks for a location for the repository to live on the local system.

After clicking Clone, you're prompted to enter any account information required to connect to the specified repository. Then a status window shows you the process is working. This dialog doesn't update very often, and sometimes not at all, so if you don't notice any changes, wait a while; eventually you're redirected to the main Git GUI window.

Adding/Committing/Deleting/Reverting

Now that you've created a repository using one of the previous means, it's time to start managing the files using the main Git GUI interface. Although it's not the best looking of applications, Git GUI makes detecting changes easy. Whenever a new change is detected in the repository, the main window reflects the change. As you can see in Figure 5-33, the changes are what the main screen is all about; it's apparent that the changes I've made are unstaged and aren't committed yet, which helps a lot.

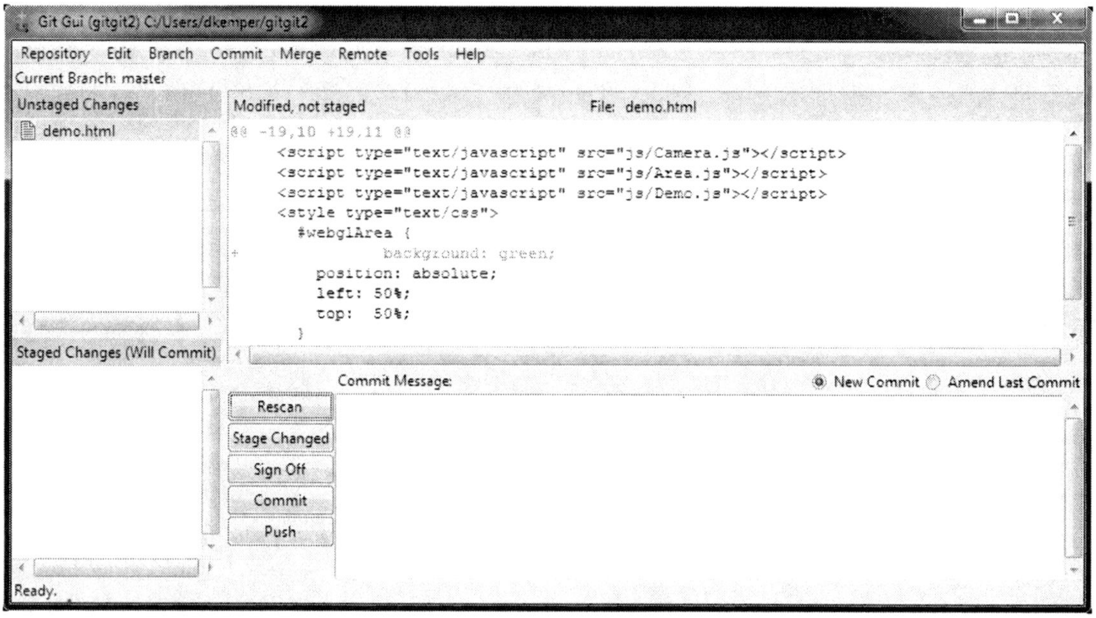

Figure 5-33. The main screen of Git GUI, showing changes (unstaged in this example)

When you're working with Git GUI, it's a good idea to scan the repositories for changes on a regular basis, as it has no automatic change detection. To do this, either click the Rescan button at lower left in the application or use the standard Refresh command (Ctrl+R). If new changes are detected, Git GUI reacts as needed.

To stage these changes to be committed, choose Commit ➤ Stage to Commit, which also has an associated shortcut key, Ctrl+T. This command works on a file-by-file basis, but the command under it— Stage Changed Files to Commit (Ctrl+I) stages all changed files to be committed. This can save a lot of time if there are in fact a lot of changes to work with. The Stage Changed button located just to the right of the Staged Changes area of the application stages all changed files with the click of a button.

After using either of these commands, any files affected are moved to a different part of the application: the Staged Changes section, which shows any changes included in the next commit. It's also possible to unstage these changes by choosing Commit ➤ Unstage From Commit (Ctrl+U), which takes the file back to being unstaged; therefore its changes aren't included with the commit.

Follow the same process for new files in the repository. If you want the new files to be committed to the repository, and therefore eligible for future tracking, follow the steps just outlined, and the files are added to the Staged Changes list.

For the instances when you're having a bad day and all the changes you've worked on need to be scrapped, you can do so in a few clicks. Head into the Commit menu and choose Revert Changes to revert the selected file back to the state it was in at the last commit or update.

When you're happy with all the changes made and are ready to perform a commit, that's also easy in Git GUI. Since the main screen of the application is centered around committing, it's no surprise that the Commit button and message box are located on the main screen too. Add a message in the lower-right dialog box, and then click the Commit button to the left of it. When you see that the list of changes to commit on the left is clear, the commit has been executed successfully.

Pushing/Pulling

If you make a lot of local changes, or you're collaborating with other users on a project, the time will come when pulling and pushing become key parts of your workflow. Of course, both of these actions are only possible when a repository is cloned, since you can't push changes to a place that doesn't exist, right? Let's start with pulling. Head into the Remote menu, and select Fetch and the name of your remote repository. This brings down any remote changes into your local copy.

As you've been through before, when the changes are brought down from the parent server, the process isn't finished until the changes are staged and then committed to the local version of the repository. All you need to do is go through the same process as before by staging all the changes and then committing them, and then the process is complete.

Pushing is as easy as pulling, if not easier. Before attempting to perform a push, it's important to ensure that your working copy is up to date, with all the changes committed. Once your local clone is in this state, go to the Remote menu again, but this time select Push or use its shortcut, Ctrl+P. This launches a dialog where you can select the location to push the changes to from the Remote: drop-down. You can also specify other options, such as using a low-bandwidth sending method or overriding remote changes (which you should avoid at all costs). When you're happy with the selection, click Push, and the changes are shipped off to the server.

Git GUI summary

Although this application isn't the best, it does allow for basic management of your repositories, and it isn't all that bad. Thanks to the layout of Git GUI, any changes you make are immediately visible, and the wording of the different sections of the window makes managing the stages easy. It also comes in useful that you can open a Git GUI window from within a Git repository; that makes this application a little more useful than some others, as you can be brought directly into the repository without having to go through the Start menu route. But Git GUI can always be improved—even small issues like the application not auto-refreshing can cause changes to be potentially lost.

All in all, this application is good enough when it comes to the day-to-day management of your Git repositories, thanks to the layout of the application and the ease of launching the window in local repositories using a right-click shortcut. If you haven't tried Git GUI, and you're not ready to make the dive into the command line, give it a shot. It gets the job done.

TortoiseGit

This is another great offering from the Tortoise series. On its Google Code project page it's described as a port of TortoiseSVN, which becomes apparent when you use it: there are a fair number of similarities in how it works, as well as in some of the core functions and features. Although this application may not have the slickness if its SVN counterpart, it's still a pretty decent app that can make managing your local Git repositories and clones a little easier.

Download and installation

The source code for the program is hosted on Google Code, and is open source. This means that all the source code and the available builds of TortoiseGit are hosted here too. You can find all this and the wiki, issues, and more at http://code.google.com/p/tortoisegit/. To get down to business, you need to pick up the required version of the application for your system. As you've been over before, you need to determine whether you're using a 64- or 32-bit system. Then, select the latest download for your version from the left menu on the project page: the highest release is always your best bet.

When it comes to installing things, the process is pretty similar to any other installation. The only real difference is the dialog shown in Figure 5-34, where you select the SSH method TortoiseGit will use. It's advisable to use the method that is selected by default, which is shown in the figure. I say this because OpenSSH isn't the best application to use and, as the dialog says, TortoisePLink integrates better with Windows. After this, the installation process is normal, so there isn't anything else to be concerned with; keep the defaults, and everything will be fine.

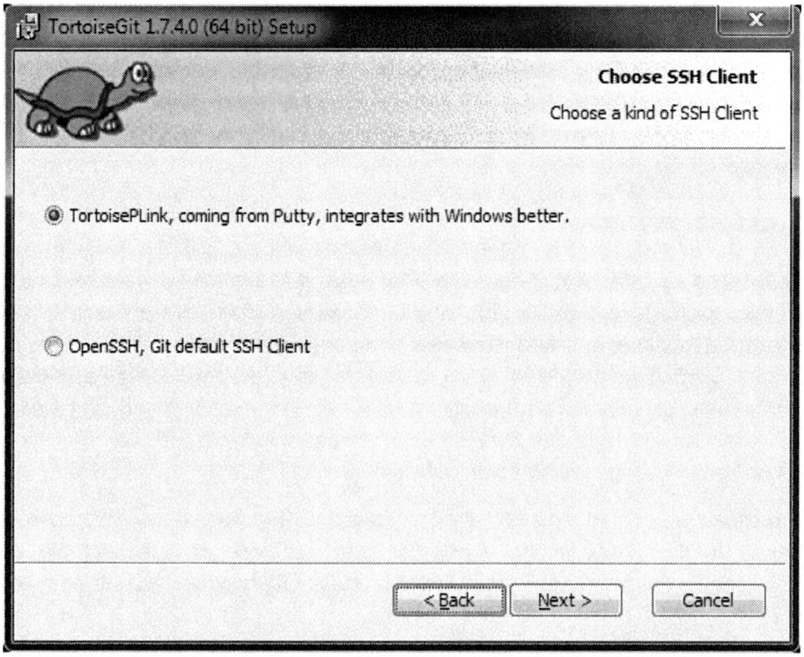

Figure 5-34. The default method for installation is selected.

Creating repositories

TortoiseGit makes creating repositories easy. The first thing you need is an empty folder to house the repository. Right-click it, and click the Git Create Repository Here button. This launches a prompt informing you of the potential to create a repository that is used in a parent-child relationship. Selecting the check box causes the repository to be bare: no files live in it, and it's only used for storing changes. The repository should end with .git, as this is a standard practice with Git repositories.

Normally you won't be making bare repositories, because you want to manage the files, right? In this case, all you need to do is select a folder (either plain or with contents in it) and go through the same process as before. This time, be sure to leave the check box unselected; this creates a normal repository. If your folder isn't empty, you're asked to confirm whether you want to proceed with creating the repository; you're warned about the potential to lose data, but in most cases it should be fine. If you have an issue with losing data, create a blank folder to house the repository, and then copy the desired files into it. This approach is slightly longwinded but still works. You don't need to do this if you don't mind the danger of potential data loss—click Proceed to create the repository. Easy.

Cloning a repository

Cloning a repository is also an easy process with TortoiseGit and can be done with a couple of clicks. The simplest way to clone a repository is to create an empty folder to house it, right-click the newly created folder, and choose Git Clone, which launches a new dialog. The first portion of the dialog is reserved for the location of the repository, whether local or remote. The default location is local, but it can be toggled to remote by selecting from the drop-down menu. If you're cloning a local repository, you can locate it by clicking the directory button and finding it on your system.

If you right-click an empty folder to clone a repository, the next field is already prefilled, because this is the location for the clone to live in your local system. You can change the location of the repository with the Browse button to the right of the field, if required. This is the minimum required to clone a repository. If the remote repository requires authentication, you're asked for the credentials after you click OK to confirm everything. The next screen shows information regarding the clone and how it's doing and, finally, a success message if everything goes according to plan.

Regardless of where your repository is located, or whether it's brand new, creating it is easy. Now it's time to look at a view that comes in very handy when you're working with the repository on a regular basis and that can speed up your workflow and ensure that all changes are treated correctly.

Checking for modifications

If you've had experience with TortoiseSVN, the Check for Modifications view will seem somewhat familiar, because it looks and works exactly the same. For those who haven't had the pleasure of seeing this view before, it allows you to see any changes that happen in the repository, from untracked files to removed files. You can close the view by clicking OK, refresh the current directory to check for changes, and commit changes. Each of the different file states has different options in its right-click menu, such as the ability to add untracked files, ready to be committed by clicking the Commit button.

Now it's time to look into the management of the repository and how to handle the files in it.

Adding, deleting, reverting, and committing

Adding files from outside the Check for Modifications view is easy: right-click the unversioned file, and select Add from the TortoiseGit menu. Selecting this option brings up a dialog listing the untracked files that have been clicked. Select the file you wish to add, and then click the Add button. This adds the file to a list of files to be committed, so when you choose to make your next commit, this particular file is included.

Deleting files is also a very simple process that can be done, once again, from the right-click menu. The TortoiseGit menu includes two delete options: Delete and "Delete (keep local)," which lets you remove files. The latter option should remove the file from being tracked but not remove it; however, it may not work and may cause TortoiseGit to crash. The former option simply deletes the file and prevents future changes from being tracked (after it's committed, of course).

If you delete a file and change your mind, you can get the file back before a commit is done, thanks to the power of reverting. To access this wonderful option, right-click some free space in the repository and, in the TortoiseGit menu, choose the Revert option. This opens a dialog addressing the changes that have been made in the repository since the last commit, from deleting files to editing files.

Committing changes in TortoiseGit is also very, very simple. Whether it's from the Check for Modifications dialog, from the right-click menu, or even from the success message when you add a file, this application gives you many opportunities to commit your files—there are Commit buttons all over the place. No matter which method you go for, when you commit your changes a new dialog launches, which lets you enter a commit message and select which files to include in the commit from the bottom of the application.

Pulling, pushing, and Sync

Since I'm talking about having buttons everywhere, another button that is conveniently placed is the Push button located in the commit success dialog. This opens the same dialog that you can access by right-clicking empty space in the application and choosing the TortoiseGit menu. This again only works if the repository has been cloned from another source, so bear that in mind when you're attempting to push changes.

It's also advisable to have your working copy up to date and fully committed before pushing, to ensure minimal conflicts and errors. All that is required when performing a push is choosing the location, which is preselected if you've cloned the repository, and clicking an OK button. This sends the changes to the remote server so they're available to everyone else with access to the repository.

Like pushing, pulling only works if you have a parent repository to pull changes from. It's also simple to perform and is located in the same menu. This time, select Pull from the menu, which launches a slightly different dialog. It still contains the familiar reference to the parent repository, but that's it for the basic pull request. This process pulls any new changes from the remote server to the local version of the repository and attempts to merge the changes with the local repository. As is the case with any pull request, the changes need to be committed before the pull is fully complete.

The Git Sync option provides a dialog that allows you to manage both push and pull requests. This window shows all changes that are to be pushed to the remote server so you can review them before any pushes are made. When you're happy with the changes, clicking one of the buttons launches that process in the

Sync window. This can come in handy if you need to perform multiple actions in a short period of time or want to consolidate the processes without needing to use several right-click commands.

Log

The Show Log option in the TortoiseGit menu lets you track previous commits in the repository. When the dialog opens, you're greeted with the list of previous commits in the top half of the window. The bottom of the dialog contains all the changed files in the selected commit. Double-clicking a particular change shows you the changes in that commit compared to the previous version.

It's also possible to search through all the commits by entering a message in the text field at upper right in the dialog. This filters the commits based on the search; if no results are found, it defaults to displaying the working directory changes. In addition to filtering by text, you can search by different dates: if you know the approximate date of a commit, the From and To calendars let you to create a range to search within, which makes finding the specific commit you're after a lot easier.

TortoiseGit summary

This application lives up to the high standards set by its Mercurial and SVN counterparts by delivering an easy-to-use system with a great feature set. As it's a direct port of the SVN version of Tortoise, users moving from SVN to Git will find the process much easier; the two applications are remarkably similar in how they function. Even if you're unfamiliar with any of the other Tortoise applications, using TortoiseGit lets you get up and running with a Git repository quickly and with without a huge learning curve. If you're working on Windows and would like to avoid using the command line for a little while longer, check out TortoiseGit; you won't be disappointed.

Mac

Now it's time to dive in the world of pretty, shiny Git applications—it's a growing trend that most applications designed for the Mac these days are pretty sexy. There are a lot of programs you can use to manage your Git repositories, but some are better than others. This section goes through some of the top choices for users, and then you can make a decision about whether to use one that I cover, search for your own solution, or *gasp* dive into Terminal.

GitHub for Mac

As the name suggests, this application is GitHub's own answer to the best GUI to use when managing Git repositories. Because it's developed by GitHub, it has a potentially big issue: you can only push to remote repositories hosted on GitHub. If you have a GitHub account, this shouldn't be much of a problem until the issue of keeping your code private comes in, but I talk about that in Chapter 11.

If you're happy to store your code on GitHub, then this application is prefect: it streamlines the workflow for pushing and pulling changes, and it's really specific to GitHub as a hosted solution. Of course, you can use the application without GitHub being in the picture; it still manages any local changes to repositories for you, but when it comes to pushing changes to a remote location, you need use a different method if that location isn't GitHub. Let's get straight into it and go over getting the application onto your Mac and linking it with your GitHub account.

Download and installation

The process of downloading and installing this lovely application is rather simple. The first thing to do is head over to `http://mac.github.com/` to download a copy. The Download link is a big orange button—you can't miss it. When you run the application for the first time, you're asked to fill in some basic information, which is used when making commits; however, if you already have Git configured with a name and e-mail, this information is already filled in.

There is also an option to install the CLI for the application to allow it to be launched from the command line. Clicking this button requires you to enter your password to confirm the installation, but that's it. Although this is an optional step in the installation, there is no real reason to skip it, as it may come in handy at a later date.

The next stage of the installation is to enter your GitHub information to allow for remote repositories to be created and for all your repositories currently hosted on GitHub to be easily cloned. You can skip this step; however, doing so means you can't push any changes to remote repositories from within the application. If you don't have a GitHub account, the installation supplies a link to allow the easy creation of a brand-new account. What do you have to lose?

Repository view

The Repository view is where all your repositories live. With a couple of clicks, you can manage them with ease. On the left side of the screen, you can see your own computer's repository and, if you set it up, a link to your GitHub account that houses all the repositories you currently have hosted on GitHub. While in the GitHub view, if you have a repository that currently isn't cloned on your computer, you have an option to clone it with one click. Clicking the Clone button prompts you to pick a location on your system for the clone to live, and the clone is complete. Easy.

Going into the My Repositories option shows all cloned repositories and any local repositories that have been added to the application are listed here. Any GitHub clones are identified because their name is prefixed with your GitHub username and a forward slash.

Creating a repository

Creating a new repository in the application is easy. The New Repository button opens a dialog that asks you to pick a name, description, and location for the new repository on your system—pretty standard stuff.

An additional option is a check box appropriately labeled Push to GitHub.com. If you select it, you have the option to pick whether the repository is private and the account to be pushed to. At the bottom of the screen, you see some information regarding the number of private repositories still available on your account, which helps keep you updated on your account status. If you try to keep the private repository option selected when you don't have any private repositories available, you're prompted by an error when you click Create Repository to complete the process.

Whether or not you decide to push the repository to GitHub doesn't affect the outcome of creating the repository in the application. Either way, you're taken back to the Repository view where your newly created repository is waiting for you. If you were to click the plus at the bottom of the screen you would go through the same process, starting from a different location.

There are also other ways to create a new repository in the application. Thanks to its drag-and-drop functionality, you can drag an existing Git repository or a project you would like to manage with Git straight into the Repository view. There's also a box at lower left in the application that suggests you drag the folders there, but really it's the same process.

Managing a repository

Whichever method you used to create your repository in GitHub for Mac, managing the repository is done the same way. When you want to manage a repository, double-click it to head into the main management view for the repository. If you happen to click the wrong repository, or you just want to switch to another one, you can either click the Repositories option at the top of the application or press Cmd+1 to get back to the Repository view. In the management screen, you can use four different views to manage your repository; let's go through each of them in more detail.

History

This view is at the top of the left navigation in the management screen, and as it suggests, it shows you the history of the repository you're currently managing. The list has the most recent changes at the top, going down in descending order and continuing until it reaches the very first commit. To help with load time, not all changes are loaded at the same time—more commits are loaded as you near the bottom of the list.

Instead of overcrowding the UI of the application with all the information from the commits, the app hides this in each of the commits. So, double-clicking a commit makes its contents available to you. In each commit, you can see the changes that were included in the commit on a per-file basis that includes syntax highlighting to make everything a bit easier to understand.

In addition, each commit includes "Revert commit" and "Rollback to this commit" options that are somewhat similar in their function. The former reverts the files included in the commit to the state they were in before the commit took place but doesn't affect any of the changes since the commit. This is used in instances when something has been committed by mistake and needs to be reverted. The latter option reverts all changes since this commit and restores your working copy to this particular commit. This allows you to branch off and make some extreme changes while having a particular commit as the parent when it comes time to merge things back in.

Changes

This view is where all the main action happens: it's where you can manage your files and then do that all-important commit to set the changes in stone, so to speak. In the Changes view, you can see all the changed files in the repository that need to be committed, including untracked files, changed files, and so on. The first item that is noticeable in this view is a Commit Message field and an optional Description field which shows if you click into the commit field. The commit message is required and is used to give a general overview of what is included in the commit; the description is optional but ideally contains a more detailed account of the changes that are being committed and any other helpful information.

The reason this view is so simple is due to how GitHub for Mac works. Unlike some other applications, all the management of the files is done from outside the app. For example, if you want to delete a file, you do that from Finder or in your editor of choice. There also isn't an option to remove or edit files from within the application, to ensure that the process is as simple as possible. You can, however, revert the changes you've made back to the most recent version of the commit from within the application, as well as ignore the file during future tracking or reveal it in Finder, all from the right-click menu of each commit.

It's also possible to show any changes that have been made to the file from the previous commit by clicking either the Expand All button or the double arrows to the right of each commit. For text files, you see new additions to the file in green and items removed in red; however, for binary file types, you can't see any differences. That's a slight disadvantage to the diffing system, but it's still a good way of seeing differences in commits, which makes life a lot easier.

Branch

Although I haven't been through branching fully yet, the way this application handles the process is simple and very easy to use. If the repository you're managing has never had any new branches created, then you see only one branch here: Master. This is the default branch for Git repositories, so seeing it as the only one listed is perfectly normal. Creating a branch is simple: pick the branch you want to branch off from, click the plus icon in the upper right of the branch to open a text field where you can enter the name of the branch, and click Branch, and the new branch is created. To switch to a new or existing branch, double-click it, and it becomes the active branch.

Merging two branches is also a very easy process in GitHub for Mac. To show the method of merging branches in the application, click the Merge View button, which slides down to reveal a new top portion of the window consisting of two boxes that contain the branches you want to merge. You can now drag and drop the branches into the Merging section of the screen to merge them. The left branch is merged into the right branch, so in most cases the right branch is the main branch. Whenever you have two branches in their respective boxes, the text at the top of the screen explains clearly what's happening, such as

```
Merging Branch into Master
```

It also estimates how many potential conflicts this will cause, which you hope is 0. When you're happy, click the Merge Branches button to start and finish the process. After the merge has completed, you need to head back into the Changes view and commit any needed changes before the process is fully complete.

Settings

The Settings tab is the last one available in the main view in the application. It offers only two options: a link to the remote repository, if you happen to have one set up already (otherwise it's blank) and a rather large Git Ignore text area where you can enter files and extensions that should be ignored and not tracked. Normally, this would need to be done manually in the .gitignore file, but this interface saves you from having to do that and makes things a lot easier when it comes to managing the repository without using Terminal.

Syncing, and pushing to GitHub

This is another large part of the application that lets you push updates to and pull updates from GitHub with ease. Rather than the push and pull functions being separate, this application uses one Sync option. This prevents you from missing changes, because performing a sync both pulls and pushes the needed changes between the local repository and GitHub. The option to sync your repository with its remote GitHub repository is located at upper right on the screen and is labeled Sync Branch. When clicked, this option runs a push and a pull in the background to ensure that everything is kept up to date. You need to have your working copy fully committed before you can run the sync, though.

If you've created a brand-new repository, you don't have a link with GitHub yet. In this case, the Sync Branch button is replaced with one that allows you to push all the changes in your local repository to a repository stored on GitHub, created from within the application. Clicking the button opens an overlay where you can name the repository, give it a description, and indicate whether it'll be a private repository. Either way, click Push Repository to create the repository on GitHub and push all the changes to it.

GitHub for Mac summary

This application manages to keep simplicity at a high level without reducing features or usability. It has a limitation in its association with GitHub, because it lacks the option to push changes to any other service. Of course, GitHub would never allow this, since it made the application, and it wouldn't want its application used for another service. If you do use GitHub on a regular basis, this app is definitely worth checking out: it's fast, easy to use, and remarkable powerful. It does seem to lag a little if you keep switching between multiple repositories, but that depends on your system and the size of the repository.

You can use this application for the day-to-day management of your local repository without using the syncing aspect. This can be achieved by using another application to push, or even diving into Terminal and making the push there. If you try the application and like how it works, there is an easy enough way to add it your workflow. So regardless of which service you use, give this application a try; you'll find how easy it is to use very appealing indeed.

Tower

If you've worked with Git before on a Mac, or thought about working with Git on a Mac, then odds are you've heard of Tower. Thanks to its great features and ease of use, Tower has become very popular and is used by people in some very well-known organizations, such as Apple, Google, Nokia, and Twitter. Even without knowing all its features, if big companies like that are using it, it must be good!

Installing Tower

Getting your copy of Tower is easy and starts by heading over to www.git-tower.com/. Here, you can either buy the app straight up for around $60 or download a 30-day trial by clicking the yellow "Download trial" button. When the download completes, you have a Zip folder containing Tower; unzip it and drag it into your Applications folder, and you're ready to go.

Creating repositories

Let's dive right in with creating repositories. It's become a standard of version control apps to allow you to add an existing repository or create one on your local system, which Tower does with ease. You can create a blank repository by clicking Create Local Repository to launch a dialog where you add a location for the repository to live and a description. There is also an option to make the repository bare, which is necessary when you want to create a parent-child relationship (the bare repository is the parent). Once you're happy with everything, click OK; the blank repository is created on your system and added into the list of available repositories in Tower.

It's just as easy to add an existing repository into Tower so you can take advantage of the app's huge feature set. To add the existing repository, click the Add Local Repository button, which asks you to locate the repository on your system and give it a name. When you've done this, click OK, and your repository is added straight into the list of repositories available for you to manage. Easy.

In Tower, it's also possible to create repositories on both GitHub and Beanstalk with the click of a button. No matter which option you choose, you need to enter a name, a description for the repository, and the credentials required to connect to the specified account. Click the specific button for the service you'd like to connect to, and that's it. After you've created the account, you're asked if you'd like to clone the newly created repository, by specifying a location and a short name, but you can choose to create the repository and not clone it. Since I'm talking about cloning repositories, let's look at that in a little more detail.

Cloning repositories

You can clone a remote repository from any location within Tower as easily as you can create a new one. To start things off, click the Clone Remote Repository link to launch a dialog in which you enter the URL of your repository, a name and location for it, as well as any credentials needed to connect to it. After you're happy with everything, click the OK button. The repository is cloned onto your local system in the location specified and added to the list of available repositories.

A quick tour

When you double-click a repository, you're taken into the main Tower window, which lets you do all the cool stuff that makes Tower the powerhouse it is. You can perform a lot of actions, but each of the features gets applied in one main view, which you look at in more detail next.

Status

This view is where a load of the action happens and is the default view you see when you head into the main window of Tower. Any file changes you make are shown here: edited, deleted, and new files are all included in this view. Depending on the status of the files, different icons make it easy to identify which changes have been made. Thanks to a useful Stage All button above the tabs, you can easily add all your changes and unversioned files ready to commit.

In addition to showing the status of files, the application also gets a badge on the Cmd+Tab menu, showing you how many files you have ready to commit. This helps to make sure changes are always committed. And thanks to Tower refreshing itself all the time, the changes are shown on the Cmd+Tab menu immediately.

When it comes to committing the file changes, you don't have far to go. The commit options are on the right side of this window: you can enter a subject for the commit, which is a quick summary of the commit, and a detailed description of the files. Although you can't commit from here, it really helps when adding the commit message, because you can see all the changes you've made and keep adding to the description without the fear of losing the message.

In this view you can also see the changes that have occurred in the files you're committing by simply clicking the file and selecting Unstaged, Staged, Base, or Current. These views allow you to see various changes. Base lets you compare the changes on the current version and how it was after the last commit; in some of the views you can also use an external comparison tool to see the changes in a different way.

Commits

The Commits view holds the history of your repository, which can be navigated using a couple of views: Recent and List. The former lets you see the message for each commit as well as a photo of the user (if they have one), a date, and a check-box option to show the files included with the commit. The latter gives you a less expansive list of the commits associated with the repository, but you can see a lot more on the screen, and a graph shows the branching and merging history in the repository.

Regardless of which view you decide to work in, the right-click menu is the same and offers a decent list of options. In addition to being able to roll back to a particular commit, create a patch from the commit, or even revert back to the commit, you can open the commit in a new window to see the changes in more detail. This option launches a dialog that shows the information for whomever committed the code, any messages used, and, if you'd like to see it, a view of all the files changes included in the commit.

While in the List view, you can also filter the results by entering a particular range. The available options for this are two commit hashes or two dates. Either option shows a smaller and more select range of commits to ensure that you find what you're looking for.

Browse

The final view Browse, which gives you the ability to look at the full file system associated with a commit so you can see it as a whole rather than on a per-file basis. By using the drop-down menu at the top of the window, you can select between commits or search for a particular one by entering a string to search against. In this view it's also possible to restore deleted files using the right-click menu, as well as view the file or save it as something else; this can come in handy when you're looking for particular versions of files or recovering an incorrectly deleted file.

Pulling and pushing changes

Tower makes a point of ensuring that pulling and pushing changes is as easy as possible, and it also allows you to perform a Fetch command whenever you'd like. You've already been through what pulling and pushing are, several times, but fetching may be unfamiliar. Fetching allows you to check for remote changes but not make any changes to your local version of the repository, so you can see if you're going to run into conflicts, if you can safely update before a feature you're working is complete, and so on.

The Pull dialog, triggered by clicking the Pull button, lets you click OK to pull any changes from the remote repository and add them to your local copy. It's also possible to perform a rebase when you pull changes from the remote repository by selecting that in the options menu. Another option gets information from all remote branches; this is selected by default. If this option is unchecked, the pull only fetches changes from the specified branch, so it's best to keep this check box selected.

Pushing is as easy as pulling, with a dialog that is just as simple. One option is the ability to force-push, which you should do with extreme caution. Force-pushing has the potential to break the remote repository, because if you can't push normally, there's most likely a reason. If you want to push your changes, click the OK button, and your changes are whisked away to the remote server.

Merging, committing, and rebasing

The merging interface for Tower isn't the best in comparison to some other applications, but it does the job. The Merge dialog, which as you can imagine you open by clicking the Merge button, is simple, as you've come to expect from the other dialogs you've looked at. The merge relies on you being in the branch you would like to merge into; if you're not, you can always change your current branch by double-clicking the specified branch in the left sidebar.

Once you're in the correct repository, select the branch you'd like to merge into your current one from the drop-down menu provided. You can also specify whether to merge all the changes with one large commit or squish the commits and whether to commit immediately after the merge. Either of these options can aid your merging process, but they are optional. When you're happy, click OK, and the merge begins.

Committing changes in Tower is as easy as you'd want it to be. Click the Commit button to get started when it's not grayed out, which is only in the Status view. If you've already entered a commit message in this view, the Commit view is prepopulated with those values, which saves you having to re-create the message.

The only additional options available when committing are signing off the commit by appending your name and e-mail address to the end of the commit message, and amending the commit by adding it to the end of the previous commit. The latter can come in handy when you have a change that you would rather have associated with a commit you just made. Either way, when you're happy, click OK, and your changes are committed.

Rebasing is similar to merging two branches, in that you do in fact merge two branches. The fundamental difference with a rebase is how it's performed. If you rebase a branch into your current branch, it brings in the changes from the other branch, as if you had just done an update. I know you're thinking "What about my changes?" Well, they're safe, don't worry. Once the changes from the other branch have been brought into your current branch, your changes are added to the end, as new commits. When it comes to reviewing your changes, it'll seem like you hadn't had a branch at all, and the changes were made within the main branch as normal commits. .

Whether to rebase your changes rather than merge them is a preference more than anything else, and it gives the advantage of making your changes go in one big line rather than two branches merged together.

You may want to perform a rebase when you're working on a new feature in your web site or application or doing some bug fixes. If there are only a couple of commits in the branch, and it was never pushed to the remote repository, then rather than committing the branch or merging it back in, you can rebase the branch in your working copy; it's as if the branch never existed, and all the commits from the branch are added into the working copy seamlessly.

Stash

I've mentioned Git Stash before in Chapter 3, and the way it works in Tower is no exception. In case you're a little unsure about the whole Stash thing, it works like this. Suppose you're working on a new feature that is only half complete, and you don't want to commit it because it'll cause issues with anybody who updates the code and may cause bigger problems. While you're working away to finish the new feature, a member of your team comes steaming over and asks for a major favor.

Apparently some work for the company web site wasn't fully finished, and the boss is going to go off if he finds out. This puts you in a bad position: you can't commit the new change for the web site now, because the feature you're working on isn't finished. Enter Stash! Rather than discard the changes, you can stash them instead. Doing so puts all your changes into a directory in the .git folder in the repository, where they're safe. After the stash is complete, your code is back its base state, as it was after your last commit. Now you can quickly add the missing feature to the web site before the boss finds out, saving both you and your colleague. To get your changes back, select the stash and apply it, and you're back where you were before. Great, eh?

Tower makes this very simple with Stash and Apply Stash buttons. To stash your changes, click the button and enter a message. Although the message is optional, I advise adding one, in case you have more than one stash (which you can do, by the way). After you save the stash, your working copy says there are no local changes, which is what you want.

To get back your stashed work, click the Apply Stash button, select the stash from the list, and click OK. This applies the stash to your working copy again. Now you're back to how you were before the stash happened, as easy as that. When you need to make quick fixes, stashing can be a godsend and save you from doing ridiculous hacks on the live server or having to use someone else's machine to perform the commit.

Tower summary

This application can make using Git a whole lot easier on the Mac, and if you haven't taken advantage of the 30 free trial, you should. You have a lot of power with some very simple actions when using Tower, and it makes you appreciate the time and effort that when into writing the application and making it to the standard it is now. Although It comes in with a single license fee of around $60 for the features it brings to the table it comes as more of an investment than anything else. It also happens to be a very easy to use application that isn't that bad on the eyes either. If you haven't used Tower yet, you need to head on over to http://www.git-tower.com/ to download the trial to see all the features for yourself, you won't regret it.

SourceTree

If you've been reading this chapter as a whole, you've been over SourceTree before, because it works exactly the same way for Git as it does for Mercurial. The interface for dealing with your Git repository changes ever so slightly and adds a new option, Fetch. If you want to use SourceTree for Mercurial, please refer to the Mercurial section and then come here to find out about the Git-specific options.

Fetch

The Fetch option allows you to check for changes on the remote repository without actually committing to the update. In reality, it's for those instances when you would rather be extremely cautious about pulling changes, maybe because you've just done some major development work and you'd like to avoid the potential pain of conflicts. Clicking the Fetch button makes SourceTree run off to the remote repository and check to see if there are any available updates. If there are, it reports back and updates the badge on the Pull button, showing the number of changes available to pull down.

The other switch from the Mercurial UI Is the renaming of Shelve to the familiar Stash, which as you know works the same way. It allows you to place any uncommitted changes in your local copy and add them into a stash file to be retrieved later. This lets you clean up your local repository and ask for updates to be pulled from the server without conflicts, or commit a quick fix without disrupting your workflow too much.

Git summary

This section of the chapter has covered Git GUI, TortoiseGit, GitHub for Mac, and Tower, which are great applications. There are others, but these are some of the best.

If you've used any of the other Tortoise applications, you have come to expect the level of quality they offer, and TortoiseGit is no exception. This application is great and lets you manage Git without needing to get your hands dirty at the command line. You can also install it alongside other applications without it interfering, so you can use it when you want to make a quick commit or clone a repository. I would say that it has the edge over Git GUI, which isn't the best applications but does keep you out of the command line, which is what you want. You can also combine the use of the two applications to allow for the benefits of Git GUI with the flexibility and ease-of-use of TortoiseGit.

On the Mac side of things you have GitHub for Mac and Tower, two awesome applications. If you're working regularly with GitHub, I can't recommend this application enough; it flows well and makes working with remote repositories really simple. It also bring a lot of great features from GitHub down to the application level, which makes it that much better to use. It does have a limitation of only being able to work with GitHub remote repositories, which is a shame, but given that the application was created by GitHub, it's no surprise. That doesn't strike out Tower, though. It has made a name for itself by being easy to use and having a lot of features on offer. If you happen to be working on a few remote systems, then definitely give Tower a try; it's so simple to use that is makes working with Git that much easier, even for those who are new to the field.

Summary

You've been through a lot of applications in this chapter, from stand-alone apps to contextual menu applications to those that use both, Although not all the applications mentioned will be for you, at least one of them may have sparked an interest—or at least that's the idea. But you may be thinking, "These applications aren't for me. I want to get straight into Terminal!" In that case, I say wait for Chapter 9—you'll love it.

At the very least, one of these applications should be able to ease you into version control in the easiest way possible, using some of the best GUI applications available, or maybe whet your appetite for playing in Terminal. Now, though, it's time to explore what you can't version control and how best to handle certain kinds of files.

Chapter 6

You Mean I Can Version Control Everything?!

Now that we've been through some of the best programs to use for SVN, Mercurial, and Git, I'm sure you're excited about having a safe backup of your files, and that you can version pretty much anything. In some cases, though, that wouldn't be the best approach, especially for certain kinds of files. We're about to go though some cases when you really shouldn't use versioning systems on some files. We will cover some options for these files and some potential solutions for versions of some bigger and more troubling files.

Why version control isn't the solution for some files

Having a versioning system in place for some files is a great idea, as we've already talked about, but in some cases, it really, really isn't. Let's dive straight in here with an example, shall we? While a website is in production, you may need to upload files to certain pages or sections, either to help with the content editing or because that's the best solution to show said content. Let's assume you're uploading 20 images while the site is in production, and these need to be transferred to a new server for the launch of the site, a standard occurrence with content-driven websites. The easiest option to deploy the site would be to add all these files into the repository you're using, and then just do a checkout or an export when you want to go live. This does work, of course, but it's not the ideal way to transfer the files. If you added all the images/files that were uploaded by the client into the repository, it would be huge in no time, and for no good reason.

The point I'm making is that uploading one-off files into a repository can in some cases be totally avoided by methods such as compressing all of the files into a zipped file of some description, such as a .zip or tar.gz file. With the compressed file you would then transfer it to the new location, unzip it, and there you are. This will increase the speed of the repository, because it'll have less information in it, and it'll stop strange conflicts that would occur if you tried to upload the folder and there was a file name clash, for example. If a site is already in production and you need to push a new theme, you may have a test.jpg file that was used during your production, but when the files are pushed, it turns out the file already exists on the server because the client has used it. The result is that you need to rename the file and change the link to it in the code—that is, unless you know you're replacing the file that already exists, in which case you can just delete it then continue to check out the new code.

That's not to say putting all your files into a versioning system isn't possible. You can quite happily add all of the images or documents you'd like into the repository. This will carry some negatives with it, though; it'll just increase the size of the repository for the remainder of the project, when those files will most likely not be updated again and will just sit in the repository, doing nothing. Plus, it'll slow down any checkouts done either for development or production because of the repository's increased size.

The same goes for files such as music and video files. These, of course, may need to be versioned for whatever reason, such as if you decided to use version control for backing up your music or photo collection or maybe even your whole user account on your computer. The majority, if not all, of these files will be one-offs, so they'll never be changed or updated while they're being backed up. You could, of course, use SVN, Mercurial, or Git to back up everything, but it's not really the best solution. In these cases, it's better to look up into the clouds for a solution, in the form of cloud storage.

Cloud storage

When something is stored in the *cloud*, in reality it's being stored in a remote location which is (hopefully) safe from crashes and securely backed up. The main distinction being that it's in a remote location, not on your machine, so you can access it in multiple locations, and if your machine breaks down your data won't have changed. The cloud itself isn't actually one central location accessed by a number of services, but more the idea that your data is stored in a location that can be accessed from anywhere (provided you have an Internet connection) and is most likely located firmly on the ground.

Nowadays, the market is inundated with cloud storage solutions. Here are a few I've worked with and a little bit about them. Cloud storage is great, because you can back up pretty much anything you want, and then it's safe. How safe, though, can be very vague in some cases, depending on the provider you have chosen to guard your precious data. If it's not fully encrypted, then they (the service) can openly look through your data, which means if they see something naughty, they can potentially freeze your account and you will no longer be able to access your files. This isn't a common thing, but before you sign up to a service, it's worth checking that they encrypt the data and that they won't go looking through it unless you give them explicit permission. If you've picked a provider you know your data is safe with, you may have access to files on the move, the ability to play your stored music, or access to a multitude of other features. With that said, here are a few of those services.

zovo

The first cloud storage provider I'll go over is zovo, which offers a number of services to satisfy your data storage needs. You can find zovo online at `http://zovo.co`, or you can just look at Figure 6-1 which shows the website itself.

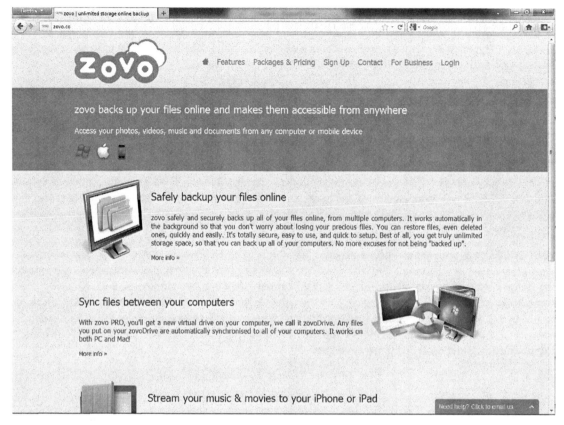

Figure 6-1. The zovo home page shows at a glance the services it offers and the platforms it works on.

In terms of cloud systems, zovo is quite new on the market, only opening its doors to the public in July 2011. If you were one of its early adopters, then may have been able to bag yourself a free account. However, if you weren't so lucky, you'll have to pick from one of the two price plans, zovo backup or zovo pro. Both accounts boast truly unlimited backup and bandwidth, a web portal for viewing files, mobile access, and the ability to sync your music, photos, and videos to an iPad/iPhone. It also has a hidden gem, a versioning system! You can see up to 30 versions of a file, and you also have the ability to revert back to a previous version. For a backup system, that's pretty damn sweet. Oh, and did I mention all data is encrypted? The data on the server is encrypted with your unique key and can only be unlocked when you're logged in either online or on one of your unlimited linked machines.

The lesser of the two packages retails for $31 per year and you still get all the nifty features I mentioned earlier. The ultimate package goes for $77 per year, and for the extra cash you get a shared folder you can access on all machines that is synced across all your machines for the files you use most often. You also get online document editing, the ability to back up photos from Facebook, Flickr, SmugMug and a whole lot of other services. You also get FTP access, one-click sharing for files and folders, priority support, and the ability to e-mail files as attachments to your zovo account.

Although it's quite a young service, you get a lot of bang for your buck. With unlimited backup and syncing to the iPhone/iPad, zovo gives you a lot of control of your data, especially with the web portal. It has a whole load of potential, and for less than $31 a year, you can't really go wrong. So if this has tickled your fancy a little bit, then check out `http://zovo.co` to sign up for an account.

Amazon Cloud Drive

This service is the cloud storage offering from the e-commerce giant, Amazon, geared toward big companies with big storage needs.

Everyone knows Amazon in some way or another, whether it's from their web services or the online super store. You may or may not be aware of Amazon Simple Storage Service, or as it's more commonly known, Amazon S3. In its raw form, Amazon S3 is more for companies who need to store special data online in a globally accessible place, but they've released a simple storage solution for the consumer, called Amazon Cloud Drive.

With Cloud Drive, you can get a free account that can hold 5GB, which is pretty sweet, and which gets linked to your Amazon account. Amazon cloud storage has a great advantage: any music you buy through the Amazon store is backed up to your cloud drive, for free. So if you went for the 5GB account, you could have 25GB of music, all backed up at no extra charge, and you would still have the 5GB to use for whatever you want. You can have a look at the dashboard for the service in Figure 6-2. The dashboard allows you to browse the files and folders you have stored within Amazon Cloud Drive and perform actions like downloading and deleting the files or folders.

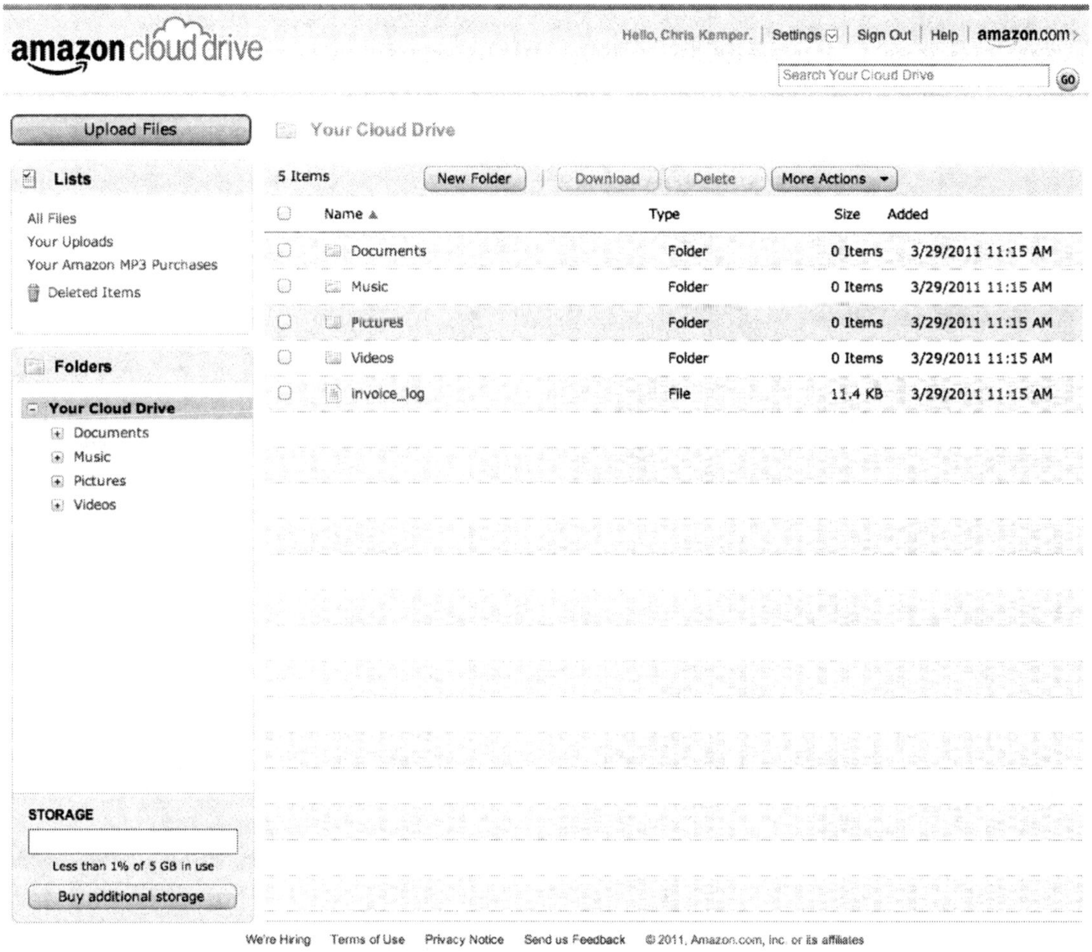

Figure 6-2. The dashboard available when you log into your Amazon Cloud Drive account, where you can manage your files and a whole lot more

This being Amazon (a name you can trust), when they say it's safe online storage, then you know it's safe! That being said, no matter how creditable the name, there is still the potential for things to go wrong. Sony learned that the hard way when the PSN network was hacked and precious user data was stolen. Sadly, though, with Cloud Drive you don't get any fancy desktop apps or sharing services; all access is through the web panel. You do, however, get Amazon Cloud Player, which allows you to play all your uploaded tunes through a browser on a number of devices, including iPhone/iPad, Android, and a range of other devices. The web interface, however, gets you access to your files from any machine, so you can always get that vital file you need while on the go.

Sadly, compared to the standard S3 services it's not all good news. It's not pay as you go. If you opt for a certain package, then you need to commit to that package. Although that's not a bad thing, for some people who are used to using S3, it's a disadvantage. Still, for most people it's still a pretty sweet deal. From 5GB you can go all the way up to 1000GB for $1000 per year. That's a pretty hefty amount of storage, but I'm pretty sure you could fill it.

Another negative for Amazon Cloud Drive is buried in its terms of service, which reads

> *You give us the right to access, retain, use and disclose your account information and Your Files; to provide you with technical support and address technical issues; to investigate compliance with the terms of this Agreement, enforce the terms of this Agreement and protect the Service and its users from fraud or security threats; or as we determine is necessary to provide the Service or comply with applicable law.*

So by agreeing, you give Amazon the right to look at your files and information, and potentially close your account, which is a bit crazy. Then again, if you have nothing to hide, they have no reason to take action, right? Wrong. There have been some cases of accounts being incorrectly closed thanks to Amazon's monitoring software picking up false positives and thinking innocent users were infringing their end-user license agreement (EULA), so it's something to bear in mind. However, if you're after a cheap backup service that does the job, then Cloud Drive could be just what you're looking for. Head over to `www.amazon.com/clouddrive/` to get more information and sign up.

ZumoDrive

Another offering in the cloud storage market is ZumoDrive. It gives you the option to upload your, well, everything into the drive, which you can access across all of your devices. This can be a great advantage when using something along the lines of a netbook or mobile device which has limited storage, so you then stream everything you need from the cloud. If you want to use a file when you're offline, you can set it to remain on your device or computer so you can make changes to it offline, then chuck it back up to the cloud when you're online again. You can find out more at `http://zumodrive.com` or, if you don't fancy heading to the site, you can just look at Figure 6-3 to get a taste of the website.

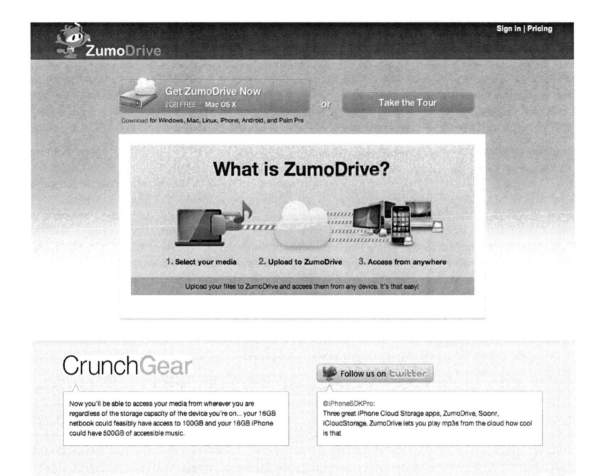

Figure 6-3. The ZumoDrive homepage gives an overview of the concept of the site and how it works.

In addition to the ability to put all your files on all your devices, you also get a few other nifty features with ZumoDrive. When it comes to music, ZumoDrive can add all of your music to your iTunes app, while the music is actually stored in the cloud. Then, your music simply streams from the cloud when you want to play it. Pretty sweet! You also get the ability to share files and folders with your friends or colleagues, which can be an advantage when it comes to collaborating. You also get a nifty feature that allows you to link any folder to your ZumoDrive, while it's in a normal location in your system. This means you won't need to move your commonly used folders into the ZumoDrive, just link them up and they'll be put in the drive for access on other machines! That's a huge advantage because your machine won't be dependent on the cloud to get the files, since they live in a normal location on the machine; when changes happen, they'll be clouded, and that's that.

Another feature you get with ZumoDrive is revisions. This, of course, is what we've been coming to terms with throughout the course of the book. As you can expect, you get all the previous versions of the file, with the option to revert. However, you don't get the ability to see the differences between text files, which could cause a problem when it comes to deciding what you need to revert to. The only issue with this is that revisions go toward your size quota, so if you make a few changes to a PSD or another large file, you could use your storage up in no time. You can, however, turn off revisions to give you a bit more control over your space, but then, you don't have revisions.

You may be a little curious now about the price point for this great service. You do get the option of a free account, where you get 1GB of space, with an additional 1GB if you complete the training section of the site. You also get the ability to gain more space by inviting more users to use the service, so if someone you invite installs ZumoDrive on their computer, then you get an extra 256MB. You can do this a total of 20 times to give you 5GB of potential extra storage. For the paid options, the largest option available is 500GB for $79.99 a month. Compared to some other services, this might seem quite expensive, and for some, not really enough space to justify the cost. Some of the features, however, such as linking folders, revisions, music streaming, and having your files on all your devices, can be quite tempting. If you're one of the tempted ones, head over to `http://zumodrive.com` to check out the packages, or if you're feeling generous, use this link and help me out getting some space `http://zumo.cc/dr/dir/1cqBZjRiZj`.

Dropbox

Dropbox is a cloud storage service which gives you a unified folder on your machine which you can use for multiple users, and that you can share with multiple users. It's one of the document leaders when it comes to cloud storing and sharing because of its quality service. You can also have a sneaky look at the default dashboard by checking out Figure 6-4.

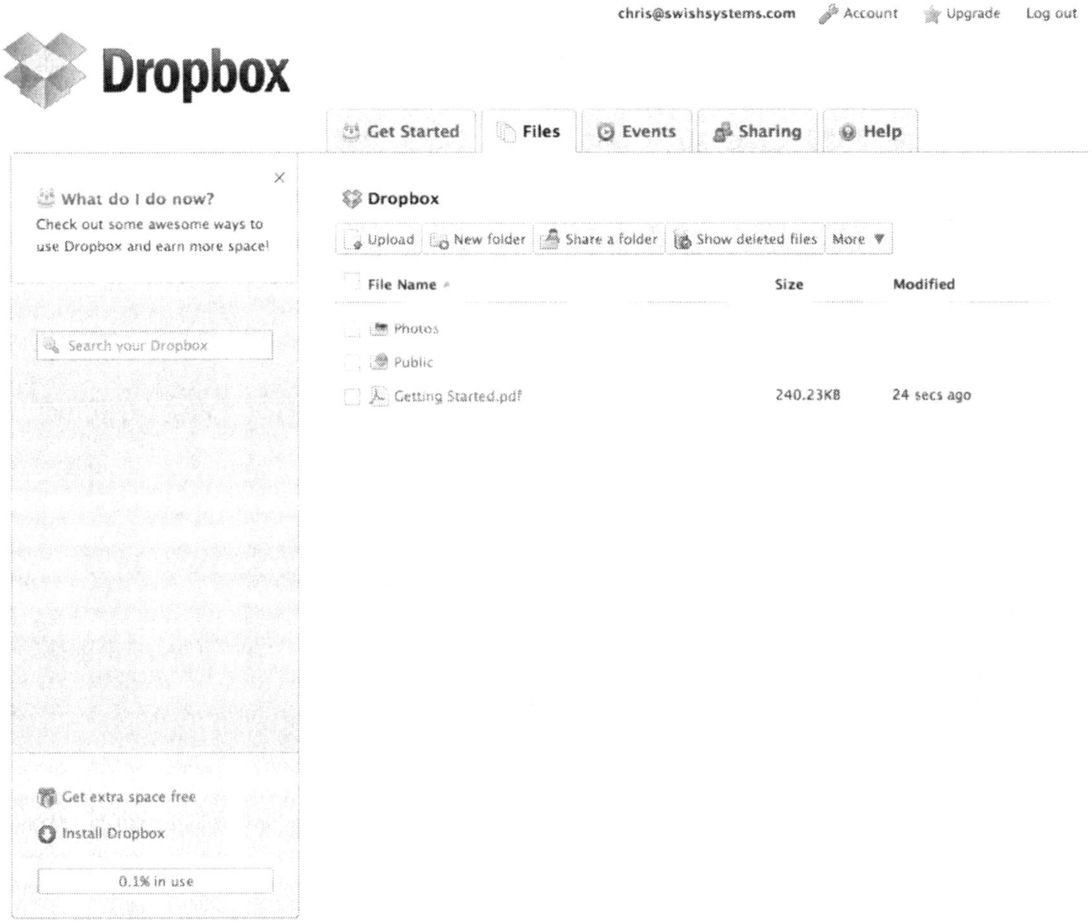

Figure 6-4. The Dropbox dashboard with a fresh account, where you can manage your files and your account

If you look at it, Dropbox doesn't actually have that many features—instead of spreading itself thin, it does what it does very well. Dropbox's main goal is sharing files with different people or computers. So if you change a folder on your laptop, within seconds that same file will be updated on your desktop, iPhone, and on the Web. No matter how many people you share the folder with, or what operating system they're using, Dropbox will be synced in most cases within seconds, no matter if it's a new file or an updated one. This can be quite useful when it comes to collaboration with other people, or just knowing that the version of the file you're looking at is always the most up to date.

Dropbox, as with most cloud storage solutions, also supports versioning of files, for those times when someone gets on your machine and deletes a huge chunk of a document, or you just need to go back. As we've been through before, you can't put a price on having revisions at your disposal because they can be life savers at times.

A lot of different companies and users have found ways to make use of Dropbox's features to make their work or leisure lives a lot easier. Companies have found uses for Dropbox for collaborating on important documents that multiple people will need to work on, or for review before sending them out to the client. Some developers also choose to have their code stored inside Dropbox, so if they change machines or even work on someone else's, they always have their most up-to-date code with them at all times.

Dropbox has also been known to be a part of complex versioning workflows for distributed versioning systems so that everyone has a code base they can push and pull from, which is similar to a remote server. For single users, people have also been known to place pretty much all of their files into Dropbox so they're backed up and readily available from any location. This also makes migrating from one machine to another easy because all you need to do is install Dropbox and there are your files.

On the cost side of things, Dropbox does offer a free solution, which gives you 2GB of storage to get you started. To gain more space, you can also invite friends, which is always a good thing! The paid solutions are as follows: for $9.99 a month you can upgrade to pro 50, which gives you 50GB of total storage. If that's not enough, you can upgrade to pro 100, which, yes, you guessed it, gives you 100GB of storage for $19.99 a month.

The final option is the Dropbox for Teams option, which is designed for organizations and bulk users and boasts up to 350GB of storage. If you do decide to go for Teams, then you'll be looking at $795 per year, but with that you get a few changes. Instead of storage being on a per-person basis, you can pool storage into teams. This allows a full team to share a much larger pool of files than would otherwise be possible. It's also possible to buy more storage but it'll cost an additional $200 for another 100GB of storage. You do also get a little more control over the versions of the files stored in the team Dropbox, which allows more previous states, and what has happened in the history of the file, such as reverts or deletions.

Although Dropbox is pretty good to work with, and many people are fine using it to manage their files and code because it syncs and is automatically backed up, there are some negatives. If you're working in a small team with a shared dropbox, and one user puts some large files into the dropbox to share with the team, then be prepared to lose some Internet speed while the sync happens. Dropbox is a bit of a bandwidth hog when it needs to be; putting in too much data to be synced at one time can pretty much destroy your current workflow, so that's something to look out for.

Using Dropbox does introduce a problem of conflicts. If you want to work on files at the same time as someone else, you might need to duplicate the changes and name them something different. Otherwise, when one person saved, that would then be the newest version; there would be no merging or anything of that nature. That is a slight negative when it comes to using Dropbox for collaborative projects.

If you fancy checking out these features for yourself, head on over to `http://dropbox.com` to sign up for a free account. If you're feeling especially generous, use my referral link to help me out: `http://db.tt/teNWe1y`.

Visual versioning

Files such as PSDs and images can be stored using the previously mentioned methods, but it's not really ideal to do so due to their size, and unless you have a good bit of diff software, there's no real way to detect differences between the file versions. This doesn't mean you can't use SVN, Git, or Mercurial to version these, but it will result in a larger and slower repository, when it isn't necessarily needed. It will, however, keep all of your changes in one location, so it would be easy to share the assets with the other members of the team, without any extra effort. When it comes to versioning visual files, you need additional solutions other than cloud storage, and one of those solutions comes in the form of PixelNovel.

PixelNovel

This option is aimed straight at designers in the form of an Adobe Photoshop plug-in. Timeline from PixelNovel allows you to version your Photoshop file by integrating with SVN, to give you access to a repository for keeping your files safe. The plug-in creates a timeline of changes for the file you're working on, which is visible right inside of Photoshop. In addition to the visual timeline, you also get the ability to add the file you're working on into the repository, if it isn't currently there. You can also revert to previous versions from the plug-in, and you can check for updates as well, right from inside of Photoshop!

For the most efficient work environment, it may be a better idea to have a single repository for each visual project. This will help keep the file size down, and also decrease the number of files that are included in each repository, which makes management easier and reduces overhead. Working with multiple users may still cause problems with conflicts, though, because SVN won't be fully able to distinguish between the versions, determine where the conflicts reside, or even identify the major differences between the files.

Having a visual timeline of the file could be very helpful when it comes to the need to revert: you can avoid having to have multiple versions of the same file and just create different iterations of the same design in one file, just making them different versions of the same file. This will generally keep local storage a lot lower and make it a lot easier to manage because all versions would be in one file, instead of multiple ones.

Adobe Drive 3

While you may not be too familiar with what Adobe Drive actually is, you may be familiar with Adobe Version Cue. As of Adobe Creative Suite 5, Version Cue has been dropped and is no longer available with the newer creative suites. Before, it was a versioning tool for PSDs, PDFs, and other visual media and you could access it from Adobe Bridge. When you saved a file, you had the option to check in a new version of the file, and you could look at all the previous versions via Version Cue. There were some issues with it, one of which being the speed at which it worked. It was worse when you had Version Cue on your own machine, although you did have the option to set it up on a network, which would increase the speed and decrease the load on the local machine. Despite that, it was still quite resource intensive, regardless of whether or not it was set up on a local machine.

As for Adobe Drive 3 itself, it's a lot better than it used to be and has many more features. In previous versions, Adobe drive was used as an easier way to connect with Version Cue by making any server created on a local network a mounted drive you could drag and drop files to. Now, though, Adobe Drive does a lot more and works a lot better! It is a bit of a challenge to set up, though. Before you can make use of its features you need a Digital Asset Management Server (DAMS). Sadly, they aren't so easy to come by. Most solutions will cost you a few hundred dollars, which can be both a hosted solution and one you would install on your own server. Once you have that in place, you can then configure Adobe Drive to connect to it, and from then on, you have the features you'd expect from a versioning system. At the moment, Adobe Drive has only just come into development; not much help is available for it beyond the articles on the Adobe website, which aren't always clear. Hopefully when it's been out a while, the cost of Digital Asset Management will come down, which will make the service a lot more usable. Until then, if you're able to get it set up and don't mind the current cost of DAMSs, the features you get from it will outweigh its current minimal support.

You still get a nice feature set with Adobe Drive. In addition to the expected versioning of your files, you can also see the status of the file you're viewing. This shows whether the file is up to or out of date, has been checked out by someone else, or is unversioned. You can also see which user has been working on the revision, which we all know can come in useful. Of course, you also have the option to add comments when adding in new versions of files, which again comes in very useful when you're reviewing changes. This is all available right inside of Adobe Bridge, so if you've used it before there will only be a very small learning curve when it comes to using this software. If you want to give it a try, you can download the Adobe Drive app for free from the Adobe website, but you will also need Adobe Creative Suite and a DAM server. If you can find them all, you'll have a great versioning system for your visual assets.

Zoom

Yet another offering in the asset management market is Zoom from Evolphin. This guy is a machine, a fast-as-fudge machine! Zoom is a full-fledged asset management system, which covers all visual assets, and also covers the document versioning side of things as well. Zoom will also help you create complex workflows, which can take you as far as the user permission level. Once you have a bunch of files committed, you'll be able to quickly look between different versions of the file to spot differences. You can also revert to a previous version with just a few clicks, which can get you out of a tight bind in some cases. To make the collaboration process easier, Zoom also has notifications to inform you about any new versions or changes to a file you've been working on. This can make it a lot easier to know when to use a file, rather than having to check if there are updates available every five minutes.

Behind the scenes, Zoom is one fast and efficient beast. Saving multiple versions of the same file could take a huge amount of space, but Zoom stores just the changed pixels, which can lead to a huge amount of storage savings. In some cases you can use up to 2000 times less storage than with conventional versioning systems. Using this unique technology also means things move a lot faster, 50 times faster in some cases, which can make a mammoth difference when you're committing files on a regular basis.

Team management is very important to Zoom; you can get very granular control over users, breaking permissions down by team, user, or project. When you check out a project, you can't do anything outside the permission set of that project, so if you only have read access for that particular project, then all you can do is look at the pretty file. This really helps to stop users making unwanted changes without the required authority, but even if a user did make an unwanted mistake, because of the versioning system that's always in place, you can always revert back if need be.

If you have a lot of teams and therefore a lot of commits and stuff going on, it'll be a little hard to keep track. Zoom has thought about this, and to save you some headaches in keeping track of it all, you get access to some fancy-pants reports to make keeping track of all the changes the team has made a whole lot easier. Oh, and did I mention the reports are in real time? That's right, kick-ass reports, all in real time.

As you can probably work out for yourself, this kind of functionality won't come cheap. Well, this is how expensive it is: you have to contact them for a price. (Whenever a company does that, you know it's going to be a nice chunk o' cash.) Despite the potentially large price tag, this is one serious asset management system and could really save a lot of time and effort by keeping your files safe and secure. So if the feature set is good enough for you to not be phased by the potential price, check it out by heading over to www.evolphin.com to take a look.

Document management

Although you can manage documents using standard version control systems, sometimes you just want a better way to visualize changes, or even a better way to store documents to collaborate with others. To that end, it's time to go through some document management systems. From now on, you'llhave some additional options when it comes to selecting a versioning system for your documents and/or text files.

Microsoft SharePoint

This is Microsoft's offering in the document-and-a-whole-lot-more-management side of things, which is known as SharePoint. Currently, its latest version is the 2010 edition, which better integrates into Microsoft's Office suite and is a lot easier to use than previous versions. Previously, you could only make the best use of its features if you were using a Microsoft operating system and browser, which for some people just isn't possible. Now, though, Microsoft has expanded its browser support to include Firefox, Safari, and, of course, Internet Explorer. This huge piece of software is definitely not aimed at individuals looking for a way to manage their teams and documents. It's for large teams that require a system for managing all aspects of their working environment.

As well as improved browser support, there have also been cosmetic improvements to make SharePoint much better to use. As far as features go, you get wikis, document management with versioning history, blogs, the ability to create websites, advanced reporting, and a whole lot more. As well as impressive features, it also has a lot of support available in the form of a forum, a whole load of videos on its features, and Microsoft's huge support network.

To run this Microsoft beast you'll need a Windows server, and not any old one; it needs to have some kick to it. You'll need a 64-bit CPU that has at least 3GHz of processing power, at least 8GB of RAM, and a good-sized hard drive that's at, like, 80GB in size. If you want to run multiple instances of the software, you'll have to ensure the server you have is top of the line. Although the tech specs are quite high because of the huge feature set it offers and the market it's aiming at, it's no surprise that you need such a highly specified machine to run SharePoint.

After hearing about the server required to run this beast, you're probably already thinking SharePoint must cost a fortune, and I'm thinking that is the case. The pricing itself isn't included on the dedicated

SharePoint website, or even on the licensing website it directs you to. To get a price, you'll need to contact someone at Microsoft, so get your credit card ready—and up the limit, because this will be a pricey one.

All in all SharePoint isn't a bad system for a company that requires its huge features and has the cash to support the server and potential cost of the software. There are some drawbacks, especially with respect to its integration with Windows, which is great for Windows users, but limits the experience for others. If you'd like to look at SharePoint 2010 in a bit more detail, head over to `http://sharepoint.microsoft.com/` to check out its features and watch some videos on how to use various parts of the system.

HyperOffice

The only thing that's got more inside of it than HyperOffice is Mr. Creosote from Monty Python's *The Meaning of Life*. (If you're unfamiliar with the reference, look it up; you should see it. If you're not interested in looking it up, Mr. Creosote is a very, very fat man who explodes from having literally the smallest of mints on top of an enormous meal. But enough of Monty Python and back to HyperOffice.) When you take a look at its feature set, you can see straight away it's not meant for average-Joe document management. This is a top-end management system. The features go from collaboration software to a calendar and even as far as mobile syncing, as well as document storage and sharing, project management, and contact management. From the outside, it's seems this guy is trying to do too many things without being too good at any one—"Jack of all trades, master of none" comes to mind.

That, however, isn't the case. These guys have thought long and hard about their management offering, and for good reason. Everything is closely linked together to allow for a better workflow completing tasks than you would normally have using a different system. Take project management, for example: if you create a task for a user to do, you can also assign documents, e-mails, contact information, external documents, and more to the task. You can also have discussions about the task, using the task itself rather than a stream of e-mails. This helps keep everything in one place so all information relating to the task is right there.

The document side of things is also quite impressive. With other high-end storage systems, you get access to either an online portal, or a desktop folder, which syncs up with the remote version. You're then able to edit the documents in your preferred program by opening it through one of these streams; then, all changes are synced back to base without any problems. You can also turn on versioning, to keep all changes to the file in case something goes wrong and you need to revert. If you need to discuss a document, you don't need to pull out an e-mail and send it to someone. HyperOffice has a discussion system built into each file, so that any discussion you need to have is right there, and it's all kept in one place. To keep you up to date with changes, you can turn on notifications, so whenever changes are made to a file, everyone who needs to know about it, knows about it. From a management point of view, you can also change the permissions of certain files and folders down to a team or user level. So if you have a document you need reviewing, but you don't anybody else to make changes to it, you can simply set the permissions to read-only and then the user can't edit the file.

Although that's only the tip of the iceberg when it comes to what HyperOffice has to offer, it's all you really need to know about. The document management side of things is quite good, for example, but that, of course, comes at a price. If you have a company with over 250 users, then you would need to pay $1,499.99 a month! That doesn't include e-mail. If you wanted e-mail service for your 250-user company, you'd have to call the company to get a price. Even on the low end of things, with five users, you're still looking at $44 a month without e-mail. As you can see, it's quite pricey. If you're still interested, `http://hyperoffice.com` is where you want to go.

MagnetSVN

We're back down to more reasonable systems with MagnetSVN. This guy doesn't try to do everything; it does one thing, versioning documents, and does it well. Sadly, you are limited to Microsoft Excel and Office on Windows, but don't let that put you off. MagnetSVN offers full integration into the ribbon interface, so it really looks the part. As for the more technical stuff, as the name suggests, it integrates with SVN whether you are using a local or remote server. (You have the option to create a local repository while installing.) You get all of the standard SVN functionality, including committing/updating/comments/history and more, which you can do right from Word or Excel, so no need to leave the program, which is always good. You can see how MagnetSVN integrates into Word by looking at Figure 6-5.

Figure 6-5. The ribbon that's added into Microsoft Word which houses all the potential actions you can perform on the open document

The merging side of things is quite clever: MagnetSVN handles the updates in a special way, which means you don't have to reload Word every time new changes come in. You can be happily working away, and if new changes come in while you're editing, they'll be downloaded. Then, when you're finished, it'll merge the changes together without losing any changes you've made. You also have the ability to lock a file. If you've finally finished working on a document and no more changes need to be made to it, you can lock the file so no further changes can accidentally be made to it unless the lock is released. It'll also display the current version of the document as you're working on it, so if the file happens to be in a conflicted state, needs cleaning up, or is currently unversioned, MagnetSVN will tell you about it so you can take the needed action.

Although this little guy is only a small application, it could come in quite useful if you write a lot of documents using Microsoft Word or you're a bit of a spreadsheet guru. You can get a fully functional free trial which is yours to use for 30 days. If you decide you love it, you won't break the bank: you can have it for a one-time fee of $19. If you want to give the trial version a go or have a better look at the features, head over to `http://magnetsvn.com`.

Google Docs

I haven't forgotten about Google. Nobody can ignore this powerhouse of a company, because of its huge size and huge product features. Whether it's to see what this Google+ thing is about, use one of the best e-mail systems on the web, or use Google Reader, nearly everyone has a Gmail account nowadays. You can also have an account if you've gone down the Google Apps route for your domain or business. Either way, whether you've paid for an account or are using a standard one, you still have access to Google Docs.

If you want a way to work on documents with other members of a team, and have your work safely backed up in the cloud, then Google Docs is amazing. Not only can you watch other people making changes in the documents in real time, you can apply useful notes to make changes to the file later on while working, right inside the document. Google being Google, you can also make a document as public or as private as you like, so whether you want to have a huge chat or a reviewing session it can all be done via the sharing settings in any Google doc.

Everyone has had the experience of knowing *what* they put in a document, but not *which* document they included it in. With the search function in Google Docs you can find the document you need, then open it straight up and edit it online without any issues. If you so choose, you can also download the document to your desktop to make any needed changes there, then reimport it into Google Docs so it's safe in the cloud once again. The search can be a real life saver—especially if, for example, you've done a quote for a client, but can't remember which important file you put the costs or timescales for the project inside of. Just do a search in Google Docs, and you will find it.

Another time saver offered by Google Docs is templates. If you produce a lot of similar documents, such as quotes, press releases, proposals, or anything like that, each can have a template for use in Google Docs to save you having to re-create items multiple times. This can save a lot of time and money. If you don't want to create your own, it's also possible to download stock templates for use in Google Docs. That's one of the perks of having a huge community around a product.

As well as all these features, Google Docs also supports revisions. When multiple users are all working on the same file, some things are bound to get unexpectedly deleted, and that's why revisions can be so useful. You can see who made the changes, and also what they changed. When you look through the previous versions, you can even see how they differ from the most up-to-date document, which can help add context to changes people have made, or give you a reason to revert if you really need one.

For this, and many other reasons, Google Docs is a great tool for versioning documents. You know your data is always going to be safe in the cloud because it's managed by the largest search engine in the world, and for the majority of us, Google Docs, Gmail, Reader, Apps, and more are free services. You really can't grumble when you get all these great services for nothing (in most cases), so if you're just using Microsoft Word and no versioning for your documents at the moment, get on Google Docs and know your work will always be safe.

Summary

We've been through a lot of different versioning systems in this chapter, from general storage solutions to those focused on certain tasks. Not only have we looked at small solutions, we've also had a glimpse of some of the larger solutions for large corporations and the feature set you can expect for the kind of cash they require.

Whatever the document type you're working with, it's always beneficial to back up your files in some way, at least by using some kind of cloud-based solution. Taking a more specific route—for example, using some of the visual versioning tools described in this chapter—offers a lot more benefits than just storing files. Using one of these tools will make looking at previous versions of images, PSDs, or PDFs a whole lot easier, and you'll get a lot more out of the service than you would just storing the file in a plain SVN, Git, or Mercurial repository. Using one of these services does add an additional cost to the development process and potentially some extra steps to the workflow, but when it comes to having a history of files that is visually appealing and useful, then any additional work or cost can be justified.

The document-management route is a little harder to justify than the visual side of things because, really, documents are just text files and SVN, Git, or Mercurial can handle those, right? Although that's technically true, having a dedicated versioning system for documents can make managing revisions of documents a whole load easier. Conventional diffing tools don't work with documents too well—looking at plain differences between two files may not be enough to enable you to appreciate the changes between the two versions.Other services will make document management and group collaboration a lot easier by using a hosted document management system that is constantly backed up, and in some cases will be easier for nontechy users to pick up and use.

Hopefully, this chapter has encouraged you to get all your previous data backed up in some way, whether it's through versioning or cloud storage. Plus, if you're working with PSDs, PDFs, Word documents or spreadsheets, there's always going to be a solution out there to your versioning problems. Now though, it's time to move on tostreamling your development process and saving time by using version control in some of the top development applications available, so let's get to it. .

Chapter 7

What Can Make My Life Easier?

When it comes to writing code, you can, in theory, use any text-based application. You could even use something like Word to write it, if you really wanted to. Of course, that wouldn't be the best of ideas, since Word hasn't been designed for writing code at all, and the features could impact negatively on your development (with the addition of styles and hidden characters, for example). Some people prefer to use basic text editors, such as Notepad on Windows, TextEdit on Mac, or even gedit on Ubuntu, as they're really basic editors and their features don't compromise your ability to develop.

Although basic editors are fine for small projects, for more complex development there are applications that are better suited and have been created for the purpose of writing code and make the process easier. These applications often carry features such as code highlighting, auto completion, keyboard shortcuts, and a load more.

There's another level of editor known as Integrated Development Environments, or IDEs, which are full-fledged development environments. These allow you do a number of things, including but not limited to, creating and working on full projects, searching said projects, building applications, expanding functionality through plug-ins, and a lot, lot more. The first IDE came about in the 1970s in the form of Maestro, which was installed on a number of top-end computers at the time, for large companies such as Boeing and Bank of America. Things have come a long way since then and there are a lot of great editors that can be used for development that work across multiple operating systems and some specialist systems used only on certain operating systems.

Everyone has their own preferred application when it comes to writing code, whether it's a cross-platform solution like Eclipse or a more platform-specific program such as TextMate. Either way, most of the commonly used editors have ways you can integrate your preferred versioning system right in the application. This saves a lot of time when performing basic actions that would otherwise require you to use another application. Although that may only take 30 seconds, doing that multiple times in a day eventually adds up!

In this chapter I'll take you through some of the most popular editors and how to get them working with SVN, Git, and Mercurial, or with at least of one of them. As per usual we'll begin with Windows, move on to Mac, and then to finish, we'll go over a few applications that work cross platform. Nice, eh?

Windows editors

There are a lot of editors available for Windows, although a few that are Windows-only have very poor version control support. The E editor has potential to be a good sport but, because it is 32-bit, and all of the Tortoise applications (TortoiseSVN, TortoiseGit and TortoiseHG) you've installed are 64-bit, it cannot pick up the necessary options from the right-click menu. If, however, you're working with a 32-bit system, and the versions of Tortoise that have been installed are also 32-bit, you'll be able to access the contect menu from the sidebar. This means that if you load a project into E, you'll be able to right-click any file or folder and perform any action that the various Tortoise applications are capable of, right within E, which makes life a whole lot easier.

Other than that, there may have been some hope that E can potentially work with TextMate bundles, but the SVN, Git and Mercurial bundles don't work at all. This comes down to certain dependencies that the TextMate bundles have to the Mac operationing system; because these cannot be replicated on Windows, the bundles fail and their functionality is lost. In terms of the versioning bundles, this means the respective SVN, Git, and Mercurial bundles don't work, so all their features are useless on Windows. If you're working on a 64-bit system and want this functionality, then it's not really possible without installing 32-bit versions of the applications, which would result in a reduction in performance and stability that isn't really worth it.

Notepad++

Notepad++ has the potential to expand its use with plug-ins, although the only plug-ins available rely on the Tortoise applications you've installed, which are 32-bit and which render the plug-in useless for 64-bit users. If you are rocking a 32-bit system, the option to use this plug-in is still available to you, and it's easy enough to install and use, too. Head over to www.switchonthecode.com/tech-news/notepadplusplus-subversion-plugin to get a copy of the plug-in, and also a nice representation of how it works.

Just in case you don't fancy heading over there, I'll give you a quick look at how it actually works. To install the plug-in, download the zip file from the previously mentioned location, and copy the contained .dll file into the following location: C:\Program Files (x86)\Notepad++\plugins or (on systems earlier than Windows 7) C:\Program Files\Notepad++\plugins. With the plug-in in the correct location, restart Notepad++ if you have it open and if not, open it.

Within the plug-ins menu there will now be a new menu option called Subversion, which contains a number of options. Thanks to the plug-in, you can know Update, Revert, or Commit either the file you are working on or all the files you have open. Although it's not the most extensive of plug-ins, it still allows you to perform a limited number of actions without leaving Notepad++—if you happen to be on a 32-bit machine, that is.

That covers SVN, but in terms of Git and Mercurial support, there is sadly a shortage. There are some plug-ins that users have worked on, but nothing that's thoroughly supported, and that's just the Git side of things. As for Mercurial, there doesn't seem to be a slither of a plug-in available which leaves the support for Mercurial and Notepad++ together at zilch.

Visual Studio

This is another application with potential to be improved but, alas, it doesn't work as planned. There is a subversion plug-in that can be installed within Visual Studio (VS), but it only allows the ability to check out repositories which offers no real benefit at all. If you go down the Mercurial route, however, there is a plug-in available to you which can be downloaded from http://visualhg.codeplex.com/. It does rely on TortoiseHG to run its commands, so you'll need to make sure that is installed before you go any further. After you've installed the plug-in, it's time to head into VS and do some configuring.

Before you can actually use the plug-in, you need to enable it within VS. Thanks to how it's set up, you can only have one versioning system enabled at once. To enable the plug-in, head into **Tools ➤ Options...**, which will launch a new dialog window containing all the settings for the application. You won't be able to see the menu you need by default, so be sure to have the "Show all settings" check box checked, which will reveal some additional options, including the one you need: Source Control. In this section there is a dropdown menu, where you can now select VisualHG from the list, which will add an additional pane to the application, which contains nothing to begin with; when you change a file, however, its path and file name will appear here.

The plug-in, sadly, doesn't allow you to create a repository directly from within VS; however, you can create one outside of the application, then interact with it using the plug-in. It allows you to commit/add files to the repository, check the status, and even synchronize with a remote repository. To access these options, just right-click the file in question, go into VisualHG, then select the action you need to perform. Clicking one of these options will launch the action in TortoiseHG, which isn't exactly direct integration into the application, but still saves you switching to a Windows Explorer window. Since we've already been through how to use TortoiseHG, I won't go into any more detail about how to perform the actions.

Despite these failings, there are some applications that work cross platform, have the ability to work well on Windows, and integrate with various source control systems. You will find out about these later in the chapter.

Mac editors

Now it's time to head into the shiny world of Mac applications, covering some of the more popular choices and maybe a couple you hadn't considered. Although you'll be installing some plug-ins or packages, some of the things we'll be looking at already exist in the applications. I'll describe those in more detail, just in case there was a feature in there you weren't aware of. But enough talking. Let's go straight into it by looking at a popular choice amongt developers: TextMate.

TextMate

This text editor has a somewhat mixed crowd in terms of users. Some people seem to shy away from it because the developer is a bit removed from the project, which results in very few updates and not much actually being done to improve the application. There has, however, been an update on the developer's blog, which suggests an early beta of TextMate 2.0 will be released soon. Whether that will happen is another question entirely. Despite the poor updates for the application, it's still a great bit of kit and is used by a large number of developers, some of whom create great plug-ins and extras for TextMate to improve its performance and usability.

SVN

TextMate has a built-in bundle that allows you to perform SVN actions while inside of it. This saves you having to switch to another app to perform basic actions. It's worth saying that if you were to use this in conjunction with an application such as SVNx, Versions, Cornerstone, or any other SVN application, then it wouldn't stop functioning or ruin your repository. You can simply hop between applications without worrying.

All you need to access the SVN controls is one keyboard shortcut: Ctrl+Shift+A. This shortcut is one to rule them all—if you were to navigate through the menu structure to find the command there (**Bundles ➤ Subversion**) you would notice that all the commands have the same shortcut (Ctrl+Shift+A). When you enter the magic shortcut, you will be shown a menu numbered from 1 to 0, then with a number of other options below. While this menu is open, you can use the number keys to do that action without clicking that item on the menu; so if you were to do Ctrl+Shift+A then 5, that would show the commit dialog for the file you have selected.

The basic functions of this bundle do work, but they don't look very nice in the process. For example, if you were to update your local copy of the code, the window it brings up would be huge, and unnecessary. It does, however, save you having to go back and forth between applications, which saves time and effort. Although you do get the option to check out changes with TextMate, I wouldn't recommend it because if something were to go wrong, you would just get errors back with no ability to input anything, which isn't so good. Another thing to be cautious of is when you get a conflict; the dialog box will show you a list of options but will not allow you to select any of them. In that instance you'd need to go back to your main application to update and then resolve the conflict from there.

Although this bundle has its downsides, when it comes to updating and committing, in most cases everything will be just fine. If you're trying to do as many commits as possible, or you're collaborating with other people on the same code, just doing that simple shortcut, then updating or committing, is quick and easy, and because of that you do more commits.

The top and bottom lines of this bundle come down to the uses for it. If you're just doing updates, commits, and adds, then it's great: if you don't use it, you should. For all the other SVN functions, though, it's not the best. For those, you'll need to have another application to back you up.

Mercurial

There isn't a Mercurial bundle installed by default, but there is one available to use, so the first thing is to add that in. The easiest way to do this is through a couple of Terminal commands, so open up a new Terminal window and add the following code into it:

```
mkdir -p /Library/Application Support/TextMate/Bundles
cd !$
svn co http://svn.textmate.org/trunk/Bundles/Mercurial.tmbundle/
osascript -e 'tell app "TextMate" to reload bundles'
```

This simply creates a folder to house the bundles (if it doesn't already exist) within TextMate's core files and settings. Then put in the directory from the previous command, to save you having to do it manually. Next, the bundle is checked out of the TextMate repository using SVN (ironic, I know). Now the bundle is in the same directory as all of the others, so all that's left to do is refresh the bundles list to ensure TextMate picks it up correctly—easy. Once that's done, you will now have the same control over your Mercurial files as you would with SVN, although this time the keyboard shortcut to use is Ctrl+Shift+M.

You're probably thinking "Great, that's it, then?" Well, sadly, it's not as simple as that. Although actions such as adding, committing, checking the status of a file, and so on will work correctly, trying to perform a pull or push will result in nothing happening. The action will not throw an error, unless you have a remote repository, in which case you will see `abort: http authorisation required` and no way to input the required information. So if you are working locally with one repository which has no other repositories to push to, this bundle will be great for you as the Commit and Add actions work just fine. Otherwise, I'm afraid you'll need to use another application for managing those Mercurial actions.

Git

As I mentioned a little earlier, there is a Git bundle supplied with TextMate that works just fine. However, there is a little configuration to be done before it'll work. If you try and use any of the commands within the bundle, the first thing you will see in the window that appears will be `sh: line 1: git: command not found` which indicates that TextMate doesn't know where Git lives on your system. Let's sort that out now. The first thing you need to do is head into Terminal. When it's open type in

```
which git
```

This will return the location of Git on your system, so be sure to copy that URL. You'll need it in just a moment. If the which git command gives you an error, head back into Chapter 3 and install Git (it's easy, honest!). With the path copied to your clipboard, head into TextMate's preferences window by clicking TextMate in the main menu, then Preferences, or by pressing Cmd+ , which will open the same window.

Once it's open, go into the Advanced section, and then click the Shell variables option. You should have at least one option in this list, which will be PATH, but you need to add a new one to the list by using the + just below the window. When the new variable appears in the list, double-click MY_VARIABLE to rename it to TM_GIT, then double-click "some value" and replace it with the path that was copied from Terminal just a moment ago. Once that's all done, it should look like Figure 7-1. Don't worry if your path is different from mine, as long as the variable is there with the path specified in Terminal, it'll be fine.

Figure 7-1. The Advanced settings menu within TextMate, which shows the application's shell variables and where the TM_GIT variable needs to be added.

If all has worked out as planned you should now be able to perform a boatload of Git commands, including pulling, adding, committing, logging, checking the status, and so on. Although you may not notice an option for Add in the Git bundle menu (**Bundles ➤ Git** or Crtl+Shift+A) you can still add unversioned files with ease. To achieve this, simply commit the file then, using the option in the bundle, when the dialog window asking for a commit message shows up, just check the unversioned file in the bottom half of the window and it'll be added, then committed. Easy.

The bundle also allows for pushing to remote branches, which is, again, awesome! After you have the remote repository, such as one on Github configured, you can easily Push any changes you need to without any issue from the application, as all authentication is done via previous configuration and SSH keys. The dialog that opens up after the Push has completed will inform you about which files have been pushed, and the message associated with the commit. Pulling also works in the same fashion, you won't get any prompts for authentication, it'll just work.

Using the Git stash option also works really well within TextMate. For example, say you have some changes that are ready to be committed, but a mega-important change comes in that has to be attended to. You can't commit what you are working on now because it's not finished, so you can just open up the trusty TextMate Git bundle, then hit stash. Now you can update and make any changes you need to and when you need the stash back, just select Pop Stash from the menu, and your changes will be added straight into the working copy as they were before, ready to be committed and pushed.

TextMate summary

Thanks to the dedication of its users, TextMate has some pretty good bundles to use right within the application; the SVN and Git bundles prove just that (sorry, Mercurial). Although TextMateis slightly let down by the lack of Mercurial support, when performing the basic actions with the SVN or Git bundles, keying in a keyboard shortcut and then a number will save loads of time in the long run, and saves having to switch to another application. The quality of the Git bundle also really helps new users get to grips with how to use it by making the motions as seamless as possible. All in all, if you want to find an application you can use with different version control types without having to switch to another application, TextMate well and truly has your back. The shortcuts and actions available for the three bundles will save a large amount of time and effort. If you like the features on offer from TextMate and you'd like to give it a try or even buy it for $59, head over to `http://macromates.com/` to get to know TextMate a little better.

Coda

Although you may not have used it, almost everyone has at least heard of Coda, thanks to its great reputation in the field of being awesome and including a huge feature set. Coda was initially created by a company called Panic back in April 2007. That year it won the 2007 Apple Design Award for Best User Experience, which isn't bad for your first year of release. Panic is also behind Transmit (an FTP client) and Unison (a great usenet browser) as well as a few other applications. Although they have a number of other applications, the guys at Panic have put a lot of work into Coda, adding in file transfers, Terminal, book, and a whole lot more features. Coda also advertises very openly that it has great integration with SVN, but sadly no sign of Git or Mercurial. That's not to say there isn't hope. Getting Mercurial and Git support within Coda is a hugely requested feature and will hopefully be coming along soon. So let's dive right into Coda and get started with SVN, shall we?

Starting with SVN

When you set up a new site in Coda, it will automatically detect the .svn files within it and pull out the repository URL. All you have to do to kick everything off is to check the enabled box, then enter your username and password and that's it. If, for some reason, you don't have the repository set up yet, you can always go back into the settings for the site you have set up and just check the box as normal, just like that.

Now that you have your source control information stored inside Coda, you have a number of actions available to you which you would usually have to switch to another application for, such as updating, adding, committing, comparing versions, and a lot more. Really, Coda lets you do anything you would need to while writing and editing code, which makes life a whole lot easier.

Committing and updating

Two actions that go hand in hard are committing and updating, which are both easy as pie within Coda. You have the option to update any file by either right-clicking it, then going to **Source Control ➤ Update To ➤ Latest**, which will update the file to the most recent version, obviously. You can also perform the same action by using Shift+Cmd+U or by going to **File ➤ Source Control ➤ Update to ➤ Latest**. From the File menu, there is also an option to update the entire site in one go, which may come in useful if you know a whole lot of changes are coming in.

When it comes to committing files, you will only be able to use the command, unless there are changes available to commit—which, of course, makes sense. In the Source Control menu, the option will be grayed out by default, unless changes are detected. If there are changes, you can Commit the file or files from either the Source Control menu (File or right-click) and if it's an individual file, you can use Shift+Cmd+M to commit it. You can also commit all changes at once by using the "Commit entire site..." option which will push all changed files to the repository.

A good action to perform regularly is "Refresh entire site" which lives in the **File ➤ Source Control** menu. This command checks the server for any changes to the files and displays the * icon next to them if they are due to be updated. The issue with this is that if the file lives within a folder, the folder itself won't display the icon. This means you need to have all the folders in the site open all the time to see changes, which in some ways makes this function useless. You can run the Refresh Status command on an individual file by using either the menu, or by using Shift+Cmd+R as a nifty shortcut.

Adding a new file

If you want to add a new file to your site while in Coda, you'll be prompted to add the file into SVN straight away. This is a really cool function from Coda as it means you can add the file there and then, and then you can't forget about it. You do have the option to not add the file, though—you can do that easily enough from the file Source Control menu and hitting "Add files", which adds the files, ready to be committed.

Coda summary

Although it lacks Git and Mercurial support, Coda is a great coding application, and if you're working with SVN, it's a dream to use. You can perform most of the important and regularly occurring actions within Coda without having to switch to another application. If you've never used Coda before, you should at least give it a try before passing judgement on its lack of Mercurial or Git support. Despite missing those key features, it's still a great piece of kit. You can download a trial over at the Panic website at www.panic.com/coda/ and, if you like it, you can buy a copy for $99.

BBEdit

This is another popular editor in the Mac world, having reached a tenth numbered release. With that number of releases comes a vast feature set, including FTP, CVS, and SVN support. That, of course, doesn't even explain how well it handles writing code and all the small and big features that justify its $49.99 price tag. You can have a closer look at the application, take it for a test drive, or buy it by going to www.barebones.com/products/bbedit and having a look around.

Yet again, there is lack of Git and Mercurial support, and searching the Web for answers on the topic will tell you to either use a dedicated application or Terminal. Although it is lacking Git and Mercurial support, it does support SVN and CVS, so let's have a gander at how to work with SVN, BBEdit style.

Starting with SVN

Although it's possible to set up projects in BBEdit, it's not required in order to perform SVN tasks (unlike a certain editor called Coda) so you can just open up your project in BBEdit by dragging the folder containing the project right into the icon for BBEdit. Once you're all set up, there are two ways you can perform SVN actions within BBEdit: either by right-clicking the file or folder in the project navigator or by using the S option in the main menu.

From the right-click menu you can Revert, Add, Commit, Update, Delete, and show the Status of any file or folder with your project. The one thing that is missing from both locations are keyboard shortcuts, so each time you want to perform an action, it'll need to be initialed from one of the two locations. This is a slight upset, but not one to be taken too heavily, as the convenience of having SVN access within the application saves time as it is.

Committing and updating

A slight annoyance with the SVN tools in BBEdit is the lack of icons in the project navigator. If a file has been modified and needs to be committed, there will be nothing to alert you of this, unless you go ahead and check the status of the project in the main S menu under Show Working Copy Status.... When the dialog pops up you may need to select the root of your repository, and whether or not you want to show available updates. Once that's all sorted, just hit Show Status and you will be shown a list of files and the state in which they are in. You can interact with the files in this window by right-clicking them to perform SVN actions on them, or by clicking them and editing them in the lower half of the window. You can, of course, just close the window and continue editing the files as you were. BBEdit doesn't mind.

The updating side of BBEdit isn't so bad, either: you have the option to update individual files or the site as a whole, depending on which option you choose. Both options live under the SVN option in the main menu. It seems a bit strange that you can't update an individual file by right-clicking it, but it's no big deal. To update the site as a whole, rather than the file you have selected just pick Update Working Copy... from the menu. If you'd rather update the files one by one, just select Update to Head... which will update the file you have selected to the latest version.

Committing works the same way as updating in BBEdit. You can either commit all the changes you've made at once, or one at a time. A slight bonus here is that a commit option is located in the right-click menu when clicking a file, so you don't always need to use the main menu for performing the action. The main menu does still contain the option to commit the file you have selected, as well as the Commit Working Copy... option, which will commit all your changes.

BBEdit Summary

That about wraps up BBEdit and its SVN support. It's a shame, really, that it doesn't also support Git and Mercurial, but there's always hope that BBEdit will drop CVS support to make room for another VCS. BBEdit is a great editor; if you're using SVN, it'll make your life a whole load easier!

Cross platform

A select few editors can work across multiple platforms, so pinning them to a particular operating system could result in the assumption that they're dependent on a particular operating system. A number of these applications are used by a whole host of developers, so anything to help save those few minutes in a day can be extremely useful. We'll start off with Eclipse, which luckily has plug-ins for SVN, Mercurial, and Git.

Eclipse/Aptana

For those of you who aren't familiar with it, Eclipse is a very popular IDE among all kinds of developers, thanks to how easy it is to customize, and the different versions available. If you're unfamiliar with it, and you'd like to download a copy of it for free, head over to www.eclipse.org/ and see what all the fuss is about. Although you can argue Aptana is a different application, in reality it's built on top of Eclipse, and thanks to that, it uses the same plug-in system. With that in mind, these steps will work on either Aptana or Eclipse. Aptana breaks out of the mold a little by being aimed towards web and mobile development. Although Eclipise is capable of handling this, Aptana has been designed with it in mind. You can get a copy of it at http://aptana.com/.

Neither application comes with any version control options available when it's first installed, but that's why it has the option of installing new plug-ins. First of all, you'll be installing Subversive, a great SVN plug-in which can be used within Eclipse and Aptana.

SVN: Installing Subversive

Although there are a few options available when it comes to choosing an SVN plug-in, the one you'll be installing is called Subversive. The other main choice in this field is a plug-in known as Subclipse, which performs the same basic functions, and is maintained by Tigris, the guys who originally developed SVN. There is no immediate problem with Subclipse as a plug-in—it works perfectly fine—but we're going for Subversive as it's slightly easier to install. Because it is maintained by Eclipse, you don't need to add any additional download sources. This plug-in is able to perform any of the basic tasks you would want it to from within the application, and possibly save you time if used often enough. The first step to take is to head into **Help > Install New Software**, which launches a new dialog window where it's possible to install new software, which is exactly what you want to do. In the dialog window, you'll need to hit Available Software Sites to make sure the correct location is in fact enabled. You'll be looking for Eclipse Helios Update Site and ensure that is checked. If you see Eclipse Galileo Repository, make sure that is unchecked, as the newer version of Subversive lives in the Helios repository. With that done, from the dropdown menu in the update window, select the Helios link then, using the search field, type in `subversive`, which will filter the list of updates. This process is very slow and can take a while to load everything, but once it's done it'll look something like Figure 7-2.

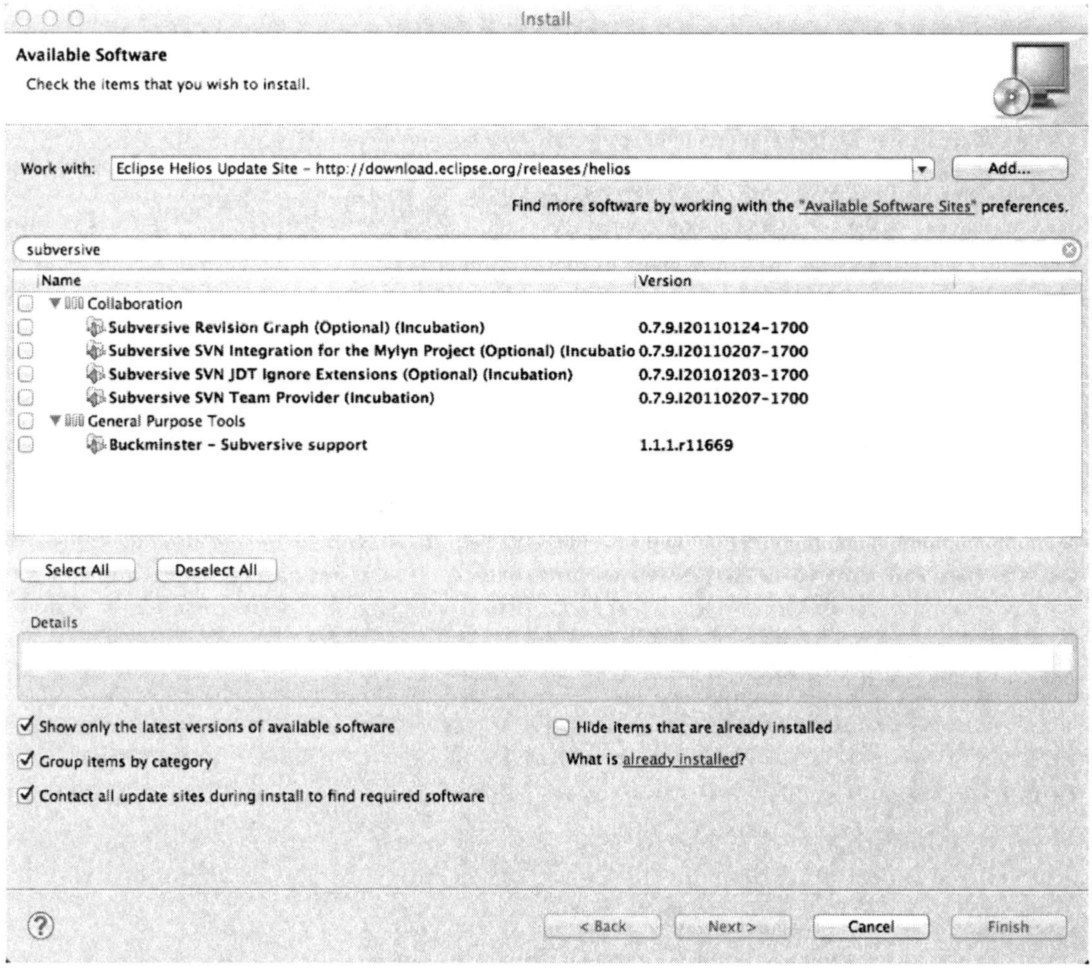

Figure 7-2. The list of available packages to install (after selecting the correct download source and searching for "subversive")

Select the four checkboxes within the Collaboration folder and hit Next, and Next again. The next screen is the license agreement, so just click the Eclipse option, and then select "I accept" and, finally, hit Finish. This will download all the software you need and after it's done you'll be prompted to restart Aptana.

When you return into the application, you'll be greeted with the dialog pictured in Figure 7-3, where you'll need to select an SVN connector to install. Here you'll be installing the second option, as it doesn't require additional software, and it works with the newer version of SVN. If you're working with SVN 1.5, then go with option 1. You can install all of the options if you'd like, but that does mean you'll be installing more stuff, which is never a good idea.

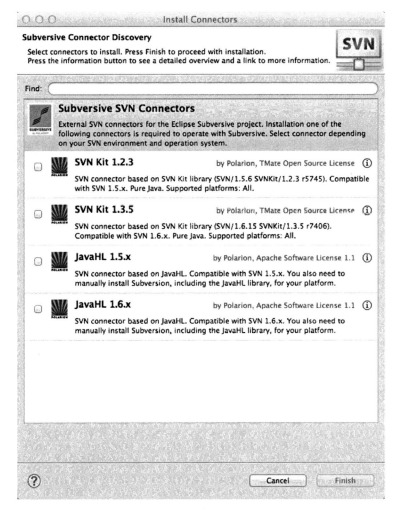

Figure 7-3. The potential SVN connectors that can be installed upon restarting the application

Once you've selected the correct option for you, hit Finish, which will launch you into another dialog to install the connector. Then hit Next, Next again, then accept another user agreement and hit Finish. When the process has completed you'll need to restart Aptana once again, for the last time, thankfully.

Checking out a repository

Checking out a new repository is easily achieved within Aptana once the plug-in is installed. To perform a checkout you'll need to create a new SVN project, which can now be selected when you create a repository by going into the SVN folder. You can get to the new project dialog by right-clicking the project pane and going into **New ➤ Project**, or by going into **File ➤ New ➤ Project**. Either gives you the same dialog.

In most cases you'll need to have "Create a new repository location" selected to allow the input of a new repository URL. You can select from an existing one (if you have any) but in most cases with new projects you'll need a new repository. In the next dialog, you'll need to enter the repository URL and the authentication required, and that's it. With the URL, be sure not to include the trunk or branches part of the URL as the plug-in prefers to do that itself.

The next part of the checkout process requires you to select which revision you would like to check out, although in most cases this will be the default: head. Once you've hit Finish, you'll be taken to another dialog asking what you would like to do with the repository. The top option will be most used as it will create a new folder to house the checked-out repository. With the top option selected, hit Finish and you'll be taken to another dialog which looks awfully familiar, the new project dialog. This time, though, just select the project that best applies to your code, such as PHP project. The final stage of the process is to pick a name and a location for the repository and you're in the closing stages. The final part of the process is to actually check out the repository to the specified folder. That's it, the repository will be checked out and added as a project.

Adding an existing repository

You won't always need to check out a new repository—for example, if you're controlling your repositories with another application, or just trying out Aptana to see how things go. If the project contains .svn folders, then after a short period of time the plug-in will pick up this information, and the association between the local and remote repositories will be made. In the event this doesn't happen (which can be down to not storing the access credentials locally) the association can be made manually, and although this is a little annoying, it's easy enough to achieve.

To start the process, right-click the project in the project explorer and in the menu, go to **Team ➤ Share project**, which will launch a dialog box. You'll be able to select SVN from the list, and hit Next. If this repository has been checked out from a remote location, all of the options as you go through the stages of the wizard should be prefilled, and if you're dealing with a local repository this should also be the case. In the event you need to specify a local path to the repository, just start the location with file:// and include the full path to the repository and it will be added without an issue. When adding in the location don't forget about the potential / at the start of the path if needed (which it would be if it was located on your local drive). This may make it start with file:///, depending on the location of the repository. After the location has been added, the other information will prefill. If not, just enter the information then keep on hitting Next until you can finally select Finish.

Adding and deleting

The Team menu when you right-click the file or folder will now have completely different contents in the form of a boatload of SVN options. When you come across an unversioned file, simply right-click it, head into Team and hit "Add to version control", which will launch a new dialog window. Inside this window, you just need to hit Ok and the file will be added to the repository. Easy. Deleting files is even a little simpler, because it doesn't involve the Team menu at all. If you want to delete the folder, then just delete it. It will be deleted in the repository after a commit has been done. With that being said, let's look at how committing and updating work.

Commiting and updating

When it comes to committing changes, it can be done on a file-by-file basis or at the top level of the repository. Whichever way you decide to commit your changes, the option can be found within the Team menu. If done from the root level, all changes made to the repository will be listed, including unversioned files, which can be added and committed directly from this commit dialog. Just select which files you would like to commit, enter a message to accompany the commit, and you're all set.

Updating is also really easy. Head into the Team menu and hit Update. When you do you may be asked for authentication details for the repository, otherwise it'll simply fetch any updates without a problem. You also have the option to update to a specific revision. You'll be asked to enter therevision number you'd like to update to and the rest is done in the background.

History

It's also possible to get information on the history of the repository with a simple click of the History option within the Team menu. This can be done at the root level to see all of the commits for that repository, or on a file to see specific changes to that particular file. Either option will open up a new tab at the bottom of the window showing all the commits associated with either the repository or file depending on what was clicked. In the pane it's also possible to revert to said revision by right-clicking the specific commit. You'll also see the revision number of the commit, the message associated with it, the author, and the date of the commit.

Git

The latest version of Aptana comes with Git support baked in, but you need to make a quick change before it'll work correctly. First you need to dive into Terminal or command line/Git Bash to run the following:

```
which git
```

This will return a path, which is where Git lives on your system. Copy this, as you'll need it in just a moment. With the code on the clipboard, head back into Aptana then into **Preferences ➤ Team ➤ Git on Mac or Unix** and **Open Window ➤ Preferences ➤ Team ➤ Git**, then in the Git Executable text field, paste the path into it. With that in place you're all set to go and, thanks to how it works, if you open a Git repository within Aptana, it will change the Team menu to be filled with all of the Git options you'll need.

Adding and staging

When you make a change within a Git repository, the change needs to be staged before it can actually be committed; the same process needs to be followed in order to add untracked files. Head into the Team menu and hit Stage, which will either add the file to be tracked when committed, or stage the changes so they can be committed. You'll get no output from running this command; however, the project panel will change accordingly and files will gain a plus (+) icon when staged. Untracked files also get marked in red so they're easy to spot.

Commiting

The commit process is rather simple too. When you have changes tracked and ready to commit, the commit command itself is found within the Team menu. A new dialog window will be launched when you hit Commit, where it's possible to add any other files that are currently unstaged, and also add a message to accompany the commit. Once you're happy with everything, hit Commit and the changes will create a new revision, just like that.

Pulling and pushing

Of course, from time to time you'll need to update your working copy with remote changes, and thanks to Aptana, you can do so without having to leave the application. In the Team menu, you have the option to perform the Pull command. You won't get a dialog popping up here, just the outcome of the pull shown in the Console tab at the bottom of the screen.

Pushing is a little different, but not any more difficult to perform. Within the Team menu, hit the Push option which will perform the Push with any committed changes. Depending on the repository setup, you may be asked for user details in order to perform the action, but after they're entered the changes will be pushed without a problem.

Status

The status command can be really useful when you're working on a project to ensure all of the changes are committed correctly. This command doesn't care about which file or folder is clicked to launch the Team menu, it'll always be performed on the full repository. You'll see the outcome of the command in the console tab at the bottom of the screen, which will show you the current status of your working copy, of course.

Mercurial

Unfortunately, Mercurial support doesn't come baked into Eclipse/Aptana so you need to install it manually. To achieve this, head into **Help ➤ Install new software** once again to start the process off. In the dialog, hit the Add button, which allows you to add another location you can download software from. In the new dialog that pops up, enter the following information:

```
MercurialEclipse
http://cbes.javaforge.com/update
```

Adding this will default the location in the "Work with:" field, which is what you want. When it loads there will be two check boxes to select, so be sure to select them both. However, if you happen to be on an operating system that isn't Windows, you'll need to open up the MercurialEclipse dropdown and uncheck the Windows binary option. With this selected on a non-Windows system, it will cause an error on the next stage of the process. Provided everything is as it should be, your "install new software" screen should look something like Figure 7-4 (with the potential exclusion of the Windows binaries).

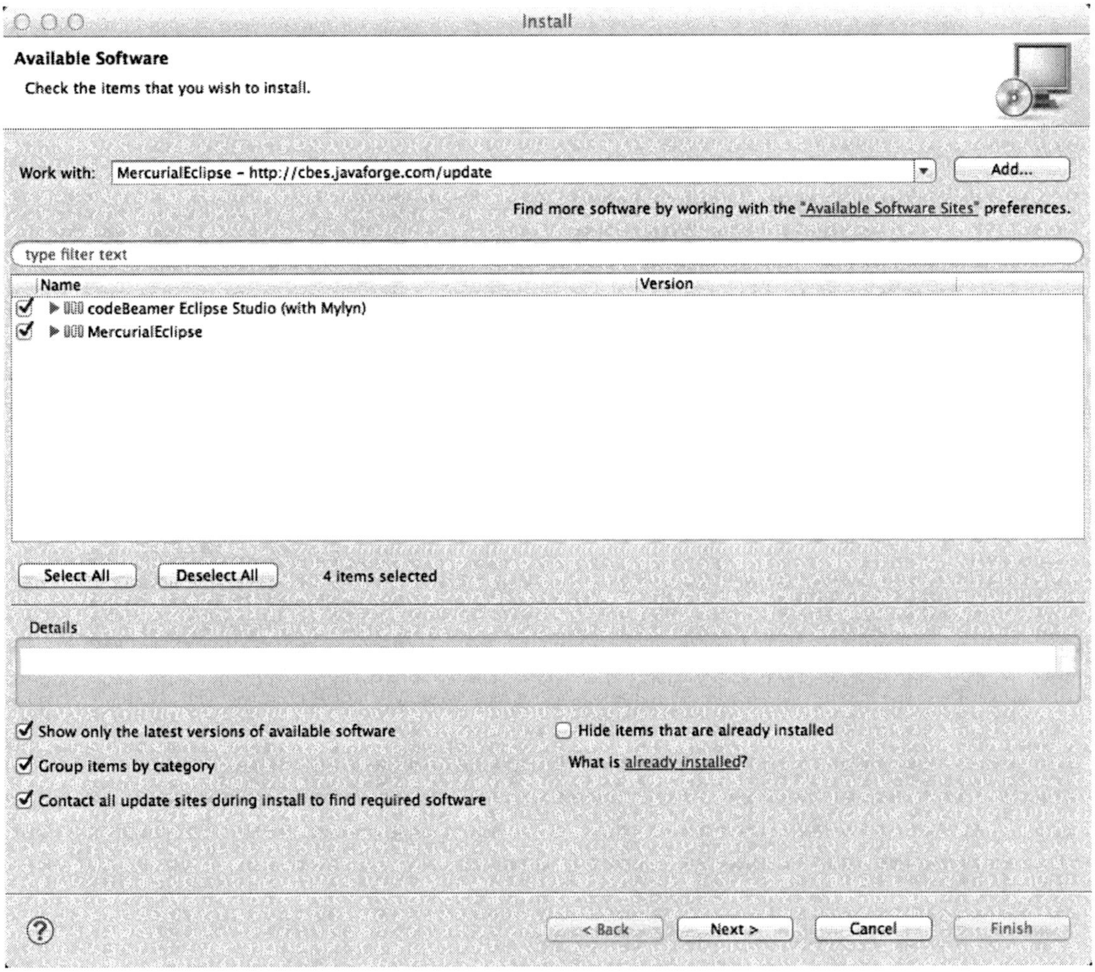

Figure 7-4. The packages available to install from the MercurialEclipse software repository.

You now need to accept the license agreements yet again, and when everything has finished downloading, a restart will once again be required. Once the restart is complete, though, Mercurial integration is a go and you can perform all the actions you need to. Let's start by looking at working with repositories.

Getting your repositories into Eclipse/Aptana

You can get your repositories into Mercurial by using one of two methods: cloning an existing repository or working with an existing repository on your system. In the case of existing repositories, all that needs to be done is to create a project out of the existing repository, and then you're all set. The plug-in is clever enough to realize that it's dealing with a Mercurial repository and changes the Team menu accordingly, just like that.

With repositories you wish to clone to get them into the application, the process is a little different. First of all, create a new project from within the application and select Clone Existing Mercurial Repository from within the Mercurial folder. This will launch a dialog asking for the URL of the repository and any other credentials required to gain access to it. You'll also be asked to pick a name and location for the cloned repository to live in on your system. Once all that information has been entered, the cloning process will begin. You'll be prompted to select a name for the main branch on your machine. To keep things easier to manage, it's advisable to leave the defaults in here. The final stage of the process involves determining whether or not you would like to import the project into the application. Just hit Finish and the process will be complete.

Adding and committing

The ability to add a file or files to the repository is really easy and, as with every other command you've looked at, lives in the Team menu. Although the option is available for all files, unless the file is untracked, it won't do anything. You won't see a prompt confirming the action, either.

Committing is also a breeze using the application. The option is always available, and doesn't take into consideration which file is selected. When inside the Team menu, it always runs from the root of the repository. When you run the command, a dialog will launch showing all of the changes that are set to be committed and the option to include them or not, thanks to check boxes. If you happen to run the command from root level, you can also see files that are yet to be added, which allows you to commit them in one go without having to add them first. Once you have the files you'd like to commit selected, just enter a message and the commit will be complete.

Pulling and pushing

We'll start with pulling first, as it's the easiest to perform. You'll need to right-click the root of the project in order to be able to see the pull action, and to run it, of course. When clicked, you'll be asked for information to connect to the repository, although it'll be prefilled in most cases; you'll just have to confirm and hit Next to go to the next stage. In said next stage you'll be asked to select which change sets you would like to pull down (if there are any, of course). If there is nothing to pull, this stage will be blank, and hitting Finish will just abort the process. If you have changes, they will be pulled to your local copy. Easy.

Pushing goes through the same process as pulling, just in reverse. You'll still have to add in any authentication details, or confirm them, as they'll most likely already be there. On the next stage of the process you'll see that all of the changes are due to be sent to the remote server, and hitting Finish will perform the push. In the absence of changes, the process will just abort upon clicking Finish, so you're covered either way.

Eclipse/Aptana summary

These plug-ins allow great interaction with each of the version control systems respectively, and work in such a way that in most cases you may have no need to leave Eclipse or Aptanaat all. If you use Eclipse as a base for your development, you should really look into getting these plug-ins installed, which will allow for better management of multiple projects using different versioning systems.

No matter what system you decide to use, whether it's SVN, Git, or Mercurial, there are very few negatives to having one or even all of these systems installed to version your code. Thanks to these plug-ins, even performing the basic actions is easy enough, and won't take any extra effort on your part. So if your project isn't currently versioned, pick a versioning system and get the code committed into it. Plus, you cannot go wrong with an open source application with free plug-ins, so there's no real reason not to give them a try.

NetBeans

Although to some people NetBeans will sound like a strange snack, to a lot of developers out there it's a great development environment and is used by a great deal of developers at different levels of skill. Oh, and did I mention that you can run it on Windows, Mac, and Linux, and because it's an open-source project, it's free to use? With open source-projects generally comes a large development community creating plug-ins and offering support, and NetBeans is no exception. You can find the various versions of NetBeans at http://netbeans.org/ where if you'd like, you can download a copy for free.

There are a few versions of NetBeans available: various Java editions, a C edition, a PHP edition, and one with everything in. The good thing is, whatever flavor of NetBeans you choose to go for, they all boast HTML5 and CSS3 support and, with a plug-in, support for SVN, Git, and Mercurial! In actual fact, support for SVN and Mercurial come out of the box for NetBeans, and a simple plug-in is required to install Git support, but I'll go through that when it comes to it. For now, though, let's have a look at how to use NetBeans to interact with our favorite version control systems, starting with SVN.

SVN

As I just mentioned, SVN support is baked right into NetBeans and can be found in a couple of locations within a project. First of all, you can access a lot of SVN commands by right-clicking a file or folder within a project and selecting the Subversion menu option. NetBeans scans the contents of the project to see whether or not it contains .svn files and serves the menu as needed. It also does the same thing for Git and Mercurial projects. The other place you can access the SVN commands offered by NetBeans is through the Team option in the main menu, which will display all the available commands, including some that weren't included in the right-click menu.

The first time you try and perform an action, you'll be prompted to enter some user details for the repository. Once those are stored you will start to notice some changes to the files in the project explorer, such as the file names being highlighted in blue when changes have been made to them and they are in a modified state.

Updating and committing

Performing updates within NetBeans is easy. As mentioned above, you can get to most SVN actions in a number of locations. When it comes to updating, it'll be easier to perform this action by selecting the top level of the project and performing the SVN update from there. This will ensure no files are missed. The easiest way to perform the update is to select that option from within the Subversion menu. When performed, no dialogs will be launched, but a progress bar will show at the bottom of the screen to allow a visual representation of the update progress.

Committing is just as simple within the application, which still lives in both locations of the Subversion options. You can commit files on a file-by-file basis, or run the commit from the top level of the application. This will list all files that have the potential to be committed, but will also include unversioned files, which saves you having to manually add each of the folders, which can still be done by using the Add option within the menu.

When a commit is launched, a new dialog window will be launched listing all the included files, and the option to add a commit message. You can also get additional options, such as a diff between this version and the base version, or the ability to exclude it from the current commit.

Status

If you right-click a file and hit Show Changes within the Subversion menu, a new pane in the window will be revealed which will show you the current state of the SVN in relation to the repository. Although this can be done on a file-by-file basis, it may be more beneficial to run this command on the Source Files directory of the project (this is created by NetBeans when you create a new project), as it will show all changes within the full project in an easy-to-view manner. Within the window you can also interact with the files by right-clicking them and choosing an appropriate action to take, and you can also select multiple files for bulk actions, which makes life a little easier.

Reverting

Undoing your changes within Nebeans is simple, thanks to the simplicity of the application. The reverting process is just as simple as the others and, again, can be accessed from both locations. This is best performed on a file-by-file basis to ensure no changes are accidentally reverted by mistake. When you choose the Revert Modifications option from the menu, a dialog option is launched which allows the choice of three radio buttons.

The first button allows you to simply revert the changes in said file or folder to the state they were in at the last commit, or base. The second option allows you to revert back to a particular commit which can be entered as an integer into the text field accompanying the radio button. The final option allows the changes to be reverted between two commits, although in theory this option doesn't have a reasonable use, so the first two options will be used most often. Once you decide which commit to revert back to, just hit the Revert button and the changes will happen in the background, with the progress indicated yet again by a progress bar.

Mercurial

Working with Mercurial in NetBeans is just as easy as SVN and can be done with the greatest of ease. As you would expect, you get access to all of the main functions you could wish to use on a regular basis. That, however, seems to be it—other than the basic operations, the Mercurial plug-in is somewhat limited. You could argue that the functions aren't advanced enough. But if you wanted to perform a major action, would you really want to do it within the application you write code in? I'll get you acquainted with the functions you do have; getting them nailed downed will still save a lot of time in the long run.

Updating

The Update option lives within the **Team > Mercurial** menu item, along with a fair few other Mercurial options. To perform an update, just hit the appropriately-named link within the menu that was just mentioned and you're off. Clicking this will open up a new dialog where you can specify the revision you would like to update from. It also shows the description, author, and date of the commit to make pinpointing the correct revision even easier. Once you hit Update the working copy will be updated and you'll be ready to go.

Committing

As mentioned previously, you need to commit changes after an update or a merge has taken place. Until you do, the changes aren't tied to a commit. Plus, you also need to commit files after you've made changes, of course. NetBeans also makes the commit process really simple, and this option is also located in the right-click option within the project sidebar in the main window. To perform a commit it's easiest to right-click the top level directory then go into Mercurial and hit Commit.

This opens up a dialog window which lists all of the files that need to be committed, including unversioned ones. As well as being able to commit them in one go, you can also add files using this method because there isn't just an Add option within NetBeans. Once you're happy and you've entered a message, just hit Commit and your bidding will be done.

Status

This command does what it says on the tin: checks the status of the file or folder you run the command on. For best results, it's advisable that you perform this action at the highest point possible to ensure no files are missed out. You can find the status action from either the right-click menu or in the Mercurial option within the Team menu, whichever floats your boat. When the action is performed, no dialog windows are launched; instead, the bottom of the application changes. If you happen to have the dialog options at the bottom of the main menu closed then it will launch a new option showing the status of the repository.

If you still have the options open, the change may be a little harder to notice as it'll simply switch the status results to being the current active tab. If you have any changes, whether unversioned files or actual changes, they'll be listed in the window here. You can also right-click the particular files and perform a couple of common actions, such as committing, doffing, or launching the file within NetBeans, if applicable.

Git

Sadly, Git doesn't come enabled out of the box, but is available in the form a plug-in you can install, so let's get that out of the way first. Head into **Tools > Plugins** to launch the plug-in dialog window. This allows you to manage upgrades to existing plug-ins and more importantly, install new ones. Head into Available Plugins to locate the Git plug-in. You can either search for it on the list or just type `git` into the search window; either way, you'll get something like what's shown in Figure 7-5.

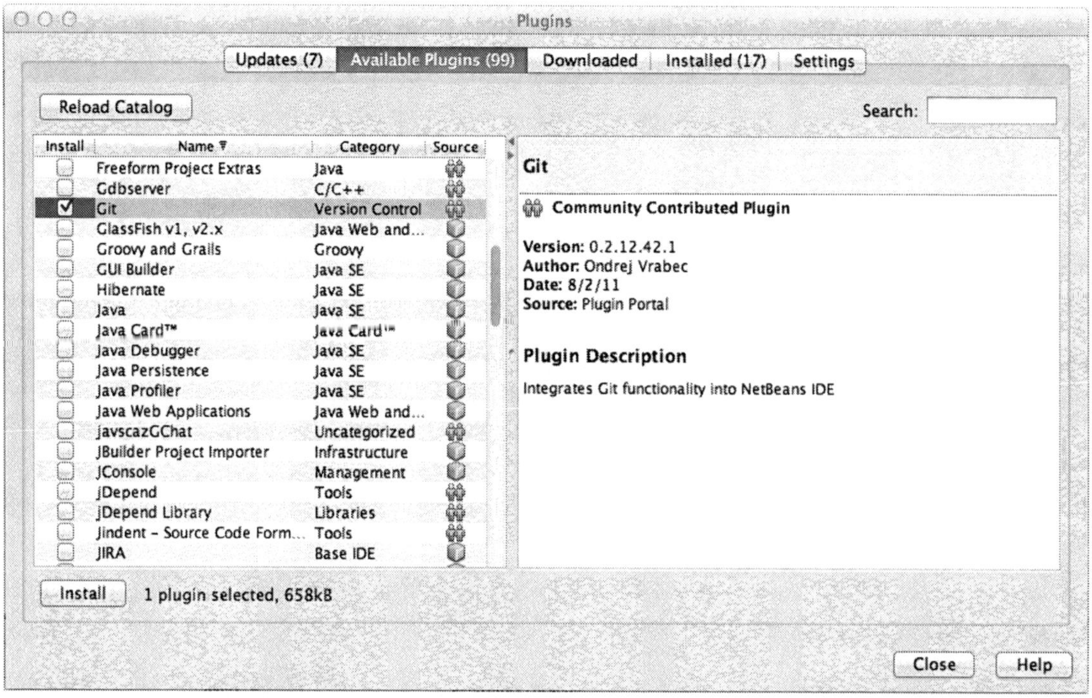

Figure 7-5. The list of available plugins, with Git selected.

Once you've found Git, select it and hit the install button, then accept the terms of use and hit Install. You'll then need to wait till it's installed; it won't take too long, so go grab a beer or cup of coffee if you don't fancy watching the process. Once it's installed, you'll need to restart NetBeans for the installation to take effect. Once it's running again, it's time to get into Git. The plug-in itself is rather full featured and if you wanted to you could perform nearly any desired Git action from within NetBeans. For now, though, we'll just look at the basic actions, starting with adding and committing.

Adding and committing

As with Mercurial, when you perform a commit with Git, you have the option to add any untracked files as well, saving the need to manually add the files before committing. You can, of course, manually add the files using the command located in the right-click menu within the projects section of the main window. Hitting the add option at the top of the project is the best idea, as it ensures no files are missed.

Performing the add function at this level will add all of the untracked files within the repository to be committed and also add all changed files to the list of files to be committed,otherwise knowing as staging the files, which it does without prompting for a confirmation of the file choice. To avoid this, you can add or stage the files on a file-by-file basis, or use the commit function, which allows you to select which files you would like to commit or add and bypass the staging process.

Whichever route you go down to get to the stage of committing, the action is the same. When the commit action is called, from either the option within the Team menu or the right-click menu, a dialog is launched where it's possible to select which files you would like to commit, and add a commit message to accompany the selected files. The message is a required field, so if you can't think of something useful to say to go with the commit, have a think about it and come back.

Show changes

You'll most likely be performing this action on a regular basis to ensure your repository is in good working order, and to make sure you haven't missed anything. The option can be found in both of the menus, and is best performed on the top level of the repository, to ensure no changes have been missed. When clicked, this option doesn't open a dialog window like some of the other actions; it will, however, change the lower half of the screen to show any changes that have been made to the repository. If you happen to have closed all the windows again, as with the Mercurial status command, this will open up a new one for you. Otherwise it can be a little hard to notice the switch.

From within the window it's possible to diff, add, revert, and commit the changes by right-clicking any file that comes up in the status window. This can come in rather useful if you happen to have forgotten about a particular file or if you just prefer managing your files from within this pane; either is just dandy.

Reverting

There may be a time when you have some files that are staged to be committed, or even some changes that you've made when you ask yourself "What was I thinking?!" At such times, you need reverting. This can be achieved relatively easily within NetBeans and, like most of the options in the Git plug-in, it lives in both menus, which makes it even easier to get to. When you launch the revert dialog, you get three options to choose from. The first simply reverts all changes you've made back to the last time they were staged to be committed, so if you have new files, or files that have yet to be staged, you won't lose any changes.

The second option really only applies when you have previously staged a file to be committed and then gone back to make the changes. This option will remove any of the unstaged changes and revert back to the staged version of the changes. As with the previous option, you can also choose whether or not to include new files and folders with the revert, which will cause them to be deleted if the check box to include them is checked.

The final revert option available is to revert any uncommitted changes that have been staged to be committed back to the way they were before they were staged. This can solve the problems caused by the accidental staging of files, or if you just want to unstage changes you weren't ready to commit yet. This option doesn't enable you to include new files and folders, as you wouldn't have tracked unversioned files (it's not possible to do that).

Pulling and pushing

Of course, from time to time you'll need to push or pull changes from a remote server, and NetBeans has you covered. Let's start with pulling. To start the process, just hit the Pull option from within either of the Git menus to get things going. In the dialog that opens, you'll be asked whether or not you want to use the preconfigured remote server options or specify new ones. If the repository you are working on is a clone, you'll just keep with the defaults here. The next stage in the process is to select which branches you'd like to update. In most cases, though, just check all of them and hit Finish to start the pull! After all the files have downloaded, you'll need to do a commit before the changes are fully merged with your working copy. Be sure to remember that, or launch "Show changes" to see exactly what's changed.

Pushing works in nigh on the same way as pulling does, just in reverse. As with Pull, you can run the push command from either menu and, when clicked, a dialog window will be launched to go through the remaining steps. The first stage is to specify remote access details, but this will default to those that have been stored within the repository in the case of cloned repositories. If you do want to enter some different details, just select the lower radio button and enter any required information. The next and final step is to choose which branches you would like to commit. You have to select at least one, or it won't let you finish and therefore complete the push.

NetBeans summary

NetBeans has great support when it comes to version control, and most if it comes from straight out of the box, which is always a good thing. There aren't many negatives when using the actions within NetBeans. Some actions such as pushes and pulls can be a little sluggish, but this is a problem you can always address by firing up another application to deal with it. Even being able to perform commits and deletes is enough to drastically increase productivity, which NetBeans does without breaking a sweat, all while being a kick-ass editor, too!

Sublime Text 2

This editor is an up and comer in the IDE world, with a lot of people seeing it as an alternative to TextMate, mainly because it actually gets updated, regularly! Sadly, unlike TextMate, it has no version control abilities built in, which results in having to play around with some packages to get the functionality you're after. If you're not using Sublime Text 2 and you fancy giving it a try, you can do so on an evaluation basis by downloading a copy to your Mac, Windows, or Linux machine from the website at www.sublimetext.com/2.

Before installing any packages, there's something else to install that makes life using Sublime Text 2 a whole lot easier: Package Control. This is a package in itself, and it makes installing new packages and a lot of other things easier. To get started, open up the console within Sublime Text by hitting Ctrl+` on Mac/Linux or Ctrl+' on Windows. This will open up the console at the bottom of the screen. With the screen open, type in the following code and hit return:

```
import urllib2,os; pf='Package Control.sublime-package';
ipp=sublime.installed_packages_path(); os.makedirs(ipp) if not os.path.exists(ipp) else
None; urllib2.install_opener(urllib2.build_opener(urllib2.ProxyHandler()));
open(os.path.join(ipp,pf),'wb').write(urllib2.urlopen('http://sublime.wbond.net/'+pf.repl
ace(' ','%20')).read()); print 'Please restart Sublime Text to finish installation'
```

This code won't do anything until the editor is restarted, so go ahead and do that now. You may see a number of errors pop up on the screen regarding github packages not existing. If this happens, run the process again and all should be well. Just in case the code changes, or you'd rather copy and paste it, the original can be found on the website here:

```
http://wbond.net/sublime_packages/package_control/installation
```

Once you have the package installed, you can open up its window by hitting Ctrl+Shift+P for Windows and Linux or Cmd+Shift+P for Mac. This window exists already within Sublime Text 2; however, all of its commands are added into it. The commands we're looking for here all start with Package Control, so type that in to filter the list down a bit. There are a lot of available options where you can find out a bit more about the packages (Discover packages) or just install them, which is what you want to do. Hit enter on Package Control: Install Packages to get everything ready.

You'll notice a loading bar at the bottom of the screen while it generates the list. If you see any dialog windows coming up for unavailable packages, just ignore them. It just means that said package has moved or has been deleted. Once they're all loaded, all of the available packages will be displayed in this list; you're looking for the Git package, so find it and hit Enter to install it. You may get some of the missing repository dialog windows again at this point, but they're unrelated to the installation. You'll see a success message at the bottom of the screen when it's finished.

Mercurial

There is a Mercurial plug-in available within the Package Control system installed earlier, called SublimeHG. Install it in the same way as before, opening up the Package Control: Install Packages option within the Command Palette (Cmd+Shift+P on a Mac or Ctrl+Shift+P on Windows and Linux) and typing in `SublimeHG`. Once installed, this now gives you two additional options in the Command Pallete: SublimeHG: HG and SublimeHG: Open HG Command Prompt.

The latter of these options just opens up a command prompt window where you can use Mercurial Terminal commands from within Sublime Text 2, but that isn't the option you're after here. The command you're looking for here is SublimeHG: HG, which when you hit enter on it, gives a list of commands you can use within the application.

In some cases, this plug-in actually doesn't run, and when you try and use any of the commands, you'll see this error:

```
[Errno 2] No such file or directory
[Finished]
```

This is down to the plug-in not being able to locate not being able to locate the Mercurial installation on the machine, so you need to set some additional configurations to help it out. To do this, you need to go into **Preferences ➤ Global Settings – User**, which will open up a new file within the editor. If you've never opened it before, it will be blank except for some curly brackets ({}). In the file, add in the following line:

```
"packages.sublime_hg.hg_exe": "/usr/local/bin/hg"
```

The second half of the setting is the location of Mercurial on your system, so be sure to replace it with the path on your system. You can find that out by using which hg in Terminal, and copying the path that gets output. With the file saved, restart Sublime Text 2 and now the plug-in should work as expected. Now that it is working correctly, all of its functionality is now available to use.

Adding and committing

You can add files in a number of ways using the plug-in, using either the add command, or the addremove command. Either will add the files for you, ready for them to be committed, along with any changed files, and doing so will show the output of this in a new file in the editor, but this isn't necessary and you can close it as needed.

When it comes to committing files, you can either commit the whole working copy or go into the specific file you want to commit and use the commit (this file) command, which, as it says, will commit this file. Either option when selected will ask you for a commit message at the bottom of the screen, then the file will be commit to the local repository. Easy.

Blame and log commands

The plug-in also allows you to perform the blame and log commands on the files of your choosing. The blame command breaks down the file on a line-by-line basis and shows you who wrote each line. The log command, on the other hand, shows when the commit committed, the date, the author, and the comment associated with the commit.

You have the choice of logging the repository either as a whole or on a per-file basis, depending on what your needs are. Just select log or log (this file), as appropriate. The blame command only works on a per-file basis, so just have the file you want to blame open, then run the command and the output will be displayed in a new file. The same goes for performing the log command, too.

SVN

Although there are a few packages available for Subversion, there aren't any valuable ones available. They're either riddled with errors or they just don't work at all. That means that any work you want to do will need to be done outside of Sublime Text 2 or by using the Terminal package to make running Terminal commands a little easier on specific files or folders.

Git

Now that the package is installed, launching the Command Palette is the best way to perform your Git actions. Typing in `Git` will filter the list down to show all of the available commands from Pushing to Pulling and Adding to Deleting. We'll start with adding and committing first, as these are some of the most frequently-used features—if you're being good and making regular commits, that is. Just as a side note, you won't see the Git options in the Command Palette unless you have a Git project open in Sublime Text 2. In case you think it hasn't installed correctly, it has.

Adding and committing

You have a couple of options within the Git menu for adding files. You can either add the current file using the option that says just that, or use Add… to bring up a list of all untracked changes. In this view, you can add one file or all the files, whichever you'd prefer. The problem with the all option, which it mentions, is that it won't include untracked files, so they will need to be added one at a time. When you perform an add command, or any command for that matter, the command itself or a confirmation message will be shown at the bottom of the application, so you know all is well.

Once you've added any changes you'll, of course, need to commit those changes into the repository, which is just as easy as adding them. In the list of Git options there are two commit commands to choose from, Commit or Quick Commit. The main commit option, when checked, opens up a new window within Sublime Text 2 to allow an in-depth commit message to be used. This, of course, comes in very useful when you're committing large amounts of code. Once you've entered your commit message, just close the window off; trying to save it or anything else will cancel the commit.

The Quick Commit option performs the same action but, instead of opening up a new file to enter a commit message, a text box will appear at the bottom of the page where you can enter your message. This comes in very handy when you need to make quick changes or bug fixes, when you just need to enter a few words, hit enter, and, boom! Everything is committed and up to date.

The only slight problem with both of these commands is the lack of being able to choose which files you are committing. Using the regular commit option lists all of the changes that you are committing within the file but doesn't give any options regarding which ones to commit. This is a little annoying, but by no means a deal breaker.

Pulling and pushing

The pull command is just as easy to use as any of the others. By now you may have realized that typing the name of the command, such as `Pull`, can filter down the Command Palette a lot more quickly than typing `Git Pull`, which can save some time. However you get to it, hitting the Git Pull command will perform the action there and then for you, and you'll see a message at the bottom of the screen informing you of the output from the pull. Easy.

The push command works in the same way as the pull command, so when you have changes that you're ready to push, just run the command and the changes will be pushed. When you perform the command, you'll see the output you would receive if you ran the command in Terminal, such as `Everything up-to-date` when there are no changes to push. You'll also see any errors with the push in this console at the bottom of the application, so keep an eye on it if you have any problems. Otherwise the push should work just fine.

Blame and log commands

It's pretty easy to take advantage of the blame and log commands using the Git package. The blame command breaks down a file on a line-by-line basis, showing the user who last edited that line, and the date that line was altered. You can run the blame command on the file you're on by selecting the option from the Command Palette and it'll launch a new file that contains the blamed file with the author of each line, and the line itself. It happens really quickly. When you're done with the file you can just close it.

The log ability is also pretty cool and you can take advantage of its speed to make quick changes and review your changes. There are two log options available in the menu: log and log all. The log all command looks at all the commits in the repository, so you can see the message associated with the commit as well as the author and the date it was committed. If you hit enter on any particular commit, a new file will open showing more information about the commit including all of the files included in it.

The other log command is specific to the file you have open, and using it brings back all of the commits that have been done with that particular file. When your list of commits comes up, you can quickly scan the comments to see if that's the file you're looking for. If you hit return with said commit selected, a diff will be launched in a new file, showing the differences between the two files, which is really handy for quick reviews of the file history.

Summary

In this chapter you've picked up some tips on how to speed up your workflow without actually having to leave your favored coding application. You've been through a number of great plug-ins that help speed up development and make committing changes so easy, you don't have an excuse not to use them. You've also looked at a number of applications (across numerous OSs), some of which you may never have used, or even known existed.

You may be curious to try a new application, given how easy some of them are to use and how great some of the plug-ins are, not to mention the benefits they would bring to your workflow. This also covers some of the popular cross-platform applications we've covered, and of course those which are specialized for a specific operating system. If none of these have floated your boat, it may be worth giving Terminal a try, especially if a coding application does not interact with your versioning system in the way you want it to. But there's a whole chapter for that later on. Now, it's time to talk about that horrible moment when you find yourself with a conflict and learn how to go about resolving it.

Chapter 8

I Have a Conflict: What Can I Do?

Before I go into anything major in this chapter, I need to cover what conflicts are and how they happen. On the basic level, a conflict occurs when two people are working on the same part of a file at the same time. When the first user commits their code, that commit is fine, because there are no changes to conflict with it. However, when the second user goes to update, then there is a problem. When the versioning system tries to merge the files together, the changes from both users are new and in the same location, so the versioning system gets confused about what goes where; as a result, it creates a conflicted file containing both sets of changes. Conflicts commonly happen when more than one person makes a change to, for instance, a width value in CSS. Since the system doesn't know which value it should use, it gets confused and conflicts the file.

No matter which system you use, conflicts are always around to bite you in the butt. Having ways to help make that process easier is always a good thing. This chapter looks at some applications that can help alleviate the strain of merging conflicted files by allowing you to do it in a nice app rather than going into a file and managing the conflict yourself. This is always an option, however, so I'll start by talking about managing conflicts manually.

Manual conflict management

Before I dive into the applications you can use to manage conflicts, let's look at what happens when you get a conflict and have to deal with it manually. This is an option you can choose, because given the time it can take to resolve beastly conflicts with programs, it may be easier to do so in the file. With that said, let's start with SVN.

SVN

While you're happy in your own little SVN world, that's generally when a conflict shows up. And when that happens, SVN takes a few steps to ensure that nothing is lost. A conflict results in a total of four files: the original file, which contains the actual conflict; your version on the file, before the conflict happened; another file, which has the revision of the file before you made any changes to it; and the most recent version of the file. If, for example, you have a conflict in a CSS file called `style`, your folder looks something like this:

```
Style.css
Style.css.mine
Style.css.r86
Style.css.r87
```

The `Style.css` file contains all of its original contents, as well as the conflict generated from your local version, and the remote version. It only contains the areas that conflict, from both files, and these are inserted in the file at the location the conflicts occurred.

The `Style.css.mine` version of the file is your local copy, before the update ran. It doesn't contain any conflicts, but it contains all the changes you made.

The `Style.css.r86` revision is the one that existed after the last update took place, before the conflict happened. Therefore, any changes that have been made since then aren't present in this version. It's classed as the BASE version of the file.

`Style.css.r87` is the newest revision of the file, which was brought down from the repository when the update occurred. This version only contains the new revisions, so conflicts exist here.

In most cases, if you open the current file (in this case, `Style.css`) in a text editor, you should be able to spot the conflict and manually fix it. Generally, as I mentioned, conflicts are caused by two different people editing the same part of the file at the same time, and in those cases you can say, "Oh, I see what they were trying to do there." When you have a conflict, the file looks something like this:

```
<<<<<<< .mine
a:hover {
  color: #818181;
}

a:visited {
  color: #555;
}
=======
a img {
  display: block;
}
h1, h2, h3, h4, h5, h6 {
  font-weight: normal;
}
>>>>>>> .r87
```

In this example, you can see where the conflict happened, because it's wrapped in lovely > brackets. If you know a file has a conflict, you can do a general search for <<<< to find it easily. In this case (or any case, really), the easiest way to resolve the conflict manually is to select which version of the conflict section to use: yours or the remote version. After that, remove any other traces of the conflict; this leaves the file a normal state again, containing the desired version of the conflicting section. Once the file has been cleaned up, you resolve the file of its conflicted state via Terminal or your choice of program. When you do that, the other files created during the conflict are removed, and that's it—conflict resolved.

In this case, the conflict is basic and easily resolved. Sometimes you get horrible conflicts: for example, an entire file that's duplicated. If you try to resolve it this way, you get a file that is a duplicate of itself, which isn't good. It may be a better idea to revert the file to the most recent version, thereby removing your changes to the file. Before doing that, though, go into the .mine file, manually copy your changes, revert, paste those changes into the file, and then commit the file again.

Resolving conflicts manually isn't often necessary, but it's nice to know how to do it in case you get a conflict that's a beast. In a nutshell, that's how to resolve SVN conflicts—by using the file itself rather than a GUI. If it's made you feel a little ill, never fear: a few options are available, and you see those in a bit.

Mercurial

When you get a conflict in Mercurial (which is a little less likely than in SVN, because the merging system is better), you always get the same format to deal with: two files, rather than SVN's four. Let's say, for consistency's sake, that you have another conflict in the same file used in the SVN example (Style.css). You have the following files:

> Style.css
>
> Style.css.orig

They are the file containing the conflicted state, and the original file before the conflict happened. This approach is due to the distributed versioning system. Since it uses change sets rather than revisions, keeping files with previous revisions doesn't apply as it does with SVN.

To resolve the conflict, you need to dive into the Style.css file and look for it:

```
<<<<<<< local
a:hover {
  color: #818181;
}

a:visited {
  color : #555;
}
=======
a img {
  display: block;
}
h1, h2, h3, h4, h5, h6 {
  font-weight: normal;
}
>>>>>>> other
```

223

The changes in the local part of the file are your changes, and the changes in other are causing this whole conflict business in the first place. If you clean up the file and remove all the > and < brackets, then the file is in a state that's ready to resolve. If you then resolve the file and commit it, you're unfortunately left with the .orig file, which you have to remove yourself. Shocking, I know, but that's how things are.

If you're dealing with a really hideous conflict, you may need to revert because it's too different for you to deal with. In such an event, dive into the .orig file and copy all your changes, perform the revert, and add the copied changes back into the main file and commit combo. It's a killer every time.

Git

Conflicts in Git are somewhat similar to those in Mercurial: they show the most recent changes at the top and changes from the other commit underneath. No additional files are created or anything like that; everything is managed from this one file and from the repository itself. In the conflicted file in question, you see something like the following:

```
<<<<<<< HEAD
a:hover {
  color: #818181;
}

a:visited {
  color : #555;
}
=======
a img {
  display: block;
}
h1, h2, h3, h4, h5, h6 {
  font-weight: normal;
}
>>>>>>> b29196692f5ebfd10d8a9ca1911c8b08127c85f8
```

In this example, the local copy of the code is located at the top of the file, and the newer version of the file is at the bottom. When you get a mess like this, which is quite rare with Git, you need to work out which changes you'd like to keep or discard. Then remove all the >> and == to leave the file in the state it would be in if a merge had happened successfully. After that, all that's left is to resolve the conflicted file by either diving into the Terminal or command line or going into your program of choice.

When it comes to manually resolving conflicts, no matter which versioning system you use, the process to resolve the conflict is always the same. First work out which version of the conflicted code is correct (either yours or the remote version), and then remove all instances of the code generated by the conflict. This also goes for files containing multiple conflicts. When the file is clean, resolve it, and it's ready to be committed. You can take this approach and use Terminal to resolve the conflict, or you can use one of many different programs to achieve the same thing.

Configuring a merge tool for use

For some versioning applications, you select your preferred merge or diffing tool from a list of preconfigured options, and that's it. If the application you want isn't included, then you may need to go to the application's forums or find out if your application is going to be added to the list of potential options. There isn't much you can do otherwise.

Terminal use is slightly different and isn't as easy to set up in most cases. On the most basic level, when you want to use a new diffing tool, you need to write a small script known as a *wrapper*, which ensures the data is delivered to the application in the correct order. This may assume that your application has its own command-line tools, meaning you can open the application from the command line or Terminal. If your application doesn't have these tools, the process is more difficult but not impossible.

When configuring your desired merge tool, you link to the wrapper script and not to the application directly. This ensures that the application gets everything it needs and opens correctly. However, one wrapper script isn't enough if you want to use the same application for versioning systems. Because each system provides different files or requires files from different locations, you need different wrappers to ensure that the configuration for each system is respected. Since the wrapper for each application and each system it works with may be different, there is no generic script that can be used as a base. That being said, Google is definitely your friend here: with a quick search, you can probably find other users who have written a solution to your needs. As an alternative, you can always contact me through e-mail (hey@chrisdkemper.co.uk) or Twitter (@Chrisdkemper), and I'll do my best to help you. To get you started, Chapter 9 includes a few wrapper scripts that should give you a better idea of how wrappers work and how to get started if you want to write your own.

GUIs

Now, on to the much easier world of using graphical tools to manage conflicts, rather than having to go into the file, remove stuff, and then commit the file again. This section looks at some Windows programs, Mac programs, and programs that can be used on multiple OSs (including Linux). That's a lot to get through, so let's go.

Windows

Although a lot of the better-known applications that look for changes are cross-platform, a few are specific to Windows. The best of the bunch is WinMerge, and you're about to go through it.

WinMerge

This lovely program is fully open source, and therefore no one person is responsible for it. That being said, it's also free, which is a great bonus in this economy. Don't let the fact that it's free make you think it's a poor-quality program—it's a great program with an equally brilliant set of features. The developers who contribute to the maintenance and improvement of the WinMerge project also use it while developing, which is often referred to as *dogfooding*. It's a great sign when the developers working on a program actively use it! Another perk is that you can integrate it straight into TortoiseSVN, which makes it appear in the context menu when you right-click a conflicted file. This saves you from having to load the files individually, which can be quite useful and save precious time.

Loading conflicts

When you load a conflicted file in WinMerge by opening it from the command line, manually dragging and dropping the file into the application, or right-clicking the file and selecting WinMerge from the menu, you get to see your version and the post-update version side by side. The file in the right column is the one that is used when the merging process is complete, so bear that in mind while you're sorting out the conflicts.

Navigating the conflicted file

While you're navigating the conflicted file, you'll use two main controls: Use Left and Use Right. This process allows you to choose which file's version of the conflict is used in the resolved file. As you move around the file, either by scrolling or by jumping between conflicts using Alt + Up and Alt + Down, conflicts are highlighted in yellow. You can see an example of this in Figure 8-1.

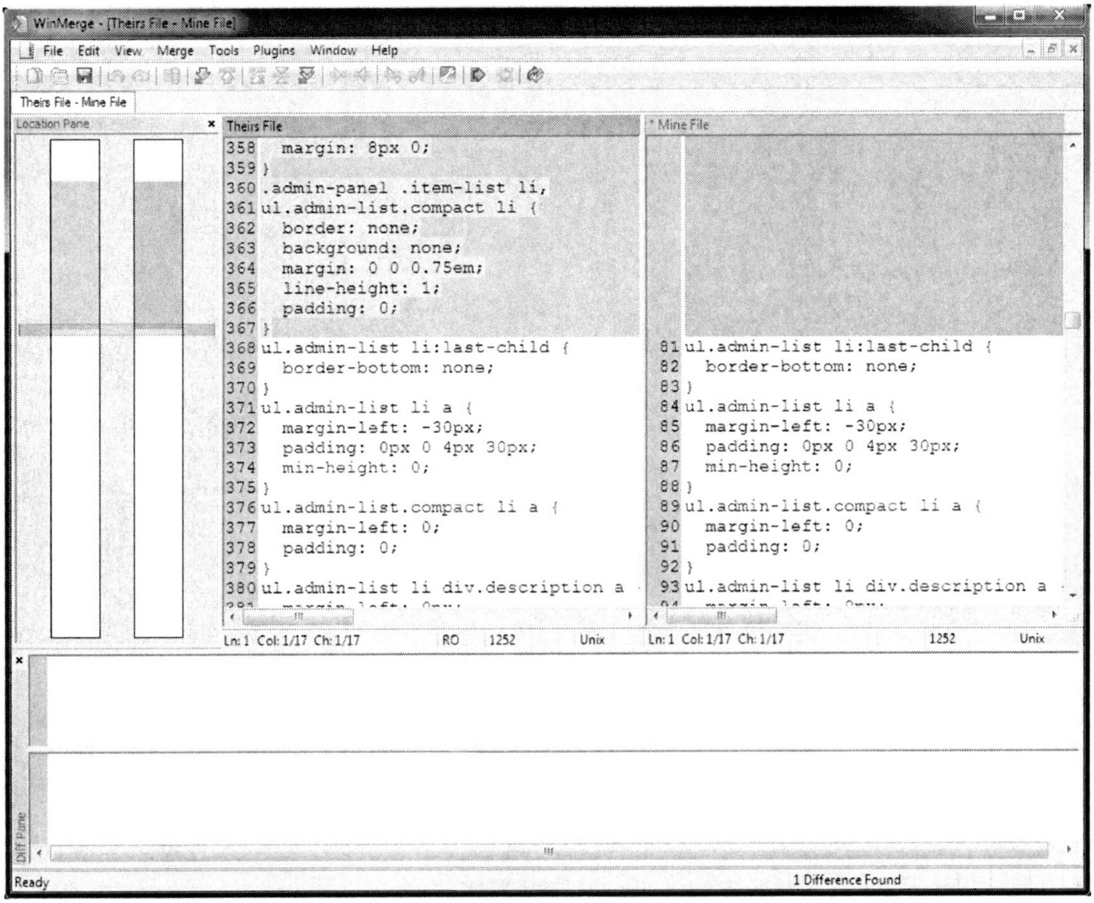

Figure 8-1. WinMerge's main screen. A section has been deleted in the local version but not in the remote version, causing a conflict.

When you select a conflict, you have a few options, the first of which is to choose whether you prefer to use the left or right side of the file. You can do this easily by using the copy-left arrow (Alt + Left) to copy the highlighted change to the left file or the copy-right arrow (Alt + Right) to copy the selected conflict to the right file. But this isn't always the best solution, which is why having the ability to drag and drop code is a great bonus. If you have a conflict where both changes are needed for the same line, you can simply drag the changes from the left side to the right and then alter the file on the right side to get the required result. Once you have the right file in the state you want it (remember, the right file is used when you save), save the file, and that's your conflict managed.

Resolving conflicts in other ways

If, for whatever reason, you get the merge wrong, and you need to resolve the conflict in a different way, then you'll be glad to know that when you save a conflicted file, a new file is automatically created: the .bak file. This is a copy of the original file that has the same file name, with .bak at the end. If you need to, you can open the .bak file and do the merging process again. (You get a new .bak file as well—it's a vicious cycle.)

You also have the option to use other controls in the app to influence your merging capabilities. One choice is to go with all the changes in either your own file or the remote version, which you can do by using either all left or all right. If you want to use all the changes from the remote file, rather than attempting a merge, it's easier to revert the file instead. This achieves the same result by discarding any changes made by you in favor of the newer version of the file.

Once you're happy with the merges you've made, you have to resolve the file manually using your preferred SVN client. Then, if you don't need it anymore, delete the .bak file created during the process. The conflict is gone, and your merge is handled. Easy!

WinMerge summary

All in all, this isn't a bad little program. It's got a half-decent feature set, and best of all, it's free! The only issue is that getting it to work with Git or Mercurial is a bit of a pain; but for an SVN diff alternative, it's OK. You can use it to manually check for differences between two files, if you happen to have both versions, by going to **File ➤ Open**, selecting the files you'd like to diff, and clicking OK. This gives you the same features as if you opened a conflicted file and means you can use it to sort out conflicts in Mercurial or Git files, just not directly from their applications.

To try this app for yourself, head over to http://winmerge.org/ and download a copy.

Mac

Developers have taken advantage of the creative freedom in OS X to create some great-looking applications. Mac-specific applications are built well and generally quite shiny. This section looks at some of the best applications for the Mac.

Kaleidoscope

If you remember Versions being mentioned in Chapter 5, then you may find Kaleidoscope a little familiar, because they were created by the same company: Sofa. You can find this application at www.kaleidoscopeapp.com/; it's possible to either buy it outright for $38 or download it for a 30-day trial.

Kaleidoscope is a very good-looking application, and you can tell that a lot of effort has been put into making it both look good and work well. The interface is very clean and easy to figure out.

Loading conflicts

The easiest way to compare two files with Kaleidoscope is to drag them both into the application, where they are placed side by side automatically. Alternatively, you can use the Open With command with the files selected, or open the application directly and then open two files that way. You can also perform multiple comparisons at the same time by opening a new tab in Kaleidoscope and then opening the files you want to compare. It's also worth noting that when you choose **File ➤ Open**, you can select multiple files, which can save you from having to run **File ➤ Open** twice. New comparisons or new tabs also support dragging and dropping files, so open the tab into which you want to drag files, and then go crazy with drag-and-drop action. You can see an example comparison of two files in Figure 8-2.

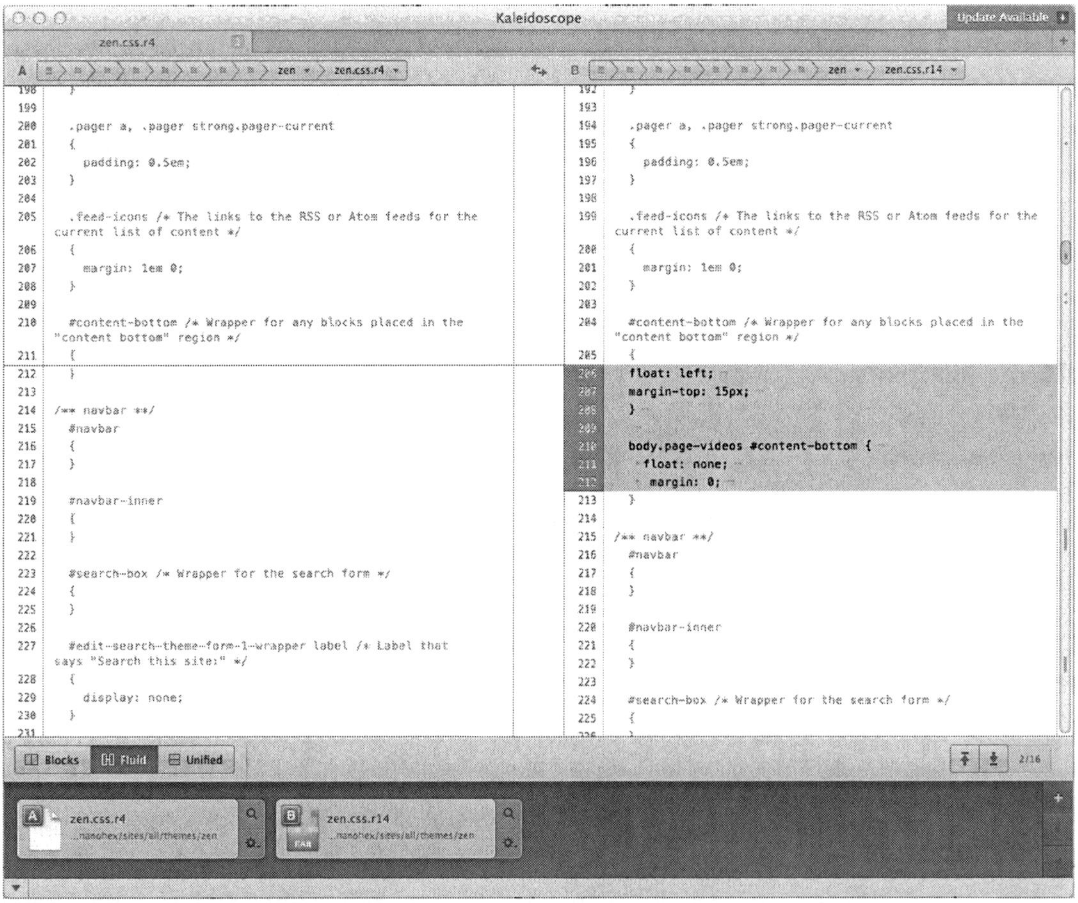

Figure 8-2. Comparision of two files in Kaleidoscope's fluid view. Additional lines have been added in the right file, and they're highlighted in green.

You also have the option to work with more than two files at any given time. If you drag and drop multiple files into Kaleidoscope, it opens a file drawer. From it, you can make any file either A or B to show differences between those two files, and you can change to another file from the file drawer at any time. You can also add files to the drawer by dragging them into the drawer directly or by using the plus icon to the right. If you have additional comparisons or tabs open, each one has its own file drawer, which helps prevent files from getting mixed up between comparisons.

Navigating conflicts: colors

Kaleidoscope offers a number of different options for navigating conflicts, including multiple views and the use of colors to show differences. Let's look at the colors first. Any added text is shown highlighted in green, any removed text is highlighted in red, and any instances where changes occur are highlighted in purple, with the specific words affected on that line in a deeper purple. The purple cases in the file don't depend on which file is A and which file is B; however, the red and green text highlighting are more relative. For example, if file B includes some text that isn't present in file A, it's highlighted in green, because the application treats file B as if it were the more up-to-date file.

If you swap the files around (using the double arrow icon located in the top-center of the main window), the same text, now present in what is in theory file A, appears highlighted in red. It's classed as deleted text, because the application believes it has been removed from file B and therefore has been deleted.

Navigating the differences in the application is a little easier when you know that the red and green highlighting show differences between the two files in a more creative manner. In addition to the double arrow, there is also an up and down combo located at lower right in the application. This lets you navigate between differences without having to scroll through the file, and it also shows you which difference you're looking at in relation to the total number next to the arrows.

Navigating conflicts: views

There are also a number of different views available to help you navigate through differences in files. This can be changed at lower left in the main window by clicking the item method you want to use.

The default option is the Block view, which blocks off any changes against the other file, making it a lot easier to identify differences if you're skimming the file.

The next option, Fluid, removes the blocked-off areas and shows the two files as they stack up next to each other. Any differences that occur between the files are shown with the previously mentioned colors, and lines show where they are located in relation to the other file.

The final view, Unified, shows only one version of the file, with all the changes included in it. To the left of the window are two sets of line numbers so you can keep track of where each difference occurs in the file. All line differences highlighted in purple are shown on top of each other, with lines from the left showing which file each of the values is from.

Search feature

As well as the previously mentioned options, Kaleidoscope also has a search feature that you can use on either file. To activate it, choose **Edit ➤ Search**, or press Cmd + F. With the search option open, select which file you want to use it with (if you're in Fluid view, then no specification is needed) and type your query, and Kaleidoscope starts searching. Any results are highlighted in yellow with the rest of the page darkened. You can also skip to differences using the arrow keys located next to the search field.

Image comparison

In addition to text files, Kaleidoscope can show differences between images, which is a cool feature. To start, add the two images to the application the same way you add text files (the file drawer works too). This time, however, the navigation controls are different. The only one that remains the same is the double arrow, which serves the same purpose as before by allowing you to switch the location of the images between A and B. The other controls are totally new.

Two-Up view

The first and default view is Two-Up, which shows the images either side by side or on top of each other. You can toggle the position of the images by selecting an arrangement to the right of the view selections. While in any of the view modes, notice that the controls to the right remain the same. The majority of them control how zoomed-in the images are, except for the hand; when it's selected, it allows you to move the image around, which is great for when you've zoomed in a lot. Figure 8-3 shows an example of the Two-Up view.

Figure 8-3: Kaleidoscope's Two-Up view showing two images side by side, ready for comparison

One-Up view

The next view is One-Up. This view shows you only one image at a time, with the ability to switch between which one is showing at the moment by using the double arrow or the A/B buttons to the right of the view controls. The cool thing about this view is to the right of the A/B buttons: a play/pause icon combo, and a drop-down containing some speed settings. When you click the play icon, it switches between the images at the specified speed, which can make it a whole lot easier to spot small differences or compare which image looks better!

Split view

The Split view is another pretty awesome Kaleidoscope feature. It places the images on top of each other and allows you to show a portion of one image and a portion of another image. This is achieved by using a line with two draggable points, which you can position to show as much or as little of one image as you want. As you would expect, the position of the images you're splitting can be swapped by clicking the faithful double arrow.

Final view

The Final view may well be the most impressive, as it tries to highlight the visual differences between the two files. As in the One-Up view, you can toggle which image is visible by using the A/B buttons, which are accompanied this time by a slider. The slider toggles the opacity of the changes Kaleidoscope has overlaid on top of the selected image. Of course, this has its best results when you're comparing two images that have been only slightly altered; otherwise it shows that the entire file is different. It can be really useful for those moments when you know an image doesn't look right, but you can't put your finger on why, and, sadly, the One-Up view couldn't help.

Integrating other applications

In addition to all these features, Kaleidoscope also integrates into other applications easily; or if it doesn't integrate directly, it has a command-line tool that can be used instead. It includes instructions and/or assets for integration with the command line, Versions, TextMate, and the SVN, Git, and Mercurial command-line options as well, which is pretty cool. You can access the Integration menu by choosing **Kaleidoscope ➤ Integration**, which brings up the dialog shown in Figure 8-4.

Figure 8-4. The Integration window, which lets you use Kaleidoscope in conjunction with other applications and the command line by following the instructions

Kaleidoscope summary

Although Kaleidoscope has an impressive feature set and allows you to look for changes in images in a few cool ways, it does have one issue: you can't directly resolve conflicts from the application. I may have heard "What?!" or "Eh?" from you, but it's not all bad, because it allows you to view the conflicts in an easy-to-see format. Then, all you need to do is manually resolve the conflicts in the file or use another diff tool.

Kaleidoscope really comes into its own with its image and text diffing. If you need to find differences between two files for QA or another reason, I challenge you to find a better interface for it.

Before you pass judgment too quickly, head over to www.kaleidoscopeapp.com/ and download the free trial. Even if it's not your main diff tool, you'll find uses for it in your workflow, such as comparing different versions of the same file. Either way, it's definitely worth a shot.

FileMerge

If you've used a Mac before, then you've already dealt with FileMerge, because it's bundled with the developer tools you installed a few chapters ago. Although FileMerge is a bit basic, it's still a great tool to use, and being free adds another plus to its list.

FileMerge integrates with a lot of programs by default, such as Versions, Cornerstone, svnX, and many more. If you decide to use FileMerge as your default conflict-management program, this is yet another perk of doing so.

Loading conflicts

When you open the application for the first time, you're given two fields, one for the left file and one for the right, as you can see in Figure 8-5. Notice the message at the bottom of the window that says "Enlarge window to specify ancestor and/or merge paths." If you do as it commands, you see an additional two fields for Ancestor and Merge, respectively.

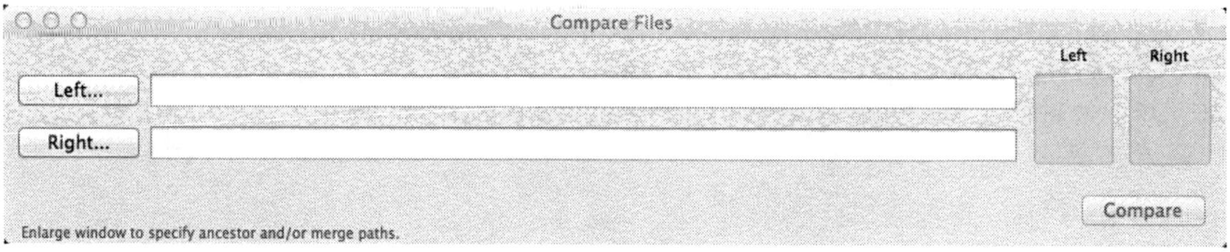

Figure 8-5. The FileMerge in which you can compare two files: one on the left and one on the right

When you have the two files side by side, the real party begins. The window is split into three sections: the two files are at the top, and the bottom half of the screen is home to the merged file—what is in the file when you click Save. Any changes are shown on the far right of the application, marked by lines of different thicknesses depending on how big the difference is between the two files.

Navigating conflicts

As you go through the changes, you can select them individually and choose which file should be used in the merged version, right or left. This can be easily controlled by using the drop-down at lower right, where you can select whether to use one side, both, or none. Selecting an option changes the bottom half of the application accordingly, so you can see how your changes affect the finished file. You can go back and change which file to use at any time. You can also make changes manually in the bottom half of the application by typing as needed. This can be handy for tidying up small bits of code that didn't merge properly, or adding little tweaks or comments.

When you've made your choices and the bottom file is finally to your liking, go to the File menu and select either **Save** or **Save As** to save your changes. If you've specified a file to use to house the merge, then you aren't prompted to select a file; however, if you went with the basic setup, you need to specify a file name and a location. Once the file has been saved, that's that; the original files are left in place. If you manually added the files into FileMerge, you may need to delete some files to clean up the working copy, such as the .mine file that comes with SVN conflicts.

FileMerge summary

Although FileMerge is a very basic application, it works really well at what it does. You could argue that it doesn't highlight the changes well enough or looks a little plain, but it allows you to merge a file relatively easily and make manual changes to the finished file. Also, its vast integration into Mac versioning applications makes FileMerge all the more appealing, plus it's free. How can you complain?

Linux

When it comes to using applications on Ubuntu and other Linux systems, they're most likely open source. In this instance, the best applications for visually assessing changes are open source and not necessarily Linux specific. With that in mind, I'll review a number of applications that work cross-platform and work on Ubuntu, too. One of these applications is Linux specific: Meld. Let's take a closer look.

Meld

Although Meld Is a basic application, it works well and is a pleasure to use. It provides some great features such as inline editing, directory comparison, tabs for multiple comparison sessions, three-way merges, and more. In addition, it's an open source application that is only available on Linux, plus it's free.

Installation

Installing Meld on Ubuntu is simple. It can be installed in the usual `apt-get` fashion, which makes the installation even easier. To install Meld, run the following command in Terminal:

```
sudo apt-get install meld
```

Loading conflicts

If you run Meld in Terminal, it opens as a stand-alone application, ready for you to use. If you select the New Comparison button at upper left in the application, it launches a dialog with a number of options, as shown in Figure 8-6.

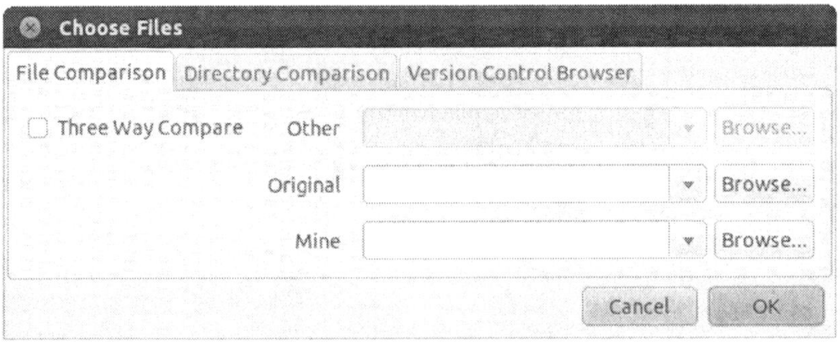

Figure 8-6. This dialog in which you create a new comparision in Meld

You can use this dialog to load files manually into Meld, using the Mine and Original fields. The first option is grayed out, but it becomes available when you select the Three Way Compare check box. You can also select the Directory Comparison tab to compare directories rather than files.

Version Control Browser

You can also select the Version Control Browser tab, where you can select a repository to scan. Selecting the directory and clicking OK scans the repository for changes; you can click any files that are outputted, and the differences are shown in Meld. This allows you to make last-minute changes before committing the files, and it gives you an easier way to review the changes you've made locally. Either way, this feature is pretty cool and not one you find in other applications.

Three-way merge

Sadly, when you use the three-way compare system in Meld, you don't get any additional ways to navigate between changes. This is slightly annoying. Despite that, it's still a way to compare three files at the same time, which you don't always get so easily. In normal cases, you use the third file as a common ancestor to make identifying changes much easier. However, you can in theory select any three files to compare; it's entirely up to you.

Navigating conflicts

In terms of navigation, Meld only has very basic tools: up and down arrows for navigating between differences. You can also scroll between the differences; they're highlighted with green for added material and red for removed material, which makes the differences easier to manage and view.

Meld summary

This is a great application, and its being free and easy to use are definite perks. Although it's only available on Linux, if you happen to be on Ubuntu or any other flavor of Linux it's definitely worth a try—you get a load of useful features.

Cross-platform

Let's look at a couple of the best-rated cross-platform applications available and see how to get them up and running on your operating system (if they're supported, that is).

Diffuse

The first cross-platform application is Diffuse, a lovely diffing app. As it's open source, you get a lot of features, which you don't always expect with free software; so if you're having doubts, I'd put them to one side for now. Let's get straight into installing Diffuse on either Windows or Linux; these two options are the best in terms of ease of installation. If you prefer to use a Mac, you need to consider MacPorts and possibly other dependencies, which aren't particularly useful at this level. If you're using a Mac, it's best to choose one of the other options suggested; but if you're on Windows or Linux, read on!

Installing on Windows

The Windows installation is a lot simpler, mostly because the nice people at Diffuse supply an `.exe` file for Windows users, which cuts the pain of having to compile anything from source. To get the file, head over to `http://sourcegear.com/diffmerge/downloads.php` and click the Win32 link to be taken to the SourceForge page that houses the program. Once it's downloaded, run it like a normal installation process. After the install is complete, a new option is added to the Start menu, and you can launch Diffuse.

Installing on Linux

Although you need to head into Terminal to install Diffuse, it's quite painless. The installation itself is only one line of code, which is in a format similar to the commands you've used. With Terminal open, enter the following command to start the process:

```
sudo apt-get install diffuse
```

This command asks for your password, but other than that it runs quickly, so no cups of team are needed this time. Once the installation is finished, you have a fully working application, ready for use. You can run Diffuse into a stand-alone application by running `diffuse` in Terminal, which launches it as desired.

Loading conflicts

Regardless of the operating system being used, one of the first things to do is open some files to compare. This can either be achieved by selecting **File > Open File** or via simple drag-and-drop. With the files in place, it's time to look at some of the basic controls of the application, starting with the various arrows.

Navigating conflicts: arrows

Diffuse includes a number of up and down arrows: to be specific, two up and two down. These arrows allow you to move between differences in the two files without the need to scroll. You can also quickly jump to the last difference by using the arrow with a link on top or below it, depending on the orientation of the arrow.

The other arrows that point left and right, or a mixture of the two, control the main functionality in the application. The two arrows to the left of the group control the movement of selections between one file and another. They can be easily identified thanks to the line located at the tip of each arrow; they look like the first and last selection arrows, but tipped on their sides, you can see all of the arrows used for navigation in Figure 8-7. For example, if you want to copy the selected chunk of code from the left file into the right file, you use the lined arrow pointing to the right; if this were the other way around, the opposite process would occur.

Figure 8-7. The arrows available when navigating changes within Diffuse.

To the right of the previous arrows are two simple left and right arrows that have a different purpose: you select an area in one of the files and then click the arrow pointing at the opposite file, and the content at the same location in the other file is copied into the selection of the selected file. If you want to take only one or two lines of a change using this method, you select the lines in the opposite file, regardless of what was there, and then click the arrow pointing toward the selection. Doing so takes the lines from the other file and copies them into the selection in place of what was selected. You can also see all of the arrows used in Figure 8-7 above.

Two-way merge

Creating a two-way merge is as easy as pie. You can either open the application and drag in two files, or click the New Two-Way File Merge button. If you have an existing merge open and click the New Two-Way File Merge button, it opens a new tab in the application where you can have multiple diffs open at once, which can be handy at times. You can add new files to the previously mentioned tab by using the File menu or the folder icon on each side of the application. You can work with the files using the controls you've already seen; then, when you're happy, save the file, and you're all set. Having the two files loaded side by side should look something like Figure 8-8.

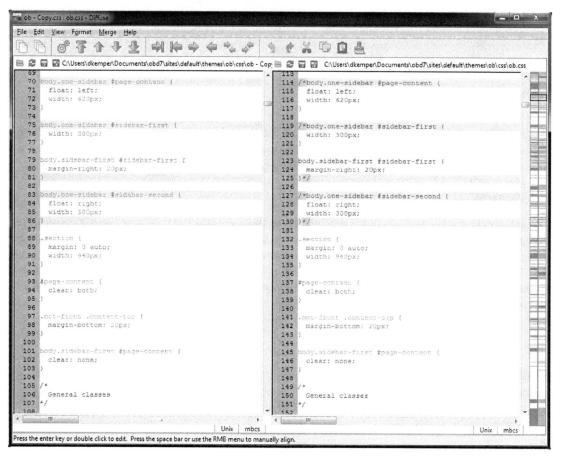

Figure 8-8. Two CSS files next to each other in Diffuse's two-way merge

Three-way merge

To launch a new three-way merge, use its button, which is the second from the left. If you have another merge or diff open, the new merge will be opened as a new, blank tab in the system; you only need to add files for it to work. The easiest way to do this is to add the files from the File option in each frame of the application. All the functions you've been over still work in the three-way state, with the addition of the Right Then Left and Left Then Right buttons, which can be used to include both sets of changes.

The last set of buttons only really shines when the buttons are used within three-way merges. These buttons are the two arrows pointing in opposite directions, with the distinction between the two being which diagonal the arrows are arranged in. The button you click determines which code in the selected files appears first in the merged center file. So, clicking Merge From Left Then Right takes the selected code from the left file and then code from the same selection on the right, resulting in the middle file being altered with the code from the left on top and code from the right underneath. In case you need another look at these arrows, they're included in Figure 8-7. When used on a two-way merge, this option leads to the code in both files being replaced by the code located in the right file, because it requires the center column to work correctly. Avoid using these buttons in a two-merge situation; but if you make mistakes, there are always the Undo and Redo buttons.

Diffuse summary

To sum up, this application is extremely powerful and should definitely be considered when you're choosing an application to manage conflicts. It also has integration with Git, Mercurial, and SVN, which makes it that much more useful. If you feel like trying out a new, powerful application, head to the web site for more information: http://sourcegear.com/diffmerge/downloads.php

Araxis Merge

This application is a merging beast that has been chowing down features and now is full. If that was lost on you, Araxis Merge is a very full-featured application, and it's currently available on Windows and Mac (sorry Linux). Thanks to all its features, the ladies and gentlemen at Araxis decided to chop the app into two versions, Standard and Pro. The annoying thing about the split is the difference in the cost: Standard comes in at $123, and the Pro version is a whopping $263—and that's without VAT! Once you've recovered after the fall from your chair, it's time to look into the features that make Araxis Merge worth that insane price tag.

As well as having integration into applications such as Versions, Cornerstone, and command-line tools, it also offers both image and binary comparisons. This lets you do comparisons that in some other applications would cause a mammoth crash. If you opt for the Pro version, there is also the additional joy of three-way merges (as shown in Figure 8-9) and the ability to achieve a form of auto-merging. This saves you the trouble of looking through the file yourself and manually managing the differences; and if it goes wrong, there's always Undo.

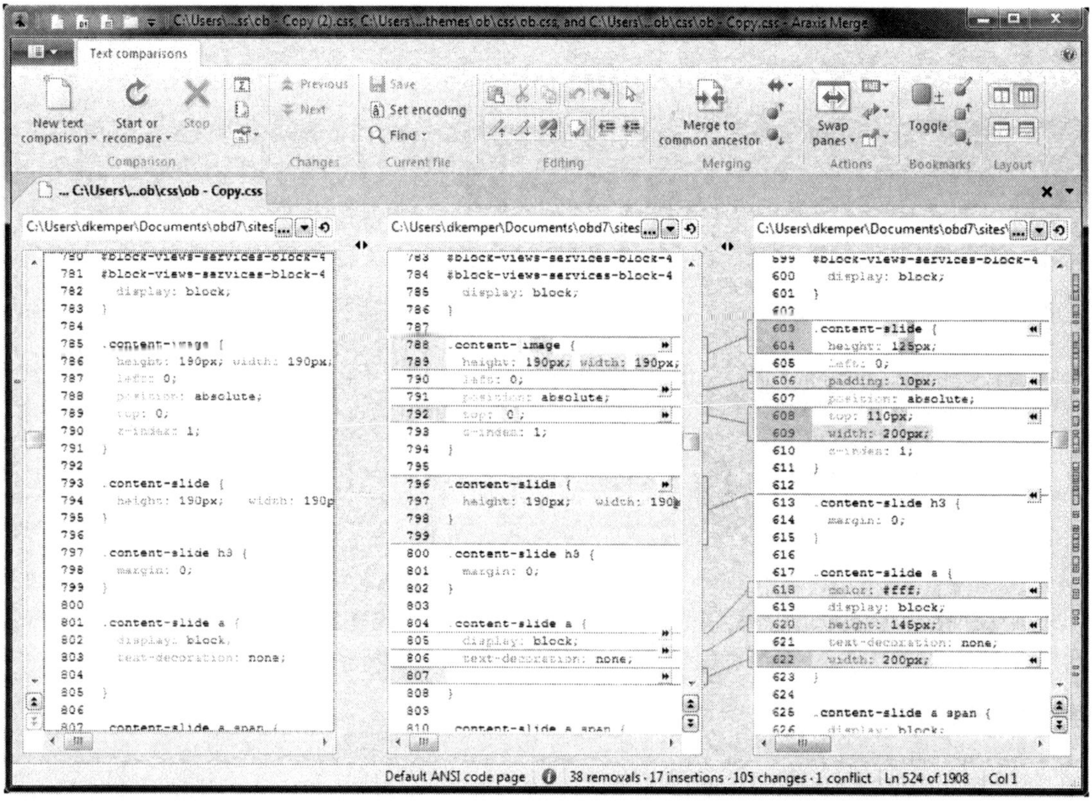

Figure 8-9. The glory that is Araxis Merge's three-way merging system, which lets you visibly work with differences between three files at once

If that's not enough, Araxis Merge also offers inline editing capabilities, folder comparisons, and a load of other features that make it the beast that it is. Of course, with applications like this, talk is cheap. It's best to dive right into the features and see what they can do.

Navigating conflicts

The toolbar used in Araxis Merge is rather simple in comparison to some of the others you've looked at, but that's not to say it's lacking in features. The tools to move changes between files are located right on the changes themselves, rather than at the top of the application, to make them easier to manage and execute. Each change has an arrow on it (which can be seen in Figure 8-9), to indicate which direction it can be sent; if you click the arrow, the change is executed, resulting in text being removed or added to the selected file. When a change is moved, it's indicated by pencil icons to the side of the change, to ensure that the change isn't lost in the sea of the file.

If a merge done within the application misses some minor details, it's also possible to edit the changes in line, which saves you from having to open an external application. This can help avoid cleaning up the file before it can be committed again, rather than having to dive into an editor, make the same change, and then commit the file.

This approach works for both two- and three-way merges; and if a change is able to go from the middle column to both the left and right on a three-way merge, it gets two arrows. Although there are some obvious benefits to three-way merging, it can easily be avoided when it comes to managing conflicts: the third column normally contains an ancestor file used as a reference only. If you happen to be using the Pro version, and you have access to the three-way merge, you can switch between the two types, clicking the three-column button and two-column button depending on which merge type you desire.

Image comparisons

Setting up an image comparison in Araxis Merge is slightly different but no more complicated. The first step is to click the New Image Comparison button, which is the third from the left in the main application. This either launches a new tab with two empty columns in it or refreshes the screen and shows the updated columns. It's worth mentioning that this tool really only works with different versions of the same image; if you use two completely different images, it results in no changes being detected—or if they are, they're nothing you couldn't have noticed yourself.

In the event that you're comparing two versions of the same image, any changes picked up by Araxis Merge are shown in red. You can also change the zoom of the images, as well as make the images swap sides or even make them sit on top of each other to help spot small, hard-to-notice changes.

Auto-merging

The last tool to talk about is the auto-merging tool, which is included in the Pro edition of the software. On the toolbar, this is indicated by two arrows facing each other. When clicked, this button merges the two outside files into the center file to create one merged file. All the changes are done by the application, and thanks to the pencil icons, you can see what is changed in the files. If the auto-merge throws a conflict, it's highlighted for you so it's easier to spot. If the conflict is of mammoth proportions, then it's also possible to undo the changes and make the merges manually; this is great for seeing whether the lazy Auto option works as desired before you manually make the changes—and if it doesn't, you can use Undo.

Araxis Merge summary

It's safe to say that the huge price tag on this application is due to its ease of use, as it's a breeze to work with. Having the ability to move changes to the relevant files by clicking the required arrow makes things much easier. With that said, the features on offer can't justify close to double the cost of the Standard application just to get your hands on Pro. The three-way merge does have its uses, and the auto-merging tool can come in handy when you're merging in branches or making large changes; but that price can't be justified.

You can, however, sign up for a free trial on the web site, which allows you to sample the Pro side of Araxis Merge for 30 days. This gives you more than enough time to decide whether you can live without it. You can also download full versions of the application, or, in the case of Mac, a version for the last three main operating system releases. You can also download an executable Windows version of the application, which makes getting started a little easier. If you're considering giving this application a try, head over to www.araxis.com/merge/ to pick up a trial, and see how well it can work for improving your workflow and emptying your pockets.

Summary

To summarize this chapter, you've been through the manual processes involved in removing conflicts from within files, rather than relying on an application. Even if you never dive into a file to fix a conflict, it's always good to be aware of the process. You also looked at several applications that help you avoid needing to go into the code to fix conflicts, or at least provide a much more usable experience when it comes to reviewing changes. All in all, handling conflicts should now be slightly less painful; and when they do come up, you'll be ready. With that behind us, it's time to take a closer look at managing your workflow without relying on an application: you can use Terminal to do it all instead.

Chapter 9

I'm Feeling Brave; Can I Do This With Terminal?

This is when things really begin to get interesting, now that we're at the point where you're willing to brave the use of Terminal and get to grips with a few key commands that can make your versioning life a little easier. In this chapter, you go through how to accomplish the most common and complex tasks you might do via an application, using Terminal commands. Are you excited? I know I am.

Since Terminal, in most cases, is the same regardless of what machine you're on (unless it's Windows), the chapter is very generalized. However, If there's something Windows users need to be aware of, it's mentioned, so everybody is on the same page. The difference on the Windows side of things is due to Command Prompt running a different coding language than the standard UNIX Terminal used on Linux and Mac. This means it uses a different set of commands for achieving certain tasks, and other tasks (such as compiling applications) aren't possible on Windows Command Prompt because of the limitations of its code.

For the majority of this chapter, you need to have a Terminal window open to work with the commands. Although in most cases it won't matter where in the file system you perform these commands, it may be worthwhile to perform the majority in your htdocs or website root directory. This will help you get into the habit of checking out and managing repositories in locations where they can be easily set up into working web sites or applications. You could technically perform these commands in any directory on your system, but if you later wanted to turn a repository that was checked out on your Desktop into a working application, it would be more complicated than if all of the repositories were in the same location.

SVN

Before I get into the commands, the first thing to do is set up a few configuration options for SVN that will come in useful later. You'll set up the programs needed when performing certain actions, such as adding commit messages, or when a conflict occurs and you would rather use an external application. This process involves adding a few configuration options in the .bash_profile file, which resides in your home directory and holds configuration options for a number of things, including SVN.

If you ran a bare setup, you may not have this file, because it's optional, but creating it doesn't take much effort. The process for working with this file on a Mac or Linux machine is the same; however, Windows causes a few problems due to the way its command line works. Because of this, you can't use a .bash_profile file, so you need another solution to add these variables into Windows; you go through separately. Setting these variables isn't required by default, but it's nice to have the applications you'd like to use in cases such as commit messages or conflicts to make them easier to deal with, and to avoid getting error messages like this:

```
None of the environment variables SVN_EDITOR, VISUAL or EDITOR are set, and no 'editor-
cmd' run-time configuration option was found.
```

This was caused by trying to commit a file without a commit message. However, if I had the SVN_EDITOR variable set, then instead of seeing the message, my editor of choice would have opened.

.bash_profile on Mac or Linux

Since Terminal on Mac and Linux works the same way, creating or modifying the .bash_profile file is a piece of cake. First, open a Terminal window, which defaults to being in your home directory when opened, indicated by the ~. If you're not in your home directory, just key in cd ~/, which takes you back there. When you're in the correct place, use the following to open the file; or, if it doesn't exist, open a blank file that uses that name when saved:

```
nano .bash_profile
```

You can of course use vi if you'd prefer. But if you don't do much in Terminal, the nano command is a lot easier to understand, as it's just a very basic editor in Terminal.

> **Note** The vi and nano commands are different text editors that be used on both Mac and Linux. As I said previously, nano is a lot easier to use, and its keyboard shortcuts are always present on screen to help. Vi, on the other hand, is a lot more complicated, and it doesn't offer any help with its commands. It's often used by people who have experience using Vim, a popular editor used by developers that looks a lot like Terminal. All you really need to be aware of here is that vi is an editor that can be used on Mac and Linux—but given the choice, go with nano.

Setting the configuration

Now that you've got the file open, it's time to actually put in some configuration options. You'll set things like which application to use when a conflict occurs, the editor to launch when making changes or adding commit messages, and so on. Before all that, though, the following is a great little code snippet that can come in very handy. This code (although it's extremely useful) is also entirely optional, and your SVN installation won't be affected if you don't use it. If you go with it, it'll show the revision you're currently working on and, if applicable, also the branch, which is pretty damn valuable and helps you keep on top these details in case they need to be referenced. It also includes a similar solution for Git, but it works as a whole, so be sure to include it all.

```
parse_git_branch() {
  ref=$(git symbolic-ref -q HEAD 2> /dev/null) || return
  printf "${1:-(%s)}" "${ref#refs/heads/}"
}

parse_svn_revision() {
  local DIRTY REV=$(svn info 2>/dev/null | grep Revision | sed -e 's/Revision: //')
  [ "$REV" ] || return
  [ "$(svn st)" ] && DIRTY=' *'
  echo "(r$REV$DIRTY)"
}

pimp_prompt() {
  local        BLUE="\[\033[0;34m\]"
  local   BLUE_BOLD="\[\033[1;34m\]"
  local         RED="\[\033[0;31m\]"
  local   LIGHT_RED="\[\033[1;31m\]"
  local       GREEN="\[\033[0;32m\]"
  local LIGHT_GREEN="\[\033[1;32m\]"
  local       WHITE="\[\033[0;37m\]"
  local  WHITE_BOLD="\[\033[1;37m\]"
  local  LIGHT_GRAY="\[\033[0;37m\]"
  case $TERM in
    xterm*)
    TITLEBAR='\[\033]0;\u@\h:\w\007\]'
    ;;
    *)
    TITLEBAR=""
    ;;
  esac
#PS1="${TITLEBAR}[$WHITE\u@$BLUE_BOLD\h$WHITE
\w$GREEN\$(parse_git_branch)\$(parse_svn_revision)
$RED\$(~/.rvm/bin/rvm-prompt v g)$WHITE]\$ "

PS1="${TITLEBAR}[$WHITE\u@$BLUE_BOLD\h
$WHITE \w$GREEN\$(parse_git_branch)\$(parse_svn_revision)$WHITE]\$ "
PS2='> '
PS4='+ '
}
pimp_prompt
```

Of course, you may not want to type all that (I wouldn't blame you), so here is the site the code came from: https://gist.github.com/790086. You can copy it and save yourself some typing time. The code is written in BASH script and broken into a few sections; the first and second parts are responsible for showing the current branch in Git, and revisions in SVN, respectively. The next section of the code, pimp_prompt(), controls the colors for the various colors that are available in the code. The final chunk of the code ties everything together and changes Terminal output using the previously defined functions and colors. With that helpful piece of code out of the way, it's time to get into some actual configuration.

SVN editor

This setting controls the editor used when performing commits, if you don't happen to specify the message flag when performing a commit (you go through that later). The editor you use can be any text-editing application on your system, although for ease and speed, I'd suggest a basic editor. You can also potentially use vi or nano (mentioned earlier), but that's up to you.

To set the editor, you need to use the following code:

```
export SVN_EDITOR=nano
```

The export is particularly important here, as it makes sure the variable is used in all future Terminal sessions, and not just the session after you enter the code and restart Terminal for the changes to take effect. In this example I've used nano, but you can equally use a non-Terminal application like so:

```
export SVN_EDITOR="/usr/bin/open -n -W -a /Applications/TextEdit.app"
```

This is broken into a few parts. The first part calls the Terminal equivalent of opening a file or file, just as if you'd double-clicked it. The next part are flags for the open command: -n tells it to open a new instance of the application, even if it's open already; -a tells Terminal it's an application; and -W pauses the command until the application is called. The -W is the most important part, because if the command didn't halt and wait for the commit message, then opening the application in this manner would be totally pointless. The last part of the command is the link to the desired application, in this instance TextEdit for Mac. For this to take effect, you need to either restart your Terminal application or run source ~/.bash_profile in Terminal to force-reload the file and save having to restart.

SVN merge

Setting this lovely variable gives you an application that can be used when the dreaded conflicts happen. This can be any application you'd like—that can do the job, of course. Sadly, unlike setting the SVN_EDITOR variable, this isn't straight forward. How you set up this variable depends entirely on which application you will be using to deal with your conflict, as different applications work in different ways. In most cases, you need to create a special shell script that configures your program of choice to use the files that SVN makes available when conflicts occur.

Mac Merge tool

Since FileMerge is enabled on your system by now, it's a safe bet to set it up as a diff tool. FileMerge has been out for a while, so a number of solutions have been written for this issue. These are overly complicated for your needs, so it's much easier to write your own.

You want to create a new file containing a line of code that configures FileMerge correctly for dealing with conflicts. The file can be created wherever you'd like, but for ease mine is in my home directory. When you have a location selected, create the file in Terminal using nano merge.sh while in your directory of choice. You can change the name of the file, but make sure it has the .sh extension. With the file open, add the following:

```
#!/bin/bash

# svn will invoke this with a bunch of arguments.  These are:
# $1 - path to the file that is the original
# $2 - path to the file that's the incoming merge version
# $3 - path to the file that's the latest from trunk (current working copy)
# $4 - path to where svn expects the merged output to be written
opendiff "$3" "$2" -ancestor "$1" -merge "$4"
```

FileMerge comes with a Terminal command (opendiff), so you don't need to call it directly, which is good. As the comments in the file suggest (the lines beginning with #), the different $s are files used in the output when SVN has a conflict; all this file does is serve them up in the correct order, with the correct flags.

With the script created, you need to make it executable, which you can do via chmod 0777 merge.sh. After that, you need to link to it in .bash_profile, like so:

```
export SVN_MERGE=/User/Chris/merge.sh
```

Now, when the l open is used in conflicts, you can manage it in FileMerge. For other applications, you need to check out their respective command-line tools to see how to use them, but you can pretty much keep to the same format shown here.

Linux merge tool

This step is actually somewhat similar to that for a Mac, but rather than using FileMerge, you use Meld as the diff tool of choice. You still need to create a wrapper for use with Meld, to ensure that everything is working correctly, but luckily it's a rather simple script thanks to Meld's meld Terminal command. As before, you need to create the file in a safe location, such as in your home directory, as I've chosen to do in this instance. When you're in Terminal at the specified location, create the shell-script file like so:

```
nano svnmeld.sh
```

This gives you a blank file. Paste the following into it, bearing in mind that the name of the file can be anything you like:

```
#!/bin/bash

# svn will invoke this with a bunch of arguments.  These are:
```

```
# $1 - path to the file that is the original
# $2 - path to the file that's the incoming merge version
# $3 - path to the file that's the latest from trunk (current working copy)
# $4 - path to where svn expects the merged output to be written
meld "$3" "$1" "$2" "$4"
```

You're keeping the comments in the file similar to those in the Mac file, because they're good to have as a reference point if you ever need to make changes down the line. With the file populated, save it, and exit the file. Now you need to make it executable, which you can do using chmod +x svnmeld.sh. The next step is setting the SVN_MERGE variable. In the .bash_profile file, add the following line:

```
SVN_MERGE=/home/chris/svnmeld.sh
```

Be sure the full path to the file is included. You need to take one final step, which is reloading the .bash_profile file. You can do this with source .bash_profile, which leaves everything configured and ready to go.

Setting up on Windows

Sadly, thanks to the nature of how the Windows Command Prompt works, the code sample used in the previous section won't work. So, if you're on Windows, you'll lose the code's functions if you're working with the default Command Prompt. You can use another package on Windows to emulate the UNIX Terminal, if you'd like to go down that road, but again it's entirely optional. If you do find that approach appealing, a few possible packages you can try out are Cygwin, Gnu On Windows (Gow), and even Git Bash. Using one of these solutions means you can use a .bash_profile file in that application, so the previous configuration method works with these applications.

With that out of the way, it's time to set up your variables on Windows—assuming you're still working with the default Command Prompt, that is. To set either SVN_MERGE or SVN_EDITOR, you need to be in an admin section in Computer (My Computer on older systems). To get into the correct location, go to Computer ➤ Properties ➤ Advanced System Settings ➤ Environment Variables (My Computer ➤ Properties ➤ Advanced ➤ Environment Variables on older systems), which launches a new dialog called Environment Variables that is just where you need to be.

SVN editor

This variable can potentially be used to enter commit messages if you don't add the necessary flag to the command (you see that in bit), so let's get right to it. In the dialog opened in the previous section, click the New button for your respective user account, which launches another dialog called New User Variable which has two fields. You could do this as a system-wide variable, but this would mean users couldn't easily override the default to set their own SVN_EDITOR variable with a different value.

In the new dialog, the variable name is SVN_EDITOR, and the value is the path to your editor of choice. The best way to get this path is to find the shortcut to the application on the Start menu, right-click it, and choose Properties. Then, copy the contents of the Target field into the Variable Value field in the original dialog (New User Variable). This sets that application as the default one used when adding a commit message; so, that is now set.

SVN merge

The process for setting this variable is the same as for the previous one. You need to create a new variable for your user account, but this time the variable name is SVN_MERGE. Getting the value of the variable works the same as with the SVN_EDITOR variable: use the right-click trick.

This variable is used when you need to work with conflicts, so it could be useful to set it; but as with the others, it's optional. Here, you set it up with WinMerge; you need to create a batch file to do so. To create the file, open Notepad and enter the following:

```
start "WinMerge" "C:\Program Files (x86)\WinMerge\WinMergeU.exe" /ub %1 %2
```

In this line, replace the path to WinMerge with the path you copied from the right-click menu. With everything in place, save the file in a safe location, using File ➤ Save As. In the drop-down, be sure to select All as the file type. Now select a name—I'm using "merge" followed by the .bat extension—and click Save. This creates the batch file for you to use. All you need to do from here is link to the batch file in the variable value field of the Environment Variable dialog. Be sure to use the full path to the file, which in my case is

```
C:\Users\dkemper\merge.bat
```

After everything is set up, restart your Command Prompt, and everything will work as you'd like it to. Easy!

Global options

A number of global options can be used with most, if not all, SVN commands. Although they're not always needed, it's good to know about them, just in case. The following are some of the better ones that are more often specified.

--username ARG

This option allows you to specify a new username to use when committing files. This can come in handy if you're working on a machine that has details saved into it, or you want to use a different name.

--password ARG

The password option is normally tied in with the username option, although it can be added on its own. When using this option, you simply put the password after the argument, and it's used in any commits that are made. Although it can be used with the username option, you're always prompted for a password when using a new username, so it's not always needed.

--dry-run

When this option is added to an SVN command, it treats that command as a test. This means you can see what would happen if you ran the command, without actually making any changes either locally or remotely. This can be very useful when you're testing large merges or double-checking that you're doing things correctly.

--force

The name says it all with this one. Adding the force option to a command is a risky business and should not be attempted unless you really know what you're doing. Playing with --force is like doing a jump using a child's tricycle: it's either going to be epic or make a mess. You can use --force if you want to delete a file that has been added but not yet committed, or to check out a repository to an already-existing location. It can also be used when you're moving files with SVN, as well as with merges.

Some instances, such as deleting files, should be fine with --force, provided you know what's going on. However, on the merge side of things, be very careful when using --force, as you can really break everything.

--revision (-r)

This allows you to specify a particular revision, or range of revisions, to use when performing certain commands. In addition, you can use a number of tokens that can refer to specific revisions and save you from working with numbers. These are shown in the Table 9-1.

Table 9-1. The potential revision variables that can be used in conjunction with –revision (-r)

Token	Definition
{ DATE }	The first revision at the selected date
HEAD	The latest version in the repository
BASE	The base revision of the file: in other words, the state it was in after the last update, before you made any changes
COMMITTED	The last commit at or before the base
PREV	The revision that has just been committed
NUMBER	A good old revision number

SVN checkout

You could say the first step with managing a repository is to check out a repository to manage. Using the following command initiates a checkout of the specified repository to the folder you specify in the command:

```
Svn checkout http://path/to/repository folder-name
```

You do have a few options with this command, one of which is to use svn co rather than svn checkout—co is the shorthand version which can come in useful when you have to perform this action on a regular basis. It's also worth mentioning that the folder you specify doesn't necessarily need to exist. If you want to check out the repository into a folder that hasn't been created yet, just replace folder-name with the name you'd like, and the folder will be automatically created.

Another option when checking out a repository is to use a dot (.) in place of the folder name. This checks out the repository in the folder you're currently in. So if you have cd'd into a directory you've been working in, and you then decide you want to check out a repository into it, simply perform svn co and replace folder-name with . to check out the repository right there. It can be a nifty trick to know, and it will save you having to do some unnecessary cd .. commands to move to the parent directory to perform the checkout.

If you leave off the folder name and simply do svn co repository, then a folder is automatically created for you to house the checkout. The folder gets the same name as the repository you're checking out; so if the repository you're checking out is called test, then a test folder is automatically created if you don't specify a folder to house the checked-out code. If you choose to check out the repository this way, be aware that if you already have a folder by that name in the same location where you perform the checkout, the process checks out into the directory anyway, regardless of whether it's empty. Keep this in mind when you're checking out repositories.

svn status

This is probably the most-used command in the svn-terminal toolkit. It shows the status of the current working copy of the repository you're in. In other words, it shows changed and new files. This therefore allows you to make sure the files you're working on are up to date. The command is as simple as svn status, is really easy to use, and is extremely useful.

While using this command, you'll come across a number of different status letters and icons that let you know the current status of the files in question. To make them a little easier to identify, I've chucked all these status items into Table 9-2.

Table 9-2. The letters and symbols that can be generated when performing an svn status or svn st

Symbol	Description
' '	The file has no modifications, so there's nothing to worry about.
A	This item has been added to the local copy of the repository, and after a commit it'll be available for others to use.
D	This file has been removed via an svn action and is scheduled to be deleted once it's committed.
M	The item has been changed or modified locally and therefore needs to be committed or reverted.
R	This item has been replaced in your working copy. This means the file was set to be deleted, but a file with the same name has been added in its place. This can commonly happen when you need to completely replace a directory/file. You have to delete it and then add the new version.

Symbol	Description
C	This is the bad one: it means the file in question has a conflict in its contents. You can resolve this problem by going into the file and fixing it yourself, or open your favorite GUI diff tool.
X	The item is present because of an externals definition.
I	This item is being ignored. This is usually achieved by using the svn ignore property.
?	This item isn't under version control— as easy as that.
!	The item in question is no longer available. This can happen when you delete or move a file without using the appropriate svn commands. This symbol can also indicate an in complete checkout or update that has left the folder in an incomplete state.
*	An update for this file is available from the server. This will most likely lead to an update or a revert being done to the file to bring it up to date.

Some people don't like typing svn status as it's too long, so to take that pain away, it has a couple of aliases to make the typing shorter. You also have the choice of using svn stat or the shorter svn st, which saves you a little typing time.

When you perform svn status or one of its aliases, you get output similar to the following:

```
A    site/css/ie.css
M    site/css/stye.css
?    site/images/bg.png
D    site/old-folder
```

As you can see, the left column shows the status of the files; in this case, there's quite a mix. Then on the right you see the location of the file within the local copy of the repository.

Showing updates from the repository

If you use one of the previously mentioned commands on its own, you see changed and newly added files in your local copy of the repository. This is fine if that's what you want to check; but if you're checking for updates to your files, then you need to add --show-updates or just -u. You may, however, get into the habit of applying -u every time you check the status of the repository, to ensure that no updates are missed. Using all the shorthand, your svn status command may well look like this:

```
svn st -u folder-name
```

This always ensures that you can see any changes you've made locally and any updates available from the main repository. You can also leave off the folder-name, and the command will run from the current directory. Adding the -u flag to the command alters the output in Terminal—you get two columns. Since the -u flag adds changes from the repository as well as local changes, the new columns show the file status on your local copy of the repository, and the revision number. Let's look at an example:

```
A                   site/css/ie.css
M      *      45     site/css/stye.css
?                   site/images/bg.png
       *            site/images/logo.png
D                   site/old-folder
```

You can see how the two extra columns have been added. The second column shows the changes from the server: for two files in this example, updates are available from the main repository. The logo.png file isn't in my working copy yet, so in the left column it doesn't have a status icon because it has no place in the local copy. With style.css, there has been a local change, indicated by the M, but the * in the next column shows that there is a newer version of the file in the repository. The third column for the file is the revision number that is available for an update; the latest repository revision is always shown here. If you see a huge list of the same number in the third column, it's showing that all those files have changes in the latest revision.

Verbose flag

One additional flag can be applied to svn status: --verbose, or -v for short. This shows you the revision information for every file in the repository. It has six columns, which it uses to show any potential status that may apply to a file or folder in the repository. The -v flag shows up something like this:

```
A   +      48     48     chris     site/css/ie.css
M          48     45     chris     site/css/stye.css
?                        lauren    site/images/bg.png
           48     48     phil      site/images/logo.png
D          48            chris     site/old-folder
! L        48     ?      ?         site/uploads
```

The -v flag gives some extra information over any of the others you've looked at. The first change is the additional two columns: the second and third to the left. They show you the status of the file or folder, and whether the file is locked, respectively. You also get an additional two columns on the right, which show you the last committed revision (that is, when it was last modified and then committed) and the author of the file.

Quiet flag

The results can be a little hectic and confusing if you don't need all the information, which is why the following option comes in so handy. The quiet flag, --quiet (-q), shows any files that have been modified or that need attention. It removes revision numbers and usernames, so you see the status of the file and nothing more. You can also combine it with -u to make a command along the lines of svn st -u -v -q: this gives you a bit more detail than svn st -u and a whole lot less than svn st -u -q, so you can see as much detail as you'd like. If you're ever in doubt about the status of a particular file, remember that svn help st is your friend.

Update

This command does as it says: it updates your local version with the most recent version of that file or folder from the repository. The command, as you may have guessed, is svn update or svn up for short.

You get a few options with this. If you run the command at the base of the repository, it simply updates the whole repository. If you're in a directory in the repository, the command updates that particular directory, which can be useful if you're working on a particular part of an application.

You can also specify individual files to update, by running the update command followed by the file name, even if that file is in another folder. You can also auto-complete the file name by using the Tab key after typing in some of the letters. This is a standard Terminal feature, but it's more useful when updating individual files. You may end up with something like this:

```
svn up plugins/my-plugin/config.php
```

Specific revisions

You can also update a file to a specific revision, just in case you need to roll back a feature or correct a terrible bug that has suddenly surfaced. Doing so requires that you know the revision number you'd like to revert to, which can be frustrating; but, sadly, that's how it works. If you don't specify a revision number along with the command I'm about to share, you get an error along the lines of

```
svn: Syntax error in revision argument
```

To avoid getting that error, use the command folder/file-name:

```
svn up -r 40 css/style.css
```

Replace the number (in this case, 40) with the revision number you'd like, and of course change the file to the one you'd like to revert.

There may be an instance where you need to revert changes because somebody didn't deal with a conflict properly, and all the hard work you did has been totally trashed. This leaves you needing to merge the two revisions, which I go over in the section "Conflicts, and how to solve them."

svn export

Exporting the repository, as you've seen, exports all the files from the repository in a specified directory, but with no .svn files. There are a few reasons you may want to export a repository (such as giving the final version of a project to a client or as a way of deploying the code to a server), but a common one is because you want to use a previous web site build as a base for a new one. In its simplest form, the export command can look like this:

```
svn export http://repository-url folder-to-house-export
```

This exports the most recent revision of the chosen repository into the folder specified. It's as easy as that. Of course, you may not want the most recent version. In that case, you can specify a specific revision number by adding the -r flag after export, followed by the desired revision number.

svn help

This is the help command you can use to find out the correct syntax and such for all SVN commands. If you run the svn help command by itself, you're given a list of the available commands available to SVN. You can also find out more information about a specific command by adding it after the command, something like this:

```
svn help export
```

This gives you the correct syntax and a description of what the export command does. The help documentation can be quite useful if you need to quickly double-check the order in which to do a command. However, it isn't that brilliant, and it can be confusing at times.

svn log

This lovely command allows you to see all the commits in a repository and comments associated with them. If you run svn log for a working copy, it shows you all commits right back to the first one, which isn't really very useful. With that being said, you can limit the number of results shown and even pull out a specific revision if you know what it is.

To limit your search to a certain number of results, you can use the following command:

```
svn log --limit 5
```

This shows you the five most recent commits and the comments associated with them. You can also specify a specific revision by replacing --limit with -r and the specific revision number you're after, like so:

```
svn log -r 3
```

This doesn't help much, though, as it only shows the commit message, the user responsible for the commit, and the time and date of said commit. To get around this, you can add --verbose or -v to the end of the command, which will include the files and what happened to them. That means a command like this

```
svn log -r 4 --verbose
```

outputs something like this:

```
r4| chris | 2011-10-25 15:18:04 +0100 (Tue, 25 Oct 2011) | 1 line
Changed paths:
   A /trunk/wp-content/theme/mytheme/css/mytheme.css
   A /trunk/wp-content/theme/mytheme/css/ie.css
```

This is a lot more useful when it comes to working out what happened in specific revisions, since you can actually see what happened.

svn import

Sometimes you're working on something outside of a repository, and you want to add it into a repository you're working with. This is what svn import is for. With this command, you can recursively commit everything in the included folder to the included project, using the following syntax:

```
svn import [Folder] [Repository URL]
```

In reality, this command just adds and then commits all the files and folders in the specified folder to the specified repository, which can of course be rather useful. Although this command can be performed without the use of a commit message, I'd advise adding one using the -m flag. You can either leave the -m without anything following it, which launches your default editor, or use double quotes to add a message. Let's looks at an example:

```
svn import newproject http://url-to-repository/trunk -m "imported new project
into the main repository"
```

This imports the folder into the main trunk of the repository, but you can just as easily import it into a branch or a folder in the trunk, as you like.

Conflicts, and how to solve them

While you're updating files or folders, the time will come when you find a conflict: you have local changes in a file, and the repository shows changes in the same place in the file. This greatly confuses SVN, and since it can't merge the two versions of the file cleanly, it puts the file into a conflicted state.

The following is what you see if you get a conflict while updating in Terminal or at a command line. This example shows a conflict in a CSS file, which is a fairly common occurrence when working on the styling of a project with other team members:

```
Conflict discovered in 'css/style.css'.
Select: (p) postpone, (df) diff-full, (e) edit,
        (mc) mine-conflict, (tc) theirs-conflict,
        (s) show all options:
```

After this, you can specify a letter to choose from; but if you press S, then all potential letters are displayed with explanations. You can see them in Table 9-3 for reference.

Table 9-3. The full list of options available when you come across a conflict in SVN

Option	Definition
(e) edit	This option opens the conflicted file in the previously specified editor—you know, the one you put in the config file. This allows the conflict to be manually removed; and when you save the change, the conflict is resolved.
(df) diff-full	This shows a full diff between the two versions, in the command line. If you happen to be working with a mammoth file, I don't recommend this option because tracking changes is a nightmare.
(r) resolved	This marks the file as resolved, regardless of its current status. Be warned: if the file is in a conflicted state, and you use this option, it'll leave the file in a conflicted state but allow it to be committed. This means the file could be committed with errors in it, so be wary of using this option.

Option	Definition
(dc) display-conflict	This option shows all conflicts (ignoring the merged version).
(mc) mine-conflict	As previously mentioned, each conflict has a *mine* version and a *yours* version. Using mc takes the local versions of the conflicts rather than the remote version.
(tc) theirs-conflict	This does the reverse of the previous option: it takes the remote version of the conflicts and discards the local version.
(mf) mine-full	This option pretty much says "F*#k you" to the incoming changes and uses the local changes that were in the file before the update. This does, however, replace any other changes in the file, including non-conflicting ones. If the author of the newer version has made a large number of changes that happen to conflict with your local copy, all those changes will be wiped out, so be careful.
(tf) theirs-full	This, as you may imagine, is the reverse of the previous option. If you realize that the changes you've made aren't that good, use tf, and the file will actively be reverted: the local version will be replaced with the most recent version of the file.
(p) postpone	This little gem leaves the file in its conflicted state, which looks just like the example at the start of the chapter. You need to manually resolve the conflict before the file can be committed.
(l) launch	Using this launches the previously configured diffing program of choice to resolve the conflict. Than can be a lot easier than sifting through the file yourself to fix the conflicts. If you didn't take the time to set the SVN_MERGE variable earlier, check out the info and set up that bad boy.
(s) show all	This shows the full list of options available when managing conflicts.

svn resolve and svn resolved

If you choose the p option or the l option from Table 9-3 but your program of choice doesn't automatically resolve conflicts, then you need to do some resolving via commands. You can use two commands here: svn resolve and svn resolved. That *d* makes a big difference in what the commands do, which is why I'll go over both, starting with the resolved option.

svn resolved

Using this command implies that you've dived into the file and resolved the conflict yourself, leaving it in a state in which it can be committed—but its status is still conflicted. This can also occur when the conflict has been resolved using another application, but the state of the file hasn't changed, so it remains conflicted. If either is the case, resolving the conflicted state of the file is as easy as svn resolved [filename], which resolves the file specified in place of [filename]. Doing so allows the file to be committed, which it can't be without the conflict being resolved first.

svn resolve

If the previous situation doesn't apply, and you decide on the p option but don't make any changes, the resolve option is for you. This option gives you back some of the options originally listed when the conflict was first discovered, but in a different way. It gives you the option to use your version of the conflicted file, the remote version, and a couple of others. Table 9-4 discusses these in more detail.

Table 9-4. When performing a resolve these options are available to use.

Option	Definition
base	The base revision of the file refers to the version after the last commit, before any changes were made locally. This option results in the loss of the remote changes, so use it with care.
Working	This option means the file is already fixed and just needs to be resolved, the same case as using svn resolved.
mine-full	This takes your copy of the changes and disregards the remote options, at times when you know you and the other person have both made the same changes, or you plain don't care about the other changes.
theirs-full	This takes all the remote changes that have been fetched from svn update and uses them to resolve the conflict, disregarding your own changes.

Now that you know about the different options, you need to know how to use them. This is achieved by following this example:

```
svn resolve - accept [option] file
```

In this command, replace [option] with one from Table 9-4, and the files will be resolved using that method.

Reverting changes

On some occasions, you need to revert your file back to its base version, or even to a specific earlier revision, which can be easily achieved, thanks to reverting.

svn diff

This lovely command really comes into use when you need to look for differences in a repository or working copy. The svn diff command, when used with no arguments, compares any changes you've made with the base version of the repository, which in most cases is either useless or not specific enough. To help with that, you can specify a file after the command, which compares that file with the base version of it. If the file has no changes, then nothing will come up in the diff; and if there are differences, they'll be output. Of course, you don't always want to perform a diff against the current and base revisions file, which is when the -r flag is your friend. If you only specify one revision, such as `svn diff -r 10 file`, it'll compare the differences in the working copy with the differences in revision 10.

You can be still more specific than that, by specifying an additional revision using a colon, like so: `svn diff -r 10:15 file`. You can also perform a diff on files in the remote repository by using the full URL of the file in place of its name, just in case that's what you need to do.

svn info

Using this command allows you to receive a little more information about a particular file or folder. If you perform the action on, say, a CSS style sheet, you get something like the following:

```
svn info sites/default/themes/mytheme/css/style.css
Path: sites/default/themes/mytheme/css/style.css
Name: style.css
URL: http://svn.chrisdkemper.co.uk/repo/trunk/sites/default/themes/mytheme/css/style.css
Repository Root: http://svn.chrisdkemper.co.uk/repo
Repository UUID: 3124cba5-3ba6-4a82-98e1-e15d6b12221f
Revision: 2087
Node Kind: file
Schedule: normal
Last Changed Author: chris
Last Changed Rev: 2042
Last Changed Date: 2011-11-03 16:07:54 +0000 (Thu, 03 Nov 2011)
Checksum: 9f7f791dc31f135c1e962e0951ce3ccf
```

Although you may never need to use this command, it's good to know it exists, just to get that extra bit of information about a particular file.

svn blame

This command is a godsend, to say the least, as it allows you to see a file on a line-by-line basis accompanied by the identity of the person who wrote each line. This can be very useful when you're looking for who wrote certain lines of code. The usage of this command is `svn blame file`, which outputs the contents of the file in Terminal along with the author of the file. It's also possible to add the -v flag to the command, which shows when each line was created. In addition, -r shows a specific version of the file, to make the debugging process a lot easier!

svn cleanup

A cleanup is required when you can't complete an update or commit, or for other reasons. You will know a cleanup is required, because you'll be told. If you do need a cleanup, you see output similar to the following when you try to perform any svn command:

```
svn: Working copy '.' locked
svn: run 'svn cleanup' to remove locks (type 'svn help cleanup' for details)
```

You then use `svn cleanup`. Provided everything has gone correctly, you shouldn't see any output from the command. If you do see output, it could mean there is a problem with your repository, in the form or read-write access. You can try to `sudo` the command to make it run successfully, or modify the file permissions on the files with `chmod`, which can help to solve the problem. If you're still having issues with the cleanup, try checking out the repository again to help remove the errors.

Deleting, moving, and renaming files

When it comes to moving or deleting files, you can't just perform the move or delete normally, as this would cause problems. If you deleted a file, then when you did an update, it would return, which isn't ideal. To get around this, perform `svn delete file` on the file and then commit it, which deletes it for you and everyone else. Moving files follows the same principle, but with different consequences.

If you move the file to another folder, then if you update the original folder, the file appears to be back again, because SVN thinks the file is missing and needs to be restored. The new location wants the file to be added, because it doesn't recognize it, which isn't what you want. You could technically delete the file from the old location and add it in the new one, but this would cause a loss of the file's history, which you also don't want.

Renaming comes into things depending on the command used. When you pick the new location for a file, it's possible to also rename the file. If you want to just rename a file and not move it, use `svn move oldname.txt newname.txt`. If you're moving the file, use `svn move file.txt folder/file.txt`. You can also specify a message when performing the action, with `-m`; however, this is entirely optional. If you fancy a change, you can use `mv`, `rename`, or `ren`.

svn add * (multiple files)

This command is used when you want to add files or folders to the repository, where you would generally perform `svn add file` or `svn add folder`. Either of these would work fine, but you can also combine wildcards when adding files. For instance, if you've just added, say, a boatload of `.png`s to your `images` folder, then you can use `svn add *.png` to add any files including `.png`. This can make adding files a lot easier, especially when the folder already contains added files so you can't just add the folder.

SVN Summary

Thanks to all these commands, you'll be a Terminal expert in no time. You've been through the process of checking out a repository, working with the files in a variety of ways, and then committing them again, which is just what you need. Remember that `svn help` is your friend; if you ever get stuck with commands, check it out, and you'll soon have your problem solved. If that fails, you can always talk to the glorious web community or drop me a line on twitter (@ChrisDKemper), and no doubt the problem will be solved.

Mercurial

As you know, this system is seen as a great versioning tool by itself, and thanks to its great development community, it's growing all the time. It's also very easy to use once you get the basics down, so let's get straight into it with some configuration options.

Configuration

You need to set a couple of things in your `.hgrc` file (or `Mercurial.ini` on Windows), in the form of the application to use:

```
[ui]
editor=nano
```

The editor can be something like `nano` or `vi` or, for the sake of Windows users, Notepad or any other editor, but be sure you use the full path to the application. It's time to set up your merge for Mercurial in the same way you did for SVN, using WinMerge on Windows, FileMerge on Mac, and Meld on Ubuntu. Since the process is totally different for Windows, I've split it into Windows and Mac/Ubuntu; let's get straight into it.

Setting up the Windows merge tool

Since you already have WinMerge installed, you need to amend your `Mercurial.ini` file and add some additional settings to enable the use of WinMerge for diffs. This code adds a new command to Mercurial, in the form of `winmerge`, which allows you to perform diffs really easily using the application. To get started, you need to add the following to the `Mercurial.ini` file in your user directory:

```
[ui]
merge = winmergeu

[extensions]
hgext.extdiff=

[extdiff]
cmd.winmerge = C:\Program Files (x86)\WinMerge\WinMergeU.exe
opts.winmerge = /e /x /ub /wl
[merge-tools]
winmergeu.args=/e /ub /dl other /dr local $other $local $output
winmergeu.regkey=Software\Thingamahoochie\WinMerge
winmergeu.regname=Executable
winmergeu.fixeol=True
winmergeu.checkchanged=True
winmergeu.gui=True
```

You may need to change the path to the `WinMergeU.exe` file, depending on your system, but you can always use the right-click ➤ Properties technique to get the path if you're in doubt. Also, with the [ui] section of the code, you should have additional information in that section already, so add in the `merge = winmergeu` line under your existing code. This code does two things: it allows the addition of a new command (`hg winmerge`), and it lets you use WinMerge to deal with conflicts when they happen.

As far as configuration goes, that's it. You can now use `hg winmerge` to show differences between your current changes in the repository compared to the base version of the files, before any changes were made. , You can make this more specific by selecting a particular file and see the differences between its base version and the current changes within it, by using `hg winmerge file`.

Setting up Mac and Ubuntu merge tools

The settings for the two systems are pretty much the same: all the configuration takes place in the `.hgrc` file, but it differs slightly depending on the applications used. Since you're going with FileMerge for Mac and Meld for Ubuntu, let's start with Mac.

Using FileMerge on Mac

The first thing you need to do is create a simple script that allows the use of the FileMerge application with Mercurial. You create the file in `usr/local/bin` because it's included in `$PATH` and the file will be safe from changes. To create the file, run the command like so:

```
nano /usr/local/bin/hopendiff
```

Then add the following code, and save the file:

```
#!/bin/sh
`/usr/bin/opendiff "$@"`
```

In this instance, `hopendiff` is the name of the command you'll be using in the `.hgrc` file in a moment. For now, though, you need to add the ability to use FileMerge as a difftool in Mercurial. You can easily achieve this by using the following script, written by Bruno De Fraine, which you can download from his repository at `http://soft.vub.ac.be/svn-gen/bdefrain/fmscripts/fmdiff`. Copy the file to your clipboard and then create a file to house it, just as you did before:

```
nano /usr/local/bin/fmdiff
```

With the file saved, it's time to head into the `.hgrc` file and add the needed configuration to allow for FileMerge to be used in instances of conflicts and for diffs as well:

```
[extensions]
hgext.extdiff =

[extdiff]
cmd.opendiff = fmdiff

[merge-tools]
filemerge.executable = hopendiff
filemerge.args = $local $other -ancestor $base -merge $output
```

You can now use `hg opendiff` as a diff tool in Mercurial. And when conflicts occur, FileMerge will have your back.

Using Meld on Ubuntu

With Meld already installed, you need to add some simple configuration to the `.hgrc` file to enable to use of Meld as a diff tools:

```
[extensions]
hgext.extdiff =
```

```
[extdiff]
cmd.meld =
```

From now on, you can use `hg meld` to perform diffs on files in your Mercurial repository.

Some global options

A number of global options can be applied to Mercurial commands to make them more specific, or even more helpful. I'll go over them now.

--rev (-r)

This flag allows you to specify a particular revision to use along with the command, such as performing a `diff` or `log` command. You can specify a revision number or, if applicable, a range of revisions, such as 3:6 or 6:3, which shows the same information but in a different order.

--verbose (-v) and --quiet (-q)

Using the `verbose` option allows you to see additional output from the commands, such as listing all the other files associated with the particular commit. The `quiet` flag removes all unneeded code from the command: you only see the bare minimum, which is the changeset information.

--patch (-p)

This flag allows you to see the contents of the files associated with particular commits. Doing this can be really useful when you want to quickly see what's changed in a particular revision, especially if you're tracking changes or you want hunt down a bug.

--dry-run (-n)

This allows you to perform a test run on any command, where the output is shown straight in Terminal. This can come in very handy when you're performing particularly intense commands, such as merges. The command is done, but no files are affected, meaning you can try anything you like without consequences.

--force (-f)

Occasionally, you'll need to use the `force` flag to perform certain actions while working with files in Mercurial. These can be things like removing files that haven't been added yet, certain merges that say they can't be done but actually are fine, and several more. Be sure you know what you're doing when using `force`, or things can go terribly wrong.

Creating and cloning repositories

You need a repository to work with before you can use these commands, and you can achieve that by either cloning an existing repository or creating a new one. Performing a clone of the repository is really easy using the following command:

```
hg clone https://bitbucket.org/tortoisehg/thg
```

This example clones the tortoisehg repository on Bitbucket into a folder called thg, which is the name of the repository. It's possible to specify a directory for the clone to live in by adding the folder name to the end of the command, like so:

```
hg clone https://bitbucket.org/tortoisehg/thg my-directory
```

If any details are required from the repository, you're asked for them before any of the changes are cloned, via prompts on the command line.

When it comes to creating your own repositories, this is just as simple as cloning a repository, if not easier. All you need to do is create a directory for the repository to live in and initialize the repository, and you're finished. You can create a repository called test by using the following:

```
mkdir test
cd test
hg init
```

Whichever method you use, there is now a repository for you to work with, which leads us right into the next section: working with the basic commands in Mercurial.

Basic file operations

In the repository, there are a number of actions you use more than others: status, add, log, and commit. Although it seems that these commands are a bit basic, in reality, you need to check the status of files, add new ones, and then commit all the changes. With that said, let's take a closer look at some of these commands and see how they work.

Adding files

When it comes to adding files, the command itself is simple and can be as little as hg add, which adds any untracked files to be tracked—after they're committed, of course. If you do hg status before actually adding the file, you should see something like this:

```
? folder/file.txt
```

The ? indicates the file is untracked and needs to be added, which I just covered. You can specify a particular file by using hg add file to be more specific, or use the plain old hg add command to add all currently untracked files. After the files have been added, if you do another hg status, it should show the following:

```
A folder/file.txt
```

This indicates that the file has been added, and it's ready to be committed.

Now, let's commit the file, but using hg commit to start things off. Doing this launches your editor to prompt you for a commit message, and you need to save the file with a message to confirm the commit. You can alleviate this issue by using the -m flag to supply a commit message, like so: hg commit -m [commit message]. This commits the file and leaves hg status clear of changes. You can also remove files in the same way you add them, by using hg remove file, which marks the file to be deleted but doesn't delete it.

Deleting files

If you delete a file, hg status shows the following output:

```
R folder/file.txt
```

This shows that the file is marked for removal. When you perform a commit, the file will be deleted; but remember that all the history of the file will remain. There is another method of removing files in the form of hg forget, which removes the file from being tracked but doesn't delete it. You can use either command, depending on your personal preference.

hg addremove

This is where the addremove command comes in, and it does just what it implies. Running hg addremove adds any new files and removes any missing files, so that when you commit, you remove the old and add the new.

You can make this more efficient by using another flag when performing a commit. If you do hg commit -A -m [message], it performs the commit, adds the new files, and deletes missing ones. Although this approach can be quicker, it can potentially cause you to add files you don't want to add, such as server-generated files. So, be sure to use it with caution.

hg revert file

When you happen to add or delete a file by mistake, and you have yet to commit, don't worry: it can be fixed. The hg revert file command takes the file back to its original status. This makes deleted files go back to normal, and added files go back to being unknown to Mercurial.

hg copy

In some instances, you need to duplicate a file using Mercurial, which of course is possible. You could technically duplicate the file outside of Mercurial and then add the new file. However, if you'd like to copy a file that way, use hg copy file newfile, which duplicates the file for you; when you perform hg status, you see that the new file has been added.

hg help

As you'd hope with Mercurial, a lot of help is available in the form of hg help, which gives you an overview of available commands. You can also use hg help command, which shows you specific help related to that particular command; this can help when you're a little stuck on a command or on which flags you can use.

hg summary

Another way to show the status of the repository, but in a more verbal way, is to use hg summary, which gives a better indication of what's changed. Rather than using letters to show the status of a file, it shows the same information using words. So, if you have five added files, the command outputs commit: 5 added; the same is true for deleted and modified files. This command also shows you which branch you're currently on, updates available, the current branch, and the parent revision.

hg annotate

When it comes to breaking down a file on a line-by-line basis, hg annotate is what you're after. Using this command on a file without any additional flags shows the revision in which the line was created, but that isn't enough in some cases. To get around that problem, you can add additional flags to the command. For example, if you add -u, you also see the user's name on each line, so you know who authored each line.

Verbose flag

If that's not enough information, you can add the verbose flag to get even more, including the user's full name and e-mail address. Another useful tip when using the shorthand version of the flags is the ability to bundle them together. For example, you can use hg annotate -u -v or even hg annotate -uv, which can save you some typing.

Moving and renaming files

When it comes to moving and renaming files, the processes and commands are the same. Although there are commands for both actions, the commands can be swapped around, so really you can use any of the following commands to move or rename a file: mv, move, and rename. Both processes require you to pick the original file first and then either the new name for the file or the new location. You can make the new location of the file in a different folder if you prefer, or keep it in the same folder and change its name, or both.

hg log

When you want to look at previous revisions and checking out the logs, that's where hg log comes in. Several options can enhance the log experience, but when you use the command without them, you see all the revisions from the repository. Each one looks something like this:

```
changeset:    4:5ed5beba9692
user:         Chris Kemper <hey@chrisdkemper.co.uk>
date:         Tue Sep 28 00:05:53 2010 +0100
summary:      Removed old forms
```

This doesn't show much in terms of changes that have been made. To resolve that, you can add -v to the mix, which shows all the files included in the commit. This is a little more helpful, but if you have a lot of repositories, it can be overkill. To make it a little less painful, you can use -r to specify a revision or range of revisions. If you put those two together, the command gives something like this:

```
hg log -v -r 4
changeset:    4:5ed5beba9692
user:         Chris Kemper <hey@chrisdkemper.co.uk>
date:         Tue Sep 28 00:05:53 2010 +0100
files:        application/modules/default/Forms/Login.php
application/modules/default/Forms/Signup.php
summary:      Removed old forms
```

You can take this another step by adding the -p flag to the command as well, which adds the actual contents of the changed files to Terminal. This gives you a more in-depth look at the changes in the file, if you need that much detail.

Going remote

When you need to pull or push changes, it's always best to use either hg outgoing or hg incoming to see if you have changes that need to go either way. Running either of these commands uses the predetermined URL to see which changes should be either pushed or pulled, depending on which command is used.

After you're happy with the changes that need to be pulled down, you can use hg pull, which pulls down any changes that are due to be pulled down. When everything gets pulled down, you need to perform an update (hg update), which adds the newly pulled changes to the working copy. This can be avoided if you add a -u flag to the pull command, which performs the update upon completion and saves you a step.

In some cases, you see the following error when trying to perform an update:

```
abort: crosses branches (use 'hg merge' or 'hg update -C')
```

This means you need to merge the changes before you can perform the update. This is an easy process and can be achieved by using hg merge, which will ideally work and merge the changes. In some cases, though, you're left with conflicts in the files that need to be dealt with before you can perform the merge. This means you need to resolve the file(s) in question before moving on. After resolving the conflict, you may once again run into problems performing the merge; since you know which files conflicted, and you've fixed the issues, you can safely use force to ensure that the merge goes through correctly.

With the merge resolved, you can perform the update, and the working copy will be in a modified state. It needs to be committed, after which everything will be back in a state of no changes: everything that needed to be committed has been committed.

hg resolve

I briefly touched on resolving conflicts, and now I'll go into a lot more detail on the subject, because you can do a lot with the hg resolve command. In the earlier example, you needed to resolve a particular file so you could merge the files again. To achieve this, you use hg resolve -m file, which marks the file as resolved.

If you're unsure which files are resolved or resolved, you can use the following commands to list all the files that are in either state:

```
hg resolve -l
```

Running this command outputs the applicable files with either R for resolved or U for unresolved files. If you accidently resolve a file before you're ready to do so, you can reset it by using hg resolve -u file, which gives you the choice to try the merge again or resolve the file manually. Using the command without any flags attempts to remerge the specified file. If you specify a particular tool to use, using --tool tool-name, then the merge is attempted in that particular tool.

hg fetch

There is a command you can use that combines pull, update, and merge in one command: hg fetch. It can save you some time when you're dealing with low-level commits, but before you can use it, you need to enable it in the .hgrc file, like so:

```
[extensions]
hgext.fetch=
```

With that enabled, use the command, and all of the actions are combined into one. If things go wrong, you can use the previous commands to fix the errors, depending on what failed.

hg push

I've covered the updating and pulling sides of things; now I you need to cover pushing. This allows you to push the changes to a remote server for centralized usage. The command itself is as simple as hg push. If you've cloned a repository, then the URL is predefined in the repository config files, so no URL needs to be specified. If you want to push to another location, or indeed to a new one, you need to specify a URL to push to. Depending on the state of the remote repository, you may need to use the force flag to ensure that the push works correctly. Other than that, ensure that the local copy is up-to-date before attempting a push, and you'll be fine.

hg diff

It's also really easy to perform diffs in Mercurial, thanks to hg diff. Without any arguments, it attempts to perform a diff on the local version of the files and the last committed version. You can be more specific by specifying particular revisions to diff between, using something like the following:

```
hg diff -r 5 -r 6 file
```

The file part of the command is optional; however, not including it compares the whole repository, so the screen is rather hectic with changes. If it's possible to specify a file, be sure to do that.

Mercurial summary

Although this is a somewhat simple overview of the Mercurial command-line usage, it's enough to show you how powerful and easy-to-use this tool is. Whether it's pushing or pulling changes, committing, or diffing, it all works together really well. And if you get into the habit of using the command, it can speed up your workflow thanks to avoiding bloated applications and doing exactly what you want to do.

Git

Git should already be set up on your machine regardless of your operating system (if you haven't set it up, go back to Chapter 3 to see how), so on that side of things, you're ready to go.

Setting up merge tools

Although Git is already set up, you need to configure some merge tools to simplify working with the repository and handling conflicts. You stick with WinMerge on Windows, FileMerge on Mac, and Meld on Ubuntu; let's get right into it, starting with Windows.

Windows merge tool

To enable WinMerge as a merge tool, you just need to add a few lines to the .gitconfig file, which lives in your user account page. If your file already has any of the sections in it, expand them with the following additions:

```
[merge]
    tool = winmerge

[mergetool "winmerge"]
    cmd = \"C:\\Program Files (x86)\\WinMerge\\WinMergeU.exe /u /e \"
```

With this addition, you need to use git mergetool to perform the required merges in WinMerge. If there's nothing to merge, you see "No files need merging," as you'd expect. You may need to change the path to the WinMergeU.exe file, depending on your system; you can find out the path using the right-click method I already talked about.

Mac merge tool

Git has support for FileMerge baked in, which makes setting it up even easier. Rather than editing the .gitconfig file directly, you can use this command to set things up:

```
git config --global merge.tool opendiff
```

Look in .gitconfig to see what just happened:

```
[merge]
    tool = opendiff
```

That really is all you need. The next time you come across a merge conflict, it'll be managed from FileMerge.

Linux merge tool

To get your Ubuntu merge tool (Meld) up and running as Git's merge tool, you need to use a wrapper script to set it up. You can find a great one at https://gist.github.com/1247554, which does just what you need. To get started, copy the contents of the file to your clipboard, and then head into Terminal and run this command:

```
sudo nano /usr/local/bin/git_merge_meld.sh
```

With the file open, paste the contents of the previous script into the file, and then save it. You need to need to make it executable, which you do like so:

```
sudo chmod +x /usr/local/bin/git_merge_meld.sh
```

Now that the file is executable, you need to ensure that Git is ready to work with it, which can be archived by using the following commands:

```
git config --global merge.tool meldscript
git config --global mergetool.meldscript.cmd git_merge_meld.sh $LOCAL $BASE $REMOTE
$MERGED
```

With everything in place, all that's left to do is run git mergetool when those horrible conflicts creep up on you, easy as pie.

Creating a repository

Before you can use any other commands, the first thing you have to do is create a repository. You can use either an empty folder or one that already has files in it; Git doesn't mind. Once you've navigated to it in Terminal (remember, cd to change directories), use git init to create your repository, ready for use. Creating a repository in a blank folder looks something like this:

```
mkdir test
cd test
git init
```

Cloning a repository

It's also possible to clone an existing repository, which can be achieved using the git clone command with a repository URL. For example purposes, let's look at cloning the HTML 5 Boilerplate project from GitHub. Since the repository allows for anonymous access, you need to add any login credentials; however, if they were required when performing the clone, you would be asked for them. The clone looks something like this:

```
git clone https://github.com/h5bp/html5-boilerplate.git
```

By default, this puts the code in a folder called html5-boilerplate because that's what the repository is called. However, you can specify your own folder after the repository, if you'd prefer for the name to be something else.

Basic commands

Now that you have a repository, it's time to manage some files and start getting to the good stuff. As with SVN and Mercurial, I'll go through the commands you'll use most often, starting with git status.

git status

You'll end up using this command a lot when playing with Git. It gives you the status of the folder you're in; or, if you specify a file or folder, such as git status folder, you get the status of that specific item. If you use git status on an empty repository, it gives you the following:

```
# On branch master
#
# Initial commit
#
nothing to commit (create/copy files and use "git add" to track)
```

As you can see at the bottom of the command, there is nothing to commit, so let's get some test files in place.

Adding files

Create a new file in the repository, either by saving a file in the folder or by using touch textfile.txt, which creates a file with that name (provided it doesn't exist). Now, if you do git status, the bottom half of the output is slightly different:

```
..
# Untracked files:
#   (use "git add <file>..." to include in what will be committed)
#
#        textfile.txt
```

The output shows that the file you just created is unversioned and also suggests you should add it.

A couple of options are available when adding files. You can do it file by file or folder by folder, by using git add file or git add folder to target specific items. However, if you're going for an initial commit where everything in the repository needs to be added, use git add to mark all the unversioned files in the repository for addition. Using git status now gives different output, something like the following:

```
# On branch master
#
# Initial commit
#
# Changes to be committed:
#   (use "git rm --cached <file>..." to unstage)
#
#        new file:   textfile.txt
#
```

The next stage in normal circumstances would be to commit the files into the repository, but let's assume a file was added by mistake and needs to be removed from the list of files to be committed. This can happen when certain files are unique per-user, so there's no need to commit them. Let's do that for the file you just added.

If you run git rm --cached textfile.txt, that file is unstaged and therefore back to the state is was before. If you run git status now, the result is the same as when the repository was first created and shows the textfile.txt file as untracked; so, if you wanted to, you could add it again.

Let's assume you do want commit the textfile.txt file. Again, you have a couple of options. It's possible to either commit the file directly or commit the whole repository in one go, taking any staged files to be committed with it. Both methods start with the same command, git commit, which when run by itself commits the entire repository. You can specify a file or folder by adding its name after the command, like so: git commit filename.txt. After the command has run, you're asked to enter a commit message, which appears in the editor you specified during the Git configuration. If you want to avoid using an editor, you can include the commit message in the command by adding -m and your message, like so:

```
git commit filename.txt -m "This is a commit message"
```

Regardless of which method you use, a message needs to be specified, and the -m flag can be added in either case. The filename.txt file is committed into the repository, and for now, that's it. For now on, any changes you make to this file can be committed as a new version, which gives you the joy of reverting to previous revisions and other great features.

Deleting files

Of course, you won't always be adding files. Sometimes you need to delete a file, which is easy too. Let's create a file that you'll delete soon after committing it. The following commands create a file, add it, and then commit it:

```
touch todel.txt
git add todel.txt
git commit todel.txt -m "To be deleted"
```

To remove this new file, all you need to use is the simple command git rm <file> or, in this case, git rm todel.txt, which deletes the file from the repository and the file itself. However, until It's committed, the file remains in limbo and isn't removed from any future commits. It's worth mentioning that deleting a file doesn't remove its history, so if you happen to delete a file by mistake, it's possible to get it back.

While the file remains in limbo, you can remove the flag to delete the file by using a couple of commands. The first move is to reset the latest version of the repository or HEAD for the deleted file. This stops the file from being committed with the deleted flag, which is half of what you need to do. The next and final stage is to get the file back, which is accomplished by checking out the file from the repository. There is a downside to this: any changes that were made to the file after the last commit are lost. To get the file back, enter these commands:

```
git reset HEAD todel.txt
git checkout - - todel.txt
```

With these two commands, the file is back to how it was before it was deleted, minus any changes that were made since the last commit.

These commands allow the majority of day-to-day management in your local Git repository, since normally all you need to do is add, commit, and delete files. Nailing these basic commands will really help you get to grips with Git in general and with maintaining your local repository.

git log

Before you go any further, let's have a closer look at the git log command, over which you have a load of control. By default, it can be a little hectic and show the wrong information for your needs, but that's why it can be customized. The --pretty flag is your friend, because it helps pretty up the output of the command, as in a couple of these examples:

```
git log --pretty=oneline --max-count=2
git log --pretty=oneline --since='5 minutes ago'
git log --pretty=oneline --until='5 minutes ago'
git log --pretty=oneline --author=<your name>
git log --pretty=oneline --all
```

These examples explain themselves and limit by count, a time limit, author, or everything. Although these work fine, it's possible to combine some replacement tokens to create a better `log` command, where you can see the ideal amount of information. The following command shows just enough information to be useful without overloading things:

```
git log --pretty=format:"%h %ad | %s%d [%an]" --graph --date=short
```

In this command, the pretty type is `format`, which allows for the use of tokens to create custom log output. Going from right to left, you have a shortened version of the commit hash, the author date, the comment associated with the commit, any tag, branch information, and, of course, the author name. The `graph` flag also tells the log to be output in an ASCII format, which keeps everything neat and tidy. The final option shortens the date format so it doesn't include the time or anything like that. This command outputs something like the following:

```
* d32dfb7 2011-10-26 | Update README repo urls [Nicolas Gallagher]
* 380c4f8 2011-10-25 | Add default font-size and line-height styles. [Nicolas Gallagher]
* 125a7a6 2011-10-23 | Remove default font-size and line-height. Close
#724 [Nicolas Gallagher]
* 1437e0f 2011-10-23 | Remove demo folder. [Nicolas Gallagher]
* 0a80eba 2011-10-23 | Remove test folder. [Nicolas Gallagher]
* 5fdb99f 2011-10-19 | adding a depends -clean. fixes #692 [Divya Manian]
```

This output is from the HTML 5 Boilerplate project you cloned earlier. If you happened to be on a branch at the time of running the log, the left side of the output would change to respect the output of the graph, giving a graphical representation of how the commits pan out.

The previous command is a little hard to type in every time. To get around that, you can create an alias to it, which lets you use it more often and more easily. To achieve this, you need to add the following lines to the `.gitconfig` file:

```
[alias]
hist = log --pretty=format:\"%h %ad | %s%d [%an]\" --graph --date=short
```

Of course, if you already have aliases set up, then add these lines below any others you have. This means from now on, you can use `git hist` to run that `log` command, which is a lot more manageable.

Reverting unstaged changes

Say, for example, you've been working on some changes to a file, but you've realized that really, you don't want those changes; you'd rather go back to the previous version of the file. That's easy to do with Git; all you need to do is check out the file again. This gets the most recent version of the file that's been committed, discards all changes made after that commit, and brings the file back to its previous state. This can be achieved like so:

```
git checkout file.txt
```

This takes the `file.txt` file back its last committed state. So, when you have unstaged changes that you want to get rid of, checking out changes is your friend.

Taking this a stage further, if you have staged the change, but you want to take it back, you can do so using the git reset command. To unstage the changes, you need to reset the HEAD revision of the file to clear the most recent changes to the file, in this case as it's being staged. With the example of the file.txt file, the command looks like this:

```
git reset HEAD file.txt
```

This takes the file back to the state it was in before it was staged. So, if you want to remove the file, all it takes is checking out the file again, and it'll be like nothing ever happened.

If you happen to go a stage further and commit the file before you realize that you made a big mistake, you can get around that too! This is what git revert is for. It allows you to revert changes you've made back to their previous states. If you have literally just performed the commit, you can use HEAD again, as it's the latest change that's been made. So you can use the following:

```
git revert HEAD
```

You have the option to add a message when performing the revert, and it's advisable to do so, just to make sure you know exactly why you made the commit.

Moving and renaming files

It's as easy as you'd expect to move a file in Git. You can use the git mv command to initiate the move. First you specify the file you'd like to move, and then the new location of the file. Alternatively, in the destination, it's possible to pick a new name for the file, just like renaming it. This can be achieved even if you don't move the file into a different directory.

Reverting to previous changes

There will be a time when you need to go back to a previous commit, which can be done easily enough by combining the git hist command from earlier to locate a vital bit of information, the commit hash. With that in hand, you can use it to check out to that particular version:

```
git checkout <commit hash>
```

This brings the repository back to that revision, allowing you to perform any actions you require while in this version. You can tag the repository if you'd like to, but that's up to you. After you've done what's needed, you can get back to the most up-to-date version of the repository by checking out the branch you were previously on, which is most likely master:

```
Git checkout master
```

Now you're back where you were before going back to the previous version, just as if it had never happened. Hazzah!

Tagging

When you're doing certain code releases, or you reach a stage in development that you'd like to tag so you can easily refer back to it, then you'll appreciate tags. Using tags gives you the ability to check out a specific tag with ease, bringing the repository back to the state it was it when the tag was created. Let's have a look at setting up some tags.

To create a new tag in the current working copy, use the following command:

```
git tag tag-name
```

This tags the current changeset with the tag name specified. You can get back to this particular version at any time by using

```
git checkout tag-name
```

Of course, sometimes tags are created by mistake, and you want to remove one. The best way to achieve this is to first use `git tag`, which lists all the tags currently in the repository. Then, to delete the tag, use the following:

```
Git tag -d tag-name
```

This removes the tag, but the history of the commit remains intact, so you don't need to worry about losing any changes; only the tag reference is deleted.

In general, you'll most likely tag the development of a project at specific benchmarks within the project. Some of these may include beta releases, feature development releases, bug fixes, and many more. It's always good to have tags recorded because you can easily go back to a tag and see the project at that stage. This can be useful for bug fixing or even for future feature development, but either way, tags are extremely useful.

Pulling changes

If you're dealing with a cloned repository, you'll occasionally need to pull in changes from the remote server to your local repository to ensure that everything is always up to date. There are a couple of ways to do this, the easiest of which is to use `git pull`, which pulls down all the changes to the local copy of the repository and merges the remote changes into the local copy. The other option in this instance is to use `git fetch`, which pulls all the changes down the local copy but doesn't perform the merge. To perform the merge, all you need to do is use `git merge`, and changes are merged into the repository.

Pushing changes

If you've already cloned a repository, pushing the changes back is a piece of cake, because all it takes is a `git push` and your changes will be sent up to the remote repository—provided the local copy is up to date before you try to perform the push. You can check out the information about the remote repository by using `git remote`, which shows the remote locations stored in the repository, but in most cases this is origin. You can then probe a little further and get more information about the origin repository by using `git remote show origin`, which shows you a load of information about the remote server. The following is from the HTML 5 Boilerplate repository mentioned before:

```
* remote origin
  Fetch URL: git://github.com/h5bp/html5-boilerplate.git
  Push  URL: git://github.com/h5bp/html5-boilerplate.git
  HEAD branch: master
  Remote branches:
    cake   tracked
    master tracked
    rake   tracked
  Local branch configured for 'git pull':
    master merges with remote master
  Local ref configured for 'git push':
    master pushes to master (local out of date)
```

If you want to push a repository that you've created locally to a remote server, either your own or a service like GitHub, that's simple, too. The first thing to bear in mind is that you can't push a repository that isn't bare: in other words, it can contain no files other than the `.git` folder. If you're managing the server yourself, be sure to initialize the repository using

```
git --bare init
```

If the repository isn't under your direct control, make sure it's just been created and is in fact empty.

The next step is to add a new remote location to the repository. By default, there won't be an origin location. However, if there is one, replace `origin` in the next example with an appropriate name for the location:

```
git remote add origin path-to-remote-repository
```

This adds the new location to the repository. All you need to do now is push the changes to it, like so:

```
git push -u origin master
```

Now, any changes in the repository are pushed to the repository. You can pull and push from it very easily in the future by using `git push <name>` or, if `origin` isn't required, `git push`.

Git summary

You've been through how to manage your repository, from the basics of creating it right up to pushing changes to a remote server, even if you haven't cloned the repository previously. You've seen how to manage your files, add new ones, delete unwanted files, and a lot more. Although you can create intricate workflows and more with Git, everything covered here lets you process the majority of actions and easily initialize and maintain your own local or remote repository.

Chapter summary

This chapter has covered a lot of ground, from SVN to Git. While you're using Terminal, it's good to remember that unless you throw around the `--force` flag command, you can't do any harm. Even if you only perform basic actions in Terminal, and perform more complex actions using a GUI, you can still improve your knowledge and become more confident in what you're doing. It's always good to remember that the `status` command is your friend and can really help out if you're unsure which command you need to use next.

Bear in mind that when you're commiting files in SVN, those changes are available to other users with access to the repository as soon as they are committed. However, this isn't the case with distributed repository; if you're working with a shared repository, then until you push those changes remotely, no other users can access those changes, and you can develop in peace.

Now it's time to head into the land of setting up remote servers for the various versioning systems you've been working with. The next chapter covers how to set up your own remote repositories that you create on your own personal server. If you don't have one, I'll recommend services you can use to achieve your goals. Let's get to it!

Chapter 10

How to Create a Server

Now comes the time to make a major leap into the world of version control and actually host the repositories yourself! In this chapter, I'll take you through how to set up respective SVN, Git, and Mercurial servers. Where possible, I'll also show you how to make things a bit more interesting by integrating with Apache and a couple of tricks to make the whole process a bit smoother.

For this chapter, you'll be using a server edition of Ubuntu as a base for all of these servers. Although there are other server options out there, such as other flavours of Linux and Windows server, I've chosen Ubuntu here for a number of reasons. Firstly, as with most other Linux distributions, Ubuntu is free of cost, which makes it much easier to try out on your own computer without actually having to spend any money. The Windows alternative isn't free, nor as easy to come by. You can download a trial, but it requires a Windows Live account which may involve signing up for an account you may never use again. Using Ubuntu also helps when it comes to hosting; there are a lot more choices out there for Linux hosting which helps keep the prices down. You can still obtain Windows hosting, achieving the level of access you need here brings the cost up, which puts it at a slight disadvantage.

The support for Linux is also great, thanks to the open-source community around it who want to spread the word and encourage other people to use it. The Ubuntu forums contain information on a number of scenarios and issues and many bloggers and developers alike have documented their experiences and expertise so you can learn from them. That's not to say the same cannot be said for Windows Server—many people have written articles on how to accomplish certain tasks on that system—but the core support base is significantly smaller than that of Ubuntu.

When you install Ubuntu server, there is an option available to install a LAMP stack during the installation. In case that's not available to you, however, I'll run through the commands anyway. If you can recall back to Chapter 3, we ran through a few commands to get everything set up and running, so this time we'll speed through them, just in case anything got missed.

Setting up the server

As mentioned, you need a LAMP stack on an Ubuntu installation for the following instruction. Of course you can use other flavours of Linux or even a Windows server, but then the following may not work. The following commands will set up a LAMP stack on Ubuntu, and get it ready for all of the other changes you'll be making:

```
sudo apt-get install tasksel
sudo tasksel install lamp-server
```

The above commands will install the basics of the server. There was an option to install phpMyAdmin in Chapter 3, so feel free to look back at that chapter to see about installing it on this server. Now you're at a point where you can move forward and create some remote repositories. To gain access to the repositories across different machines, you'll need to ensure you have a domain name pointing at the server, which is an address you can use to access the system. In these examples, I'll be using the domain chrisdkemper.co.uk, which is my personal domain name.

It is possible to use these services with just an IP address and no domain name; however, if you want to take advantage of sub-domains, giving the domain name is greatly recommended. If you're totally unsure about the whole domain name thing, that's fine. We'll have a brief run through, just to make sure we're all on the same page.

Domain names and DNS records

Having a domain name is a pretty widely established thing in the web industry. It allows you your own personal space on the web that you can put on business cards, bios, or just mention in conversation. The domain name itself is really just an easy way of accessing an IP address, which is the numbed address that allows access to your web space. The problem with IP addresses is that they're rather hard to remember. If I said 209.85.229.103 to you, it would most likely mean nothing, just like 209.85.229.105 or 209.85.229.99. However, if I were to say google.co.uk, that would make a lot more sense. The IPs that were just mentioned are all Google's, as well as a whole load more I'm sure, but rather than getting people to remember the numbers, they have an address mapped to those numbers to make it easier to access. But if you were to put one of those IP addresses into the address bar of a browser, it would still resolve to Google.co.uk.

Now that you know the importance of domain names, it's time to look into how they work. Each domain name has a few records that control where it points in the form of the DNS record and the name servers. The name servers aren't really important, and will be dependent on where you register your domain name, such as 123-reg or Go Daddy. There isn't much of a difference between the two services; they both give you full access to your domain names and are similarly priced. The interface for 123-reg is slightly easier to use, which gives it the edge over Go Daddy's cluttered control panel. Also, Go Daddy does a lot of sponsorship deals, which means you can always pick up a bargain when registering your domain; however, this means there will be a lot of ads present.

The DNS records control where the various parts of the domain point, including e-mail and the A record, which controls which IP address the domain points to. If you were to buy a new domain name, this would be blank, so you would replace it with the IP address you'd like it to point to, then save the form. Now, depending on the domain, it'll take different amounts of time to propagate the Internet, so for a while the domain may work for some people and not others, but generally after 24–48 hours the whole Internet will be aware of the change.

A few good hosting providers

For those of you that don't have any web space yet, or don't have any control of the space you're working on, this section is for you. The hosting game is one many people choose to opt out of, because it can be really confusing. I'll try to numb the pain as much as possible here. The following are services where you get root access to your particular chunk of web space, which allows for any amount of customization you'd like to use. These guys can be used for hosting applications, websites, repositories, or even all three. It just depends on what you'd prefer to use. All of the offerings below are VPSs or virtual private servers, which are, basically, full server packages in the cloud for you. These guys will give you root access to the server, and even install an OS for you with a couple of clicks. If you do look into any of the following, or even go hunting for a provider yourself, be sure they support an Ubuntu distribution—the newer, the better!

Linode

These guys are a dedicated VPS company, so virtual private servers are all they offer, and they do it really well. You have a few options to use when signing up, mainly having to do with the amount of RAM and traffic you'd expect to have on a monthly basis. Hosting a couple of repositories, or even a website, won't use up a huge amount of bandwidth (that is, of course, assuming you're not mega popular, and are not pushing and pulling a lot of files in and out of your repositories).

Currently Linode 512 is the smallest package offered, which gives 512MB RAM, 20GB of storage, and 200GB of data transfer for $19.95 a month. This is more than enough to work with and, in reality, if you're only using this for repositories might be overkill. But having the ability to manage the server however you like and having the option to host additional sites are great.

When you log in, your control panel gives you a number of options, including being able to restart your Linode server, clone it, back it up, or even ditch it and install a new OS instead. You also get comprehensive graphs to show data usage and so on. It's also possible to set up notifications when you're getting close to your caps so you can either calm down or get more space.

You're also under no crazy contract with Linode. You can get your money back if within seven days you decide you want out; otherwise, you just pay on a month-by-month basis, with no long-term commitment. If you're looking for a good place to start, with a server that will handle a large chunk of traffic and allow you to host pretty much anything, check out www.linode.com to see for yourself.

Media Temple

Although you may not know exactly who Media Temple (mt) are, you'll no doubt have seen them as sponsors of events, or you may even own one of their super-soft t-shirts. As well as being great sponsorship partners and givers of super-soft t-shirts, they also offer a wide range of top-notch web hosting products. Although we're looking at the dedicated server option, they also offer standard hosting packages, and some intense packages intended for the big dogs out there.

They have a number of Dedicated-Virtual (dv) servers available, starting with 512MB RAM, 20GB storage, and 350GB data transfer. That comes in at a price of $30 a month, and with that come the quality and high standard of hosting that Media Temple are constantly working to improve, in-depth analysis tools, a number of OS choices, and a whole lot more. They also offer a great amount of support on both their website and via Twitter. It's also possible manage your (dv) server from a handy iPhone app, which can make doing a quick restart or checking stats a breeze.

This barely scratches the service of the level of service, quality, and standards offered by Media Temple. They're always improving their products to make things more efficient, faster, and generally just better. You can see for yourself by heading over to the website at http://mediatemple.net/roadmap. While you're there, you can check out the products they have on offer and maybe even sign up for their high-quality service.

SVN

Now that we have all of that out the way, it's time to get into the good stuff and set up an SVN server so you can start hosting your own repositories. Now that you have a server to work with, you need to install some additional packages before it's possible to host any repositories at all, so let's get right into it.

Getting started

The first thing to do is make sure everything is up to date, and then install Subversion and its equivalent Apache package. Using the following commands will perform the update, and then install the packages:

```
Sudo apt-get update
Sudo apt-get install subversion libapache2-svn
```

The next step is to create a location to store the repositories. This can, in theory, be anywhere in the system, but a common location is in the var directory within the file system, so you'll be creating a folder called svn-repos in there. Feel free to change the name or location of the folder, just be sure to remember it for later. The following command will create the folder:

```
Sudo mkdir /var/svn-repos/
```

This creates the repositories' house. Now you need to actually create some repositories, which can be done using the following commands. You'll also be adding the trunk, branches, and tags directories into the repositories here to ensure the repository is in the correct format.

```
Sudo svnadmin create --fs-type fsfs /var/svn-repos/project_test
```

```
Sudo svn mkdir -m "initial setup" file:///var/svn-repos/project_test/trunk
Sudo svn mkdir -m "initial setup" file:///var/svn-repos/project_test/branches
Sudo svn mkdir -m "initial setup" file:///var/svn-repos/project_test/tags
```

Of course, in the above, just replace project_test with the desired name of the repository, and repeat as needed for additional repositories.

Managing users

Now you need to manage the users for the newly created repository, which requires a few initial steps that won't need to be re-created for future use. First of all, you need to create a new group to hold all of the SVN users. This is to ensure they can access the repositories by checking them out, and so on. Use the following command to create said group:

```
Sudo groupadd subversion
```

With the group created, it's now time to change the ownership of the repository folders to Apache, and make them a part of the previously created group. To achieve this, the files will be owned by www-data, which is a user created by Apache when it's installed. This means that since Apache owns the repositories, they can be viewed through it in the browser, but because the repositories are in the subversion group, any users in the group can view them, too. The following commands will set that process up; like the groupadd command, this won't need to be done again).

```
Sudo chown -R www-data:subversion /var/svn-repos/*
Sudo chmod -R 770 /var/svn-repos/*
```

Now that's all set up, the next stage is to manage the users for the repository. How this is done depends on personal preference: you can either have one set of users for all repositories or a set of users for each repository. Some people prefer to have more control over each repository, but if you want to work on all repositories, you'll need to add yourself to the password file, multiple times. In this example, it'll only be me who's working with this repository, so using one password file for all repositories is good enough. Now I need to create the file, which is done like so:

```
Sudo htpasswd -c /var/svn-repos/users chris
```

The htpasswd command is a function used by Apache to add users to a password file and to give access to certain parts of the server; the -c flag creates the file, if it doesn't exist. The users part of the URL is actually the file itself, which doesn't have an extension, so don't let that catch you out. The final part is the user you'd like to create. Add the name in first—in my case, chris—then, upon pressing enter, you'll be asked for a password, then to confirm said password. This can be repeated as needed for other users; just remove the -c flag if the file already exists.

Integrating with Apache

Everything is coming together now. You have a repository and users for the repository, so now comes the part that links everything together: the integration with Apache. At the moment, you have no way to access the repositories because there isn't an address mapped to the location, which is where Apache virtual hosts comes in.

First, there needs to be a virtual host set up to handle the address you'll use for the repositories; in my example, I've chosen svn.chrisdkemper.co.uk for the sake of ease, although this could in theory be anything you'd like. If do take the sub-domain approach, be sure to set up the relevant DNS records to be sure it actually points at your server. Following is the basic virtual host for that address; in this case, there won't be anything in the DocumentRoot of the address, so going to svn.chrisdkemper.co.uk wouldn't resolve an address, which is pretty standard practice so nobody stumbles upon your repositories.

```
<VirtualHost 178.79.159.153:80>
        DocumentRoot /srv/www/code.chrisdkemper.co.uk/public_html/
        ServerName svn.chrisdkemper.co.uk
</VirtualHost>
```

This isn't enough to route the respective repositories, but it's a start. You need an additional chunk of code which will do the rest of the work, and make all the action happen, as follows:

```
<Location />
        DAV svn
        SVNParentPath /var/svn-repos/
        AuthType Basic
        AuthName "Chrisdkemper Repositories"
        AuthUserFile /var/svn-repos/users
        Require valid-user
</Location>
```

The above can be used in a couple of ways. In this example, it will take into account every repository listed in SVNParentPath, which can actually be individual repositories if you so choose. Using one <Location> tag only allows for one password file to be used, which is represented by the AuthUserFile option. To achieve a password file per repository, you would need to create the multiple files, and use a <Location> tag for each repository, ensuring that the SVNParentPath was set to the specific repository each time.

If you combine these two chunks of code together, you get the following.

```
<VirtualHost 178.79.159.153:80>
        DocumentRoot /srv/www/code.chrisdkemper.co.uk/public_html/
        ServerName svn.chrisdkemper.co.uk

        <Location />
                DAV svn
                SVNParentPath /var/svn-repos/
                AuthType Basic
                AuthName "Chrisdkemper Repositories"
                AuthUserFile /var/svn-repos/users
                Require valid-user
        </Location>
</VirtualHost>
```

After modifying the vhosts, you'll need to restart Apache to make the changes take effect so, provided you've done so, you should now be able to check out the repositories using the URL specified, followed by the repository name. Taking everything you've set up until now, this would be the following:

```
http://svn.chrisdkemper.co.uk/project_test
```

You should now be able to access said repository by either putting the address into the browser or by checking out the repository using Terminal or your program of choice. When prompted for login information for either method, just specify a user that was added during the setup process and that's it! The repository should now function as a normal repository, which is just what you want.

You're up and running!

You now have a working SVN server which can be used to host all of your repositories and all of the files within. You can also add users, or even have a set of users per repository, however you'd like. Given that it's so easy, why wouldn't you want to set up your own server?!

Mercurial

It's time to head into Mercurial land, and set up a server which can be used to share repositories over the Web. This can be a public repository, or you can add other users to allow better collaboration. I'll go through the steps of setting up the server, right from installing Mercurial to serving it online through Apache. I know you're excited, so let's dive right in!

Getting started

First things first: you need to ensure that you have Mercurial installed on the server and that the actual server is up to date, which is done like so:

```
sudo apt-get update
sudo apt-get install mercurial
```

You now have Mercurial installed on the server and it's ready to be used, so the next stage of the process is to create a folder to house all of the repositories. This folder can be placed anywhere on the file system; however, for consistency, I'll be putting mine inside /var to keep it consistent with the SVN repository I created earlier. There will also be some other configuration files within the hg folder, so be sure to name it appropriately. The final stage of the process is to make sure the directory that will house the repositories is opened by Apache, which is what the chown -R www-data:www-data hg/repos command is for. This enables the repository to be viewed in the browser through Apache—after you've enabled it, that is. With that all said, let's get right into the code:

```
cd /var/
sudo mkdir hg
sudo mkdir hg/repos
sudo chown -R www-data:www-data hg/repos
cd hg/repos
mkdir test
cd test
hg init
```

With the directories created and a test repo initialized, you now need to get the first of two configuration files needed for the repository to function correctly. Before that, though, there are a few options that can really help with managing your repositories, in the form of .hgrc file configurations. If you create the file in the repository, there are a huge number of options available. The following are rather useful, and you can adapt them as needed for your repositories:

```
[web]
contact = Chris Kemper <hey@chrisdkemper.co.uk>
description = Test Mercurial repository.
allow_push=chris,craig
allow_read=chris,craig
```

The allow_read and allow_push variables allow you to specify users that are allowed to access the repository. These are optional values, but if you're using one user's file (more on this later) then this can come in useful if you want to easily restrict access to one particular repository.

The first configuration file in question is hgweb.conf, which will live in the previously created hg folder, which for me is in /var. For the minimum level, you just need to show where the repositories reside within the server, so you'll need to create the file by using either your vi or nano to create the nonexistent file, and then save it. Using nano the code would be as follows:

```
nano hgweb.conf
```

Then, with the file open, just copy the following code inside, then save it.

```
[collections]
/var/hg/repos = /var/hg/repos
[web]
push_ssl = false
style = gitweb
```

The last file you need is hgweb.cgi, a copy of which can be taken from the Mercurial examples (it's pointless to re-create a file from scratch when a perfectly decent example is available). You also need to make sure this file is executable, so use chmod to change its read-write status. The following code will copy the file from its example location into the /var/hg folder, which will, of course, change if you want to store the repositories in another location. The following code will copy the file, and make it executable.

```
cd /var/hg
sudo cp /usr/share/doc/mercurial/examples/hgweb.cgi .
sudo chmod a+x hgweb.cgi
```

With the file copied, it'll need to be edited using your favorite editor and modified slightly to include the path to the config file, hgweb.conf, which in my case lives in /var/hg/hg.conf. After the file has been altered, it'll look something like this:

```
config = "/var/hg/hgweb.conf"
```

Managing users

You now need to create some users to allow access to the server, which is pretty easy when it comes down to it. To keep everything together, I'm placing my users file in the root of my hg folder. The file is created, and users added to it as follows:

```
cd /var/hg
htpasswd -mc hgusers chris
htpasswd -m hgusers craig
```

When this command is run, you'll be asked for a password for the user, then to confirm said password, but after the confirmation the user will be added to the file. The -mc flag creates the file if it doesn't exist—in this case the file is hgusers and the user being added is chris. As you can see with adding craig there's no need to use the -mc flag as the file already exists, so -m is used instead. You can add as many users as you like using this method, just repeat the command and alter the name as necessary. Now that you have users created, this part of the configuration is done. You now need to move on to some Apache configuration in the form of a vhost to house all of the Mercurial repositories, but before you do that, you need to create another config file.

In this instance you need to create the main.conf file, which can reside anywhere you want; however, I'm putting it inside of /etc/apache2/hg, since it's needed by Apache and it makes sense for it to live within the apache directory. The hg folder within /etc/apache2/ doesn't exist, so you'll need to create it. The following commands will create the file and the folder for it to live in:

```
cd /etc/apache2/
mkdir hg
cd hg
nano main.conf
```

Inside the file, you need the following code:

```
ScriptAliasMatch ^(.*) /var/hg/hgweb.cgi$1
<Directory /var/hg>
  Options ExecCGI FollowSymLinks
  AllowOverride All
</Directory>
```

In the code above, you can see a reference to the /var/hg/hgweb.cgi file, which will need to be changed if you choose a different location for the file. The <Directory> tag also contains a reference to the root of the Mercurial repositories, which will need to be altered if you choose any other path.

Integrating with Apache

How your server is set up will determine where the following code will go—it'll either be a file by itself, the name of which is the virtual host itself, or just go inside one big vhosts file. If you're unsure on this, your hosting provider should have documentation on setting up and editing Virtual Hosts. Either way, the following code will allow you to access the repository through Apache, clone the repositories locally, and also commit files as needed:

```
<VirtualHost 178.79.159.153:80>
        ServerAdmin webmaster@localhost
        ServerName hg.chrisdkemper.co.uk

        DocumentRoot /var/hg
        <Directory />
                Options FollowSymLinks
```

```
                    AllowOverride None
            </Directory>
            <Directory /var/hg/>
                    Options Indexes FollowSymLinks MultiViews
                    AllowOverride All
                    Order allow,deny
                    allow from all
            </Directory>

            ScriptAlias /cgi-bin/ /usr/lib/cgi-bin/
            <Directory "/usr/lib/cgi-bin">
                    AllowOverride None
                    Options +ExecCGI -MultiViews +SymLinksIfOwnerMatch
                    Order allow,deny
                    Allow from all
            </Directory>

            ErrorLog /var/log/apache2/error.log

            # Possible values include: debug, info, notice, warn, error, crit,
            LogLevel warn

            CustomLog /var/log/apache2/access.log combined
        Alias /doc/ "/usr/share/doc/"
        <Directory "/usr/share/doc/">
            Options Indexes MultiViews FollowSymLinks
            AllowOverride None
            Order deny,allow
            Deny from all
            Allow from 127.0.0.0/255.0.0.0 ::1/128
        </Directory>
            Include /etc/apache2/hg/main.conf
        <Directory />
            AuthType Basic
            AuthName "Mercurial repositories"
            AuthUserFile /var/hg/hgusers
            Require valid-user
        </Directory>

    </VirtualHost>
```

Let's break up the important parts of the file to see what's most important.

```
    ServerName hg.chrisdkemper.co.uk
```

The ServerName variable is the virtual host being used for the repository; this will need to be changed to meet your needs. The ServerAdmin is used when a 500 error occurs on the server and the e-mail address supplied is shown in this instance.

```
    DocumentRoot /var/hg
    <Directory /var/hg/>
    ...
    </Directory>
```

The above two variables will need to be adjusted to whatever you have set to your Mercurial root, since they're /var/hg for this particular setup. The following line refers to the last configuration file you created, so just alter it as needed to suit where it's stored on your system:

```
Include /etc/apache2/hg/main.conf
```

This code snippet links the users file to the repository to allow for authentication to the server, and allow users to access the repositories. In this instance, the file is applied to all repositories and locations on the virtualhost, however you can use individual users' files for specific repositories by including multiple versions of the snippet, then replacing the / with the path to the repository, surrounded by quotes.

```
<Directory />
    AuthType Basic
    AuthName "Mercurial repositories"
    AuthUserFile /var/hg/hgusers
    Require valid-user
</Directory>
```

With all of these changes in place, all you need to do is restart Apache and the changes will take effect. This can be achieved by using the following command:

```
sudo /etc/init.d/apache2 restart
```

That's it! You're now all set up and ready to go. If you go straight to the virtual host address, you'll see all of your repositories rendered through Apache, and you'll need to log in with valid credentials to access it. You can also clone to the repositories by using virtual-host/repository-name or, in this instance, http://hg.chrisdkemper.co.uk/test.

Git

Unlike the other two processes, setting up a Git server is rather complicated and carries with it a huge amount of choices on how to do it. Don't let that worry you, though, I'll be taking you through everything step by step, so you could be running your own Git server in no time at all! I'll also take you through some things I haven't touched on before, and a number of third-party processes that help everything along. I'll also be showing you how to create SSH keys and more; it's going to be great!

Getting started

First of all, you'll need to install some additional tools, including (if you don't have it already) Git. To install everything you need, run the following commands:

```
sudo apt-get install git-core
sudo apt-get install gitolite
sudo apt-get install git-daemon-run
```

With that taken care of, you need to head back onto a local machine to run a few commands. On Windows, you'll need to open up the Git Bash to run these commands. If you have the joy of a Mac or Linux machine, you'll be able to run these commands in the standard Terminal window, so whichever system you're on, ensure you have the needed program open. You'll be generating SSH key-pairs, which are used to allow communication between your local machine and the server. If this seems familiar to you because you've created a key before, you'll need to do something slightly different when generating the key to give it a different name.

When you run the command to generate the key ssh-keygen you'll be asked a number of questions when generating the key; if you've never generated a key before, all of the defaults will be fine. If you have created a key before, when asked for the file to store the key, the default location will be in brackets. Take a copy of that value and append something like .git to the end of the file, which will differentiate it from the other keys in the folder. If you use all of the defaults, the output of the command will look something like this:

```
ssh-keygen
Generating public/private rsa key pair.
Enter file in which to save the key (/Users/Chris/.ssh/id_rsa): /Users/Chris/.ssh/id_rsa
Enter passphrase (empty for no passphrase):
Enter same passphrase again:
Your identification has been saved in /Users/Chris/.ssh/id_rsa.
Your public key has been saved in /Users/Chris/.ssh/id_rsa.pub.
The key fingerprint is:
9b:0b:50:1f:d4:f1:4b:00:e7:ee:5f:d6:18:de:14:b7 Chris@ChrisMac
```

You may also have a randomart image with the output, but this isn't needed to finish the process so don't worry either way. There is an additional step if you've generated keys before because, at the moment, the new key won't be considered when it's needed,, because the system doesn't know it's there. To remedy this, you need to create a configuration file, which tells the system to include the new file when calls to the ~/.ssh directory are made, which is done as follows:

```
touch ~/.ssh/config
chmod 600 ~/.ssh/config
echo "IdentityFile ~/.ssh/id_rsa.git" >> ~/.ssh/config
```

This basically creates the config file, and adds the line IdentityFile ~/.ssh/id_rsa.git to it, telling SSH to acknowledge the file. There are a lot more options you can place into the config file, such as pointing specific hosts at certain files, and more, but for now all you need is for the file to be picked up.

Gaining access to the server

The next stage is to copy the public-key file to the server so when you attempt to connect to the server, the two halves of the file can communicate and you can gain access to the sever. To achieve this, use the following command, modified with your information for the server:

```
scp /Users/Chris/.ssh/id_rsa.pub user@gitserver:/tmp/chris.pub
```

In the above, change the SSH access details (user@gitserver) as needed to access your server and also change the chris.pub part to whatever user you're currently adding (chris, in my case). If you're planning to work on multiple machines but retain the same username, then you might want to make a slight change to the above. If I were to have a home and work machine, I wouldn't require multiple users for this, as gitolite has a way of dealing with this case. Rather than just naming the file chris.pub, I would instead call it chris@work.pub or chris@home.pub because gitolite is smart enough realize that "chris" is the username used by both. Just something to bear in mind if you do plan on working on multiple machines.

Provided the copy has executed correctly, the public key you need is now on the server, ready for use. You now need to head back to the server and use this public key in gitolite which is the package used to managed all of the repositories. To accomplish this, you need to access the gitolite user account, which is automatically created when the package is installed and then, using the key, add it to the configuration of the package for later use. This can be done by using the following commands:

```
chmod 666 /tmp/chris.pub
su gitolite
gl-setup /tmp/chris.pub
```

This will set up a number of things, including repository administration access to the user specified, which in this case is "chris". It also means this repository can now be cloned, which allows for the creation of new repositories, users, and more. Let's get the repository cloned, shall we?

Cloning the repository

Head back to your local machine and clone the repository. For ease, I'll show you how to do this in Terminal, but feel free to use your application of choice. You'll also need to change the server address to your own in the following:

```
git clone gitolite@server:gitolite-admin
```

With the repository cloned, it's time to open up the config file, located in conf/gitolite.conf, which should look something like this:

```
repo    gitolite-admin
        RW+     =    chris

repo    testing
        RW+     =    @all
```

Let's create a test repository to ensure everything is working, which can be done by adding the following:

```
repo    test
        RW+ = chris
```

In both cases repo is the name of the repository and RW+ shows the users that can access the repository. You can use @all, as in the testing repository, which will allow all the users added to access the repository, or add additional users on another line, like so:

```
repo    mytest
                RW+ = chris
        R = craig
```

You'll notice I've only used R for "craig" which gives him read access, but not the ability to commit, so just tweak as necessary. Of course, to actually give access to "craig" he would need his own public key file (craig.pub) which will have been created by him and sent to you to be added to the admin-repository.

With the changes made and any new users created, and their public keys living in the keydir/ directory, they need to be pushed up to the remote server in the form of a git commit. This is done as follows:

```
git commit -m "Added mytest repo" conf/gitolite.conf
git push
Doing this will give output similar to the following:
Counting objects: 7, done.
Delta compression using up to 4 threads.
Compressing objects: 100% (3/3), done.
Writing objects: 100% (4/4), 365 bytes, done.
Total 4 (delta 1), reused 0 (delta 0)
remote: Already on 'master'
remote: creating test...
remote: Initialized empty Git repository in /var/lib/gitolite/repositories/test.git/
```

The important part of the above is remote: Initialized empty Git repository in /var/lib/gitolite/repositories/test.git/, which tells you that the new repository you created has been initialized. You can now check out the newly created repository by using this command:

```
git clone gitolite@server:test
Which will give the following output:
Cloning into test...
warning: You appear to have cloned an empty repository.
```

This is exactly what you want: you have a blank repository to play with and it means that the server is running correctly. You can now use this repository and any others you created just like you would a hosted solution. Just bear in mind, if you move computers, you'll need to add another public key for yourself as you went through above. There is a slight negative to creating the repository this way, which is the inability to view your repositories online. This is a consequence of how the repositories are stored, which is a shame, but for a kick-ass server, it's a fair price to pay.

Summary

If you so choose, you could now have a server for SVN, Mercurial, and Git, respectively. Although the idea of setting up a server might be scary, once you itemize things and go through it slowly, it's not actually that difficult to do. With this knowledge you can go and set up servers all over the place, and even help out others who are having a little bit of trouble setting up their own servers. Even if you're still not convinced about getting your own server to set up repositories on, it's worth it to just set up a copy of Ubuntu on a virtual machine. It could cost you as little as nothing (depending on the emulation software used—Virtual box is free!) which means that these server creation processes can be tried out with no money spent and no damage done!

Chapter 11

I Don't Have a Server, What Other Options Do I Have?

In this chapter, it's time to cater to those of you out there who don't have a server at your disposal and are looking for a third party to host your code repository. If you happen to fall into this category, or if you're just interested in looking at what's out there because the idea of managing your own repositories worries you a little, then this chapter is for you. We'll be going through some third-party solutions for hosting SVN, Git, and Mercurial repositories. Some of them may even be able to help you if you have multiple repositories using multiple versioning systems. The prices we'll be looking at in this chapter are valid as of early 2012, but it may be worth double-checking the respective websites for the most current pricing.

Beanstalk

The first option available to you is Beanstalk, a great-looking hosting solution. If you've used Versions before, you may have already heard the name, or even had a look at the website. If you're unfamiliar with Versions, it's a Subversion (SVN) GUI available for the Mac (discussed in Chapter 5, if you'd like to know more about it). With Beanstalk, you can host both Git and SVN repositories but, sadly, no options for Mercurial hosting are available. Beanstalk does the whole hosting thing rather well with a decent feature set. You can see the welcome page for Beanstalk in Figure 11-1.

Figure 11-1. A shot from the Beanstalk homepage where you can see an overview of the features it has on offer

Features

All Beanstalk accounts (including the free version) come with private repositories, SSL encryption, and daily backups as standard. With the paid accounts, you get a few additional features including FTP/SFTP deployment, web hooks, and your data backed up every five minutes. Across most hosting systems, these are pretty standard features to expect when hosting a repository, but one additional feature Beanstalk does offer is a great looking and easy-to-use interface. If you check out Figure 11-2 you can see this for yourself.

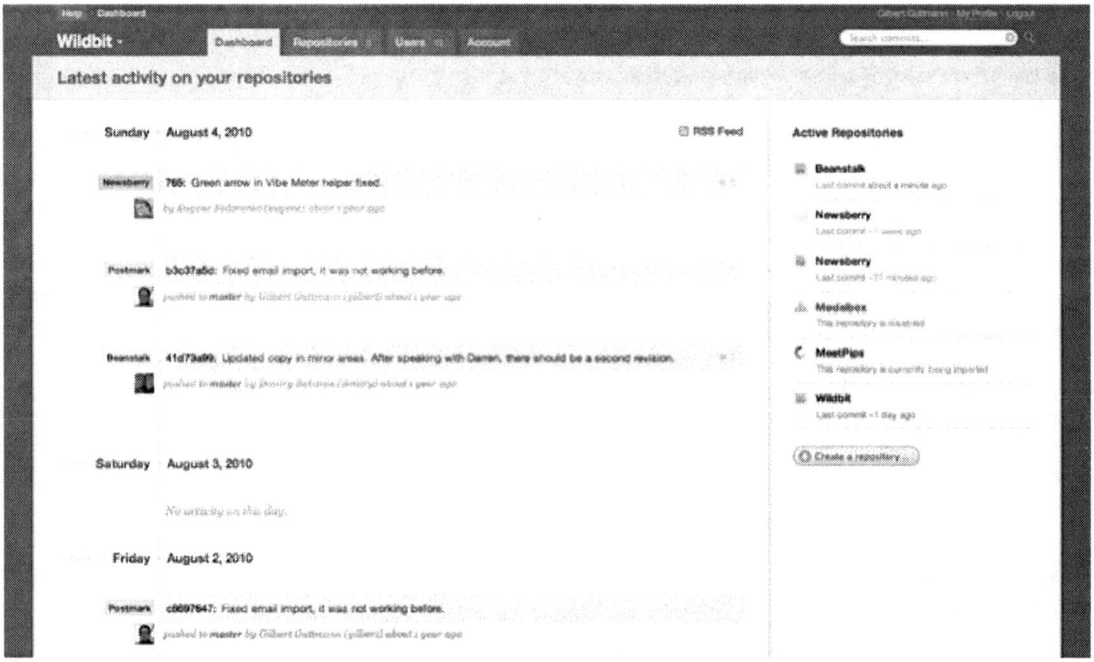

Figure 11-2. The dashboard when you log into your Beanstalk account; you can see recent activity on your account, both your own and that of other members of your team. There's also a link to create a new repository, right on the dashboard.

Beanstalk also gives you some nice user management tools to create permissions on a per-user, per-repository basis, which can come in really useful when you're managing a team. On the main home screen, each commit is labeled by user, with any comments included. This allows whoever is leading the project to keep up to date on which commits are coming in, and if they're on time. Other features of Beanstalk include commit hooks, the Beanstalk API and related applications, code previews, and good options for deploying your code. We'll look at these now.

Commit hooks

If you go with a paid option, you'll get access to commit hooks. Commit hooks can be integrated with third-party applications such as Kiln, Basecamp, Freckle, Twitter, and more to keep you on track and organized with your projects. For instance, if you integrate your Beanstalk commits with Basecamp, every time you make a commit, notification messages will be added to your Basecamp project. Beanstalk can also log time for you if you include tags in your commit messages, which is invaluable for a lot of developers.

API and applications

There is also an API available to all users, which means if you fancy getting your hands dirty with a bit of development then you can integrate the system in some cool ways. A few people have been busy with the

Beanstalk API and created some cool products, including a couple of iPhone and iPad applications to allow users to remotely access their Beanstalk account and check things are going smoothly, which you can download on the App Store. You can also check these out yourself on the Beanstalk website.

Code preview

Another snazzy feature you get from using Beanstalk is the code preview. You can preview files as they would be on your server or local machine. As well as that, you can view all files in the repository in an easy-to-read format with syntax highlighting. The same highlighting follows through all code previews when looking through past revisions and changes, which saves you having to handle and review changes in another application, since Beanstalk can do that for you.

Deploying your code

One of the best features of online repository hosting is being able to deploy your code straight from the web interface. This means reviewing your code changes and deploying the latest revision can be done in a snap within Beanstalk. In the paid plans, you can manually and automatically deploy to your server using FTP/SFTP, but if you move up to the business plan you can deploy your code to multiple servers at once. Business plans also come with a 100% uptime service-level agreement, so might be worth your while if you have a lot of projects to manage.

Support

The support you get with Beanstalk is fantastic. It offers Live Chat and FAQs that can help you sort out most issues, but the main win with Beanstalk's support is the guides. The guides go from basic introductions to version control on to best practice. Although you won't need it now—thanks to this lovely book—Beanstalk offers some great getting-started tutorials with version control, setting up SSH keys, and all that kind of stuff. (I covered SSH keys in Chapter 10 in connection with setting up a Git server, so you can check that out if you're curious.).

Pricing

Beanstalk has a competitive pricing structure for this kind of service and, as you'd hope, there is a free account to allow you to test the waters before diving into a plan. If you do choose to go with a paid plan, there is no commitment and no contracts involved, and if you fancy upgrading or downgrading at some point, that's fine, too. The free account gives you one repository, one user, and 100MB of space, which for the sake of hosting a personal repository or testing out the service, is a great amount to use. Have a look at Figure 11-3 to see the full pricing plan Beanstalk has to offer.

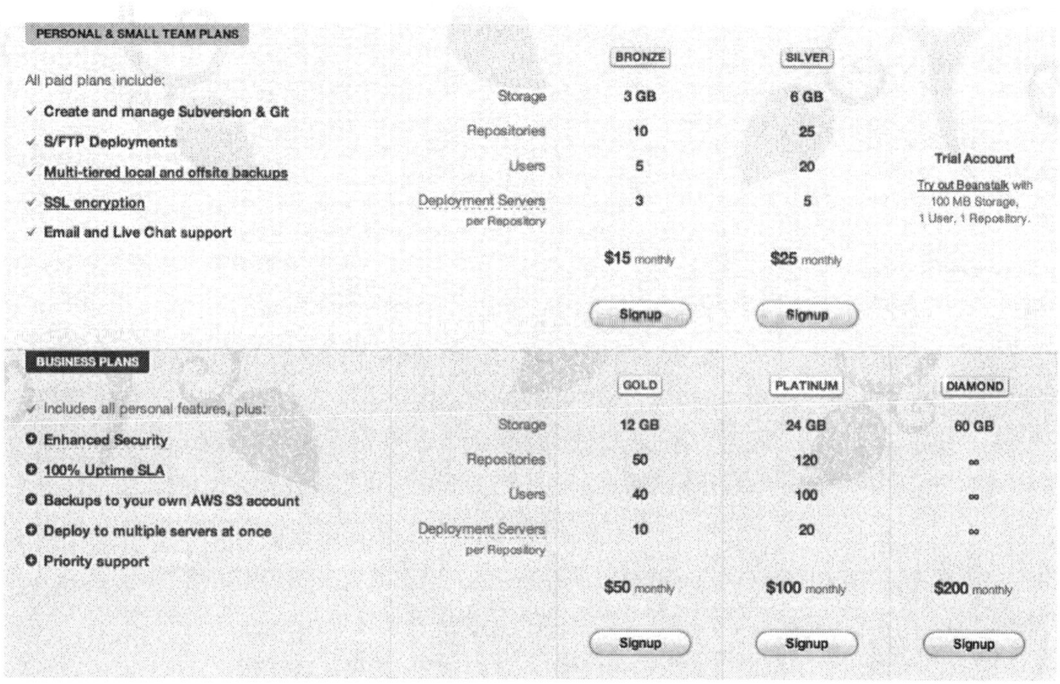

Figure 11-3. The prices for the various packages offered by Beanstalk, from the *Bronze* package, right up to the *Diamond* one.

To sum up Beanstalk

Thanks to Beanstalk's great reputation and user-friendly interface, it's gained quite a few reputable partners, including our good friends Versions and GitTower, as well as PixelNovel and Rackspace. All in all, Beanstalk is a great application to use, and it's great to look into if you want a low-cost repository hosting solution for hosting your source code.

You can give it try with a no-obligation free account where you can have a taste of the features without the commitment. If you're willing to give it a go, head on over to http://beanstalkapp.com/ to have a look round the site and maybe even sign up for an account.

Springloops

Springloops is another hosted solution for Git and SVN. The gorgeous web interface allows you to manage your repositories, from viewing individual commits to see where everything went wrong, to managing your team and assigning them on a per-repository basis. Your Springloops data is hosted in a secure data center with real-time back-ups, so no sweat on potential security issues. (See Figure 11-4.)

Figure 11-4. The Springloops home page gives links to the various sections of the site. It also shows screenshots of the various displays available to you in the Springloops dashboard.

Features

Signing up to Springloops is a breeze; with a simple one-page sign-up form your Springloops account is set up for you. You can migrate any existing repositories to be managed by Springloops or create a new project to have a repository created for you. Once you have your project set up, your dashboard keeps you updated with any commits from the team and other activity on your repositories, which you can see in Figure 11-5. Your activity feed can also be accessed via an RSS feed, for those who choose to use this option.

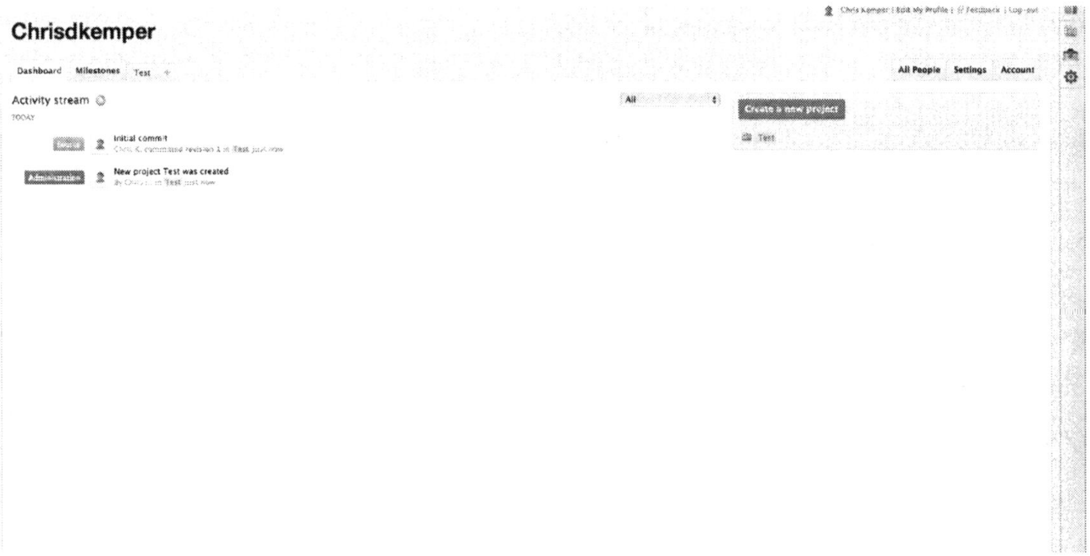
Chrisdkemper
Dashboard
Milestones
Test
All People
Settings
Account
Activity stream
Initial commit
Administration
New project Test was created
Create a new project

Figure 11-5. The dashboard for Springloops, where you can see your recent activity, also gives you the option to create new projects and subscribe to the RSS feed, if you choose to do so.

As well as the cracking repository hosting, all Springloops accounts come with a few additional features that complement your workflow. These include milestones, per-project wikis, ticket tracking, and team management. It's safe to say, if you were to get a Springloops account, you could quite happily manage a project through the application itself. Figure 11-6 shows examples of pricing.

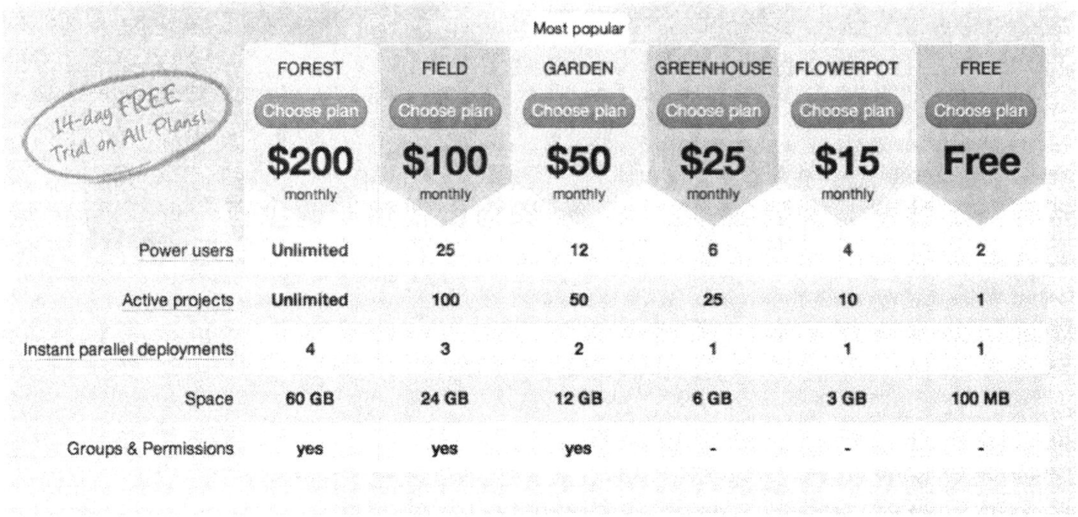
Most popular
14-day FREE Trial on All Plans!
FOREST
FIELD
GARDEN
GREENHOUSE
FLOWERPOT
FREE
Choose plan
$200 monthly
$100 monthly
$50 monthly
$25 monthly
$15 monthly
Free
Power users: Unlimited, 25, 12, 6, 4, 2
Active projects: Unlimited, 100, 50, 25, 10, 1
Instant parallel deployments: 4, 3, 2, 1, 1, 1
Space: 60 GB, 24 GB, 12 GB, 6 GB, 3 GB, 100 MB
Groups & Permissions: yes, yes, yes, -, -, -

Figure 11-6. Springloops pricing for its various packages, ranging from Free to Forest

Multiple deployment servers

Within Springloops you can set up multiple deployment servers, such as a production server and a development server, for when you're working in multiple environments. Springloops makes deploying your code a dream: you simply select the revision you want to deploy from a dropdown and send it off or, if you prefer, have your repository set up to deploy on each commit. The only trouble can arise when you're working with a team on multiple repositories; some pricing plans restrict how many parallel deployments you can have going on, so there might be some waiting around.

Integrated milestones and tickets

The integrated milestones and tickets in Springloops function in the same way as an issue-tracking system would, allowing you to create tickets against milestones to help track bugs and progress. This is where Springloops shoots above most of its competitors, by including real-time project management within your repositories. Tickets can be assigned to a milestone and team member so you can get a real-time idea of progress on a project. There is also the ability to integrate with Basecamp if you so choose, and no doubt more applications will be added as time goes on.

Viewing files

Viewing files from the repository is a very easy process, which means you do code reviews online, whether you want to view the file as it is, or as raw code with its snazzy highlighting to make viewing easier. A brilliant feature is the image comparison tools, which allow you to compare two images via three methods to spot differences between them. This can come in very useful—especially to designers! One comparison style allows you to do a side-by-side comparison of the selected images to spot potential differences. If that isn't good enough, you can try out the difference method, which places one image on top of another to see the differences by using different tools to show the image below, which is pretty cool!

Project wiki

One of the latest and greatest features of Springloops is the wiki section for each repository. This is perfect for big teams that need a central knowledge base for a project; everyone can be kept in the loop with vital details which can be kept constantly updated rather than requiring a slew of e-mails. Because the wikis are on a per-repository basis, management is kept to a minimum. This ensures no irrelevant data will be included, saving time and effort, which is great.

Pricing

Pricing for Springloops is competitive for what it offers. There's a big range of pricing plans, ranging from *Free*, for individuals or small teams, *Flowerpot*, which is aimed at small teams with a few projects, all the way up to *Forest*, which allows an unlimited number of users and projects with 60GB of storage. There's a 14-day free trial available for all plans, but if you just have one project to host then the free plan could be enough. Check out Figure 11-6 to get a better understanding of the pricing structure.

To sum up Springloops

If you're tempted to check out Springloops (which you should) then head over to www.springloops.com/ where you can have a look at the features or even sign up for a free account. It has a great user interface which is easy to use and navigate, along with features that work well. Its deployment feature can come in really useful if you're working in a client-facing environment where you need to deploy changes at regular intervals, or even irregular intervals. Whether you're in a large team or just a lone wolf, you can find some great features in Springloops, so check it out!

Unfuddle

Although Unfuddle is not one of the best looking choices out there for online repository hosting, it is a choice well worth examining. As the good people say, it's not always about looks, it's about the data, or brains, however you want to look at it. Off the bat, Unfuddle offers both SVN and Git hosting (sorry, no Mercurial here) as well as a plethora of other features you would expect to see from a keen player in the game.

Features

Regardless of the plan you decide on, each Unfuddle plan offers a similar set of features, with a couple reserved for the higher end of the scale. For starters, each account gets unlimited repositories, which you don't often see from hosted services—so if you're able to keep your sizes down to the space specified in your package, then you can have as many as you like, although you can only have one active project at a time. This means that you may have multiple repositories but, because only one project can be active, all repositories will be associated with that project. So, for example, if you wanted to work on a project that wasn't active, you could still host it with Unfuddle, but you wouldn't be able to use any other features alongside that particular project.

Unfuddle does have some useful features, such as a dashboard, bug tracking and milestones, notebook pages, messages, different pricing plans, as well as an API. Let's look at these now.

Dashboard

Your dashboard gives you access to everything you need to see while you're logged into your account. You can keep track of messages, milestones, recent activity on the projects, tickets, and more. You can also filter down the tickets on the dashboard to include all projects, or maybe just a particular one you are working on. Either way, the dashboard allows you to quickly get an overview of a project on one screen, and the different sections are color coded depending on status, such as red for overdue milestones or green for completed ones.

Bug tracking and milestones

Every Unfuddle project comes with project management tools such as bug tracking and milestones, which is an essential tool when you're keeping track of deadlines and issues. You can associate a particular bug with a project or file and it'll stay active in the system until it's been fixed. You can also create milestones that are associated with a particular project. Really, milestones are just another name for tasks with dates, but either way they allow you to set goals with dates, and if you miss a particular milestone, then your dashboard will show that by coloring the late task in red. You can, however, export the tasks into an iCal or RSS format to allow for management outside of Unfuddle, which is great for people working on the move.

Notebook pages

You also get Notebook pages within your Unfuddle projects. On the free plan, you only get three Notebook pages, but all paid plans offer unlimited pages. Notebook pages is a useful tool that acts as a project wiki, usually comprising technical specifications and reference documents. These pages are also versioned, so you'll never lose any documents once they're inside the notebook. You can also attach files to your Notebook pages in the paid plans and, using Unfuddle tags, you can link pages together to create a makeshift online "book."

Messages

Although the free plan only allows you two users, each account comes with messaging for communicating with other members of your team, which is, of course, essential when working as part of a big team and not always in the same office. Messages also allows your team to ask questions, get feedback, and keep up with documents, as well as attach files to messages. Although this does seem slightly similar to e-mail, the messages used here will be contained in a central location. This gives the benefit of keeping them safe, and you can give access to other members of the project really easily. Doing this via e-mail would require forwarding multiple e-mails to any new recipient(s), which isn't very elegant. Sometimes messages will be in the wrong order, or attachments can be left off, and so on. Using messages ensures every user gets the same information at the same time without any problems. An easy way to look at Unfuddle's messaging feature is to think of it as a project blog, so you can post when the project is kicking off, when a major bug needs to be fixed, when a client gives good feedback, that kind of thing! It's just perfect to keep everyone in the loop, especially for those on the team that aren't in the position to always hear feedback directly from a client.

Differences between pricing plans

One troubling thing about Unfuddle is that an SSL (secure sockets layer) connection is only available to the higher-tiered paid plans. SSL provides you with a secure connection when you transfer data to and from Unfuddle, which on some services just comes as standard on all plans. Although this can be a problem for some, it's not a huge issue unless the data you are transferring is extremely confidential and you cannot allow anybody to see it. In most cases, the information stored in repositories is just development files, which don't need to be protected with a lock and key. Also, unless somebody is intentionally trying to get your data and hacks your connection, your data is in no real danger. Understandably, some users don't always require this kind of connection, but it seems odd to only include it on packages that cost more than $24 a month.

On all paid plans you can archive projects, which comes in useful given that the number of active projects is always limited, regardless of plan. By archiving a project, you still have access to all of the information associated with the project, such as tickets, messages, and milestones, but in a read-only format. This means you can still retrieve useful information from the project and reinstate it if necessary. Code repositories for projects are always active, you just can't manage them with Unfuddle. This allows for a flexible system to maintain all of the projects you need to, but any archived projects don't affect the amount of active projects you have going.

On the top two account levels, you unlock time tracking for use on your active projects. This time tracking system works on a ticketing basis, where you assign a ticket to a user, and the user is able to log time on that ticket based on how long they spent working on it—easy. Then using the reports Unfuddle offers, you are able see how well the team has been working across projects, or on a per project basis.

API

Unfuddle also has an API available for you to play with, although at the time of this writing it was still in public beta. The API allows you to access the same features that your account has access to, which allows you to either make an Unfuddle-based application or tie it into your existing workflow.

An online repository system wouldn't be complete without a view of your source code online, and Unfuddle delivers just that. You can view any revision of your files online using Unfuddle whenever you like, and you can even compare two different versions side by side to help spot differences. Sadly, you can't view any other file types in this format, such as images or PSDs. In those cases, an external application would need to be used but, for what it does, Unfuddle's code comparison tool is quick and effective.

Pricing

As mentioned before, Unfuddle comes with a free account, as well as an additional four others ranging up to up to $99 a month for the *Enterprise* plan, which is aimed at very large teams. Even with the free plan, you still get a reasonable 200MB of storage for your projects, which isn't too bad, although in comparison to the 10GB Enterprise plan it might not be enough. You can have a better look at the feature set for yourself in Figure 11-7, which includes a breakdown of prices per plan, or at http://unfuddle.com/about/tour/plans.

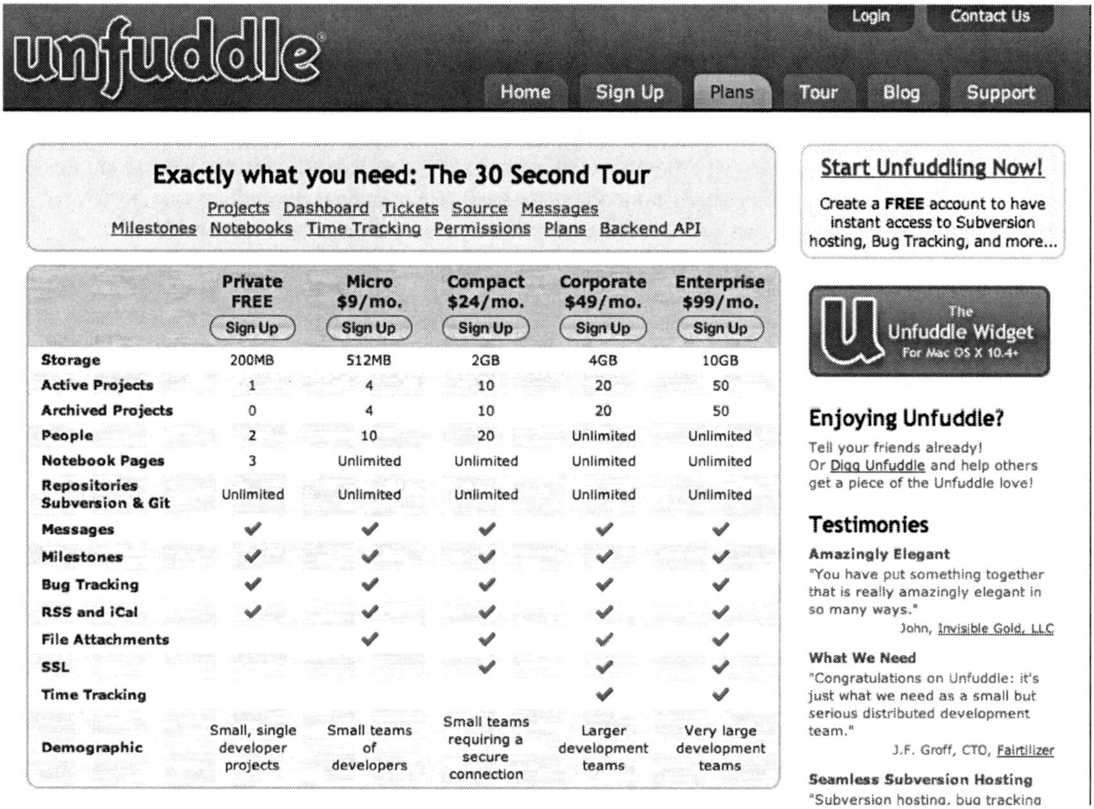

Figure 11-7. Unfuddle's available plans and features ranging from *Free* to *Enterprise* ($99) and all the features in between.

To sum up Unfuddle

Unfuddle offers a well-rounded set of features for your Git and SVN repositories, especially with the project management tools included. You can centralize your whole development system within Unfuddle, with issue tracking, messaging, pages, and more. In addition, you can also customize Unfuddle for your needs using the API. Although it may not be your thing right now, you may fancy playing with it one day and developing your own features. The pricing in Unfuddle is also very reasonable, on a par with the other players in this space. You can check out their website at www.unfuddle.com to see what their plans can offer you or even sign up for a free plan to have a browse around the features.

Google Project Hosting

Unsurprisingly, online project hosting is yet another service Google offers through their Google Code offerings. The service is for open-source projects and, along with most Google products, it's fast, free, and reliable. Google's mission is to support the open source community, which means there are no private repositories on Google Project Hosting (GPH). Users are encouraged to collaborate and host projects that encourage good practice and standards.

Google Project Hosting isn't geared to the developer working on private, client projects—your projects must be open source to enable collaboration to build better software and a better community. If you'd like to join forces with other developers on a project, Google Project Hosting is the place to put your code.

Features

To get started on GPH, you need to create a Google account, which I imagine most will already have. But once you're set up with that, you can host Git, SVN, and Mercurial repositories on GPH, with 2GB of storage and 2GB of download hosting. A Google account isn't necessary to browse projects or to check out code, but to create and comment on an issue you have to have a Google account. Other beneficial features of GPH include hub, the project wiki, issue tracker, and integrated source code browsing, which we'll look at now.

Hub

Once you've created a project on GPH, your project will have a hub created for it on the Google servers. From here, you can add a summary of your project. An overview of all updates to your project will be shown and the people involved in your project will be listed. People that are a part of your project can have one of three roles:

- Owners can create issues, comment, edit the wiki, commit, create downloads, and edit anyone else's actions.

- Committers can do all of the above except delete data and edit anyone else's actions.

- Contributors can only add and comment on issues and add comments to the wiki. All permissions can be upgraded/downgraded.

Owners can add packaged downloads of their code, which users can quickly grab instead of checking out the code and managing the revisions. This is usually your best bet for getting the latest stable release of a project.

Project wiki

The wiki acts as a reference guide to all aspects of the project, from FAQs to a high-level road map of the direction the project is going in. It's up to the project owners and committers to maintain the wiki to make sure it's an up-to-date resource on the project, but contributors can add comments to the discussion as well. The wiki ties in with GPH's mission to encourage collaboration and promote good practice in software development, by allowing everyone to talk about the project and offer support.

Issue tracker

There's also an issue tracker within your GPH projects, which is simple and flexible enough to adapt to any developer's workflow. Depending on what part you play in the project, you can add different types of issues, from defect reports to enhancement requests. Issues can be marked as *accepted*, *started*, and *needs info* to keep everyone in the project loop. Useful filtering means finding issues and tracking them is simple and powerful for developers.

Integrated source code browsing

GPH offers integrated source code browsing, which allows you to navigate through the repository itself with useful syntax highlighting. You can also edit the files in browser, and submit the code edits as a patch to the owner of the project. This also allows for easy code review, as you can browse changes to files and see where things have been modified.

To sum up Google Project Hosting

Obviously, GPH won't be suited to all developers, but for those of you looking for an active, collaborative, and growing development community to get an open-source project's ball rolling, this is a perfect place to host your repository. Check out http://code.google.com/projecthosting/ to read more about Google's philosophy. If your project meets the bill to be used on GPH then you will have access to a huge number of features that will really help push your project along—and it's free. If you're running an open-source project, you should really consider giving Google Project Hosting a go.

Assembla

Assembla is an all-encompassing tool for development teams, offering SVN, Git, and Mercurial hosting as well as project management and collaboration tools such as ticketing and issue management, wikis, file management, team messaging, and so much more, which we'll get into later. This tool will work great with agile teams too, as Assembla integrates managing stand-up and scrum reports.

Features

Assembla users create *spaces* to manage all of their tools. The first feature we're going to look at (and the most important one, in this case) is how Assembla handles repository hosting. As you should always hope with hosting services, your data is safe and secure, with 99.9%+ uptime. You can get started in seconds by creating a new repository or importing an existing one and inviting team members. In addition to repository hosting, other positive features include the ticketing system, group chat, and wiki tool, which we'll look at now.

Repository hosting

Your Assembla repositories are enhanced by a unified activity stream to keep all of your team members up to date, made up of a real-time feed of commits, code reviews, and builds. E-mail notifications can be set up to send summaries to your inbox or, if you prefer, you can take advantage of commit hooks to integrate with other systems. For those who really need to stay in the loop, you can post space activity to a Twitter account.

Within your space, there's an integrated code browser with full syntax highlighting, showing changesets and diffs clearly and making them incredibly easy to manage. Within the code browser, you can view files "as a web page'" to instantly see your HTML pages rendered as pages with CSS, JS, and images.

For code reviews, you can take advantage of Assembla's inline code commenting. Comments can be made within the code browser and tracked within the project space, eliminating the need to explain or comment on code via e-mail.

Deploying code is made incredibly easy with Assembla. Code deployments can be made manually to any external server with FTP or SFTP, or you can even schedule automatic deployments on commit, hourly, daily, or weekly. Multiple servers can be added for staging and production releases. For those with a more complicated build process, you can integrate with services such as Capistrano and Cruise Control.

One of the most useful features of Assembla repository hosting is the ability to publish static websites from files and directories inside your repository. This is perfect for showing off new designs to clients or experimenting with your code in a production environment.

If you choose a pro subscription, you'll have access to more than 25 tools that Assembla provides to streamline your workflow and help your team collaborate. There are too many to possibly mention, but I'll go through the best in show now.

Ticketing system

Assembla's ticketing system is enhanced for agile teams, giving you a real-time dashboard of tasks with multiple view options—from the *Ticket List view*, which gives your team a compact view of important tasks. The *Card Wall view* acts like a sticky note board, where tasks can be dragged and dropped into sections called *New*, *Working*, and *Review*. The last view is *Agile Planner*, which sorts tasks into a Stories/Features column where you can drag tasks into a coherent schedule. Your tasks are scheduled with milestones, which can be integrated into a timeline including releases, sprints, and iterations, flexible for anyone's development workflow. This tool is tightly integrated with your code repositories—commit comments can open/close and comment on issues.

Customers and clients are also brought into the issue tracking process, allowing your clients to submit feature requests, bug reports, and the like, which can also be integrated with your code repos.

Group chat

An awesome feature Assembla has for distributed teams is group chat with built-in video. The activity stream is fed into the chat so team members can discuss the latest code changes, ticket activity, and messages in real time. The real benefit of this is that the chat is persistant, so the notes you make when on the chat are available when you come back later, or even if you didn't participate in the first place. This gives people who missed the whole chat or chunks of it the chance to see the whole thread and get straight back up to speed. The video side of things becomes impressive thanks to its being in-browser, so anybody can join straight in without needing to use another service. It also allows for multiple users to chat at once, so nobody is left out. In addition, any commits, ticket updates, wiki entires, or any other activity is added into the chat in real time, so you won't miss anything coming in if you get distracted with the conversation, which is really cool.

Wiki tool

There's a wiki tool for specifications, instructions, ideas, and anything you feel is relevant to the project. All wiki pages are versioned, so you can always restore pages to a previous state. You can use simple commands to link your wiki entries to tickets and commits, too! All of these awesome collaboration and management features are available with paid plans of Assembla. For those who don't want to jump into a paid plan, you can try a free plan. Assembla's free plans give you the option to choose a single tool for trial, whether it be SVN hosting or Standup/Scrum reporting.

Pricing

There are a lot of price plans to suit all teams on Assembla. If you're a smaller team that only needs repository hosting and some foundation-level tools such as issue tracking, the *Starter* and *Single* packages will serve you well. For bigger teams and enterprise-level projects, you can take advantage of the *Group* and *Professional* pricing plans, which offer repository hosting as well as all advanced tools. If you just want to try out Assembla, or you're a single user looking for a system to use, there is also a *Free* account available. You can take a closer look at the pricing by heading to www.assembla.com/plans where you can see all the available plans and the prices and features of each.

To sum up Assembla

Assembla offers an incredibly complete package for development teams, not just as a repository hosting service but as a space to manage all of your team's activity and enable collaboration at a higher level. That also comes with some seriously impressive features such as extremely useful video chat and message boards. You also get wiki tools, ticketing, and a wholte lot more so have a closer look at www.assembla.com/ or even sign up for a free account and try it out.

XP-Dev

XP-Dev offers both repository and project hosting, geared towards agile teams. XP-Dev hosts Subversion, Git, and Mercurial repositories, and boasts rock-solid security and reliability with their subscription plans, including SSL/SSH secure access to all projects and repositories and real-time back-ups. All plans come with some handy project tracking solutions, too.

Features

First things first: repository hosting. XP-Dev offers you some documentation on getting up and running with your project repositories, whether you're importing a repository from a dump or creating a new one, which you definitely need as it isn't as straightforward as you'd hope. Once you've got your project set up, you'll get a project dashboard, where you can configure your source control. There are also useful iteration statistics and performance charts that build up once your team starts committing and deploying code changes, especially useful for agile teams. Recent changes across the project are also monitored here, such as any repositories being added or any changes in the project management tools. To manage your changesets and to do code reviews, you can use the online web repository browser, which allows you to view file contents and diffs between different revisions.

A niggle when you're setting up code repositories and projects is that you can't use the same name for your project/repository as *any other* on XP-Dev, so if you want to create a repository called Blog Website, for example, you'll have to add more personalization because it's more than likely that it already exists.

Other features that may make you choose XP-Dev over others include project management aspects, commit messages, wiki sections and integration—all of which we'll look at now.

Project management aspects

Projects can be marked as open source on XP-Dev by simply checking a box. This opens up your project dashboard to the public, allowing everyone to view any part of the project. You can designate *project writers* to be able to make commits to your project. Once your project is marked as open source, everyone, including web crawlers, will have access to your project. Of course, projects can be kept private, too, and with XP-Dev's secure access this is guaranteed.

Since XP-Dev is geared toward agile software teams, it facilitates stories, tasks, and bugs for project management. They're quite simply defined for those not familiar with agile teams: *stories* are business requirements, *tasks* implement the business requirements, and *bugs* are defects discovered in your system.

Commit messages

Commit messages also get a whole lot more powerful with XP-Dev. You can take advantage of WebHooks to integrate your commits with a whole range of project management tools such as Basecamp, FogBugz, Fixx, and Twitter. Using specialized keywords and IDs in your commit messages, you can perform actions on tasks as you commit, such as marking them as fixed and even logging time on them. This can be a great feature if you're working in a fast-paced environment and you need to switch projects a lot, or even if you're always working on a specific ticket on a project. Normally without this functionality, you would need to commit the code and then potentially log into another application to log time and then resolve the ticket you were working on, which can require three different services. Even when your tickets and time logging are managed in the same place, if you have to switch applications after committing your code, you can get distracted and not log time, or even forget about it entirely. This is why this functionality is so useful; you can commit the code, then comment on the issue you're working on, mark it as resolved, and then log time in it, all in one go! This also gives an additional bonus of making your commit messages more specific, and giving a reference to what was being worked on at what time in the form of a ticket. This becomes really useful when looking back through changes to find out exactly what was being worked on at the time and so on.

Wiki section

You can add multiple team members to your project and give them per-project access rights, giving them access to a wiki section for all of your documentation, specs, and ideas. In the wiki it's also possible to link to diffent issues and tickets within the system, which can make for more specific posts which are then more helpful to the team. For example, if a client comes back with a problem that happens a lot, you can use the ticket they created as a reference point, then write a wiki post on how to solve the problem. You also have access to a full history of the changes to the wiki post, just in case something happens. If any changes are accidentally made, you have the history there to back you up.

Integration

XP-Dev is optimized to integrate with Trac, an open-source issue tracking system (check it out at http://trac.edgewall.org/). You can link your SVN commits to Trac tickets and manage your Trac user permissions with ease, as well as a load of plug-ins already at your disposal, such as time tracking and estimation and tagging. If Trac isn't an application you use, XP-Dev also has integration with Basecamp, FogBugz, Lighthouse, DoneDone, Fixx, and Twitter. If you'd rather keep everything together, you can just use the built-in bug and time-tracking tools, which work just as well.

Pricing

XP-Dev pricing is based on how much storage space you need. There are no limits on the amount of projects and users you can have active, from the Pro Small plan at $5 a month with 2GB of storage, to the Enterprise Medium plan at $100 a month with 90GB storage. Every paid plan comes with a standard level of high security, all project tracking solutions, and Subversion, Git, and Mercurial support.

There's a free plan that comes with 200MB of Subversion hosting, only two projects and no back-ups/SSL access, which is enough to get you acquainted with the XP-Dev system. However, if you choose this option, your project dashboard will be littered with banner ads, which in some cases can completely overpower your project activity. If you want to have a closer look at the features and pricing, head to http://xp-dev.com/pricing to see everything in more detail.

To sum up XP-Dev

If you're willing to put the user interface flaws aside, XP-Dev is packed with all of the features you need to manage your repositories and your projects, and the solid security and reliabilty it offers with all of its paid plans is a bonus. Its commit message tools can also save a whole lot of time when it comes to managing tickets and time, as you can perform multiple actions at once, which really helps things. You also get the ability to integrate with third-party applications to manage your time, or you can just use the built-in tools to keep everything together. It's also easy on the wallet, because you only pay for what you use. To dig deeper, check out http://xp-dev.com.

Codesion

Codesion is a reputable project and repository hosting solution, with a high-profile user base that includes Intel, BBC Worldwide, and Stanford University. Codesion offers up to enterprise-grade hosting for your Git and Subversion repositories, as well as integrated project management tools, whether you're a small development team or a large agile software development team.

Features

You can get started with Codesion in five minutes, and once you've subscribed to your plan you can get straight into setting up your team and repositories with their clean, polished AJAX interface. It's great to see a hosted service that gets you up and running so quickly—instead of spending valuable time setting up source control, you can spend your time building your products. Codesion offers you brilliant support, too, to take the headaches out of any issues that might arise (I'll get into that later). Other benefits include FrogSAFE technology, commit options, and deployment, which we'll look at now.

FrogSAFE

Codesion prides itself on its FrogSAFE technology, which manages projects for optimum levels of security, reliability, and speed. This technology distributes server load across multiple service-optimized clusters to always give users maximum speed with the service—one of the foremost advantages of using a hosted solution.

Commits

A lot of elements of version control have been simplified with Codesion, especially for Subversion users. You can easily upload your SVN repositories with a quick wizard, using either a dump file or shared drive access. As well as easy uploads, Codesion has a drag and drop auto-commit feature that allows you to use SVN more like a network drive; you can map your SVN drive to your PC, drag and drop your files, and they are automatically committed to your repository.

Your Codesion commits can also be integrated with a whole range of project management services. Commit hooks integrate with services such as JIRA, Rally, and Pivotal Tracker so you can automatically publish your code activity to your projects, as well as connect your commits to your tickets and artifacts to automatically update them.

Deployment

Codesion also boasts one-click deployment, including parallel deployments. You can deploy your repositories to your private server, live production environment, or even cloud hosting such as Amazon EC2/S3 and Google App Engine. You can set up *recipes* of combinations of repositories to certain servers to deploy, too, to avoid configuring settings multiple times.

Unlike most services, you can get a custom domain name plan allowing you to configure your URLs to your company's URL, as well as being able to customize your account's workspace and e-mail templates with your company's logo for a more professional look.

Codesion offers both unified tracking, wiki, and document sharing tools within the service, but if you'd prefer to use your usual hosted project management tools such as Bugzilla, Trac, and ScrumWorks, these are included in Professional and Enterprise plans.

Support

Support is second to none on Codesion. On *Team* plans, you get a custom support plan, an up to two-day incident response time, and free Subversion training. If you subscribe to the *Enterprise* plan, your incident response time is only one hour, with a 24/7 telephone support line, a custom support plan, and a 99.9% uptime service level agreement. This level of support is essential to any developers, especially those working on an enterprise level, who need the reliability and security that Codesion can offer.

Pricing

Codesion has multiple levels of pricing within the diffferent editions of hosting they offer. Most small development hubs could opt for the *Team* Edition, with pricing ranging from $6.99 a month for two projects, two users and 2GB of storage to $99.99 a month for unlimited projects, 50 users and 50GB of storage. The Team Edition doesn't have as complete a set of features, lacking hosted agile management, personal branding, and integrated project tracking tools such as wikis and document sharing.

Upwards from the Team Edition, there are *Professional* and *Enterprise* Editions, with more bands within both. Professional Edition offers all of the feature set, with two different bands, depending on your team type. Depending on how many users you have, the prices can skyrocket, from $225 for 10 users to $1,038 for 50 users. The company doesn't actually reveal pricing for the Codesion Enterprise edition, but judging on the extensive support, security, and infrastructure they offer, the price will be up there in the thousands.

To sum up Codesion

Codesion is marketed towards bigger development powerhouses, judging from some features that just aren't necessary for smaller teams, such as dedicated servers for your repositories, but you can't go wrong with the concrete security, reliability, and scalability. This is perhaps a hosted solution that you might progress to, but not start up with.

If you're interested in giving Codesion a test-drive, you can sign up for the free plan for a 200MB hosted repository for one user and one project. All plans come with a 30-day trial, too, if you're interested in their paid editions. Check them out at `http://codesion.com/`.

BitBucket

If you were to scour the net for the best Mercurial hosting site, one of the best would be BitBucket. If you've ever heard of Jira, SourceTree, or Confluence, then you may know the creators of BitBucket, because it's from the same company, Atlassian. As a standard, BitBucket offers Git and Mercurial hosting with an option to import an SVN repository to Mercurial. Just a warning, though: the last option isn't as amazing as it sounds. You'll lose all the history in the repository and it'll be as if you had started again. They do, however, offer some pretty good guides on how to convert an SVN repository properly, which is pretty awesome.

Features

BitBucket has many positive features. As a starting point, you get the ability to create both private and public repositories to host your code. Although having public repositories is a normal feature, offering both public and private with no additional charge isn't. Having either option means you can show your code to the world or hide it away for later, and if you change your mind, it's as easy as checking or unchecking a box.

If you do make the choice of a public repository, then BitBucket will create a nice page for you which you can share on the Web and attract attention to your project. Users can also take a copy of your code and even begin contributing—or not. It's up to you whether or not the commits are accepted.

Wiki and issue tracking

BitBucket also offers you a wiki and issue-tracking tools as standard across all accounts, with the ability to make either one private or public. Each project you create on BitBucket will get its own wiki and issue-tracking tools (no sharing between projects here), and if you decide to have the wiki public, but the issue tracking private, that's all fine. To add the tools to your project there is just a simple check box in the admin panel, so you can choose to enable features or not. The choice is yours.

With the issue tracker comes the ability to add milestones and versions to the code. As an admin, or even as a user, this gives you a clear indication where the issue lies and how to go about fixing it. You can also assign different types to the issues; whether they are bugs, feature requests, or just tasks, they can all be logged and associated with specific milestones or versions.

Commits

Every commit, big or small, is tracked within BitBucket and gets its own URL, so if you want see what was in a certain commit, that's fine—just find it on the project page and give it a click to see who the commit was pushed by and any changes made. This process is also made a lot easier by the syntax highlighting which makes the code a whole lot easier to read and understand.

Managing users

With your BitBucket account also comes the ability to manage the role any user can have on a per-project basis. Each user can one have one of four roles:

- The *Reader* role is only necessary for private repositories, as it allows access to view the repository, but nothing else. Making the project public nullifies this role. Readers can also take copies of the code but not push any changes.

- This is when *Writers* come in; they can push changes back into the repository as well as view it.

- The next level of control is the *Administrator* role, which can do everything the Writer can do, but in addition can also manage the users. This means they can add and remove different users to the projects they are an Administrator of.

- The only remaining role is the *Owner*, which is nigh on the same as the Administrator, with one big difference: they created the project and therefore have the ability to delete it.

In addition to the four roles, users can also be grouped to make it easier for Administrators to know what's going on. This may come in useful if you have some freelancers working on a project you're managing, as it allows you to separate them off the main user base. You can also set default roles depending on the group which, for private repositories, could be quite useful when granting users access to view the repository.

REST API

For those of you who don't mind playing with a REST API, BitBucket has one you can use to integrate with pretty much anything on the site. Using the API, you have the ability to interact with commits, pages on the wiki, issue tracking, and pretty much anything else you can think of. If you happened to go "Huh?!" when you read about the REST API, not to worry; on a basic level, it's just a set of commands you can access with various HTTP addresses, and the chaps at BitBucket have already done some of the hard work for you. If you would like to use the REST API, you can integrate with e-mail, Twitter, Jenkins, JIRA, Pivotal, and Lighthouse, to name a few, right out of the box. This allows you to work with applications you're already familiar with while still hosting your code on BitBucket, which is always good news.

Pricing

Atlassian has taken a slightly different approach when it comes to pricing for BitBucket services. Rather than having a tiered system, each customer gets the same features, and you actually pay for more users. It may sound a little crazy, but it seems to work well for these guys. The free account will give you five users who can access and write to the repositories you're hosting, but will not restrict any of the features because you're a free user.

As you move up the ranks for accounts you get more and more users. You can also upgrade and downgrade from your control panel without obligation, which is a bonus in itself. If you have a look at Figure 11-8 or go to `https://bitbucket.org/plans` you can see the full pricing structure, which tops out at $80 a month for unlimited users.

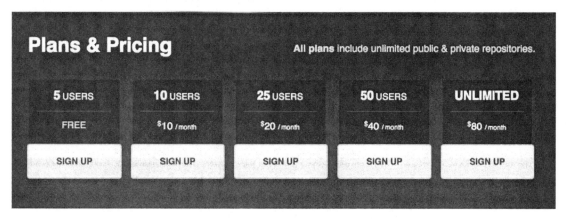

Figure 11-8. The pricing and plans used by BitBucket

Although the top dog unlimited price may be too much for some, if you're a student you may be in luck. If you register with a student e-mail address, once it's validated you'll be automatically upgraded to an unlimited student account,—which is great for students, who always seem to get everything free (I'm not bitter about not being a student anymore, honest . . .). The same can also be achieved for community projects; you just need to apply using a form on the BitBucket website and you'll also receive the love that is a free unlimited account, once you've been approved.

To sum up BitBucket

Although BitBucket is quite a popular hosting option with a lot of users currently using it, I think its main appeal is its pricing. The features it offers, really, are standard across any hosting platform that's serious about competing with the big guys, but offering free unlimited public *and* private repositories makes it stand out. Also, since you only pay for the users you need rather than the features you want, you can be sure you're paying the lowest price you need to. There's no need to grumble about paying for the top package because it offers that one feature you really want.

Anyone out there who doesn't really want all of their code to be public, but also doesn't want to host their own repositories, should seriously consider BitBucket as an option. Head on over to `https://bitbucket.org` to sign up for a free account. You can't really lose, it's free!

CodebaseHQ

Another big contender in the fight for being the best source code hosting solution is CodebaseHQ. This guy brings a whole load of great features to the table, as well as SVN, Mercurial, and Git hosting, which just makes it even more appealing to customers using another hosted solution, or those that just want to dip their toe in and test the waters.

Features

If you sign up for a CodebaseHQ account, you can rest assured your data is safe, as well as being backed up on a nightly basis. All uploaded data is also stored in redundant storage arrays. The CodebaseHQ site also makes a point of mentioning that any data uploaded is owned by whoever uploaded it. Although you would assume this is a given, it's nice to know nobody behind CodebaseHQ will ever attempt to steal any of the code hosted on their servers. This is the case with most services, but with CodebaseHQ it is broadcast openly, which helps build confidence in the service and makes you feel safer about hosting your code on their systems.

Issue tracking

If you opt to become a paying customer at CodebaseHQ, one benefit you will have is issue tracking, which is quite clever in how it works. You can, on a basic level, create tickets and assign them to users, as well as track any changes made to the tickets, both who made the change and what they changed. It's also possible to assign a custom status to each ticket, along with custom priorities, so if something really needs to be looked at pronto, you can create a status to do that. Along with the priority, it's also possible to classify a ticket by different types, depending on what it is such as bug, task, and so on. Each one is cleverly integrated into the project search, too, to make finding specific tickets a whole lot easier. If one search was particularly complex, you can save it to allow it to be used again and again.

Managing projects

You can also manage projects by creating milestones, which give a visual indication of when you can launch a certain release of the project being developed. You could, for example, create a milestone which had all of the bugs reported in the current version and contains issues with the bug type associated with them.

The commit messages can play a very key role in CodebaseHQ if you want them to, by integrating right into the issue-tracking system. By using certain keywords in the commit messages, it's possible to update the status of a ticket through just committing the code. This allows for a much better workflow and allows whoever is maintaining the tickets to see how everything is progressing much better.

Code tasks

A really cool feature offered when hosting your repositories with CodebaseHQ is the *Code Tasks* tool. When you commit code that contains TODO, FIXME, OPTIMISE, and BUG tags it automatically creates a report allowing you to see where changes still need to be made, which is pretty damn impressive. You also have the ability to run the blame command on any file within a repository so you can, in other words, see which user has written every line of said file. This comes in really useful when you need to fix bugs or just find out who wrote a certain line of code.

When viewing your code online, you have the joy of syntax highlighting to make viewing code even easier, as well as the ability to diff between commits to see exactly what has changed between different versions. It's also possible to set branches of your code to be downloadable archives, which can come in really handy for releasing code changes, or allowing a client to view work you've done without giving them direct access to the code itself.

Pricing

CodebaseHQ takes the tiered pricing structure route, giving you increasing features as you go through the account levels. That being said, it's not as bad as it sounds. There is a free account available which allows you one project, 50MB of space, two users but, sadly, no wikis or time tracking. This would be quite suited to one user who just wants to test the waters of CodebaseHQ without committing to a price plan. However, if you sign up for any of the accounts, you will receive a 15-day free trial and the ability to upgrade, downgrade, or cancel at any time.

The first paid plan is *Tiny*, coming in at $7.56 a month. With that you get the wiki, time-tracking tools, three active projects, 500MB of space and ten users. You also get unlimited archived projects and repositories, which are standard across the account levels. The only thing you don't get is the ability to brand your project pages, which isn't really that important to most people. So this account would be ideal for small teams or users who want to take advantage of the wiki and time-tracking tools.

The remaining plans all include branding, unlimited users, and an increasing amount of active projects and space. The *Large* package is the biggest on offer, in which you get a massive 60 active projects, 10GB of space, and a $60.46 price tag. If the offering in this plan isn't enough for you, just drop the guys at CodebaseHQ a line and they can set you up with whatever you need. You can also check out Figure 11-9 or go to `www.codebasehq.com/packages` to see the full details of the available plans.

		Large	Medium	Small	Tiny
How much?		£40 / month	£21 / month	£13 / month	£5 / month
		$60.46 / month	$31.74 / month	$19.65 / month	$7.56 / month
		€47.85 / month	€25.12 / month	€15.55 / month	€5.98 / month
		15 day free trial	15 day free trial	15 day free trial	15 day free trial
		Signup	Signup	Signup	Signup
Active Projects		60	30	15	3
Archived Projects		unlimited	unlimited	unlimited	unlimited
Disk Space		10GB	4GB	2GB	500MB
Repositories		unlimited	unlimited	unlimited	unlimited
Users		unlimited	unlimited	unlimited	10
Time Tracking		✓	✓	✓	✓
Wikis		✓	✓	✓	✓
Branding		✓	✓	✓	—

Figure 11-9. A great overview of the plans, features and pricing offered by CodebaseHQ

To sum up CodebaseHQ

You do get a lot of cool features when you are a paying customer and if you write a lot of code, the Code Task feature is a huge help to project managers and developers alike. Even without it, the fact that you can host unlimited repositories of potentially different types is a huge bonus. This means that if you were to change to a new source control type, you wouldn't need to switch services.

Although the free account misses out on the time-tracking and wiki features, it still gives you the chance to really try out what you can, and if you do decide to start paying, for the sake of $5 a month, it's totally worth it. If you want to review the features yourself, or sign up for a free account, head over to www.codebasehq.com and check it out. You won't regret it.

GitHub

If you've dabbled with source control before on any level, there's a good chance you will have heard of GitHub. Although it hosts Git, and Git alone, it's more than just a site to host your source code. Many developers use GitHub as a way of sharing code examples with the world. It can be used as a reference point for potential employers, as well as offering the opportunity to get involved with other open-source projects.

GitHub makes a huge deal about its social aspect, especially since its tag line is *Social Coding*. Everything about GitHub is centered around the social aspect of sharing, from its Developer profiles to the ability to follow other developers and see the work they're doing. If you explore GitHub, you can see the most popular and active projects on the site and a whole load of other features, which try as much as possible to get you involved with other people.

Features

Every account on GitHub allows for unlimited public repositories and contributors, so if you don't mind being in the public eye, you can have as many helpers and repositories as you like, which is pretty damn cool. It is possible for you to work with private repositories, but you need to pay for the the privilege.

For those of you out there who have to work in places where the internet isn't as open as you would like it to be, and the firewall is always causing you problems, GitHub may be able to help. A lot of other providers only give you one way to connect to your repository, and that's it; Not GitHub, though. As well as the standard HTTPS, they also offer the git protocol and SSH connectivity option, and if that's not enough, there are also additional ports available for firewall problems.

Issue tracking

One of GitHub's many features is its issue tracking abilities, which have been designed to keep on top of bugs, and focused on milestones and releases. As well as being able to assign issues to different users, assign custom tags and colors, and create milestones to track changes against, you also have a few tricks with commit messages. Using certain keywords alongside an issue number allows you to do certain actions when committing, such as commenting on issues, closing them, marking them as fixed, and a whole lot more.

Reviewing code

The various tools GitHub offers for reviewing code are what sets it ahead of its rivals. Whenever a commit is pushed to the repository, it can be commented on but, in addition, you can comment on a line-by-line basis, which can be used to discuss the good and bad points of the code, or start a discussion on how to improve it. Not just that, GitHub offers a unique way to review branches and work with them, and because it's so easy, it's common to find that repositories on GitHub have a lot more branches than projects hosted with other source code solutions. You can easily compare the different branches, and how the branch would cope if it was merged into the main branch, which makes it easy to decide which branches can be scraped, or if it's merging time. If you only need to make a small change before the branch would be ready, it's possible to edit the file online to save from updating pulling and pushing code, which can be a time saver for small issues.

Wiki

Although including a wiki with a hosted project isn't all that special, GitHub does it just a little bit differently. With GitHub, wikis are powered by gollum, an open-source wiki engine created by GitHub, plus they were actually built in Git. This gives you the ability to do anything to it you would a normal Git repository. Most important, you can export it and back it up without any major problems. It's also possible to play with the features, add new ones to make little tweaks—anything you want, really. If you're feeling particularly generous, you could even contribute to the project on GitHub—it's hosted there after all.

Forking

GitHub also makes forking as easy as possible, which again helps build the community aspect and get more people involved in more projects. In this instance, you would fork the code base and make your changes, then when you pushed it, it would enter a queue so that the owner of the project could decide whether or not the feature is worth implementing. Not just that, though. You can also see if the new feature will cause conflicts and commit on the fork to start a discussion about it. The fork queue allows you to easily asses all these potential changes in one go and, as a bonus, it works on all good smart phones too!

All of these features give you a lot of data to work with, and GitHub gives you some great analytics tools to allow you to see who's making the most changes, commits, and so on. When it comes to users forking your code, it's often hard to track to who's doing the forking and actually what they're doing. GitHub thought of that, and created a network graph to allow you to see all of this information in an easy-to-understand format. You can see an example of the HTML5-boilerplate Network Graph in Figure 11-10.

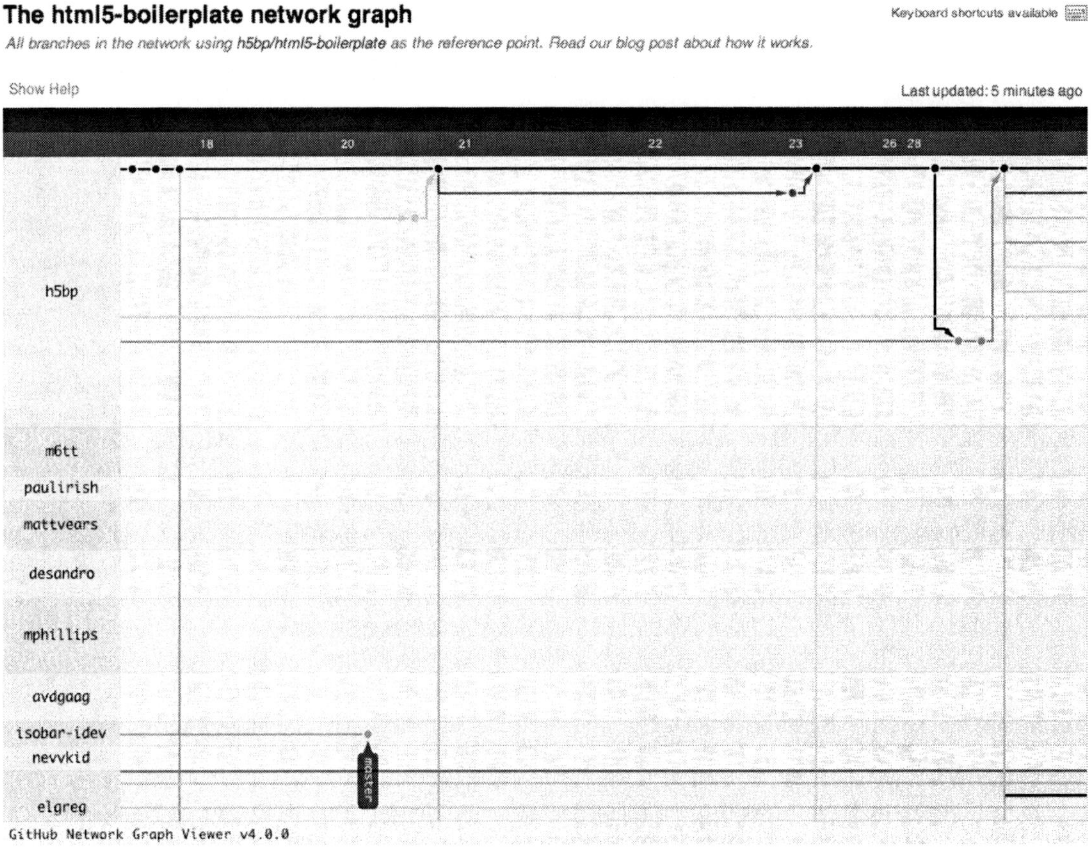

Figure 11-10. This shows a network graph generated from the HTML5-boilerplate project on GitHub. You can see different users that have participated on the project and how the various branches exist and have been merged back into the main master branch of the project.

Pricing

With the paid accounts on GitHub, you're pretty much paying for private repositories and the number of users who can work on those private repositories. The smallest of these packages is $7 a month, which gets you five private repositories and one additional contributor. The plans keep on increasing in repositories and users until you hit the business plans, where the users then become unlimited and you're paying for additional repositories.

If you check out Figure 11-11 or go to `https://github.com/plans`, you can see all the available plans on offer, but you'll notice the biggest and best plan is *Platinum*, which is a mammoth $200 a month, where you get 125 repositories and unlimited users to work on them.

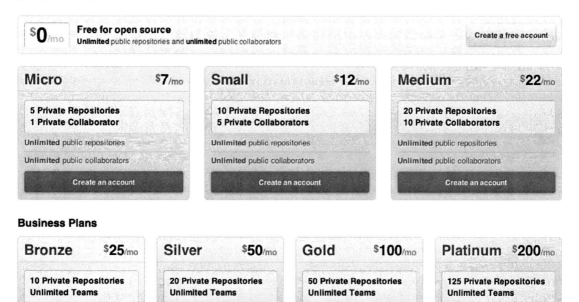

Figure 11-11. The overview of the different packages offered by GitHub and the prices associated with them, as well as the number of repositories and users you get with each

To sum up GitHub

It's safe to say that GitHub is one of the top choices when it comes to hosting Git repositories, and the best when it comes to hosting public repositories. It's also helped to create a more social side to coding with its huge community elements and by encouraging people to help improve other people's projects by forking.

Even if you don't really use Git as a versioning system, it seems that every developer should have a GitHub account, even just to show off code snippets or small projects you've done. Having an account also allows you to help out on other people's projects and take advantage of all those community features on offer.

From a hosting point of view, GitHub is easy to use and includes a whole load of guides, tips, and tutorials to get you set up, even if you're not confident with the whole Git thing. Whether you make the choice to host your code on GitHub or not, if you are a developer and you don't have an account, I would advise you set one up. Even if you never use it for hosting big projects, having your code in an accessible place can be great when it comes to getting work, finding contributors for projects, or even just sharing something awesome you've made with the world.

Head on over to `http://github.com` now to review all the features for yourself, and maybe even sign up for an account so you can start forking some of the cool projects hosted there, or make that first commit on a brand new Git-backed project.

I'm still not feeling these services, what else is available?

Although I've gone through some great solutions for hosting your source code, using one of those solutions isn't always for everyone. That really only leaves you with a few options.

- The first is to store your code locally on a storage drive on your personal network. This, of course, has its disadvantages, the great one being having to keep that code backed up all the time. Using this solution also eliminates the ability to work remotely, unless you have the knowledge to allow access to the drive from remote locations, but even that has implications of its own.

- The other slightly more difficult option is creating your own server and managing it yourself. There are a fair few bonuses with working this way, one of which is the joy of setting up your own server and working with it. Since this is a decent alternative to working with a third party, there's an entire chapter on it in this book. If you fancy having a stab at setting up your own server, check out Chapter 12. You won't be disappointed.

Summary

We've covered a lot of ground in this chapter, going from SVN-only services to Git-only services and even covering those with support for all three VCSs. In most cases these services offer a lot more than just hosting your code, including issue tracking, wikis, group chat, and a whole lot of other features. These can be a great resource to ensure all the information about a project—including the time logged on it, issues assigned to it, the users working on it, and so on—are in one central, safe place.

That does come with a price, but if you're not really a technical person, these services can be a great asset to you or even your team by saving you time and effort. Although unlocking some of these features can cost a lot of money using certain providers, you always have the option of giving it a go yourself, which we'll get into next in Chapter 12.

Chapter 12

Why Branching Is Great

Wouldn't it be great if your code could exist in a parallel universe, where you could make changes to it in one version without impacting another version? Well, with branching, you can.

SVN, Git, and Mercurial all have ways you can branch your code. In this chapter I'll show you what a branch is, when you can use branches, and how to create them in SVN, Git, and Mercurial. I'll finish the chapter by stepping through a worked example of creating a branch, committing code to it, then merging it back into the main line of development.

What is a branch?

In a version control system a *branch* is code that diverges from the main line of development. If you think of it in terms of a tree, the trunk would represent the main line of development (as it does in SVN), with the branches diverging from the trunk at various points.

I mentioned a *parallel universe* right at the start of this chapter; when you create a branch you can think of this as causing a split in your codebase. From that point onwards, your code can exist in two parallel futures, completely independent from one another.

When you create a branch, it inherits its history from the main line of development up until the point it was created. Going forward it has its own commit history, and almost behaves like its own repository.

In a moment I'll show you how to create a branch in SVN, Git, and Mercurial. Before I do that, let's have a quick look at two of the main uses of branches in software development.

When can I use branches?

Although you aren't restricted in any way when it comes to using branches, the two main ways they are employed are as release branches and feature branches.

Release branches

Release branches are used to "freeze" the code base on a project prior to a release. When a team is working on a project, part of the team will form the release team. They'll create and work from a release branch, fixing bugs, polishing the product, and working with the testing team, to get it ready for release. Meanwhile, the rest of the team can continue working on the main line of development, perhaps with features planned for the next release.

Once released, a project's release branches will be used for ongoing maintenance against that particular release until it is no longer supported. For example, if a customer reports a problem against Version 1.0 of your product, you'd check out the release-1.0 branch, fix the problem, and commit your changes to the release-1.0 branch. At the same time, another customer could have reported a problem with Version 1.1. You could then check out the release-1.1 branch, fix the problem, and commit your changes. If it turns out that either of the bugs reported still exists in the main code base, these fixes could then be merged back into your main line of development.

Feature branches

Feature branches are used whenever you need to work on something that could lead to your main branch —trunk, master, or default—becoming unstable. Unlike release branches, they are only temporary and only kept for as long as it takes to implement the feature. Features might include testing out a new database abstraction library, trying out a new version of a third-party API, or rewriting a search function using a new or different algorithm. Either way, you wouldn't want your experimental code ending up in your main code base until you were sure it was stable.

Feature branches, being only temporary in nature, tend to get deleted once they have been merged back into the main code base.

TOPIC BRANCHES

Related to feature branches are topic branches. They are essentially the same as feature branches, as they are created to implement a specific feature or bug fix, and form an integral part of the workflow for developers using Git and Mercurial.

The master or default branch would represent the stable form of the code. Whenever a developer starts work on a user story, new feature, or bug fix, they'd create a topic branch named according to whatever it is they're about to work on, hack away on that branch until done, committing their work to it regularly as they go, then merge their branch back into master or default.

In older version control systems like SVN, excessive branching is not something that is encouraged, largely due to the significant cost of merging code between branches. Some would argue that excessive branching shows signs that something is wrong somewhere along the line. In Git and Mercurial, as you will see shortly, creating branches is incredibly lightweight. Switching back and forth between branches is almost instantaneous. Creating and merging branches is an integral part of the daily workflow for many developers.

How do I create a branch?

Before we go any further, let's see how to create a branch in SVN, Git, and Mercurial, and the difference between how SVN creates a branch and how Git and Mercurial do it.

SVN

To create a branch in SVN you use the svn copy command:

```
$ svn copy -m "Creating foobar branch…" \
                  http://path/to/repository/trunk \
                  http://path/to/repository /branches/foobar
```

When you create a branch like this, SVN takes whatever's in trunk and puts a copy of it in branches/foobar. Under the covers, SVN uses a hard link by pointing the new directory at an existing tree. This helps avoid duplicating large amounts of data. SVN will use the hard link whenever it can. It will only duplicate data when it is absolutely necessary to tell the difference between versions of objects. These "cheap copies" are cheap in terms of time and space. Creating a branch on the server is a near constant-time operation.

Once the branch has been created, you can switch your working copy to use it by using the svn switch command:

```
$ svn switch http://path/to/repository /branches/foobar
```

Alternatively you can check out a copy of the branch into a fresh working directory:

```
$ svn checkout http://path/to/repository /branches/foobar
```

Git

To create a branch in Git, use the git branch command:

```
(master)$ git branch foobar
```

To start using the branch, you'll need to check it out with git checkout:

```
(master)$ git checkout foobar
```

To see a list of branches in a repository, you can use the git branch command with no arguments. The current branch will be shown with an asterisk next to it:

```
(foobar)$ git branch
* foobar
  master
```

Unlike with SVN, this branch will exist *on the client* and not on the server. That's not to say you can't push your branch to a remote. If you've got a central repository called `origin` you can push your branch to it by passing the name of the branch to `git push` like so:

```
(master)$ git push -u origin foobar
```

Under the covers, when you create a branch, all Git is doing is creating a pointer to a commit: creating a branch involves nothing more than creating a file that contains the 40-character SHA1 checksum of the commit the branch points to. As such, branches are really cheap to create and destroy, and form a large part of the Git workflow for a lot of developers.

Mercurial

Like Git, when you create a branch in Mercurial it is also created on the client, and not the server. There are four ways to branch in Mercurial: clones, bookmarks, named branches, and anonymous branches. You can also mark a branch as closed to indicate it should no longer be used.

Clones

Branching with clones involves cloning the whole repository. This is similar to the way SVN creates a branch by copying files to another directory. To create a branch as a clone, you'd do the following:

```
$ cd ..
$ hg clone hgdemo hgdemo-branch-clone
updating to branch default
6 files updated, 0 files merged, 0 files removed, 0 files unresolved
```

You can then use the clone to edit files and commit changes. Changesets can be sent between the two repositories using `hg push` and `hg pull`:

```
$ hg commit -m 'changes from clone'
$ cd ../hgdemo
$ hg pull ../hgdemo-branch-clone
pulling from ../hgdemo-branch-clone
searching for changes
adding changesets
adding manifests
adding file changes
added 1 changesets with 1 changes to 1 files
(run 'hg update' to get a working copy)
$
```

Bookmarks

Bookmarks are pretty similar to how Git creates branches. They're effectively named pointers to particular changesets that automatically update when new commits are made. To create a bookmark you'd do the following:

```
$ hg bookmark feature-1
$ hg bookmark feature-2
```

To switch to using a particular bookmark you use the hg update command:

```
$ hg update feature-1
0 files updated, 0 files merged, 0 files removed, 0 files unresolved
```

Bookmarks aren't part of the Mercurial core, but come as an extension that ships with Mercurial core. To enable it you just need to add this to your repository's .hg/hgrc file:

```
[extensions]
bookmarks =
```

As bookmarks ships with Mercurial, it knows where to find it. You don't need to pass it a path after the equals sign.

Named branches

Named branches are created with the hg branch command. You pass it the name of the branch you want to create, and Mercurial creates the branch and switches your working directory to use the new branch:

```
$ hg branch foobar
marked working directory as branch foobar
```

You can check which branch you're on by running hg branch:

```
$ hg branch
foobar
```

You can see a list of all branches by using the hg branches command. Bear in mind that this will only list branches with commits, though:

```
$ hg branches
foobar                         8:3818fceb8cf0
default                        4:d95f6c9ee7e1 (inactive)
```

All changesets on a named branch have the branch name stored in their metadata.

Anonymous branches

Anonymous branches let you update to any revision and commit. They are the fastest way to create a branch in Mercurial, but there's no descriptive name for the branch, so you'll have to write good, meaningful commit messages if you want to remember what a branch was for at some point in the future.

Because anonymous branches have no name, you'll have to use hg update --check REV—where REV is the revision number or hash of the commit—to switch between them.

Closing branches

To close a branch you pass the --close-branch switch to the hg commit command. For example:

```
$ hg up -C foobar
$ hg commit --close-branch -m 'closing foobar, not a good idea from the start'
$ hg up -C default
```

When a branch is closed, it is listed as such when running the hg branches command:

```
$ hg branches
default                         4:d95f6c9ee7e1
foobar                          8:3818fceb8cf0 (closed)
```

To only list the active branches, pass the --active switch to the hg branches command:

```
$ hg branches --active
default                         4:d95f6c9ee7e1
```

A worked example

Suppose you've written a website that displays events on a map. The site has been running a while, and the original version uses Google Maps and the Google Maps API for the map display. Recently you've heard lots of cools things about OpenStreetMap and the OpenStreetMap API and want to explore whether OpenStreetMap could be used to reimplement the site's mapping functionality.

This "experimental feature" is perfect for a feature branch. Let's look at how to handle this using SVN, Git, and Mercurial.

SVN

First you'll need to create the branch. This is done using the svn copy command:

```
$ svn copy -m "Experimental openstreetmap branch" \
                    http://path/to/svn/repository/trunk \
                    http://path/to/svn/repository/branches/openstreetmap
```

```
Committed revision 21.
```

That creates the openstreetmap branch on the server. But, if you run svn info, you'll see that your working copy is still pointing at trunk:

```
$ svn info
Path: .
URL: http://path/to/svn/repository/trunk
Repository Root: http://path/to/svn/repository
Repository UUID: a5e2b20c-f7b4-4d29-8eda-c5bf649c34ce
Revision: 25
Node Kind: directory
Schedule: normal
Last Changed Author: ianoxley
```

```
Last Changed Rev: 25
Last Changed Date: 2011-11-08 18:47:30 +0000 (Tue, 08 Nov 2011)
```

You've got two choices to get your working copy pointing at the feature branch: you can either use svn switch to switch your current working copy to point to the openstreetmap branch, or you could use svn checkout to check out a copy of the branch into an entirely separate working directory.

- svn switch sends only the minimal set of changes necessary to make your working copy reflect the branch directory. As you've just created this branch from trunk, you wouldn't expect there to be too many changes, if any.

- svn checkout will typically take longer than svn switch, as it's effectively checking out the whole repository again, albeit a different branch. You could pass svn checkout the -r argument, specifying a recent revision, or even HEAD, to minimize the amount of data that has to be pulled down from the repository. Nevertheless, some people prefer this approach, as they're less likely to get confused about which branch they're working on.

For now, use svn switch:

```
$ svn switch http://path/to/svn/repository/branches/openstreetmap
At revision 27.
```

If you run svn info again, you'll see that you are now on the openstreetmap branch:

```
$ svn info
Path: .
URL: http://path/to/svn/repository/branches/openstreetmap
Repository Root: http://path/to/svn/repository
Repository UUID: a5e2b20c-f7b4-4d29-8eda-c5bf649c34ce
Revision: 27
Node Kind: directory
Schedule: normal
Last Changed Author: ianoxley
Last Changed Rev: 27
Last Changed Date: 2011-11-15 20:27:26 +0000 (Tue, 15 Nov 2011)
```

Now you can hack away, testing and coding the new feature until it's finished and you're ready to commit your changes to the branch:

```
$ svn status
M       js/map.js
$ svn commit -m 'OpenStreetMap API integration'
Sending         js/map.js
Transmitting file data .
Committed revision 23.
```

With the code committed to the branch, it's time to merge the new feature back into trunk. To start with, you switch back to trunk; if trunk has been updated while you've been working on the openstreetmap branch you should automatically get the updates added to your working copy:

```
$ svn switch http://path/to/svn/repository/trunk
U    index.html
Updated to revision 30.
```

Now you're ready to merge your openstreetmap branch into trunk. Well, almost ready. When you run svn merge you'll need to tell it which revision you want to merge *from* and *to*. In this case, the *to* revision will just be HEAD. The *from* revision will be the revision when you created the openstreetmap branch. You did remember to write that down, didn't you? You didn't? Don't worry, because you can run svn log and pass it the --stop-on-copy switch; this will stop at the revision when you created the branch (if you remember, the command to create the branch was svn copy, hence --stop-on-copy):

```
$ svn log --stop-on-copy http://path/to/svn/repository/branches/openstreetmap
------------------------------------------------------------------------
r29 | ianoxley | 2011-11-15 21:55:49 +0000 (Tue, 15 Nov 2011) | 1 line

Fixed equality check in isLoading function
------------------------------------------------------------------------
r28 | ianoxley | 2011-11-15 21:53:50 +0000 (Tue, 15 Nov 2011) | 1 line

OpenStreetMap API changes added to map.js
------------------------------------------------------------------------
r27 | ianoxley | 2011-11-15 21:50:47 +0000 (Tue, 15 Nov 2011) | 1 line

Experimental openstreetmap branch
------------------------------------------------------------------------
```

This tells you your openstreetmap branch was created on revision 27. You can pass this number to svn merge.

To help avoid any nasty surprises, you can run svn merge with the --dry-run switch first. This will show you the result of the merge will be *without* making any actual changes to the working copy:

```
$ svn merge -r 27:HEAD --dry-run http://path/to/svn/repository/branches/openstreetmap
--- Merging r28 through r30 into '.':
U    js/map.js
$ svn status
# nothing is output
```

As you can see, when you run svn status after the dry run, no changes have been made to the working copy.

Everything looks OK with the dry run, so you can go ahead and run the merge:

```
$ svn merge -r 27:HEAD http://path/to/svn/repository/branches/openstreetmap
--- Merging r28 through r30 into '.':
U    js/map.js
$ svn status
 M      .
M       js/map.js
```

This time, running svn status shows that there *are* some modified files in the working copy, as a result of the merge. You'll need to check that everything is OK, and that all unit tests pass, before committing the merged files to trunk:

```
$ svn commit -m "Merged openstreetmap experimental branch to trunk -r27:HEAD"
Sending        .
Sending        js/map.js
```

```
Transmitting file data .
Committed revision 31.
```

> **Note** *SVN doesn't contain any internal mechanism to track merges. When merging and committing changes such as in the example above, SVN doesn't know that the changes to trunk came from a merge; all it sees is some local modifications that are being committed. The user therefore needs to manually track merge information, otherwise situations could arise where the same change is accidentally merged twice.*
>
> *The recommended best practice to guard against this is to mention the revision, or range of revisions, that are being merged into your branch.* svn log *can then be used to check which changes are already in your branch the next time you need to run* svn merge.

When you merged your branch above, everything went smoothly and there were no conflicts. Sooner or later, though, conflicts will arise after a merge:

```
$ svn merge -r 27:HEAD --dry-run http://path/to/svn/repository/branches/openstreetmap
--- Merging r31 through r33 into '.':
C    js/map.js
Summary of conflicts:
  Text conflicts: 1
```

When all the conflicts have been resolved (see Chapter 8), you'll have to commit your changes as before.

> **Note** *When you get a conflict after a merge, the files created by SVN are named differently to what they are when* svn update *produces a conflict. A conflict from an update produces files named* filename.mine, filename.rOLDREV, *and* filename.rNEWREV, *whereas a conflict from a merge produces* filename.working, filename.left *and* filename.right.

Don't forget: if a merge goes horribly wrong, you can always back out and start again by running svn revert:

```
$ svn revert js/map.js
Reverted 'js/map.js'
```

Git

Let's go through the same steps with Git, from creating the branch to merging the code. We'll also look at how you can squash commits to keep your master history nice and tidy.

First, create the openstreetmap branch from master:

```
(master)$ git checkout -b openstreetmap
Switched to a new branch 'openstreetmap'
(openstreetmap)$
```

The -b switch you passed to git checkout tells Git to create a new branch, called openstreetmap. When you create a branch in this way, you'll immediately be on that branch. You can see this by the change in the command prompt, because I've got it configured to show the name of the current branch. You can also see your current branch by typing in git branch. The current branch is the one with the asterisk next to it:

```
(openstreetmap)$ git branch
  master
* openstreetmap
```

> Tip: Changing your command prompt to show the name of the current branch you're working on is a very handy trick. It makes it really easy to see at a glance which branch you're currently working on. It's also really easy to set up. You just need to add this line to your .bashrc file:
>
> PS1='${debian_chroot:+($debian_chroot)}\u@\h:$(__git_ps1 "(%s)")\$
>
> Save and exit, then type source ~/.bashrc to load the changes into the shell. Next time you're in a Git directory, the name of the current branch will be displayed in your command prompt.

Now you can hack away on the new feature, commiting changes to your branch as you go:

```
(openstreetmap)$ git status
# On branch openstreetmap
# Changes not staged for commit:
#   (use "git add <file>..." to update what will be committed)
#   (use "git checkout -- <file>..." to discard changes in working directory)
#
#       modified:   js/map.js
#
no changes added to commit (use "git add" and/or "git commit -a")
(openstreetmap)$ git add -u
(openstreetmap)$ git status
# On branch openstreetmap
# Changes to be committed:
#   (use "git reset HEAD <file>..." to unstage)
#
#       modified:   js/map.js
#
(openstreetmap)$ git commit -m "Mapping code changed to use the OpenStreetMap API"
[openstreetmap d2e5287] Mapping code changed to use the OpenStreetMap API
 1 files changed, 3 insertions(+), 1 deletions(-)
(openstreetmap)$
```

When the feature is finished, it's time to merge the changes back into master. First, you should update openstreetmap to make sure it includes any changes that were made to master since you began working on the branch. Do this using git rebase:

```
(openstreetmap)$ git rebase master
Current branch openstreetmap is up to date.
```

What does git rebase do?

git rebase replays your local commits against another branch, or the updated upstream head. Let's look at an example. Imagine you're working on the branch topic and make commits A, B, and C. While you were doing this, someone else has pushed commits F and G to master. From the topic branch, when you execute git rebase master, Git will:

1. Store all commits made to topic that are not in master to a temporary area

2. Reset the current branch to master

3. Reapply the commits saved in step 1 to the current branch, in order

Before step 1 begins, your commit history looks something like this:

```
        A---B---C topic
       /
D---E---F---G master
```

After step 3, your commit history will now look like this:

```
                A'---B'---C' topic
               /
D---E---F---G master
```

Notice that your first commit A now appears after commit G?

If Git can't complete the rebase automatically, you'll have to manually intervene and resolve any conflicts, and run git rebase --continue to carry on with the rebase. On some occasions you might need to run git rebase --skip to skip a commit causing a merge to fail. If you need to back out of a rebase run git rebase --abort; your current branch will be back at the state it was in before you ran git rebase.

Squashing commits

Your openstreetmap branch is up to date, so you're OK to go ahead and merge your changes back into master. But before you do, you decide to clean up your commits and squash all your smaller commits from the day's work and combine them into one. You do this using git rebase -interactive (or git rebase -i) mode:

```
(openstreetmap)$ git rebase -i HEAD~4
```

This will open up your default editor containing the last four commits (the last four because you typed HEAD~4):

```
pick 6bd5441 Fixed typo in coords variable name
pick 26cd1ca Updated code to draw points on the map
pick 419f05e Added code to create the map with Open Street Map
pick 2b4bf69 Mapping code updated to use the OpenStreetMap API

# Rebase d2e5287..2b4bf69 onto d2e5287
#
# Commands:
```

```
#  p, pick = use commit
#  r, reword = use commit, but edit the commit message
#  e, edit = use commit, but stop for amending
#  s, squash = use commit, but meld into previous commit
#  f, fixup = like "squash", but discard this commit's log message
#  x, exec = run command (the rest of the line) using shell
#
# If you remove a line here THAT COMMIT WILL BE LOST.
# However, if you remove everything, the rebase will be aborted.
```

You decide to squash all your commits on the openstreetmap branch into one, leaving the top line as pick and changing the other three lines to squash:

```
pick 6bd5441 Fixed typo in coords variable name
squash 26cd1ca Updated code to draw points on the map
squash 419f05e Added code to create the map with Open Strect Map
squash 2b4bf69 Mapping code updated to use the OpenStreetMap API

# Rebase d2e5287..2b4bf69 onto d2e5287
#
# Commands:
#  p, pick = use commit
#  r, reword = use commit, but edit the commit message
#  e, edit = use commit, but stop for amending
#  s, squash = use commit, but meld into previous commit
#  f, fixup = like "squash", but discard this commit's log message
#  x, exec = run command (the rest of the line) using shell
#
# If you remove a line here THAT COMMIT WILL BE LOST.
# However, if you remove everything, the rebase will be aborted.
#
```

Save the changes and exit the editor. The editor will then reopen, this time with all the commit messages from the last four commits ready for you to edit:

```
# This is a combination of 4 commits.
# The first commit's message is:
Fixed typo in coords variable name

# This is the 2nd commit message:

Updated code to draw points on the map

# This is the 3rd commit message:

Added code to create the map with Open Street Map

# This is the 4th commit message:

Mapping code updated to use the OpenStreetMap API

# Please enter the commit message for your changes. Lines starting
# with '#' will be ignored, and an empty message aborts the commit.
# Not currently on any branch.
# Changes to be committed:
```

```
#    (use "git reset HEAD <file>..." to unstage)
#
#          modified:    js/map.js
#
```

You combine the commit messages so they look like this:

```
Mapping code updated to use the OpenStreetMap API

Added code to create the map with Open Street Map
Updated code to draw points on the map

Fixed typo in coords variable name

# Please enter the commit message for your changes. Lines starting
# with '#' will be ignored, and an empty message aborts the commit.
# Not currently on any branch.
# Changes to be committed:
#    (use "git reset HEAD <file>..." to unstage)
#
#          modified:    js/map.js
#
```

Save and exit the editor. The last four commits will be squashed into one, which you can check by running git log -1 to print out the last log message:

```
(openstreetmap)$ git log -1
commit 04225c93bc465c5621d12aed5c7cc3bff79dff5d
Author: Ian Oxley <ian@example.com>
Date:    Tue Nov 15 17:39:25 2011 +0000

        Mapping code updated to use the OpenStreetMap API

        Added code to create the map with Open Street Map
        Updated code to draw points on the map

        Fixed typo in coords variable name
```

Let's continue by merging the openstreetmap branch back into master. First, you need to check out the master branch, then call git merge and pass it the name of the branch you want to merge into master, which in this case is openstreetmap:

```
(openstreetmap)$ git checkout master
Switched to branch 'master'
(master)$ git merge openstreetmap
Updating 50b8d4b..d2e5287
Fast-forward
 js/map.js |   27 +++++++++++++++++++++++----
 1 files changed, 23 insertions(+), 4 deletions(-)
```

Remember when you did a merge with SVN? You had to commit the files that were changed by the merge yourself. With Git you don't have to; as long as there are no conflicts there'll be nothing to manually commit. You can see this by running git status:

```
(master)$ git status
# On branch master
# Your branch is ahead of 'staging/master' by 1 commit.
#
nothing to commit (working directory clean)
```

What would've happened if the merge had detected a conflict? You'd have seen something like this:

```
(master)$ git merge openstreetmap
Auto-merging js/map.js
CONFLICT (content): Merge conflict in js/map.js
Automatic merge failed; fix conflicts and then commit the result.
(master|MERGING)$
```

Type in git mergetool and it will open your configured merge tool with the first conflict (resolving conflicts is discussed in more depth in Chapter 8):

```
(master|MERGING)$ git mergetool
Merging:
js/map.js

Normal merge conflict for 'js/map.js':
  {local}: modified
  {remote}: modified
Hit return to start merge resolution tool (kdiff3):
```

You can then edit the files and resolve the conflict as you see fit. (If there were any more conflicts, the mergetool would move on to the next one, and so on, and so on, until all conflicts had been resolved.) Once you're done, you'll need to commit the changes you made to resolve the conflict:

```
(master|MERGING)$ git status
# On branch master
# Your branch is ahead of 'staging/master' by 2 commits.
#
# Changes to be committed:
#
#       modified:   js/map.js
#
```

Once the changes have been committed, the conflict is marked as resolved:

```
(master|MERGING)$ git commit -m "Resolved conflict when merging openstreetmap branch"
[master dff235a] Resolved conflict when merging openstreetmap branch
```

If you decided to abandon the merge partway through, you need to type in the following:

```
(master|MERGING)$ git merge --abort
```

The output of git status *does* tell you that master is now ahead of the staging remote by one commit. You can fix that by pushing your changes to staging:

```
(master)$ git push -u staging master
Counting objects: 7, done.
Compressing objects: 100% (4/4), done.
Writing objects: 100% (4/4), 487 bytes, done.
```

```
Total 4 (delta 2), reused 0 (delta 0)
Unpacking objects: 100% (4/4), done.
To /home/ianoxley/dev/gitdemo/
    d2e5287..04225c9  master -> master
Branch master set up to track remote branch master from staging.
```

Now that the openstreetmap branch has been merged into master, one final thing to do is to delete your feature branch:

```
(master)$ git branch -d openstreetmap
Deleted branch openstreetmap (was 04225c9).
```

Mercurial

Finally, let's look at the same example in Mercurial.

First, you create the same openstreetmap branch that you created in SVN and Git. As you're using Mercurial you'll be creating the branch from default:

```
$ hg branch openstreetmap
marked working directory as branch openstreetmap
```

It looks like you're on the new branch straight away. You can type in hg branch to check:

```
$ hg branch
openstreetmap
```

Yes, indeed you are. Now you can hack away on the new feature, just like you did with SVN and Git, and commit to the branch as you go:

```
$ hg commit -m "Refactored code to use OpenStreetMap API"
```

Once the feature is complete and all changes have been committed to the branch, it's time to merge the branch into default:

```
$ hg update default
1 files updated, 0 files merged, 0 files removed, 0 files unresolved
```

This merges your openstreetmap branch with default and puts you back on the default branch. The hg branch command will confirm this:

```
$ hg branch
default
```

hg log will confirm that your changes made in openstreetmap are now in default:

```
changeset:   7:811e1430c3c1
branch:      openstreetmap
tag:         tip
user:        Ian Oxley <ian@example.com>
date:        Wed Nov 16 00:19:06 2011 +0000
summary:     Added default map holder
```

```
changeset:    6:e2a7724067c6
branch:       openstreetmap
user:         Ian Oxley <ian@example.com>
date:         Wed Nov 16 00:17:58 2011 +0000
summary:      Added null and undefined check to draw function

changeset:    5:2e113221dfac
branch:       openstreetmap
user:         Ian Oxley <ian@example.com>
date:         Wed Nov 16 00:15:31 2011 +0000
summary:      Updated docs
```

If Mercurial detects a conflict during a merge, it'll open your configured merge resolution tool so you can resolve the conflict (you can read more about conflicts in Chapter 8).

Once you have resolved any conflicts, you'll need to remember to commit your changes. Fortunately, Mercurial gives you a helpful reminder:

```
0 files updated, 1 files merged, 0 files removed, 0 files unresolved
(branch merge, don't forget to commit)
```

If you want to tidy up your commits a bit and squash them into one, just like you did using git rebase --interactive, you'll first have to install an extension called Histedit. Use Histedit extension (http://mercurial.selenic.com/wiki/HisteditExtension) to get the same functionality as git rebase --interactive.

To install and enable Histedit you'll need to add this to your .hgrc file:

```
[extensions]
histedit = ~/path/to/histedit/hg_histedit.py
```

This makes the Histedit command available to you. To use it, pass it a revision; any changesets from that revision onwards will be available for **hist**ory **edit**ing:

```
$ hg histedit 10
```

This will open up your editor, presenting you with a similar-looking file to that what you saw with Git:

```
pick d775eff029f0 fixed typo in variable name
pick acc3f0d19218 merged experimental branch

# Edit history between d775eff029f0 and acc3f0d19218
#
# Commands:
#  p, pick = use commit
#  e, edit = use commit, but stop for amending
#  f, fold = use commit, but fold into previous commit
#  d, drop = remove commit from history
#  m, mess = edit message without changing commit content
#
```

Edit the commits using the commands available (listed at the bottom of the file). Save the file, then Mercurial opens the commit messages in your editor ready for you to amend:

```
fixed typo in variable name
***
merged experimental branch
```

Make your changes, then save the file and close the editor. Mercurial will then apply the changes to the commits:

```
1 files updated, 0 files merged, 0 files removed, 0 files unresolved
1 files updated, 0 files merged, 0 files removed, 0 files unresolved
0 files updated, 0 files merged, 0 files removed, 0 files unresolved
saved backup bundle to /path/to/repo/.hg/strip-backup/d775eff029f0-backup.hg
```

Running hg log will show the updates to your commit history.

Summary

In this chapter you looked at branches. You saw what a branch is, how branches can be used for releases and feature development, and how you can create branches in SVN, Git, and Mercurial (including the four different ways to create a branch in Mercurial). Finally, I walked you through a worked example of creating a feature branch, checking out the branch, making changes, committing code to the branch, and merging changes back in to your main line of development. You also saw how you can manage your commit history in Git and Mercurial by squashing commits before making changes public.

Chapter 13

Hooks, and Why They Can Be Useful

Hooks are commands, or scripts, that are triggered by events occurring in your repository. These events occur when you commit, push, and pull. Hooks have access to environment variables, can receive arguments containing revision information, and allow you to control whether a particular repository event can proceed or gets blocked. They live in, but are not checked in to, your repository, and a given event can have a hook that fires before, during, or immediately after said event—for example, pre-commit, commit, and post-commit. In this chapter, you'll have a look at what hooks are available in SVN, Git, and Mercurial, how you can enable hooks, and finally look at some examples of what you can do with hooks.

SVN Hooks

If you look in the `SVN_DIR/hooks` directory you'll see a set of template hook files listed. As you `svn update` and `svn commit` away, you'll mostly be interested in the following hooks.

start-commit

This hook runs before the commit transaction has **start**ed. It is passed three arguments: the path to the repository, the username of the person doing the commit and, since SVN 1.5, a colon-separated list of the capabilities of the SVN client making the commit.

> **Caution** *This list of capabilities is self-reported by the client. The `start-commit.tmpl` contains a warning that you should not make any security assumptions based on this list of capabilities, or even assume that this list has been reliably reported.*

The hook's exit status is used to determine whether the commit should be allowed to continue. To stop the commit from occurring, a non-zero exit status should be returned and any data written to stderr will be sent back to the SVN client.

pre-commit

This hook runs *after* the SVN transaction has been created but *before* it is actually committed. It is passed two arguments: the path to the SVN repository and the name of the transaction about to be committed.

If the hook wants to stop the commit from continuing, it should exit with a non-zero status. As with the start-commit hook, any data written to stderr by the hook will be sent back to the SVN client.

What does a non-zero exit status mean? A program runs in a process. When a process finishes, it passes a small numeric value to its parent process. This exit status, also known as a return code, indicates success or failure: an exit status of zero indicates success; any non-zero exit status means an error occurred.

The pre-commit hook can be used to check for nonempty commit messages, or to check that commits to your bugfixes branch include a ticket number from your bug tracking system in the commit message.

post-commit

The post-commit hook runs after a successful commit. It is passed two arguments: the path to the repository and the new revision number from the fresh commit.

The exit status of this hook is ignored, though, as it can have no influence over the commit (because it has already been committed).

As it runs after a successful commit, this hook can be used to send out e-mail notifications containing details about the commit.

pre-revprop-change

Revision properties in SVN aren't actually versioned themselves. The pre-revprop-change hook, together with its counterpart post-revprop-change, which you'll meet very shortly, make it possible for you keep track of changes to these values using an external system, such as a log file or a database, if you need to.

> **Note** *When I say that the revision properties aren't versioned, it means that any successful change to them is destructive because the old value will be lost forever. It is recommended that this hook be used to back up the old value somewhere.*
>
> *Because of the destructive nature of changes to revision properties, this hook must exist for these changes to go through. If an attempt is made to change a revision property without the pre-revprop-change hook being enabled, SVN acts as though the hook is there and has returned a non-zero status.*

This hook runs just before a revision property is added, modified, or deleted. It is passed four arguments: the path to the repository, the revision being changed, the username of the person making the change, the property being set on the revision, and whether the property is being **A**dded, **M**odified or **D**eleted.

The usual rules apply regarding the exit status of the hook: any non-zero status will stop the property from being changed.

post-revprop-change

This hook complements the `pre-revprop-change` hook above, and won't actually run unless the `pre-revprop-change` hook is enabled as well.

It runs after the revision property has been changed, and is passed the same four arguments that are passed to `pre-revprop-change`: the path to the repository, the revision being changed, the username of the person making the change, the property being set on the revision, and whether the property is being **A**dded, **M**odified or **D**eleted (denoted as A, M, or D).

Like the post-commit hook, the exit status of this hook is ignored, because the change to the revision property has already been done at this point.

This hook could be used to send out an e-mail, for example, notifying users of the new value.

> User permissions
>
> SVN runs hooks as the same user that owns the process that is accessing SVN. More often than not this will be the Apache user (#TODO add reference to setting up svn server).

Git Hooks

Git hooks live in the GIT_DIR/hooks directory. By default, when you create a new Git repository, ten sample hooks are created in there. Let's go through each of them to see what they are, and when they are run.

pre-commit

This hook is called by `git commit`, and is passed no arguments. You can use this hook to verify what is about to be committed, for example, by running unit tests.

If the script wants to stop the commit, it should first issue an appropriate message explaining why the commit was stopped, before exiting with a non-zero status.

commit-msg

This hook is called by `git commit` and is passed one argument: the name of the file containing the commit message (which it is allowed to edit).

If the script wants to stop the commit, it should first issue an appropriate message explaining why the commit was stopped, before exiting with a non-zero status.

post-commit

This hook is called after a successful commit. Like the pre-commit hook, it receives no arguments.

The post-commit hook is mainly used for notification, as it cannot affect the outcome of git commit.

prepare-commit-msg

This hook is called by git commit, and receives two arguments: the file containing the commit message, and a description of the commit message's source. Its purpose is to edit the commit message file—for example, to comment out the "Conflicts:" part of a merge commit.

pre-rebase

This hook is called by git rebase, and is passed two arguments: the upstream the series was forked from and the branch being rebased.

If the hook wants to stop git rebase from running, it should exit with a non-zero status. As with the commit hooks earlier, issuing an appropriate message before exiting is a good idea, otherwise no-one will know why the rebase failed.

The example pre-rebase hook in GIT_DIR/hooks/pre-rebase.sample shows how to prevent topic branches that have already been merged from being rebased again, thus avoiding rebasing already published history.

post-receive

This hook runs on a remote after you git push to it, and will execute once after all refs have been updated. It receives no arguments but is passed, on standard input, the old value, new value, and ref name for each ref being updated.

The outcome of git push isn't affected by this hook.

post-update

This is similar to the post-receive hook in that it runs on a remote after receiving a git push, but this hook runs once per ref that is updated (post-receive runs once after all refs have been updated). The name of each ref being updated is passed as a parameter to post-update.

As it can't influence the outcome of a git push, this hook tends to be used for notification.

update

This hook runs on a remote after it receives a git push from a local repository. It is invoked just before updating the ref on the remote repository.

It runs once for each update, and is passed three parameters: the name of the ref being updated, the old object name stored in the ref, and the new object name stored in the ref.

The update hook can use its exit status to influence the outcome of the ref update (zero for success, non-zero for failure). Any messages for the user can simply be echoed back to them.

pre-applypatch

This hook is invoked by git-am, which is used when applying patches submitted via e-mail. It runs after the patch has been applied, but before the commit is made.

pre-applypatch doesn't get passed any parameters. A non-zero exit status will prevent the working tree from being committed.

applypatch-msg

As with pre-applypatch, this hook is invoked by git-am, and is passed the name of the file that holds the commit log message.

A non-zero exit status will stop the patch from being applied.

Mercurial Hooks

Unlike SVN and Git, Mercurial doesn't come with a set of template hooks for you to rename and make executable. That's not to say it doesn't support hooks; it does. To enable them, you need to add an entry in your .hgrc file, with the name of the hook and the script it should execute.

Following is a list of hooks supported by Mercurial:

prechangegroup

This hook runs *before* starting to bring a group of changesets into the local repository from elsewhere. It would run once per hg push, hg pull, or hg unbundle.

The exit status is ignored.

changegroup

This hook runs *after* a group of changesets is brought into the local repository from another repository.

pretxnchangegroup

This hook runs after the external changesets have been brought into the local repository, but before the transaction has completed and the changes made permanent.

If the hook decides the current operation should be aborted, it should exit with a non-zero status.

preoutgoing

This hook runs before any changesets are sent from the local repository to a remote repository, for example, after a hg push command.

The hook can use a non-zero exit status to stop the current operation.

outgoing

This hook is run after the changesets from the local repository have been sent—for example, after hg push has completed.

incoming

This hook is similar to changegroup, in that it runs when bringing changesets in to the local repository from another repository. The difference is that, where changegroup runs once per group of changesets, incoming runs once for each individual changeset within that group.

precommit

This hook runs before a commit is started.

A non-zero exit status will abort the commit.

commit

This hook runs after a new changeset has been created in the local repository.

pretxncommit

This hook runs *after* the new changeset has been created, but *before* the actual transaction has completed.

To stop the commit from being made permanent, the script should exit with a non-zero status.

preupdate

This hook runs before an hg update or hg merge.

It can stop the operation with a non-zero exit status.

update

This hook will run after hg merge or hg update has completed.

pretag

This hook is run before creating a tag.

It can stop the tag from being created with a non-zero exit status.

tag

This hook is run after the tag has been created.

> **Note** *Mercurial hooks can return slightly different status values depending on whether they're being run as an external process, such as a shell script, or in-process as a Python script. Shell commands/scripts should behave the same as they do for SVN and Git; a non-zero exit status aborts the current operation and a zero exit status allows it to proceed. Python scripts, on the other hand, return True or False. True behaves the same as a non-zero exit status and aborts the current operation, and False behaves the same as a zero exit status and allows the current operation continue.*

As was said at the very start of this chapter, while hooks do live in the repository, they aren't actually checked in to the repository. As such, they aren't propagated when cloning, or pulling from, a repository. This is good from a security standpoint: if hooks *were* propagated this way, would you be comfortable having arbitrary code executing on your system? But it can also pose a challenge when it comes to managing a repository across a team.

For a start, you cannot assume that everyone working on the repo will have the same hooks. Good documentation can aid you here, letting developers know which hooks need setting up and what they need to do. But even in cases such as on a corporate intranet, where a site-wide ~/.hgrc file is in use to let all users see the hooks, it will still be possible for a user to override site-wide hooks: they could disable them by setting them to an empty string, or edit the hook script and change the intended behavior.

Enabling Hooks

As was mentioned earlier, both SVN and Git repositories come with hook script templates and samples. They can be found in

- SVN_DIR/hooks for SVN, where SVN_DIR is the directory where you created your repository on the server

- GIT_DIR/hooks for Git, where GIT_DIR is the .git folder in your local repository

By default they're all disabled, but enabling them is simple enough.

Enabling Hooks in SVN

All the default hooks are in files with a .tmpl file extension. To enable one of these hooks

1. Create a copy of the hook script without the .tmpl extension.

2. Make the script executable (none of the .tmpl files are).

To do this via the command line you'd need to type in something like the following:

```
$ cd /path/to/svn/repository/hooks
$ cp pre-commit.tmpl pre-commit
$ chmod +x pre-commit
```

Enabling Hooks in Git

To enable one of the sample hooks in Git, you follow an almost identical process:

```
$ cd /path/to/git/repository/.git/hooks
$ cp pre-commit.sample pre-commit
```

The only differences are that you're renaming a .sample file instead of a .tmpl, and you don't need to make the script executable (because it already is). Since Git 1.6, the hook scripts in GIT_DIR/hooks are all executable by default. If you're running a version of Git prior to 1.6, you'll need to run chmod +x filename as with the SVN hook above.

> **Tip** If you're on Windows, to make the script executable you'll have to give it a file extension that Windows knows it can execute, such as .exe or .bat.

Enabling hooks in Mercurial

Unlike SVN and Git, Mercurial repositories don't come with a set of default hook scripts that you can rename to enable them. Instead, to create a hook in Mercurial, you need to add an entry to your .hgrc file containing shell commands, or the path to the script you want the hook to run.

> **Note** Although Mercurial repositories don't come with a .hg/hooks directory containing sample hook files, Mercurial does ship with quite a few bundled hooks. They can be found in the hgext directory, which can be found in the Mercurial source tree or, if you installed via a binary package, wherever your package manager put Mercurial.

Mercurial hooks can either use shell commands or Python scripts:

- Shell commands run as an external process and, while they can issue Mercurial commands, have no direct access to the Mercurial API.

- Python scripts run in-process and do have access to the Mercurial API. Because they run in-process, Python scripts execute faster than the external process shell commands, so they are a good choice if you require high performance. If performance isn't too much of a concern for you, then shell commands should suffice most of the time.

Shell commands can get hold of Mercurial data via environment variables. When set as environment variables, the original variable name is capitalized and prefixed with HG_. For example, to make the variable foo available, Mercurial would create the environment variable HG_FOO and set its value to match that of foo. Mercurial exposes other data in the same manner—for example, HG_NODE. Python scripts get access to variables via keyword parameters passed to the Python function.

Defining multiple actions for a Hook

Unlike SVN and Git, Mercurial makes it possible to define more than one action per hook. So you might have one hook to check the format of the commit message, then some further actions on the same hook to check for the existence of a bug ticket number in the commit message, for example, and to run some unit tests. They'd be called something like pretxncommit, pretxncommit.bugticket, and pretxncommit.unittests.

When multiple actions are defined for a hook, the main hook comes first, followed by the rest, sorted alphabetically by extension.

As with variable names, give your hooks meaningful names. That way it'll be easier to remember what each hook does.

> Hooks and security
>
> The user a hook script executes as differs depending on the version control system being used. This is something you should be aware of, as it could impact the security of your system.
>
> With SVN, the hooks are run on the server and are run using the same user account that the web server process runs as; on a typical LAMP stack this will be the Apache HTTP user.
>
> With Git, all hooks—both those run on the client and those run on the server—are run as the current user. The same goes for Mercurial as well—unless you're pulling over http or SSL, in which case hooks are executed as the user running the server process. Because hooks can run with the same privileges as your user account, and because hooks can contain arbitrary executable code, it's not a good idea to run a hook unless you completely understand what it does and have a good idea who created it.

Hooks in action

Let's have a look at some hooks in action to see how you can use them to help solve common problems.

Preventing empty commit messages

Every developer working with SVN will, at some point or another, have run svn log and seen something like this:

```
------------------------------------------------------------------------
r12 | ianoxley | 2011-11-08 18:32:14 +0000 (Tue, 08 Nov 2011) | 1 line


------------------------------------------------------------------------
r11 | ianoxley | 2011-11-08 18:32:13 +0000 (Tue, 08 Nov 2011) | 1 line
```

```
-----------------------------------------------------------------------
r10 | ianoxley | 2011-11-08 18:32:12 +0000 (Tue, 08 Nov 2011) | 1 line


-----------------------------------------------------------------------
r9 | ianoxley | 2011-11-08 18:32:10 +0000 (Tue, 08 Nov 2011) | 1 line


-----------------------------------------------------------------------
```

Contrast this with the following, where the commit messages give lots of information about the changes being committed:

```
-----------------------------------------------------------------------
r16 | ianoxley | 2011-11-08 18:47:30 +0000 (Tue, 08 Nov 2011) | 5 lines

jQuery added

jQuery is included in the main index.html, just before the closing </body> tag. We're➥
 using the latest jQuery available from Google's CDN.

-----------------------------------------------------------------------
r15 | ianoxley | 2011-11-08 18:45:46 +0000 (Tue, 08 Nov 2011) | 7 lines

CSS and JS folders added.

The css folder contains the reset.css file. This is based on the reset.css from Eric➥
 Meyer that can be found at http://meyerweb.com/eric/thoughts/2011/01/03/reset-revisited/

The js folder contains the main.js file, currently empty, but now included in the main➥
 index.html.

-----------------------------------------------------------------------
r14 | ianoxley | 2011-11-08 18:41:42 +0000 (Tue, 08 Nov 2011) | 5 lines

Article structure added.

Main article on the page layed out, with header, section and footer tags.

-----------------------------------------------------------------------
r13 | ianoxley | 2011-11-08 18:39:46 +0000 (Tue, 08 Nov 2011) | 5 lines

Homepage template added.

Skeleton HTML only, with a main container element and the main page title.

-----------------------------------------------------------------------
```

If you're working on a bug fix and are trying to work out when the change that introduced the bug was committed, meaningful commit messages like these can be a big help.

To prevent your SVN log from filling up with empty, meaningless commit messages, you can use SVN's pre-commit hook to check that a commit message has been entered. If you remember from earlier, the pre-commit hook runs after the transaction has been created but before it is committed. You can inspect the message and issue a non-zero exit status if it's empty to stop the commit.

In actual fact, the default pre-commit hook that is in the SVN_DIR/hooks directory contains the code you need (unless you happen to be on a Windows platform, but I'll address that problem shortly). You can copy the tmpl file and make it executable like you saw earlier:

```
$ cd /path/to/svn/repository/hooks
$ cp pre-commit.tmpl pre-commit && chmod +x pre-commit
```

Now, if you open the pre-commit file in your favorite text editor, you'll see something like this:

```
REPOS="$1"
TXN="$2"

# Make sure that the log message contains some text.
SVNLOOK=/usr/bin/svnlook
$SVNLOOK log -t "$TXN" "$REPOS" | \
    grep "[a-zA-Z0-9]" > /dev/null || exit 1
```

All you're interested in at the moment is preventing empty commit messages, so the other code that is in the file can be commented out or removed for now.

If you're running SVN on Windows, this code won't be much use due to its reliance on *nix shell scripting. One alternative is to use the following batch file, which does the same thing (see www.anujgakhar.com/2008/02/14/how-to-force-comments-on-svn-commit/). This should be saved as SVN_DIR/hooks/pre-commit.bat:

```
@echo off
::
:: Stops commits that have empty log messages.
::

@echo off

setlocal

rem SVN sends through the path to the repository and transaction id
set REPOS=%1
set TXN=%2

rem check for an empty log message
svnlook log %REPOS% -t %TXN% | findstr . > nul
if %errorlevel% gtr 0 (goto err) else exit 0

:err
echo. 1>&2
echo Your commit has been blocked because you didn't give any log message 1>&2
echo Please write a log message describing the purpose of your changes and 1>&2
echo then try committing again. -- Thank you 1>&2
exit 1
```

In Git and Mercurial, non-empty commit messages are enforced by default without the need for any hooks. If you try and commit something without a commit message you'll be stopped in your tracks:

```
# An empty commit message in Git
$ git commit -m ''
Please enter a commit message with details of the changes made.

# An empty commit message in Mercurial
$ hg commit -m ''
abort: empty commit message
```

OK, so you've seen how to prevent empty commit messages by enabling the pre-commit.tmpl that comes with SVN. I've also shown you how to set up the equivalent hook on Windows using a batch file. Next, we'll look at how to ensure your commit messages conform to a predefined format.

Checking a commit message contains a bug ticket number

You've seen how you can make sure all users enter a commit message. What about making sure that certain information is in the commit message? Suppose you're getting ready to release some major new features on a web application and are now busy fixing bugs on a release branch prior to the site going live.

Each commit to this branch should contain a ticket number for the bug you've just fixed. It should be in the format #1234, and be preceded by the word *fixed* or *fixes*. You can enforce this policy by using the pre-commit hook in SVN :

```python
#!/usr/bin/python
import os, sys, string, re

SVNLOOK = '/usr/bin/svnlook'
MIN_LENGTH = 10
TICKET_NO = '(F|f)ixe(s|d) #\d+'

def precommit(repo, txn):
    log_cmd = '%s log -t "%s" "%s"' % (SVNLOOK, txn, repo)
    log_msg = os.popen(log_cmd, 'r').readline().rstrip('\n')

    if len(log_msg) < MIN_LENGTH:
        sys.stderr.write("Please enter a commit message with details of the changes
made.\n")
        sys.exit(1)
    elif not re.search(TICKET_NO, log_msg):
        sys.stderr.write("Please make sure your commit message includes the ticket number
of↩
 the bug being fixed.\n")
        sys.exit(1)
    else:
        sys.exit(0)

if __name__ == "__main__":
    if len(sys.argv) < 3:
        sys.stderr.write("Usage: %s REPOS TXN\n" % (sys.argv[0]))
    else:
        precommit(sys.argv[1], sys.argv[2])
```

The lines in bold are where you're checking for the bug ticket number. You may also have noticed the bit of code before that that does a similar thing to your first hook; this time you're not only checking for an empty commit message, but also checking that the commit message meets a minimum length.

> **Note** *Instead of using shell scripting, Python was used to implement this hook. I've done this partly to show that you can write hooks in any scripting language (you could even create your own executable file if you really wanted to, as long as it was named accordingly, such as, pre-commit), and partly so that you don't have to reimplement it as a batch file for Windows users. If you are on Windows, though, you will have to install a version of Python, unless you'd prefer to reimplement this yourself as a batch file, of course.*

To do the same checks on the commit message in Git you'd use similar code, but would use the commit-msg hook instead:

```python
#!/usr/bin/python
import os, sys, string, re

MIN_LENGTH = 10
TICKET_NO = '(F|f)ixe(s|d) #\d+'

def commitmsg(path):
    with open(path, 'r') as f:
        log_msg = f.read().rstrip('\n')

    if len(log_msg) < MIN_LENGTH:
        sys.stderr.write("Please enter a commit message with details of the changes made.\n")
        sys.exit(1)
    elif not re.search(TICKET_NO, log_msg):
        sys.stderr.write("Please make sure your commit message includes a ticket number.\n")
        sys.stderr.write("Commit messages should include the phrase:\n")
        sys.stderr.write("\tFixes [ | fixed ] #1234\n")
        sys.stderr.write("Where 1234 is the id of the bug in the bug tracking system.\n")
        sys.exit(1)
    else:
        sys.exit(0)

if __name__ == "__main__":
    if len(sys.argv) < 2:
        sys.stderr.write("Usage: %s PATH\n" % (sys.argv[0]))
    else:
        commitmsg(sys.argv[1])
```

The actual code that checks the commit message is pretty much the same. Where this differs is in how it gets hold of the commit message: with SVN you used svnlook and the revision and transaction parameters, whereas with Git you use the path file holding the commit message and read the message from there.

Since you used Python for SVN and Git, try and implement the same hook in Mercurial using shell commands. Split it out into two actions: `minlength` and `bugid`:

```
[hooks]
pretxncommit.minlength = test `hg tip --template {desc} | wc -c` -ge 10
pretxncommit.bugid = `hg tip --template {desc} | grep -i 'fixe\(s\|d\) #[0-9]\+'` >
/dev/null
```

This example has shown how you can check the text in a commit message to make sure it conforms to a predefined format. We've also looked at writing hooks in something other than shell commands by writing the hook using Python (Ruby, Perl, and other scripting languages should work just as well). In the next example, I'll show how you can use an external command-line tool in a hook, and how you can use the output from an external tool to determine your hook's exit status.

Running JSLint tests before committing changes

JSLint is a tool for checking the quality of JavaScript code. It was built by Douglas Crockford, the author of *JavaScript: The Good Parts* (O'Reilly, 2008). It checks that JavaScript contains the "good parts'" discussed in his book, and warns you if it includes any bad parts.

Using JSLint Utils (http://projects.mikewest.org/jslint_utils/) you can create a hook to verify your JavaScript source code each time someone makes a commit. The code, implemented here for a Git pre-commit hook, will look something like this:

```python
#!/usr/bin/python

import os, sys, string, re
from glob import glob

JSLINT = '/path/to/jslint-utils/scripts/run-jslint.sh'
JSLINT_OK = '^jslint: No problems found in .+\.js$'

def precommit():
        # Current working directory should be the root of the git repo
        os.chdir('js')
        js_files = glob('*.js')
        cwd = os.getcwd()

        for f in js_files:
                abs_file = cwd + '/' + f
                log_cmd = '%s %s' % (JSLINT, abs_file)
                log_msg = os.popen(log_cmd, 'r').readline().rstrip('\n')

                if not re.search(JSLINT_OK, log_msg):
                        sys.stderr.write(log_msg + "\n")
                        sys.exit(1)
                else:
                        continue

        sys.exit(0)

if __name__ == "__main__":
        precommit()
```

You're simply looping through all the JavaScript files and passing each one to the `run-jslint.sh` script. Any output that you receive back from JSLint that doesn't report "no problems" triggers the non-zero exit status.

In this example, an external process is run on the code being committed to check it meets certain criteria, and the output of that process is shown to decide the exit status of the hook. Our final example will look at enabling e-mail notifications for commits in Mercurial.

Sending e-mail notifications of commits

Finally, let's have a look at two ways you can get Mercurial to send e-mail notifications of commits.

The quickest way to get this set up is by adding the following one-liner to your hooks section in your `.hgrc` file:

```
[hooks]
commit = SUBJECT=$(hg log -r $HG_NODE --template '{desc|firstline}') hg log -vpr $HG_NODE | \
        mail -s "commit: $SUBJECT" hgcommit@example.com
```

Here you're running some hg commands to extract some info about the commit, setting the environment variable `SUBJECT` using this info, then piping this to the mail command

While it's nice to enable this in one line of code, you might find that you need more control over the e-mail, and need to include more information about what was changed. A better option might be to use the Notify extension that comes with Mercurial. You can configure it in your `.hg/hgrc` file, and set it to send out one e-mail per changeset, or one e-mail per group of changesets (all those from a single pull or push). Other configuration options follow.

from

Who the e-mail is sent from; for example, youremail@example.com.

host

The host of the smtp server; for example, mail.example.com.

baseurl

The base URL of the repository when accessed via the Web.

test

Whether e-mails actually get sent. By default, this is false and data gets output to stdin. This is really useful for debugging and testing everything is configured to your liking before you start sending out real e-mails.

config

This is the path to the config file containing subscription info. It can be maintained separate from the main repository, if you wish. One benefit of doing this is that users can update subscription info and push changes.

strip

This is the number of path separators to strip from the repository path. For example, if your repositories are located in /home/hg/code, and you're working on the repository in /home/hg/code/web/feeds, setting strip = 4 will strip /home/hg/code from the front of the path—that is, everything up to and including the fourth path separator—and matching subscribers against web/feeds.

template

The template used to send out the e-mail.

maxdiff

The default is 300 lines, but you can set this to more or less as you see fit. If a diff exceeds maxdiff, the excess number of lines are truncated. Setting maxdiff to zero will omit diff info from the e-mail.

sources

This lets you specify which sources of changesets will trigger notification e-mails. For example, you might want to only send e-mails when receiving changesets from remote users. Possible values are

- *serve*: Changesets sent to / from remote repo via http or ssh

- *pull*: Changesets sent via pull from one repo to another

- *push*: Changesets sent via push from one repo to another

- *bundle*: Changesets sent to / from a bundle

You can specify multiple values for sources, so it's not uncommon to set sources = serve pull push bundle.

Here's how all this might look when added to your .hg/hgrc:

```
[extensions]
hgext.notify =
[hooks]
changegroup.notify = python:hgext.notify.hook

[email]
from = mail@example.com

[smtp]
host = localhost

[web]
baseurl = http://hg.example.com/

[notify]
sources = serve push pull bundle
test = True # change to False to really send emails
config = /path/to/subscriptions.conf
```

```
template = \ndetails:    {baseurl}{webroot}/rev/{node|short}\nbranches:
{branches}\nchangeset: {rev}:{node|short}\nuser: {author}\ndate:
{date|date}\ndescription:\n{desc}\n
maxdiff = 300
strip = 5
```

Now, if you pull some changes in from another repository, you should see what would be included in your e-mail notification if test = False:

```
ianoxley@ubuntu:$ hg pull ../foobar
pulling from ../foobar
searching for changes
adding changesets
adding manifests
adding file changes
added 1 changesets with 1 changes to 1 files
Content-Type: text/plain; charset="us-ascii"
MIME-Version: 1.0
Content-Transfer-Encoding: 7bit
Date: Wed, 04 Jan 2012 00:18:41 +0000
Subject: hgdemo: Created package.json file for the notify library
From: mail@example.com
X-Hg-Notification: changeset d4e201488890
Message-Id: <hg.d4e201488890.1325636321.-394310582@ubuntu>
To: hgusers@example.com

details:    http://hg.example.com/hgdemo/rev/d4e201488890
branches:
changeset: 17:d4e201488890
user: Ian Oxley <ian@example.com>
date: Wed Jan 04 00:18:07 2012 +0000
description:
Created package.json file for the notify library

diffstat:

 package.json |  8 ++++++++
 1 files changed, 8 insertions(+), 0 deletions(-)

diffs (12 lines):

diff -r 3c85b93d8c9a -r d4e201488890 package.json
--- /dev/null    Thu Jan 01 00:00:00 1970 +0000
+++ b/package.json       Wed Jan 04 00:18:07 2012 +0000
@@ -0,0 +1,8 @@
+{
+    "name": "notify"
+  , "description": "User notification library"
+  , "version": "1.0"
+  , "homepage": "http://hg.example.com/notify"
+  , "main": "./notify.js"
+  , "keywords": ["notify"]
+}
(run 'hg update' to get a working copy)
```

When you're happy with how you've got `notify` configured, just set `test` = `False` to start sending out real e-mails. More information on setting up and configuring the notify extension can be found on the Mercurial wiki (`http://mercurial.selenic.com/wiki/NotifyExtension`).

So that was two ways to configure Mercurial to send out e-mail notifications when a repository is updated. The first method was a terse one-liner to send out a short summary. The second method used Mercurial's notify extension to send out detailed information on exactly what was changed.

Summary

In this chapter you learned what hooks are, and which hooks are available in SVN, Git, and Mercurial. You also saw how to enable the default hooks that come with SVN and Git repositories, and how to enable hooks in Mercurial by adding them to your `.hgrc` file. Finally, I showed you some hooks in action with some example scripts that helped to reject commits with empty commit messages, enforce bug ticket numbers in commit messages, verify your JavaScript code with JSLint, and send out commit notification e-mails.

Chapter 14

Upgrading from CVS
and Converting Repositories

Although I haven't touched on CVS very much in this book, it's worth noting that some people do in fact still use it. In a nutshell, SVN is the reworked version of CVS—they're both centralized systems—but SVN just does it way better. Although the most common upgrade path to use would be to go from CVS to SVN, I'll also cover going to Git, and Mercurial, too.

You may be wondering why you would actually want to migrate your repository to another system when you could potentially just start all over again using a new versioning system and disregarding your history. Of course, this applies to some cases where the history of the code doesn't necessarily matter, but for the majority of cases, the repository history is just too important to lose. As a system, CVS is outdated compared to the systems of today, and there are numerous advantages to migrating your repository to a newer system. These span from ease of use and management to getting more features and more stability, as well as better branching support, and the ability to version symbolic links. These shortcomings may push some people to want to migrate to a newer system without losing their precious history, and that's why this chapter is here.

Although only covering the things I've just mentioned would be more than enough to make all of you CVS users out there happy, it leaves a hole whereby some users of SVN, Git, or even Mercurial fancy a change to a different versioning system, so I'll cover that as well. I'll start, of course, with CVS, showing the different upgrade paths available and how to achieve them, and then I'll go on to the usual: SVN, Mercurial, and Git. So let's start with porting CVS to SVN.

CVS

To perform the majority of the conversions from CVS, you'll need to install an additional package called cvs2svn. This package was created by Tigris (the creators of SVN) to make migration from CVS to SVN easier. Although the name suggests you can covert to SVN, that's not the case. It has Git support built in, and it's used as a base for the Mercurial conversion. Installing it, however, causes a lot of problems. Although it will run on both Windows and Mac, getting the configurations correct to run it without a problem is huge, mainly down to dependencies on gbdm support. There is a Homebrew package for cvs2svn, but it won't install due to missing gbdm support.

It does, however, install like a dream on Ubuntu, which is where I'll be taking you through the process. Although this isn't ideal for some, knowing the package has installed correctly is a definite bonus. To get cvs2svn installed, just head into a Terminal window and enter `sudo apt-get install cvs2svn`, which will as expected ask you for your admin password, and then to confirm whether or not you're OK with it taking up the storage space it requires. When the process is complete, you should be able to enter cvs2svn into Terminal and, upon pressing enter, you'll see all the possible options available for it, which means everything has installed successfully.

Changing to SVN

With cvs2svn installed, the process of converting a CVS repository to SVN is rather painless, but you need to make sure of a couple of things first. You must have access to the server version of the CVS repository, which contains the CVSROOT folder, otherwise the converter will just complain that the folder doesn't exist. You can copy the file system directly from the server—you don't need to set up any local versions of CVSROOT or anything like that. All the converter cares about is that the file system is correct and it has the CVSROOT folder. Now, provided you have all that, it's time to get started. First of all, you need a blank SVN repository to house the converted code, which has to be a local one.

```
svnadmin create --fs-type fsfs my-svn-repository
```

Of course, just change the name of the repository to whatever you'd like it to be, and run the command. With the repository created, you're ready for the actual conversion, which is done by running the following command:

```
cvs2svn --existing-svnrepos -s my-svn-repository/ cvs-repository
```

This command will perform the conversion and when it's completed you'll have an SVN repository that's ready to check out and then be used as normal. This is great if you're performing the conversion on your server, because it can then be used like any other repository. But what if you want to use this repository somewhere else? You can dump the SVN repository, ready for it to be imported to another location, or even to a hosted solution such as Beanstalk or Springloops. Running the following command will dump the SVN into a file that can be uploaded or used as needed:

```
svnadmin dump my-svn-repository > file.dump
```

This file can now be used as needed, but if you do want to reimport the file into another SVN repository you have direct access to, ensure the dump file is on the same server, then run this command to import the file:

```
svnadmin load svn-repository < file.dump --force-uuid
```

The `--force-uuid` flag helps ensure the future safety of the repository by making sure there are no conflicts with users. Now that the repository has been dumped and potentially reused, you have freedom from your CVS repository, and you're free to use SVN to your heart's content. You can, of course, repeat the steps as needed to achieve the conversion of multiple repositories, but for now, let's look at going from CVS to Mercurial.

Turning CVS into Mercurial

Unlike the SVN conversion of CVS, the Mercurial conversion requires your CVS repository to be checked out, and you can still access the remote version of the repository. So before attempting the conversion, be sure to have your CVS repository checked out and the actual repository accessible by your machine. If it cannot connect to the repository, the conversion will fail. Assuming all of this is in order, to start the conversion process, you need to make sure the Mercurial extension you're going to use is enabled. To do so, head into Terminal, then into your home directory, and open the `.hgrc` file in either nano or vi, whichever floats your boat. Since nano is the easier command, let's go with that.

```
nano .hgrc
```

With the editor open, ensure the following lines are present in the file. If you already have the [extensions] option present in the file just add `hgext.convert=` to the line underneath. If you don't have either, then just copy the following into the file:

```
[extensions]
hgext.convert=
```

To exit the nano editor, just hit Ctrl+X to exit then, when prompted to save changes, hit Y, then enter, and the changes will be written to the file. With the extension enabled, you now need to navigate to the location of the CVS repository, just to make the command easier to execute. Once there, use the following command to start the process off:

```
hg convert path-to-cvs-repo new-hg-repo
```

Running this command will start the whole process, and you will see the following message while the repository is scanned:

```
initializing destination new-hg-repo repository
scanning source...
```

You'll see this message for longer if it's a bigger repository, so if it takes a while it's not that it's not running, it's just taking a while. When the repository has finished converting, you'll have a repository that's ready to be used as you'd like, although when you first head inside, it'll seem empty. To remedy this, be sure to perform an `hg checkout`, which will checkout the master branch, and therefore populate the repository with the files, nice and easy.

CVS to Git

The conversion from CVS to Git, sadly, isn't as easy as the other two; however, in reality it isn't too bad. When the conversion completes, you'll be left with a dump file, which can then be imported into a Git repository as needed. The conversion tool you want to use is included in cvs2svn (I know, ironic, right?), so if you don't have that installed, a `sudo apt-get install cvs2svn` will fix that. With the package installed, you now need to dive into its documentation and copy a file mentioned there, as you cannot perform the conversion without it. The easiest way to get the file in an easy-to-edit location is to copy it to said location, using the following commands:

```
cd /usr/share/doc/cvs2svn/examples
sudo cp cvs2git-example.options.gz ~/
```

The sudo is needed here to allow the copy to happen; otherwise, you'll just get a permission denied error. Using this command will copy the file to your home directory, where it's possible for you to unzip it, and then modify it for your needs. To unzip the file, use the following command, which is inside the home directory:

```
gunzip cvs2git-example.options.gz
```

The file is now unarchived and it means you can go ahead and edit it, which you should do now in your favorite editor, which doesn't have to be a Terminal editor; you can just use plain old gedit, which you can open by double-clicking the file. With it open, the most important thing to do is map the users from the CVS repository to the Git format. In the file this code block looks like this:

```
author_transforms={
    'jrandom' : ('J. Random', 'jrandom@example.com'),
    'mhagger' : ('Michael Haggerty', 'mhagger@alum.mit.edu'),
    'brane' : (u'Branko Čibej', 'brane@xbc.nu'),
    'ringstrom' : ('Tobias Ringström', 'tobias@ringstrom.mine.nu'),
    'dionisos' : (u'Erik Hülsmann', 'e.huelsmann@gmx.net'),

    # This one will be used for commits for which CVS doesn't record
    # the original author, as explained above.
    'cvs2svn' : ('cvs2svn', 'admin@example.com'),
    }
```

Add any users from the CVS repo in here, to ensure they're mapped correctly. Otherwise, the default username will be used, which is fine, but may result in some commit data being lost. The u before some entries signifies the entry needs to be encoded in Unicode format, rather than the default utf-8. You can change the fallback user by altering the following line:

```
ctx.username = 'cvs2svn'
```

As well as mapping the users, you also need to map the location of the CVS repository on your system. Be sure to use the full path here; the script will fail if you use anything other than the full path. If you choose the root of the repository then the CVSROOT folder will also be included and not ignored, so you may wish to make the path more relevant to specific modules. In my case, my project path is as follows:

```
run_options.set_project(
    # The filesystem path to the part of the CVS repository (*not* a
```

```
# CVS working copy) that should be converted.  This may be a
# subdirectory (i.e., a module) within a larger CVS repository.
r'/home/chris/Desktop/cvs/MyProjectsAwesomeName,
```

Another option that needs to be changed within the file is the location where the dump file will be placed after the process has completed. In my case, that is the following (however, you can adapt it for your needs):

```
ctx.output_option = GitOutputOption(
    # The file in which to write the git-fast-import stream that
    # contains the changesets and branch/tag information:
    '/home/chris/git-dump.dat',
```

There's one last option that needs to be changed within the file, and that's the location of the blob file, which will contain all the revision information when the repository is imported. In my file, I've set the location to the home directory, same as the others, and it looks like so:

```
    # The file in which to write the git-fast-import stream that
    # contains the file revision contents:
    GitRevisionRecorder('/home/chris/git-blob.dat'),
)
```

With the file altered and in place, you're ready to perform the conversion. If there are any errors in the file, the process will fail and the error message will be shown. In most cases, this'll be due to a path being incorrect or in the wrong case. Once you correct the problem, just run the command again and it should all be fine. The command in question is as follows:

```
cvs2git --options cvs2git-example.options
```

If you happen to have changed the name of the .options file, then amend the command as needed, but if everything has worked correctly, you should have a file that's ready to import into a Git repository, so let's do that now.

```
mkdir new-get-repo
cd new-get-repo
git init
cat ../git-blob.dat ../git-dump.dat | git fast-import
```

You will now have a Git clone of your CVS repository with all of the history intact. You may want to open up a GUI editor of some kind to clean up any potential loose ends caused from the conversion, such as some tags and branches, but for the most part, the conversion should work as needed.

CVS migration summary

If you are one of the people who wanted to get away from the limitations of CVS and get yourself onto a better and more modern system, you're now in business. You'll get all the perks of the shiny new versioning system you always wanted, and get to keep all of your precious history; it's wins all around. For those of you are a little hesitant about going through the conversion because you'll need to learn a new system or you might lose something, don't worry. Your original repository is safe during the conversion, so don't let that trouble you. Plus, if you want to try out one of the systems before making the jump, you can just install it and have a go at versioning some code the modern way. Now, though, it's time to cater for those of you who fancy migrating between our chosen systems, so let's dive right in with migrating from SVN.

SVN

The time may come when you want to convert an existing SVN project to a distributed versioning system, either Mercurial or Git. We'll have a look at Mercurial first, and go through the processes of converting it from SVN repository to a functioning Mercurial one.

SVN to Mercurial

There are a multitude of different methods you can use to convert SVN repositories, including some even supplied by Mercurial, but they aren't very good. We're going down the hgsvn route, which can be installed as follows:

```
Sudo apt-get install hgsvn
```

This should be everything you need to run hgsvn; however, if you get the following error when trying to use it, there is an additional package you need to install:

```
hgimportsvn http://url.to.repo/repo
Traceback (most recent call last):
  File "/usr/bin/hgimportsvn", line 5, in
    from pkg_resources import load_entry_point
ImportError: No module named pkg_resources
If you get the above, run the following, and the error should no longer happen.
Sudo apt-get install python-setuptools
```

You should no longer get the previously mentioned error. With that out of the way, let's actually get to converting the repository, which is done like so:

```
hgimportsvn http://url.to.repo/repo folder-name
```

This will do the initial setup of the repository, and start the process of everything. You can also use a local version of a repository, if you happen to already have it checked out. Either way, specifying a folder name is optional, and if no option is added then the name of the repository will be taken. After this process is complete, there is another step that needs to be taken, which will actually get all of the revisions and map them to Mercurial commits. Change into the newly imported repository, then run the following command:

```
hgpullsvn
```

All of the history will be pulled in and converted to commits, just as we wanted. If for some reason the process gets interrupted, just run hgpullsvn again and it'll resume where it left off. Once the process is complete, you'll have a repository that is half SVN and half Mercurial. By that, I mean there are both .hg and .svn files, then just a lot of .hgignore files to tell the repository to ignore said .svn files. You can leave the repository in this state, or clean it up a bit, and since we're going for full conversion, you should do that. The following will remove all the .svn files, and the .hgignore files, allowing you to make a fresh start. Once inside the repository directory, use the following commands:

```
find . -name .svn | xargs rm -fr
find . -name .hgignore | xargs rm -fr
```

Now this repository is fully Mercurial and can be used just like a regular repository. Depending on how your repository was set up, you may want to remove the branches and tags directories, as they aren't needed, and move the trunk directory.

```
hg mv trunk/* .
rm -r tags
rm -r branches
```

Now your repository is ready to use, and in a format that it would have been, had used Mercurial in the first place. It could be worth keeping a copy of the old repository, just in case anything goes wrong, but in most cases you'll be fine.

SVN to Git

If you're up for joining the Git crowd from SVN, there are a number of ways to do it, and I'll show you an easy way to do that right now. To achieve this, you'll need an SVN repository, and to install the git-svn package, which can be done using the following command:

```
sudo apt-get install git-svn
```

With that installed, you need to run a few commands, then everything will be set. First of all, you need to map all of the users correctly, which can be done by using the following command to output a file of all the users used in the repository.

```
svn log -q | awk -F '|' '/^r/ {sub("^ ", "", $2); sub(" $", "", $2); print $2" = "$2
<"$2">"}' | sort -u > users.txt
```

If you open that file, you'll see something like the following:

```
chris = chris <chris>
```

You'll need to change any users into the following format:

```
chris = Chris Kemper <hey@chrisdkemper.co.uk>
```

Do the above for all the users, and you'll have a file that contains all the user information needed for the Git conversion. The next stage is to use the git-svn package to perform a clone of the SVN repository. Run the following command to achieve this, but be sure that the users.txt file from the previous step is in the same directory you're running the command in (such as the home folder) or it'll fail. It'll also fail if any users are missing from the users.txt file; however, you can always amend the file and run the command again; it'll resume where it left off.

```
git svn clone [SVN URL] --no-metadata -A users.txt --stdlayout ~/temp
```

This will perform the clone of the repository, map all of the commits to the new user format, and place the code in the ~/temp directory. The next step will be to convert any SVN ignore files to the Git equivalent, which is done like so:

```
cd ~/temp
git svn show-ignore > .gitignore
```

```
git add .gitignore
git commit -m 'Convert svn:ignore properties to .gitignore.'
```

With that done and committed, you'll need to create a bare, blank repository which will soon house the repository that currently lives within the ~/temp directory. The following commands will create a repository in the home directory called bare.git, and it'll also rename the default branch from master to trunk, which will make for a smoother transition.

```
git init --bare ~/bare.git
cd ~/bare.git
git symbolic-ref HEAD refs/heads/trunk
```

Next up, you need to push the repository from ~/temp into the newly created bare repository, which is done like so:

```
cd ~/temp
git remote add bare ~/bare.git
git config remote.bare.push 'refs/remotes/*:refs/heads/*'
git push bare
```

At that stage, you no longer need the ~/temp directory, so feel free to delete it, unless you want to keep ahold of the files for old time's sake. You need to rename the default branch from trunk back to master, so do that now.

```
cd ~/bare.git
git branch -m trunk master
```

Now you're nearing the final stages, so you need to do some cleaning. At the moment, the branches and tags aren't actual tags and branches yet, which the following code snippet will sort out, but looping through them all and creating actual branches and tags, as needed.

```
cd ~/bare.git
git for-each-ref --format='%(refname)' refs/heads/tags |
cut -d / -f 4 |
while read ref
do
  git tag "$ref" "refs/heads/tags/$ref";
  git branch -D "tags/$ref";
done
```

That is the repository converted and ready to go! Being a bare repository, it's possible to push it to a remote service such as GitHub, BitBucket, or even your own server, whatever you'd like to do. If you'd rather just keep it on your system, just clone it and you can use it just like any other Git repository.

Mercurial to Git

There is a great tool to accomplish a conversion of Mercurial to Git and it's called fast-export. To make use of the tool, you first need to grab a copy of it, so head over to http://repo.or.cz/w/fast-export.git/ and download the snapshot of the most recent version of the code, then download it to your local machine, ideally in a directory close to the Mercurial repository you'd like to convert.

With the code downloaded, make sure it's unarchived and accessible from the Terminal; you'll need to access it soon enough. The next stage is to create the Git repository that will house the converted Mercurial code, and then change into it, which can be done by altering the following for the repository name of your choosing.

```
mkdir new-git-repo
cd new-git-repo
git init
```

Now comes all of the magic, which happens by running the following command, slightly modified for your needs, of course. Just make sure you're inside the new Git repository when running the command.

```
../fast-export/hg-fast-export.sh -r ../mercurial-repository
```

The `fast-export` folder will, of course, change depending on what yours happens to be called, and also depending on where it's located on your system. When you run this command, you'll see all the changesets in the Mercurial repository fill the Terminal as they're converted to Git. When the process is finished, if you were to do an `ls -la` you would see just a `.git` folder in the repository, and nothing more. To actually see the files, you'll need to perform a checkout, like so:

```
git checkout
```

This will bring in all of the changed files, so you can continue on using the repository with all of the history intact, nice and easy!

Git to Mercurial

The best way to achieve a conversion from Git to Mercurial is to use Mercurial's own `hg convert` extension, which is baked right in; you just need to enable it, which is really easy to do. First, head into your home folder within Terminal, and open up the `.hgrc` file in your favorite Terminal editor, either `vi` or `nano`. Given that `nano` is easier to use, we'll go with that here, so enter the following commands in Terminal:

```
nano .hgrc
```

With the editor open, paste in the following code, or if you happen to already have the [extensions] option in the file, just add `hgext.convert=` below. If don't have any of this, just copy the following into the file.

```
[extensions]
hgext.convert=
```

When you've finished making your changes, hit Ctrl+X to exit. You'll then be asked whether or not you'd like to save the changes you made to the file. Just type Y then hit enter and the changes will be committed. Now the extension is enabled, it's time to give it a try. Change into the directory that houses the Git directory you'd like to convert, then use the following command, altered for your needs, of course:

```
hg convert git-repository new-hg-repository
```

When you hit enter, you'll see the following message for a length of time, depending on how big the repository is:

```
initializing destination new-hg-repository repository
scanning source...
```

If you're dealing with a rather large repository, you'll see this message for a while. It, sadly, isn't the fastest of processes. Once the process actually begins, you'll see all of the commits being transferred in reverse order— you know you're getting closer when the numbers get smaller—until, finally, it'll be complete. You'll need to perform an hg checkout to see the resulting files and, then, you're converted and ready to rock and roll.

Mercurial or Git to SVN

There won't be any walkthroughs to cover this scenario, as it's rather counterproductive. Although there might be a case where it's needed, going from a distributed system to a centralized one isn't advised. If you're working with Git or Mercurial, it's a much better idea to keep at it and improve your knowledge than to go back to what is in some respects a lesser system.

Summary

We've blasted out of the CVS stone age into the better-equipped and more awesome world of SVN, Mercurial, and Git. Now you can enjoy the benefits of moving into the modern age, whether that's in the form of the distributed version control goodness that is Git or Mercurial, or what is in theory CVS 2.0 with SVN.

This chapter has also taken you through the process of moving from a centralized system to a distributed one—for those of you who'd like to take the plunge from SVN to Mercurial or Git—and even shown you how you can switch teams in the distributed world from Git to Mercurial (or the other way around). With this knowledge, you can go through the world knowing that if you see a fellow developer still working with CVS, you have the skills and the power to bring them into the light and make their life better, which is always a good thing!

Appendix

Terminal Commands

This appendix will run through some of the basic and more frequently used commands you'll be dealing with while working in the Terminal for SVN, Mercurial, and Git. If you've forgotten a command or you need to refresh yourself on things, just have a look through to find the command you need. If it's not there, use the respective help commands, which are detailed below.

SVN

There are a number of commands you'll use more often than others while going about your day-to-day version control business using SVN. These can be seen below in a quick-reference format, just in case you forget about them.

Checking out a repository

To perform a checkout of a remote repository, just use the following command:

```
$ svn checkout http://path-to-repository folder-name
```

If the folder name isn't specified in the repository, then the repository will be checked into a folder with the same name as the repository itself.

Alternative: co

Adding files

You can easily add single or multiple files using `svn add`, like so:

```
$ svn add file folder file2 file 3
```

You can also use a wild card for selecting multiple files with the same name or file type, such as:

```
$ svn add *png
```

Committing files

When you use the `svn commit` command without any specific flags, it'll commit all of the changes to the repository and then launch your specified editor to add a commit message. You can, however, specify files to commit and a message in the command, like this:

```
$ svn commit file folder/file2 folder2 -m "Relevant commit message"
```

Alternative: `ci`

Log

Using this command allows you to see information about previous commits either within the repository in general, or specific to a file. You can use the command on a basic level, as with the following, to show a log of all the commits in the repository.

```
$ svn log
```

You can also limit the amount of items shown by using `--limit` followed by the desired number, get more information by using `--verbose` (-v), or less information by using `--quiet` (-q). These can also be used in conjunction with each other and one particular file or folder, like so:

```
$ svn log --limit 5 -v
```

Updating

To update your repository with the latest changes from the server, use the following:

```
$ svn update
```

You can also update to a specific revision of a particular file by simply specifying the file after the command. You can also update a particular file to a certain revision by using the `--revision` (-r) flag, like so:

```
$ svn update -r 6 file
```

Alternative: up

Reverting

You can revert back to the BASE version of a file (thereby getting rid of all local changes you've made that haven't been committed) really easily by using the svn revert command. You'll need to specify a file, but it's just as easy as

```
$ svn revert file
```

You can also revert any changes within a folder, but using the --recursive (-R) flag, like so:

```
$ svn revert folder -R
```

Deleting

There will be a time when you need to remove files from future revisions, which is easily achieved with the svn remove command. This will prepare the file to be deleted, but it won't actually delete it until an svn commit is done. You can delete it there and then by adding the --force flag to the command. If you have a change of heart, and would rather not delete the file and have yet to commit it, just perform an svn revert on it and it'll be restored to its original state. To perform the delete action, use this command:

```
$ svn remove file
```

Alternatives: del, remove, rm

Cleanup

To perform a cleanup on your local directory after a commit or update got interrupted, run svn cleanup like so:

```
$ svn cleanup
```

Status

You can get the status of all of the files and folders within a repository by using the svn status command. You can also include remote changes and new files by adding --show-updates (-u) to the command, like so:

```
$ svn status -u
```

Alternatives: stat, st

Performing a diff

You may wish to perform a diff between two versions of a file using SVN. This is easily achieved by getting the revision numbers you'd like to compare against (potentially with svn log) and using the following:

```
$ svn diff -r 1:2 file
```

In place of revision numbers, you can also use: HEAD, BASE, COMMITTED, or PREV depending on your needs.

Branching

Creating a branch in SVN is essentially copying the current version of trunk into the branches directory with an alternative name. To perform the branch, `svn copy` needs to be utilized, like so:

```
$ svn copy -m "Creating foobar branch…" \
                    http://path/to/repository/trunk \
                    http://path/to/repository /branches/foobar
```

Switch to a different branch

If you're working with branches, you'll need to switch your checked out repository to the branch, so you can add changes and so on. To achieve this, the `svn switch` command is used in the following fashion:

```
$ svn switch url-to-branch
```

Just replace the URL for the branch to switch to it, or the URL of the trunk if you're moving back from a branch to trunk.

Merging

If you want to merge a branch back into the repository, you can do so rather easily. Before doing so, you need to find the revision where the branch was created, which can be achieved using `svn log` and the `--stop-on-copy` flag, like so:

```
$ svn log --stop-on-copy http://path/to/svn/repository/branches/branch
```

The last revision listed will be the one you need, as the merge itself will merge the changes in from the branch at the revision where it was created, right up to the most current version. This can be done by using the following, where the branch was created on revision 10:

```
$ svn merge -r 10:HEAD --dry-run http://path/to/svn/repository/branches/branch
```

You can also use the `--dry-run` flag on the command to test the output of the command without actually making any changes to the repository.

Resolving conflicts

When you happen to come across a conflict, you have a number of options when for solving it. The first option is simply setting the file to resolved, assuming you have manually fixed the conflict, which is done like so:

```
$ svn resolved
```

The other option is to resolve the conflicted file using `svn resolve` and use one of the various files created by SVN when the file became conflicted to do so. The options available to you are base, working, mine-full, and theirs-full, which are used in the following way:

```
$ svn resolve --accept option file
```

Moving or renaming files

The command used either to move or rename a file in SVN is actually the same. In essence, renaming a file is simply moving it without changing the location, just the name. Below is an example of this:

```
$ svn move oldname.txt newname.txt
```

Alternatives: mv, rename, ren

Blame

If you need to get a line-by-line breakdown of a file to find out who produced each line and when, svn blame is the command you need. To use it, just use the following, and replace the file with your desired file. (You can also add --verbose (-v) to the command for extra information.)

```
$ svn blame file -v
```

Help

If you're stuck with a command, or if you want to see all of the available commands, just use the help command in SVN, like so:

```
$ svn help
```

This will list all of the commands in SVN, but you can get more help on a specific command by using

```
$ svn help command
```

Mercurial

Just in case you're working away in Terminal and you happen to forget a Mercurial command, these are some of the most frequently used commands, so you can have a quick glance and get on with your Terminal awesomeness.

Creating a repository

When you need to create a repository on your local machine, just use this command:

```
$ hg init
```

This created a repository inside of the folder you're currently inside, so just create the folder outside of Terminal (or in Terminal using mkdir folder-name), cd into it and use the command. Easy.

Status

While making changes to the files in your repository, it's always best to keep checking the status of the repository, which can be done like so:

```
$ hg status
```

Alternative: `st`

Checking out/updating

When you pull in new changes from a remote source, you need to update your local version of the code with the new changes. To do this, you can simply use the following command:

```
$ hg update
```

If you need to switch branches, do so in the same way, using the above command and then the branch name, like so:

```
$ hg update -c branch-name
```

The –c in the above disregards any changes you've made locally, so be sure everything is committed before you use it.

Alternatives: `up`, `checkout`, `co`

Pushing changes

If you're working with a remote repository, you'll need to push changes to it quite often. To do so, just use this command:

```
$ hg push
```

You can also specify a location manually, just in case you have a reason for doing this, by adding it on like so:

```
$ hg push path-to-repository
```

Pulling changes

As with pushing, if you're working with a remote repository, you'll need to get the changes from it quite often, which is easily achieved by using

```
$ hg pull
```

You can also perform an update at the same time by adding the –u flag, like so:

```
$ hg pull -u
```

Committing changes

When you've made changes, whether by adding files or altering them, you'll need to commit those changes to the repository, which you can do really easily by using

```
$ hg commit
```

It's also possible for you to specify a commit message by adding –m to the command and adding your message in quotes, just like this:

```
$ hg commit -m "Useful commit message here"
```

Alternative: `ci`

Adding files

When you have new files in your repository, you'll need to add them before changes you make to them will be tracked. This can be done using `hg add`, which when used by itself will add all untracked files to the repository. If you'd rather only add one or two files, they can be specified after the command to ensure only those files are added, like so:

```
$ hg add file file2 folder
```

Removing files

There will be a time when you have to remove files that you no longer use and you'd like to stop them being tracked any further. To remove the file, just use `hg remove file`, which will mark that file to be deleted on the next commit. If you don't want to wait till the commit to remove the file, you can always use the `--force` flag to delete the file there and then.

Alternative: `rm`

Adding and removing

There is a command that'll allow you to save time by performing two actions in one. If you happen to have files you need to delete and ones you need to add, then `hg addremove` may be just what you're looking for. This command will delete any missing files and add any new ones, so if you've deleted the file in browser, this will pick it up, and mark it to be deleted.

Blame

The time will come for whatever reason when you want to examine a file line by line to see who made the changes and why they happened. This is where `hg blame` comes in; it'll show the author, the date the revision was created, and the revision ID. To use the command, just use `hg blame file` and the output will be shown in the Terminal.

Alternative: `annotate`

Resolving

After you've had a conflict, you'll need to resolve the file before it can be committed, which is why there is a command to do that. The command in question is `hg resolve`, which does what it says, really. Once the file is ready to be resolved, just use the command, like so:

```
$ hg resolve -m file
```

It's also possible to mark all unresolved files as resolved by removing the file reference. This isn't always adviseable, however, as you could resolve a file you aren't meant to yet.

Moving or renaming files

When renaming a file, Mercurial treats it like you're copying the file to the same location, only with a different name. The same goes for when you're changing the location of the file; Mercurial treats it like you're copying the file to its new location, then deleting the old one. Either way, the command is used like so:

```
$ hg rename original-file new-file-location
```

Alternatives: move, mv

Reverting changes

If you've been working on a file, but then decide you'd rather go back to the version before you started making changes, then hg revert is for you. If you want to just revert the file to the last revision, then you can use the command with no arguments, like so:

```
$ hg revert file
```

It is also possible to revert back to a specific revision by adding the -r flag to the command, like this:

```
$ hg revert file -r 10
```

In this example, 10 is the specified revision. Just change that to your specified revision.

Cloning repositories

If you'd like to have a repository as a parent that you push changes to (such as a remote one), before that's possible you need to clone the original repository using this command:

```
$ hg clone
```

You can also add --noupdate, which will cause the clone to only bring the repository and not the working files, which is what you'll need if you want to clone this repository in the future.

Merge

When you're working with a remote repository, there may come a time when you cannot perform a clean update, possibly because of merge conflicts or big differences between the remote and local changes. On a basic level, you can use hg merge, which will attempt to resolve the conflict itself. If you happen to make a mistake for whatever reason, then the following update command can be used to check out a clean copy of the changes so you can try again:

```
$ hg update --clean .
```

The dot in the above needs to be included, so don't leave it out.

Help

If you get stuck with a particular command and want a bit more information about it, that's when hg help can be really useful. Without any arguments, this command will output all of the available Mercurial commands you can use, and a brief explanation of what they do. You can, however, specify a particular command after hg help to see more detailed information about it, such as the flags and arguments it accepts, like so:

```
$ hg help update
```

In this example, I've used the update command; just replace that with your specified command and you'll have help in no time.

Branching

Creating branches is really easy. Just use hg branch branch-name and you'll be ready to go with the newly created branch. When the branch is created, you are automatically switched to it, so any commits you make now will be to the new branch. If you don't make any commits, though, and switch to another branch, it'll be removed, so bear that in mind. You can switch back to the default branch by using hg checkout default to make the switch. If you use the hg branch command without any arguments, it'll show you the current branch you're on, just in case you were unsure.

You can also see a full list of the branches you have in your repository by using hg branches -a, which will list them for you to have as a reference.

Git

While working in Terminal from time to time you may forget a specific command or how to use one. This little guide is here to refresh your memory and give you more of those "Oh yeah!" moments while you're working.

Adding files

The git add command has a few uses within Git, since it both adds untracked files and stages changed files to be committed. Without any arguments, the command won't be of any use, and you'll need to combine it with a dot to add all untracked files or to stage all changed files to be committed. You can also specify individual files by using git add file if you'd rather not add everything in one go.

Creating a repository

If you want to create a new repository, just use the git init command within the folder you would like to contain the repository and you will then be able to commit changes into it, just like that.

Cloning a repository

If you want to work from a remote location, or you're setting up a workflow of some description, you may have a parent or remote repository you'll need to clone so that in future you can push changes to it. To clone a repository, just use `git clone repository-location folder-name` which will clone the repository into the specified folder name. This is entirely optional, however, and if the folder name is omitted, then the folder will take the name of the repository instead. There are a lot of other things this command can do, so if you're in need of a little help, `git help clone` is a great resource.

Checking out branches

The `git checkout` command is mainly used for switching between branches, where you would use `git checkout branch` to switch between your branches really easily.

Alternative: co

Branching

Creating branches in Git is really easy, since all you need to do is `git branch branch-name` and the branch is created. It's also possible to see a list of all the branches in your repository by using `git branch -a` to list all of them. This, however, doesn't switch you to the branch, but there is a version of `git checkout` which allows you to do this in one step, in the following form:

```
$ git checkout -b branch-name
```

This creates a new branch and switches to it in one go, which can save you some time. To delete a branch, you can also use `git branch -d branch-name`, which will delete it and its changes.

Help

As with the other systems, sometimes you forget the arguments for certain commands, or even the commands themselves. You can use `git help` to refresh your memory, and even use `git help command` to get more information on a specific command.

Committing changes

After you've made changes to files and staged them with `git add`, it's time to commit them to the repository. You can either run this on a per-file basis, by using `git commit file file -m "useful commit message"` or all at once, by using `git commit . -m "useful commit message"`, which will commit all staged files to the repository. If you've made a mistake and you want to unstage some changes, this can be done using `git reset HEAD file` which will take it back to before it was staged.

Log

You can see the commit information for your repository using the `git log` command, which shows the information on your previous commits. You can also perform a log on a specific file to see all the commits containing that file with `git log file`, and even limit the number of results shown by using the –n flag, like so:

```
$ git log file -n 5
```

It's also possible to limit the log by author with the `--author` flag and a lot more, which you can see in more detail by using `git help log` to see all of the available options.

Status

This command will be one of the most frequently used during your day-to-day development, as it allows you to see the current state of the files within your repository and if there is anything you need to stage, commit, or add. The command in question is `git status`, which will give the status of the branch you're currently in.

Alternative: `st`

Merging branches

A time will come when you need to merge the changes from one branch into another. To do this, you need to make use of the `git merge` command, which can be utilized in the following way:

```
$ git merge branch
```

This will merge the specified branch into the branch you're currently inside so, before proceeding, be sure to perform a `git status` to find out which branch you're on, and to ensure the merge is performed how you'd like it to be.

Moving or renaming files

A time will come when you need to move a file from one destination to another or rename it, for whatever reason. Both of these tasks, as with the other systems, are performed with one command. Just use `git mv source destination` to perform either action, whether it's renaming a file (`git mv oldname newname`) or moving one (`git mv file folder/file`).

Pulling changes

When working with a parent repository, you'll need to ensure your repository is up to date with the latest changes, which is achieved by using `git fetch` to pull from the remote repository. After `git fetch` has completed, you'll need to merge the changes into the repository using `git merge` with no arguments. These two commands can be easily shortened by using `git pull` instead, which performs a `git fetch` and `git merge` for you, in one command.

Pushing changes

As with pulling, you need to ensure any changes you've been working on are pushed to the remote repository on a regular basis, which is achieved by using `git push`. If you've cloned from a repository to create this one, using `git push` with no arguments will push your changes without a problem.

Removing files

When you need to remove files, doing it with Git is easy. All you need to do is use `git rm file`, which will instantly delete it. Once you commit it, the file will no longer be tracked and you will be unable to make any changes to it. If you've had a change of heart, using `git reset HEAD file` should restore the file, but if that fails using `git reset --hard HEAD` will reset the entire commit to the previous version, so use it with caution.

Index

H, I, J

K

L

M